"The Fool

16

that willingly provokes a woman
has made himself another evil angel,
and a new hell, to which all other torments
are but a pastime."

Beaumont & Fletcher
"Cupid's Revenge"
1 6 1 2

John Webster
"The White Devil"
1 6 1 2

What do 12

the dead do, uncle? do they eat,
hear music, go a-hunting and be merry,
as we that live?"

"no coz, they sleep."

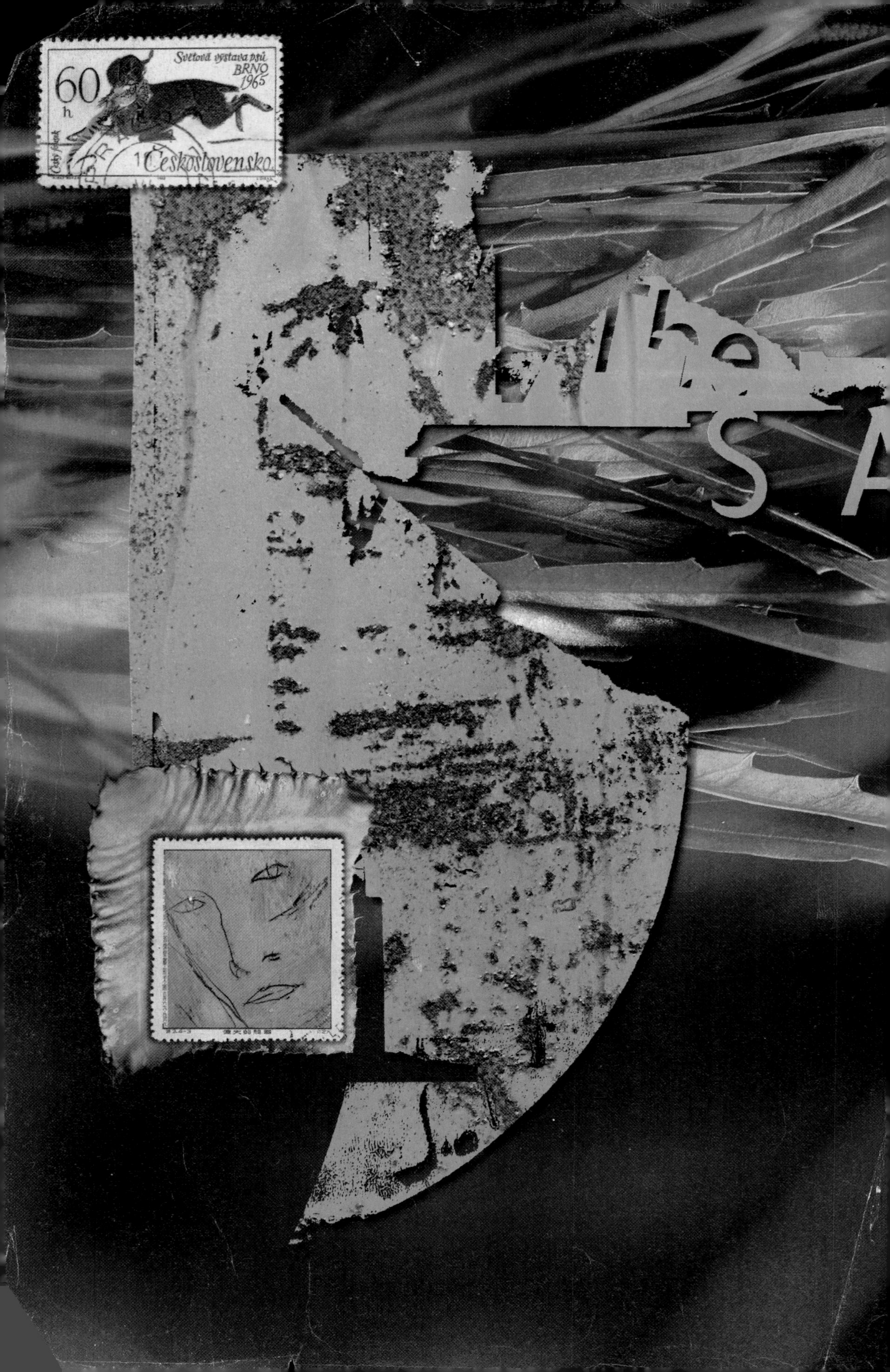
60
h
Světová výstava psů
BRNO
1965
Československo
The
S A

The Kindly Ones

SANDMAN

Writers
Neil Gaiman

Artists
Marc Hempel
Richard Case, D'Israeli
Teddy Kristiansen, Glyn Dillon,
Charles Vess, Dean Ormston,
Kevin Nowlan Colorist
Daniel Vozzo

Separations
Android Images

Letterers
Todd Klein
Kevin Nowlan

Covers ✿ and Design
Dave McKean

✿ Photo of Ruby on page 72 by permission of **Sheila Metzner**.

Introduction by
Frank McConnell

THE SANDMAN featuring characters created by
Gaiman, Kieth and Dringenberg.

published by DC comics. cover and compilation
copyright © 1996 DC comics. all rights reserved.
originally published in single magazine form
as the sandman 57-69 and in vertigo jam 1.
copyright © 1993, 1994, 1995 DC comics.
all rights reserved.

DC comics, 1700 broadway, new york, ny 10019
a division of warner bros. -
a time warner entertainment company
printed in canada.

1-56389-205-7 (trade paperback)

cover and publication design by
Dave McKean
third printing

PRESIDENT & EDITOR-IN-CHIEF
Jenette Kahn

EXECUTIVE VICE PRESIDENT & PUBLISHER
Paul Levitz

EXECUTIVE EDITOR AND
EDITOR-ORIGINAL SERIES
Karen Berger

EDITOR-COLLECTED EDITION
Bob Kahan

ASSOCIATE EDITOR-ORIGINAL SERIES
Shelly Roeberg

ART DIRECTOR
Robbin Brosterman

VP-CREATIVE DIRECTOR
Richard Bruning

VP-FINANCE & OPERATIONS
Patrick Caldon

VP-LICENSED PUBLISHING
Dorothy Crouch

VP-MANAGING EDITOR
Terri Cunningham

SENIOR VP-ADVERTISING & PROMOTIONS
Joel Ehrlich

VP & GENERAL COUNSEL
Lillian Laserson

EXECUTIVE DIRECTOR-PRODUCTION
Bob Rozakis

At this point, it's almost completely without point to talk about the fact that neil gaiman is a virtuoso storyteller and probably a genius, or that the entire run of the sandman, which achieves its exalted, tragic catastrophe and fulfillment in "the kindly ones," is one of the most extraordinary events in the history of comics. he's won more science fiction, fantasy, and comics awards than is healthy for a human being - not the least of his accomplishments is that, with all this recognition, he remains a lovely guy - so he doesn't need any new

salaams. and as for the work itself, all you have to do is open any sandman, to any page, and, if you can read at all, you gasp, and when you get your breath back you realize that you're just where all great art is designed to take you: in the presence of the holy.

and that's not a word - "holy" - that i use lightly. amiri baraka, back when he was leroi jones, wrote that art is whatever makes you proud to be human. that is one hell of a good definition of art, and also of the religious impulse, which is after all just the artistic impulse wearing a different hat: the desire to say or see something that convinces us we matter, that our messy, brief lives have a sense, a direction, a clear vector, despite their messiness and brevity. art isn't "order out of chaos": that's god's problem, whoever he/she is. art is the dream of order out of the sense of chaos: the three-cushion shot to the eight ball, the hewn stone that looks like the god apollo, charlie parker improvising on "how high the moon," or fred astaire, even if he's only walking across a room. or "the kindly ones." you hold in your hands one of the most stunning stories of the last half century - in any medium.

peter straub concluded his afterword to an earlier sandman story arc, "brief lives," by writing, "if this isn't literature, nothing is." i couldn't agree more passionately. (i just wish straub hadn't said it first.) as soon as the academic critics get off their famously insensitive butts - i work with them, so trust me, these guys would sleep through the second coming - as soon as they get off their butts and realize it's okay to admire a mere comic book, you'll see dissertations, books, annotations galore on the sandman, and then on the great comics writers - alan moore, frank miller, will eisner, the list is so long - who were his "precursors." gaiman would hate this comparison, being a modest fellow, but he's done for comics what duke ellington did for jazz in the thirties: produced work of such overwhelming magnificence that even the invincibly snobbish and the terminally tone-deaf have to dig it.

dream dies at the end. sorry to bus[t] your bubble, but this is a tragedy - as classically a tragedy as has been written in a long time - so you should know, a[t] the outset, how it's going to end: or do you want hamlet, maybe, to realize i[t] was all just a silly mistake, marry ophelia, and settle down in a nice condo in a really good part of denmark? dream dies at the end, and part of the wonderfulness of "the kindly ones" is the way it makes that death, in the manner of all great tragedy, seem so inevitable and so finally - not too strong a word - enriching.

dream dies. but how can an anthropomorphic projection o[f] consciousness die, really? well, it can't although in another way it can. in the last episode, dream of the seven endless morpheus, the shaper of form, the very principle of storytelling, does indeed die - or possibly commits a complicated form of suicide - only to be replaced by another aspect of himself, a new dream who is himself and yet is not, is subtly and crucially different because humans can no more live without telling themselves stories than you or i can kill ourselves by holding our breath

GAIMAN HAS SAID REPEATEDLY THAT THE SANDMAN WOULD CONCLUDE WHEN THE STORY BEGUN IN THE FIRST ISSUE WAS COMPLETED. TO MANY WHO HAVE FOLLOWED THE BOOK THROUGH ITS FIVE-YEAR DEVELOPMENT, THAT OFTEN SEEMED A HEROIC, BUT RATHER RASH, CLAIM. "THE KINDLY ONES" ENDS WITH MONTHLY ISSUE #69, AND WITH THAT ISSUE, HE MAKES GOOD HIS PROMISE. IN THE FIRST ISSUE, DREAM IS IMPRISONED (IN 1916) BY A BLACK MAGICIAN IN ENGLAND, ONLY TO ESCAPE AND RECLAIM HIS KINGDOM IN 1988, THE YEAR, OF COURSE, WHEN SANDMAN FIRST APPEARS. ONE OF THE ENDLESS, ONE OF THE SEVEN MORE-THAN-GODS WHO ARE, IN FACT, THE CONSTITUENTS OF HUMAN CONSCIOUSNESS ITSELF, HAS BEEN TRAPPED BY A MERE MORTAL: HAS BEEN TAUGHT PAINFULLY THAT HE IS NOT ONLY A TRANSCENDENT PROJECTION OF HUMAN CONSCIOUSNESS, BUT THAT HE IS, AFTER ALL, DEPENDENT UPON HUMAN CONSCIOUSNESS FOR HIS EXISTENCE. AND IN "THE KINDLY ONES," DREAM, FIVE YEARS AFTER HIS ESCAPE (GAIMAN IS METICULOUS ABOUT TIME-FRAMES), ACKNOWLEDGES HIS DEPENDENCE ON THE ORDINARY STUFF OF HUMAN LIFE AND ACCEPTS - OR ENGINEERS? - HIS DEATH AND TRANSFIGURATION INTO A NEW DREAM, INTO A VERSION OF HIMSELF MORE HUMAN - THE NEW DREAM IS THE EXALTATION OF THE CHILD, DANIEL - THAN HE THINKS HE COULD BE.

THAT'S THE BASIC PLOT OF "THE KINDLY ONES," AND THAT'S THE PLOT OF SANDMAN ALTOGETHER: DREAM'S DAWNING REALIZATION OF THE POIGNANCY OF MORTAL LIFE, AND OF HIS OWN INESCAPABLE IMPLICATION IN THAT POIGNANCY. THE KINDLY ONES, THE ERINYES, THE FURIES, THE EUMENIDES, CHASE DOWN HIS LIFE THROUGHOUT THIS BOOK BECAUSE HE HAS KILLED HIS SON, ORPHEUS: AT ORPHEUS'S REQUEST, TO BE SURE, BUT NEVERTHELESS HE HAS KILLED HIM. AND WITH THAT ACT DREAM HAS ENTERED TIME, CHOICE, GUILT, AND REGRET - HAS ENTERED THE SPHERE OF THE HUMAN. IN CHAPTER ELEVEN, AFTER HE HAS LEFT THE SECURITY OF THE DREAMING, THE FAIRY NUALA, WHO HAS SUMMONED HIM, ASKS HIM THE QUESTION THAT MAY BE THE CENTRAL SECRET OF THE TALE. "YOU . . . YOU WANT THEM TO PUNISH YOU, DON'T YOU? YOU WANT TO BE PUNISHED FOR ORPHEUS'S DEATH."

AND THE NEXT FRAME, DREAM'S RESPONSE, IS SIMPLY A WORDLESS, TIGHT CLOSE-UP OF HIS TORTURED FACE. (THAT'S AN EFFECT, BY THE WAY, THAT NEITHER A NOVEL NOR A FILM COULD ACHIEVE WITH THE SAME FORCE, SINCE A NOVEL WOULD HAVE TO DESCRIBE HIS FACE, AND A FILM COULD ONLY GIVE US AN ACTOR TRYING TO IMITATE THAT BLEAK MASK OF REGRET. THE COMIC, IN MARC HEMPEL'S BRILLIANTLY REDUCTIVE DRAWING STYLE, GIVES US THE THING ITSELF.)

I mentioned the inevitability of the tragedy. and inevitable it certainly is. of all gaiman's story arcs, this one has the clearest and most driven momentum of plot. we begin and end with the kindly ones, the furies themselves, but in their aspect not as the furies but as the fates: young clotho, who spins the thread of life, maternal lachesis, who measures it, and old atropos, who cuts it off. this is the archaic triple goddess, who has appeared in sandman from the second issue, and whose power is even greater than that of the endless.

it's absolutely characteristic of gaiman's imagination, though, that these all-powerful goddesses are represented as three women of varying ages, spinning yarn and having tea in a cozy english cottage - even though the oldest does have a dead mouse instead of a cookie with her tea. that layering of the mythic and the everyday is what gives the book its inimitable tone, the tone you also catch in joyce, faulkner, and thomas pynchon.

but there's more. notice that the conversation among the ladies at the opening is deliberately constructed to refer to the act of telling the final major tale in the sandman series. "what are you making him them," asks clotho of lachesis in the third frame of the first chapter. "i can't say that i'm terribly certain, my popsy," she replies. "but it's a fine yarn, and i don't doubt that it'll suit. go with anything, this will." the story begins as a story about storytelling, but also as a story - one of almost mythic simplicity - in its own right: without, sorry for the pun, dropping a stitch.

in fact, eight of the thirteen chapters begin, in the first frame, with a thread of some sort running across the panel, and with a comment that applies equally to the telling of the tale and to the tale itself: "well? how long is it going to take (chapter two)?" "i think it's going to be bigger than i planned (three)." "i wish i could be sure i was doing the right thing (four)." and so on, and so on.

now, this is the kind of writing literary critics like to call "postmodern": letting the reader know you're conscious of what you're doing at the very time you do it. and a writer like gaiman is smart enough to realize that kind of performance is about as "modern" as the odyssey or the divine comedy. the great storytellers have always wanted to tell us as much about the business of storytelling as about the stories themselves. gaiman's opening frames, with their running threads and their comment upon the tale itself, are simply his way of emphasizing that the tale possesses him as much as it does us - and that the thread of story will lead to its inevitable end, however many knots and snags develop in its unraveling.

and knots and snags do develop, thank god. approximately the first forty issues of sandman, brilliant as they are, appeared desultory: stories of genius, but without a clear center, without a clear direction. and then, beginning with "brief lives," the whole thing began to take on an overwhelming speed and shape: the byways and digressions of the early tales began to coalesce into one, stunning, final movement: a comparison to symphonic structure isn't inappropriate here.

and that final movement is the book you're about to read.

GAIMAN HAS INVENTED SO MANY CHARACTERS, SO MANY STORYLINES, OVER THE COURSE OF THIS - OKAY, I'LL SAY IT - EPIC. HE HAS REINTRODUCED TEUTONIC, GREEK, EGYPTIAN AND JAPANESE GODS, ALL OF THEM WITH ABSOLUTE ACCURACY AND RESPECT; HE HAS MADE UP DELIGHTFUL CHARACTERS FROM THE REALM OF DREAM, LIKE THE PRIM LIBRARIAN LUCIEN, THE SMART-ASS PUMPKIN MERVYN; AND HE HAS INTRODUCED US TO FALLIBLE HUMAN BEINGS, FROM THE FECKLESS ROSE WALKER TO THE ARROGANT, QUASI-IMMORTAL HOB GADLING TO THE BITTER, HALF-CRAZED LYTA HALL. ALL THESE, AND MORE, APPEAR IN "THE KINDLY ONES" - JUST THE WAY A SYMPHONY'S FOURTH MOVEMENT SHOULD INCLUDE THEMES FROM THE FIRST THREE. THERE'S SOMETHING SERIOUSLY AND A LITTLE SCARILY DICKENSIAN IN ALL THIS. LIKE DICKENS, WHO ALSO WROTE FOR SERIAL PUBLICATION (WHICH MEANS YOU CAN'T GO BACK AND REVISE YOUR LAST CHAPTER, BECAUSE IT'S ALREADY IN PRINT), HE THROWS AN IMPOSSIBLE NUMBER OF BALLS IN THE AIR, KEEPS THEM ALL ALOFT DURING THE ACT, AND THEN GATHERS THEM ALL INTO HIS ARMS AS HE TAKES A BOW. "WHAT DID WE MAKE? WHAT WAS IT, IN THE END?" ASKS CLOTHO OF LACHESIS, IN THEIR COZY HOME, AT THE VERY END. "WHAT IT ALWAYS IS," LACHESIS ANSWERS. "A HANDFUL OF YARN; A LITTLE WEAVING AND STITCHING; SOME EMBROIDERING PERHAPS. A FEW LOOSE ENDS, BUT THAT'S ONLY TO BE EXPECTED." IF THERE'S A MORE SATISFYING END TO A RECENT WORK OF FICTION - OR A BETTER DEFINITION OF WHAT FICTION IS - I'M SURE I DON'T KNOW IT.

DOES THIS MEAN GAIMAN IS A MIND LIKE MOZART, WHO HEARD EVERY DETAIL OF A COMPOSITION CLEARLY FROM THE FIRST NOTE, OR LIKE CHARLIE PARKER, WHO WOULD BEGIN TO IMPROVISE AND THEN WEAVE HIS RANDOM PHRASES INTO A PERFECT PRISTINE WHOLE? I CAN'T GET A STRAIGHT ANSWER OUT OF HIM ON THIS, AND MAYBE HE DOESN'T KNOW HIMSELF. NO MATTER: IF YOU DON'T REALIZE THAT WOLFIE AND BIRD ARE EQUALLY GREAT SOULS, THEN YOU SHOULDN'T BE LISTENING TO MUSIC AT ALL. (TRY KENNY G.)

THE POINT IS THAT THIS STORY IS A MAGNIFICENT PARABLE ABOUT THE HUMANIZATION OF MYTH; ABOUT HOW THE VALUES OF REGRET, RESPONSIBILITY AND THE AWFUL DUTIES OF LOVE OUTWEIGH EVEN THE POWER AND MAJESTY OF THE GODS WE INVENT AND THEN WORSHIP. THE VERY LAST STORY ARC, "THE WAKE," INTRODUCES THE NEW DREAM (DANIEL THAT WAS, MORPHEUS THAT IS NO LONGER) TO THE FAMILY OF THE ENDLESS: DESTINY, DEATH, DESTRUCTION WHO HAS LEFT HIS POST, DESIRE, DESPAIR, AND THE WONDERFUL DELIRIUM WHO WAS ONCE CALLED DELIGHT. IT IS A CODA: A GRACEFUL, SOLEMN, MELANCHOLY FAREWELL TO GAIMAN'S ASTONISHINGLY ORIGINAL BLENDING OF MYTH, FOLKLORE, COMEDY, AND HUMAN STRIVING AND HUMAN CONFUSION. WE CAN'T TALK ABOUT ITS INTRICACIES, ITS PLOTS-WITHIN-PLOTS, ITS WIT, OF ABOVE ALL ITS RICH, INEXHAUSTIBLY ALLUSIVE LANGUAGE: THERE'S NO SPACE.

For the three witches, fates, norns and graces of sandman - issue by issue, put it to bed, this book is for: the three wired sisters who have midwifed sandman, nurtured it and,

Shelly Roeberg, Alisa Kwitney & ABOVE ALL, SANDMAN'S FAIRY GODMOTHER: Karen Berger. With gratitude, Neil Gaiman

introduction by Frank McConnell

frank mcconnell got his ba at notre dame and his ph.d. at yale the year sergeant pepper came out. he taught at cornell when the doors were big; at northwestern between the fall of nixon and the rise of the clash; at uc santa barbara while reagan doodled, bush dawdled and clinton diddled.

what we can say is that if this isn't Literature, then nothing is - quoting brother straub - and, more, that this is the stuff of which Literature itself is made: learned, complex, straightforward, funny, melancholy, and irresistibly humanizing.

(also in east berlin the year before the wall came down - he claims no credit.) has written a lot of books and essays and four detective novels, all better hidden than the secret testament of eliphaz (which, by the bye, doesn't exist). does not, he insists, know what became of the cat halloween night nineteen-eighty-five and can not get neil gaiman to have a brandy and beer chaser before lunch. so far.

THERE'S A DREAM IN WHICH HUGE FACELESS WOMEN WITH WOLVES ASTRIDE THEM ARE CHEWING AT MY ENTRAILS AND LEGS. THEY HAVE SHARP TEETH.

ALTHOUGH THIS IS PAINFUL AND UNPLEASANT, IT IS NOT HORRIFYING.

IT BECOMES HORRIFYING WHEN I FUMBLE AT ONE OF THEM, TRYING TO GET HER TO LOOSEN HER GRIP. HER HEAD IS HUGE AND BLANK AND MY HAND GOES THROUGH THE FLESHY THIN SKULL OF IT, HAIR AND GOOP STICKING TO MY FINGERS, WHICH FLAIL IN THE EMPTINESS.

SHE HAS NO BRAIN, AND WHEN I REALIZE THIS I BEGIN TO THRASH AND SCREAM, DESPERATELY.

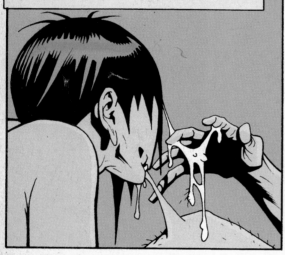

UHN.. UHN.. UH...

I WAKE, SWEATING AND MEWLING, IN A HOTEL ROOM ALONE. THE RED NUMBERS SAY 02:14 IN THE DARKNESS.

THERE'S A MOMENT OF FEAR IN THE RETURNING TO SLEEP. A HESITATION: THERE ARE DARKNESSES BEYOND THE CURTAIN OF WAKING, AND THE SHADOW-PLAYS CLUTCH AT MY HEART...

TOO LATE.

I'M GONE.

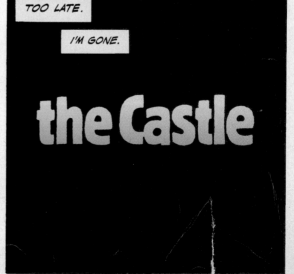

the Castle

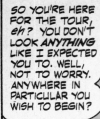

SO YOU'RE HERE FOR THE TOUR, eh? YOU DON'T LOOK *ANYTHING* LIKE I EXPECTED YOU TO. WELL, NOT TO WORRY. ANYWHERE IN PARTICULAR YOU WISH TO BEGIN?

NO?

VERY WELL.

WELL, LET'S START IN MY AREA OF RESPONSIBILITY. I'M THE *LIBRARIAN*, YOU KNOW.

MOST PEOPLE DON'T REALIZE HOW *IMPORTANT* LIBRARIANS ARE.

I RAN ACROSS A BOOK RECENTLY WHICH SUGGESTED THAT THE PEACE AND PROSPERITY OF A CULTURE WAS *SOLELY* RELATED TO HOW MANY LIBRARIANS IT CONTAINED.

POSSIBLY A *SLIGHT* OVERSTATEMENT. BUT A CULTURE THAT DOESN'T VALUE ITS LIBRARIANS DOESN'T VALUE IDEAS AND WITHOUT IDEAS, WELL, WHERE *ARE* WE?

THE LIBRARY OF DREAM IS THE LARGEST LIBRARY THERE NEVER WAS. I'M SURE ALL *YOUR* BOOKS ARE IN HERE.

WHAT'S THAT YOU SAY? YOU HAVEN'T *WRITTEN* ANY BOOKS?

OF *COURSE* YOU HAVE. *HERE'S* ONE.

IT'S CALLED "*The Bestselling Romantic Spy Thriller I used to think about on the bus that would sell a billion copies and mean I'd never have to work again!*"

NOT EXACTLY THE *CATCHIEST* OF TITLES, IS IT?

LET'S GO OUTSIDE.

2

WE'RE *STILL* ROUNDING UP STRAY STORIES THAT VANISHED OVER THE UNFORTUNATE SIX DECADES THAT MY LORD MORPHEUS WAS... UNAVAILABLE...

THERE YA GO *AGAIN*, LOOSH. YOU CAN'T JUST COME *RIGHT* OUT AND *SAY* IT, *huh*? NOW *ME*, I'M A STRAIGHT*FORWARD* KINDA GUY, Y'KNOW?

I MEAN *SOME* OF US AREN'T AFRAID TO CALL A SPADE A GODDAMN SHOVEL.

LEM*ME* TELL IT.

THE BOSS WAS *LOCKED* UP IN A GLASS BOX INNA GUY'S BASEMENT FOR THE BEST PART OF THIS CENTURY. NEKKID AS A JAYBIRD, ALL ALONE.

YOU SHOULDA *SEEN* THIS PLACE. SCRATCH THAT, YOU WOULDNA *WANTED* TO SEE IT. I MEAN, WE'RE TALKING A REAL *MESS*...

YOU CAN CALL ME *MERV*. ME AND MY GUYS, *WE* DO THE *REAL* WORK AROUND HERE. I MEAN, NEXT TIME *YOU* HAVE A DREAM, YOU GIVE SOME THOUGHT TO *WHO* PAINTED THE SKY.

Hmm? NO, IT'S NOT *ME*.

MOSTLY IT'S BORIS OR TINY.

Phhht.

HEY, IT'S BEEN GOOD *TALKIN'*, BUT YOU KNOW, HEY, *SOME* OF US HAVE GOT *JOBS* TO BE GETTIN' ON WITH. I MEAN *REAL* JOBS, NOT LIKE JUST WATCHIN' *LIBRARIES* OR NOTHIN'.

GET YOUR *HEAD* OUTTA THE *CLOUDS!*

NOT *YOU*, KIDDO. I WAS TALKING TO *TINY*. HE GETS HIS HEAD IN THE CLOUDS, HE'LL BE SNEEZING FOR *DAYS*.

OKAY, LOOSH. I GOT STUFF TO GET ON WITH.

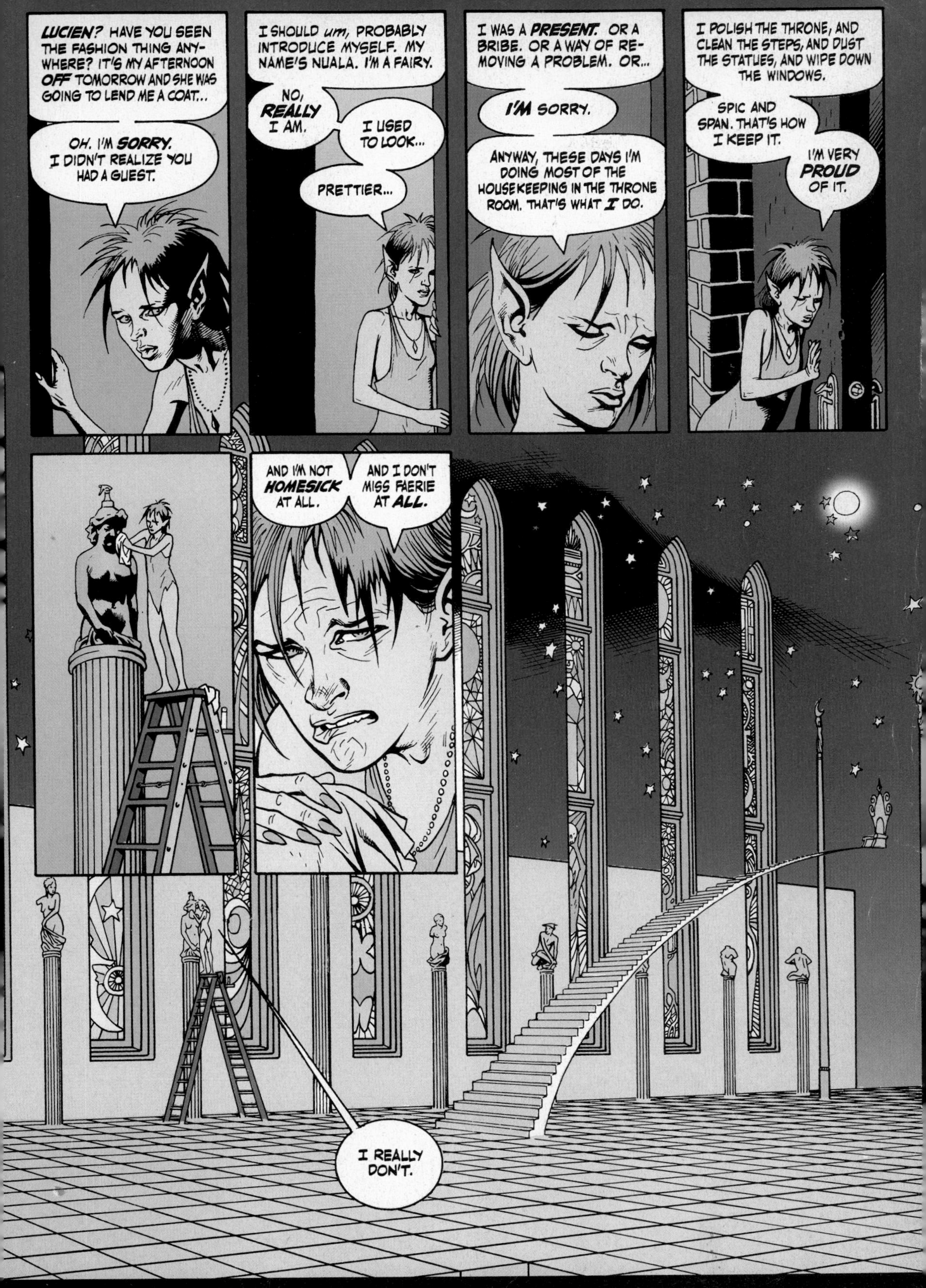
LUCIEN? HAVE YOU SEEN THE FASHION THING ANY-WHERE? IT'S MY AFTERNOON OFF TOMORROW AND SHE WAS GOING TO LEND ME A COAT...
OH. I'M SORRY. I DIDN'T REALIZE YOU HAD A GUEST.
I SHOULD um, PROBABLY INTRODUCE MYSELF. MY NAME'S NUALA. I'M A FAIRY.
NO, REALLY I AM.
I USED TO LOOK...
PRETTIER...
I WAS A PRESENT. OR A BRIBE. OR A WAY OF RE-MOVING A PROBLEM. OR...
I'M SORRY.
ANYWAY, THESE DAYS I'M DOING MOST OF THE HOUSEKEEPING IN THE THRONE ROOM. THAT'S WHAT I DO.
I POLISH THE THRONE, AND CLEAN THE STEPS, AND DUST THE STATUES, AND WIPE DOWN THE WINDOWS.
SPIC AND SPAN. THAT'S HOW I KEEP IT.
I'M VERY PROUD OF IT.
AND I'M NOT HOMESICK AT ALL.
AND I DON'T MISS FAERIE AT ALL.
I REALLY DON'T.

GREAT **VIEW**, huh?

NOW **YOU'RE** A NEW FACE. WORKING WITH LUCIEN, huh?

OOPS. **MY** GOOF. I'M MATTHEW. I'M THE RAVEN. NOT **A** RAVEN-- **THE** RAVEN. THAT'S ONE OF THE WEIRD THINGS ABOUT THE DREAMING--IT'S A KIND OF ONE-RAVEN-AT-A-TIME SORT OF PLACE.

I WASN'T **ALWAYS** A RAVEN. BUT PEOPLE CHANGE. I GOT A CHOICE, AND JESUS, THAT'S MORE THAN **MOST** PEOPLE GET.

LOOK. SEE THAT **MOUNTAIN?** WELL, HALFWAY UP THERE'S A LITTLE CAVE AND THAT'S WHERE I HANG WHEN I'M NOT HERE, WITH MY LADY EVE.

I'M HER RAVEN.

BUT I'M THE **BOSS'S** RAVEN TOO--HE WAS THE GUY WHO LET ME STAY HERE. AND HE'S NOT A **BAD** BOSS, ALL THINGS CONSIDERED.

I ASKED EVE ONCE WHAT HAPPENED TO THE **OTHER** RAVENS OF DREAM, OVER THE YEARS. I'M NOT THE **FIRST.** UH-**UH.** NOT BY A **LONG** SHOT.

DON'T THINK I **EVER** GOT A STRAIGHT ANSWER OUTTA HER.

NOT **REALLY.**

I'D **HATE** TO DIE AGAIN, Y'KNOW? I'D REALLY **HATE** THAT.

I WISH SOMEONE WOULD **TELL** ME.

5

IT-IT'S NOT *REALLY* A, AHH, SECRET. WHAT H-HAPPENED TO THE RAVENS. I'D *KNOW* IT IF IT WAS. AND I WUH-WOULD'NT TELL. RUH-*REALLY* I WOULDN'T.

I-UH, I-UH, I-UH, *HMM*, SHOULD PERHAPS INTRO-*DUCE* MYSELF. INDEED. I AM ABEL.

AND UH THIS IS MY ERR FRIEND GOLDIE.

meeeeep.

HE'S A *GARGOYLE*. I MM KNOW A GUH-GREAT MANY SECRETS ABOUT HMM GARGOYLES.

M-MY HOUSE IS ALL MUH-MADE OF SECRETS. JUST LIKE MY, UH, HMM, BU-*BROTHER'S* HOUSE IS MADE OF MYSTERIES. HE'S MY NUH-*NEIGH*BOR.

LUH-LUH-*LOVE* THY...

THEY'RE OVER THERE, BY THE GER-GER-GRAVEYARD. THE HOUSES. *SEE*, THEY LOOK *AFTER* US.

MY UH BROTHER'S NUH-NAME IS CAIN. WE'RE THE VERY B-*BEST* OF FRIENDS IN THE WHOLE *WORLD*.

IN THE WHOLE WIDE WORLD.

OOPS.

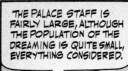

THE PALACE STAFF IS FAIRLY LARGE, ALTHOUGH THE POPULATION OF THE DREAMING IS QUITE SMALL, EVERYTHING CONSIDERED.

WE'RE HOPELESSLY UNDERSTAFFED.

NOW. WE COULD VISIT FIDDLER'S GREEN. OR WE COULD--

Lucien?

What exactly are you doing?

I AM SHOWING YOUR GUEST AROUND THE PALACE AND ITS ENVIRONS, MY LORD.

An.

My guest?

YES, LORD.

Does this look like my guest to you, Lucien?

Ah.

OH DEAR.

Well, no matter. So you have shown a dreamer the castle. It will do no harm.

And have you learned anything from your visit to my palace, mortal dreamer?

No?

Well, all of you come here, sooner or later. This place is the heart of all your dreaming, after all.

7

But you have seen very little, mortal dreamer. Would you like to stay longer?

After all, there are a thousand thousand other sights to see here in the dreaming. And many things to learn...

THEN I HEAR A BELL RINGING, SHRILL AND INSISTENT.

I'M LOOKING AROUND THE CASTLE TO SEE WHERE IT'S COMING FROM...

I WANTED THE NOISE TO STOP, WANTED TO FIND OUT WHO I WAS TALKING TO.

I KNEW HE COULD TELL ME SECRETS, KNEW THAT HE KNEW WHO THE WOLF-WOMEN WERE, KNEW THAT HE KNEW THE REAL TRUTH BEHIND EVERY DREAM I'D EVER HAD...

THE BELL PIERCES MY DREAMS, AND I ROLL OVER, RELUCTANTLY, AND STRETCH OUT AN ARM.

GOOD MORNING: THIS IS YOUR EARLY-MORNING ALARM CALL. IT'S 7:15 A.M.

OH. THANKS...

I KNOW I WANTED TO CARRY ON SLEEPING. I DON'T REMEMBER WHY ANYMORE.

SOME KIND OF WEIRD DREAM.

I DON'T EVEN REMEMBER WHAT IT WAS, NOW.

OH WELL...

IT COULDN'T HAVE BEEN THAT IMPORTANT.

IT WAS ONLY A DREAM, AFTER ALL.

END

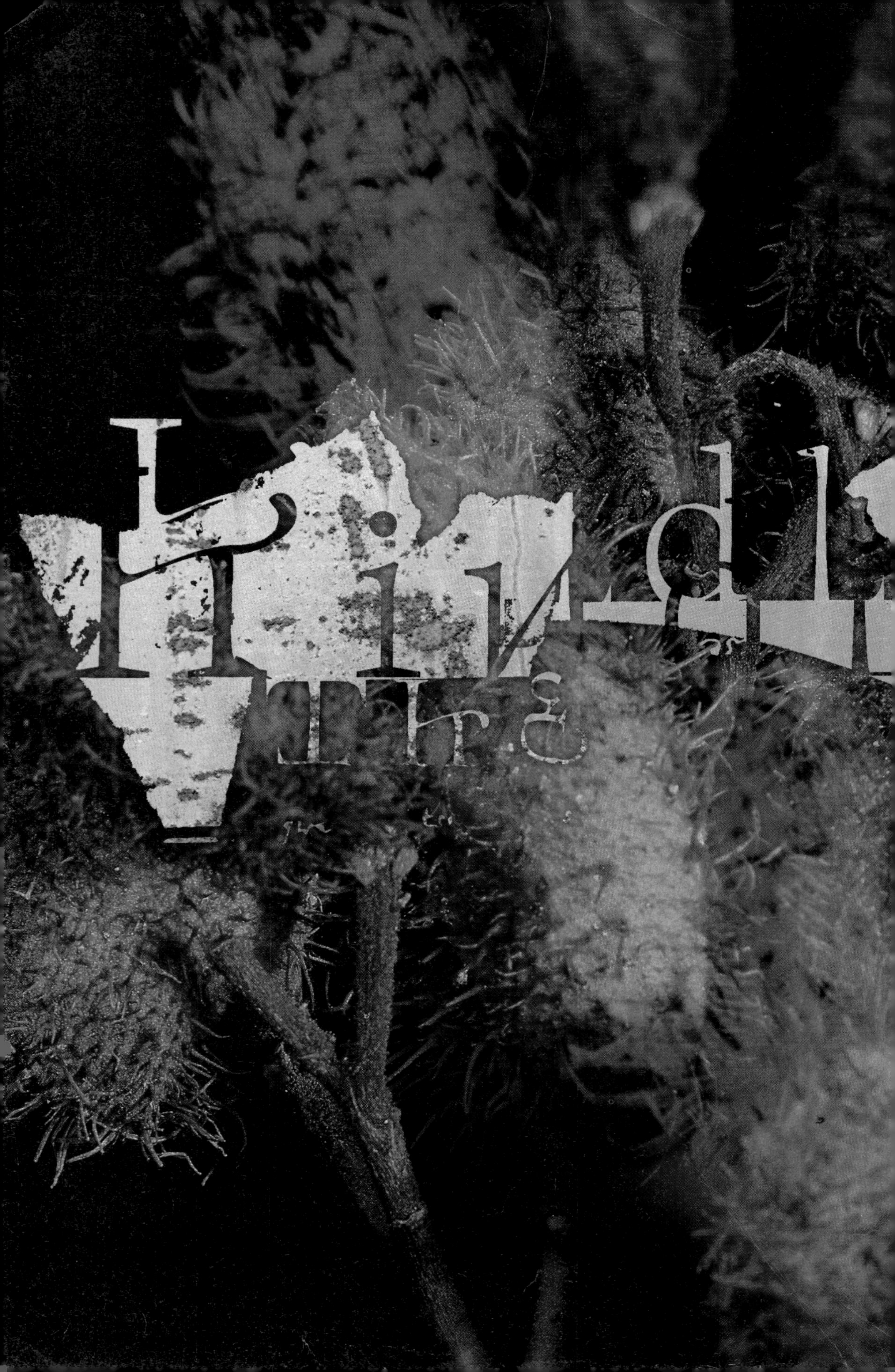

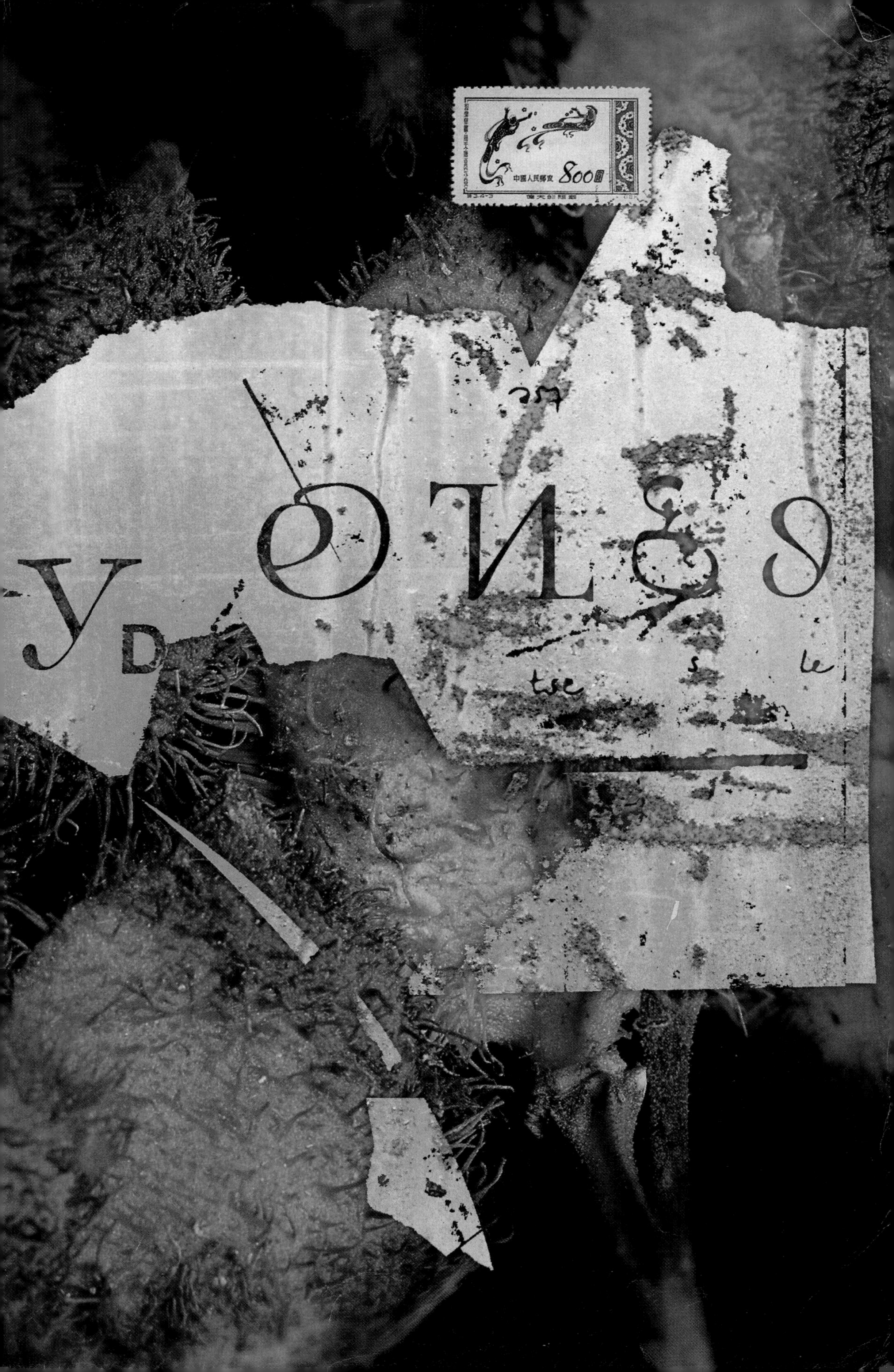
中國人民郵政
800圓

part
ONE

k c   tse   s

Edlen Tewrdanck entweichen sein eg...

...t die on alle arbeyt die welt hat ge...

...der frager·der hey\ lis geyst ist de...

...m bey seinem lebē wiewol sich der ser krümet schon begriffen· oſ Got de...

...it vnk die ewige ma...

IS IT READY YET? ARE YOU DONE?

NEARLY. *THERE* WE GO.

THERE WE ARE. ALL READY FOR YOU TO MAKE INTO SOMETHING WONDERFUL.

THAT'S ME DARLING GIRL....

WHAT ARE YOU *MAKING* HIM, THEN?

I CAN'T SAY THAT I'M ENTIRELY *CERTAIN*, MY POPSY. BUT IT'S A FINE YARN, AND I DON'T DOUBT THAT IT'LL SUIT.

GO WITH *ANYTHING*, THIS WILL.

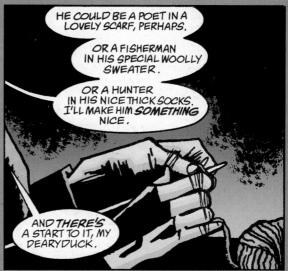

HE COULD BE A POET IN A LOVELY SCARF, PERHAPS.

OR A FISHERMAN IN HIS SPECIAL WOOLLY SWEATER.

OR A HUNTER IN HIS NICE THICK SOCKS. I'LL MAKE HIM *SOMETHING* NICE.

AND *THERE'S* A START TO IT, MY DEARYDUCK.

TEA?

I'D LOVE A CUP, MY DOVE.

AND FOR ME.

TEA FOR THREE, THEN.

CAN'T SAY I'VE EVER BEEN TOO FOND OF BEGINNINGS, MYSELF. *MESSY* LITTLE THINGS. GIVE ME A GOOD ENDING ANY TIME. YOU KNOW WHERE YOU *ARE* WITH AN ENDING.

WHOOSH!

NOW THEN, YOU MUSTN'T *SAY* THINGS LIKE THAT. YOU *KNOW* YOU DON'T *MEAN* THEM.

PURL ONE, PLAIN ONE, PURL TWO TOGETHER...

WHY, THAT'S WHAT I LIKE ABOUT MAKING THINGS FOR PEOPLE. YOU CAN START OFF IN BIRMINGHAM AND FINISH IN, WELL, TANGANYIKA OR SOMEWHERE.

THAT'S NOT MESSY, MY CHERUB. THAT'S *EXCITING*.

EX*CIT*ING MY AUNT BANANA!

WHAT'S SO EXCITING ABOUT IT?

WELL, EVERY ONE WE MAKE'S *UNIQUE*. NEVER SEEN BEFORE, NEVER SEEN AGAIN.

HMMPH. I DON'T KNOW WHY *THAT'S* EXCITING. IT'S NOT LIKE ANYONE *NOTICES* WHAT WE DO. NOT LIKE ANYONE *CARES*.

AND THEY'RE ALWAYS *COMPLAINING*: THEY DON'T LIKE THE FIT OF IT; TOO LOOSE-- TOO TIGHT-- TOO DIFFERENT-- TOO MUCH LIKE EVERYONE ELSE'S.

IT'S NEVER WHAT THEY WANT, AND IF *WE GIVE* THEM WHAT THEY THINK THEY WANT THEY LIKE IT LESS THAN EVER.

"I NEVER THOUGHT IT WOULD BE LIKE THIS." "WHY CAN'T IT BE LIKE THE ONE I HAD BEFORE?"

I DON'T KNOW WHY WE BOTHER.

WE BOTHER BECAUSE WE HAVE NO CHOICE. BECAUSE THAT IS WHAT WE ARE, IN THIS ASPECT.

HMMPH. WHO WANTS WHAT WITH THEIR TEA, THEN?

WHAT DO WE HAVE?

WE'VE GOT GINGER SNAPS, FLORENTINES, SPONGE CAKE AND FORTUNE COOKIES.

AND... WELL I NEVER, THERE'S A MOUSE IN THE TRAP. AFTER THE GINGER SNAPS, *I'LL* BE BOUND.

2

I'LL HAVE A GINGER SNAP, PLEASE.

I'LL TAKE A FORTUNE COOKIE, I THINK, MY PETAL.

≥Snf≤ THEN I'LL HAVE THE MOUSE.

RIGHT. TEA'S READY.

READ ME THE FORTUNE, WILL YOU, POPPET? I WANT TO FINISH THIS FIRST.

I DO LOVE TO HEAR FORTUNES.

"A KING WILL FORSAKE HIS KINGDOM; LIFE AND DEATH WILL CLASH AND FRAY; THE OLDEST BATTLE BEGINS ONCE MORE."

WE'VE HAD THAT ONE BEFORE, HAVEN'T WE?

IT'S DEFINITELY FAMILIAR, DEARIE.

RIGHT. I THINK THAT ONE'S GONE ON LONG ENOUGH.

DO YOU THINK SO? I RATHER LIKE THIS ONE. I THOUGHT MAYBE IT COULD BE A LITTLE LONGER...

YOU'RE TOO SOFT. BOTH OF YOU. MUCH TOO SOFT.

ALL GOOD THINGS, EH? ALL GOOD THINGS...

GOT TO FINISH SOMETIME.

SNIP

3

SAND!

THERE'S SAND ALL *OVER* THE BED. WHY, YOU, YOU *LITTLE*--

LYTA, HONEY, CALM DOWN.

I'M SORRY, CARLA. BUT JUST *LOOK* AT THIS.

IT'S SAND. SO?

SO, DANIEL WAS SLEEPING IN MY BED. I PUT HIM DOWN FOR HIS NAP, THERE.

NEXT THING YOU KNOW, THE SHEETS ARE *COVERED* WITH SAND.

WELL, SO HE MUST'VE BEEN PLAYING IN A SANDBOX OR SOMETHING.

YOU KNOW KIDS. ALWAYS FILLING THEIR POCKETS WITH STUFF.

MY KID BROTHER, JORDAN, *HIS* KID BROUGHT ALL THESE TINY LITTLE FROGS INTO THE HOUSE. WE *NEVER* FIGURED OUT HOW, MUST'VE FOUND THEM IN THE GARDEN OR SOMETHING.

NEXT THING YOU KNOW, THE WHOLE HOUSE IS *CRAWLING* WITH THESE TEENY TINY LITTLE FELLAS.

HOP, RIBBIT! HOP, RIBBIT!

Hop wibbif. Hof wibby.

CAN YOU SAY FROG? HUH, DANIEL? FROGGIE?

Hob wibble.

4

YOU STILL UPSET? C'MON, HON. IT'S NOT AS IF HE DID IT ON *PURPOSE* OR NOTHIN'. IT'S JUST SAND.

BUT HE *HASN'T* BEEN PLAYING IN THE SANDBOX.

LYTA, GIRL. *LOOK.* HOW ABOUT IF WE TAKE HIM OUT FOR A WALK. *HUH?* WE COULD GET SOME ICE CREAM?

Icecweam?

UH-UH. CARLA. NO *WAY.* I'M TRYING TO DIET.

NO PROBLEM. *YOU* CAN HAVE SOME OF THAT FROZEN YOGURT SHIT, AND WATCH *ME* GORGE MY FACE ON DOUBLE-CHOCOLATE CHIP. YOU WANT ICE CREAM, DANIEL? HUH?

Icecweam! Icecweam! Icecweam!

♪ ONE SHOE OFF AND ONE SHOE ON. ♪

HEY, DIDDLE DIDDLE, THE CAT AND THE FIDDLE. HERE'S A FLOWER FOR A PRETTY LADY.

♪ THE COW JUMPED OVER THE MOON. ♪

MUST'VE BEEN A MIGHTY FINE JUMPER, THAT OLD COW. MOON'S A LONG WAY UP, AND IT'S AWFUL COLD.

♪ LITTLE DOG ♪ LAUGHED TO SEE... ♪

WHAT DO *I* SEE?

HELLO, LITTLE BOY. YOU WANT A FLOWER, HUH? PRETTY FLOWER?

5

GET *AWAY* FROM HIM.

JUST A PRETTY FLOWER, PRETTY LADY? I THINK HE LIKES IT.

♪ ANNA DISH RANNA WAY WITHA SPOOOON. ♪

YOU. GET. AWAY. FROM MY SON. OR YOU'LL--YOU'LL--YOU DON'T *TOUCH* MY SON--

UNDER-STAND ME?

I...

I'M--AHHH--I--UH--HH--I--SNFFFF--AHHHH--AHHHH...

YOU DIDN'T HAVE TO DO *THAT.* HE'S JUST A HARMLESS CRAZY.

I'VE SEEN HIM DOWN HERE A DOZEN TIMES, GIVIN' OUT HIS FLOWERS, OR BEGGING FOR A LIGHT, OR FOR CHANGE.

31 FLAVO

LYTA, YOU'RE *SHAKING.*

I AM? MAYBE I'M JUST UNDER PRESSURE.

YEAH. MAYBE.

I--I OVERREACTED, DIDN'T I?

UH-*HUH.*

TWO SCOOPS OF CHOCOLATE-CHOCOLATE CHIP, A SCOOP OF THAT PINK YOGURT SHIT FOR MY FRIEND AND SOME VANILLA FOR THE KID.

Pint yodurt ship

CARLA, PLEASE. *LANGUAGE.*

6

YOU THOUGHT ANY MORE ABOUT TAKING ERIC UP ON THE JOB OFFER?

HE DOESN'T NEED AN ASSISTANT. *HE JUST WANTS TO GET INTO* MY PANTS.

HONEY, YOU KNOW THAT ISN'T TRUE.

YEAH. MAYBE. I JUST WOULDN'T FEEL GOOD ABOUT LEAVING DANIEL ALONE.

SO YOU GET A BABYSITTER. YOU CAN AFFORD IT.

I DON'T KNOW. MAYBE I'M OVERPROTEC-TIVE OR SOMETHING. BUT I DON'T WANT TO LET HIM OUT OF MY SIGHT.

SOMETIMES... WHEN HE'S SLEEPING... I GO IN THERE, AND JUST WATCH HIM, LISTEN TO HIM BREATHE.

JEEESUS, DANIEL.

I SUPPOSE IT'S LIKE HE'S ALL YOU HAVE LEFT OF HECTOR. IT'S KIND OF NATURAL YOU'D BE, WELL, A LITTLE BIT CAREFUL.

MM. MAYBE.

I DON'T KNOW.

DANIEL, CAN'T YOU EVEN STAY CLEAN FOR JUST FIVE MINUTES?

BUT IF ANYTHING HAPPENED TO HIM. IF ANYONE HURT HIM, IF ANYTHING HAPPENED...

YEAH, I KNOW. IF ANYTHING HAPPENED YOU'D JUST DIE.

I WOULDN'T DIE, CARLA.

IF ANYONE HURT DANIEL, I'D KILL THEM.

7

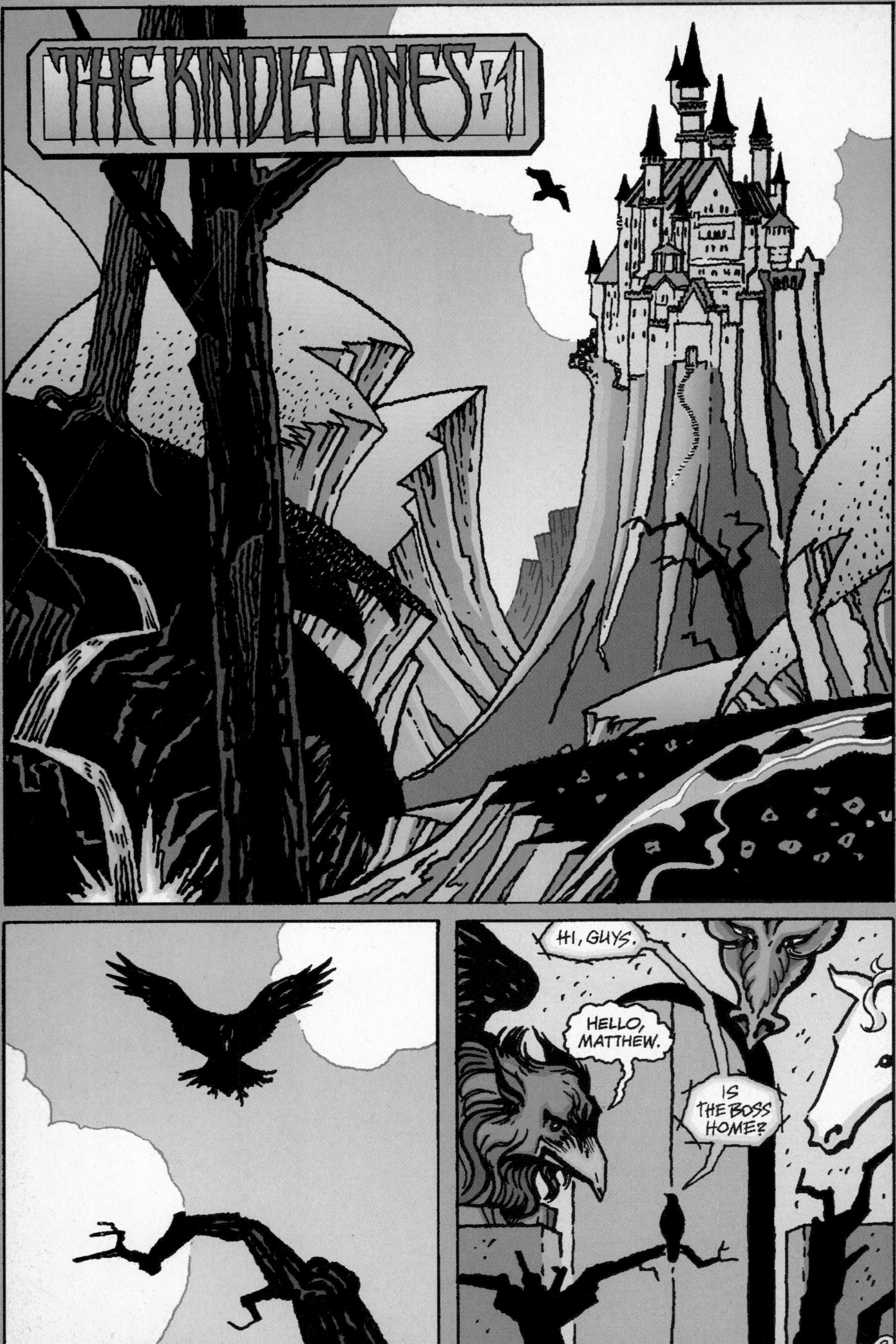
THE KINDLY ONES: 1
HI, GUYS.
HELLO, MATTHEW.
IS THE BOSS HOME?
8

CERTAINLY.

IT'S JUST HE HASN'T SENT FOR ME IN A WHILE. I FIGURED MAYBE HE WAS *TRAVELLING* OR SOMETHING.

NO. HE IS IN RESIDENCE.

OH.

WELL. I'LL BE GOING IN, THEN.

THE DOOR WILL OPEN FOR YOU, MATTHEW. YOU ARE WELCOME HERE.

HEY. Y'KNOW. I WAS *WONDERING.*

HOW LONG HAVE YOU GUYS BEEN *DOING* THIS GIG? THIS GUARDING THE DOOR BIT? I MEAN, HAVE YOU *ALWAYS* DONE THIS? OR DID YOU DO ANYTHING *BEFORE?*

I MEAN, WERE YOU *PEOPLE* OR SOMETHING?

WE WERE ALWAYS AS WE ARE. A GRYPHON, A WYVERN, A HIPPOGRIFF.

YEAH? SO YOU'VE ALWAYS GUARDED THE DOOR TO THE CASTLE?

WE ARE DOORKEEPERS, MATTHEW.

WE TAKE OUR STRENGTH AND OUR AUTHORITY FROM OUR LORD. WHEN *HE* WAS IMPRISONED AND POWERLESS, SO WERE *WE.*

THAT WASN'T QUITE WHAT I MEANT. I WAS WONDERING MORE ABOUT HOW YOU GOT *INTO* THIS GAME.

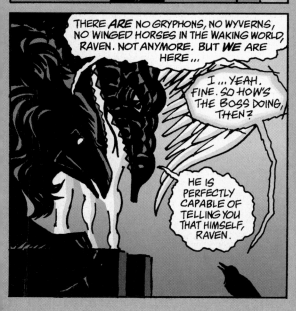

THERE *ARE* NO GRYPHONS, NO WYVERNS, NO WINGED HORSES IN THE WAKING WORLD, RAVEN. NOT ANYMORE. BUT *WE* ARE HERE...

I ... YEAH. FINE. SO HOW'S THE BOSS DOING, THEN?

HE IS PERFECTLY CAPABLE OF TELLING YOU THAT HIMSELF, RAVEN.

9

HEY, MERV.

HEY, MATTHEW. HOW'S IT HANGING?

HOW'S *WHAT* HANGING? I HAVEN'T HAD ANYTHING HANGING SINCE I WAS ALIVE.

HEY, NO *OFFENSE* MEANT. IT'S JUST A FIGURE OF SPEECH, Y'KNOW. IT'S THE KIND OF THING US GUYS *SAY* TO EACH OTHER. *JEEZ*, IT'S NOT LIKE I *MEANT* ANYTHING OR ANYTHING.

UH, RIGHT. LISTEN, MERV, YOU SEEN ANYTHING OF THE *BOSS* RECENTLY?

JUST THE USUAL.

"MERVYN, BUILD AN OCEAN OVER *HERE*, KNOCK DOWN THAT CITY UNDER THE WILLOW TREE OVER *THERE*. AND INCIDENTALLY, MERVYN, *THIS* TIME REMEMBER THAT ICE IS CUSTOMARILY COLD."

LIKE I DON'T HAVE *ENOUGH* TO DO. I TELL YA, SOMETIMES I COULD JUST TELL HIM WHERE TO *STICK* HIS GODDAMN JOB.

SO, UH, *MERV.* YOU'VE BEEN AROUND A WHILE. DO YOU REMEMBER ANY OF THE RAVENS BEFORE ME?

LIKE I'M GOING TO *FORGET* THEM? ALWAYS DROPPING FEATHERS IN THE HALLS AND SHITTIN' ON MY CLEAN FLOORS AND, JEEZUS, THE STUFF YOU BIRDS *EAT.*

NOT THAT I'M *PREJUDICED* OR NOTHIN'.

WHAT *HAPPENED* TO THEM, MERVYN? HOW DID THEY... LEAVE?

WHO HAS *TIME* TO KEEP TRACK OF YOU PEOPLE? SOME OF US HAVE *REAL* JOBS, BIRDIE.

WE CAN'T *ALL* PERCH ON THE BOSS'S SHOULDER, LIVE IN A CAVE, EAT DEAD RATS AND CRAP ON THE FLOOR.

RIGHT?

HEY, LISTEN, WHEN YOU SEE THE BOSS, YOU WON'T TELL HIM WHAT I SAID ABOUT THE JOB.

HE'D, Y'KNOW.

I MEAN, *WE* KNOW I'M A KIDDER, YOU AND ME, IT'S A *GUY* THING, BUT HE *MIGHT*, I DUNNO, TAKE IT THE WRONG WAY.

YEAH. RIGHT. NO PROBLEM.

10

HEY, NUALA.

HELLO, MATTHEW.

I THOUGHT MAYBE THE BOSS WOULD BE HERE.

NO. HE ISN'T HERE. I HAVEN'T SEEN LORD MORPHEUS FOR SOME TIME. I DON'T KNOW *WHERE* HE IS, REALLY.

BUT I'M KEEPING THE THRONE ROOM NICE AND CLEAN. FOR WHEN HE COMES BACK.

RIGHT.

NUALA?

WHY DO YOU DO THIS STUFF? ALL THIS CLEANING AND POLISHING? I MEAN, DOES HE MAKE YOU DO IT?

MAKE ME DO IT? NO. LORD MORPHEUS HAS NEVER...ASKED ANYTHING OF ME...

THEN WHY DO YOU DO IT?

I HAVE TO DO SOMETHING.

11

HI, LUCIEN.

MATTHEW.

WHATCHA READING?

AN UNWRITTEN PLAY BY JOHN WEBSTER. A BANQUET FOR THE WORMES.

ANY GOOD?

YES. VERY GOOD. "WEBSTER WAS MUCH POSSESSED BY DEATH AND SAW THE SKULL BENEATH THE SKIN," HE DID, YOU KNOW. HE REALLY DID.

YEAH? YOU MEAN LIKE HE HAD SOME KIND OF X-RAY VISION?

NO, NOTHING LIKE THAT.

I WAS KIND OF WONDERING. HAVE YOU GOT ANY BOOKS HERE ON RAVENS?

CERTAINLY. MANY THOUSANDS OF THEM.

WELL, COULD I, LIKE, CHECK ONE OUT SOME TIME OR SOMETHING?

CERTAINLY.

SO, UH, WHERE'S THE BOSS?

HE'S WORKING, MATTHEW.

RIGHT. SO WHERE'S HE WORKING?

LOOK, LUCIEN, I WANT TO TALK TO HIM. IT'S BEEN, WHAT, TWO MONTHS? SIX? A YEAR?

TIME'S SO SCREWY IN THIS PLACE.

SOMETIMES IT SEEMS LIKE A HUNDRED YEARS SINCE I DIED.

LUCIEN? WERE YOU EVER ALIVE?

I DON'T THINK SO, NO.

YOU DON'T THINK SO?

I CAN REMEMBER THE TITLE, AUTHOR, AND LOCATION OF EVERY BOOK IN THIS LIBRARY, MATTHEW.

EVERY BOOK THAT'S EVER BEEN DREAMED. EVERY BOOK THAT'S EVER BEEN IMAGINED. EVERY BOOK THAT'S EVER BEEN LOST.

MILLIONS UPON MILLIONS OF THEM.

THAT'S WHAT I REMEMBER. IT'S MY JOB. OTHER THINGS...I FORGET SOMETIMES.

HE'S DOWN BY THE SHORE, MATTHEW.

MAKING NIGHTMARES.

12

Matthew?

I do not recall sending for you.

I KNOW THAT, BOSS.

Well?

WELL, IT'S BEEN A WHILE. I WAS WORRIED ABOUT YOU.

Worried?

About me?

WHAT'RE YOU MAKING, THEN?

A nightmare.

I KINDA FIGURED THAT.

I am making the Corinthian.

YOU'RE WHAT?

Making the Corinthian once more.

I made the first one a long time ago, Matthew. Before poor Orpheus was born, I crafted him. Now I craft another.

WHY?

Why?

THAT'S WHAT I SAID. WHY? I MEAN, YOU ALREADY HAD TO DESTROY HIM ONCE...

SEEMS KIND OF... ODD... TO START HIM OFF AGAIN.

I created the Corinthian to be the dark mirror of humanity, Matthew.

13

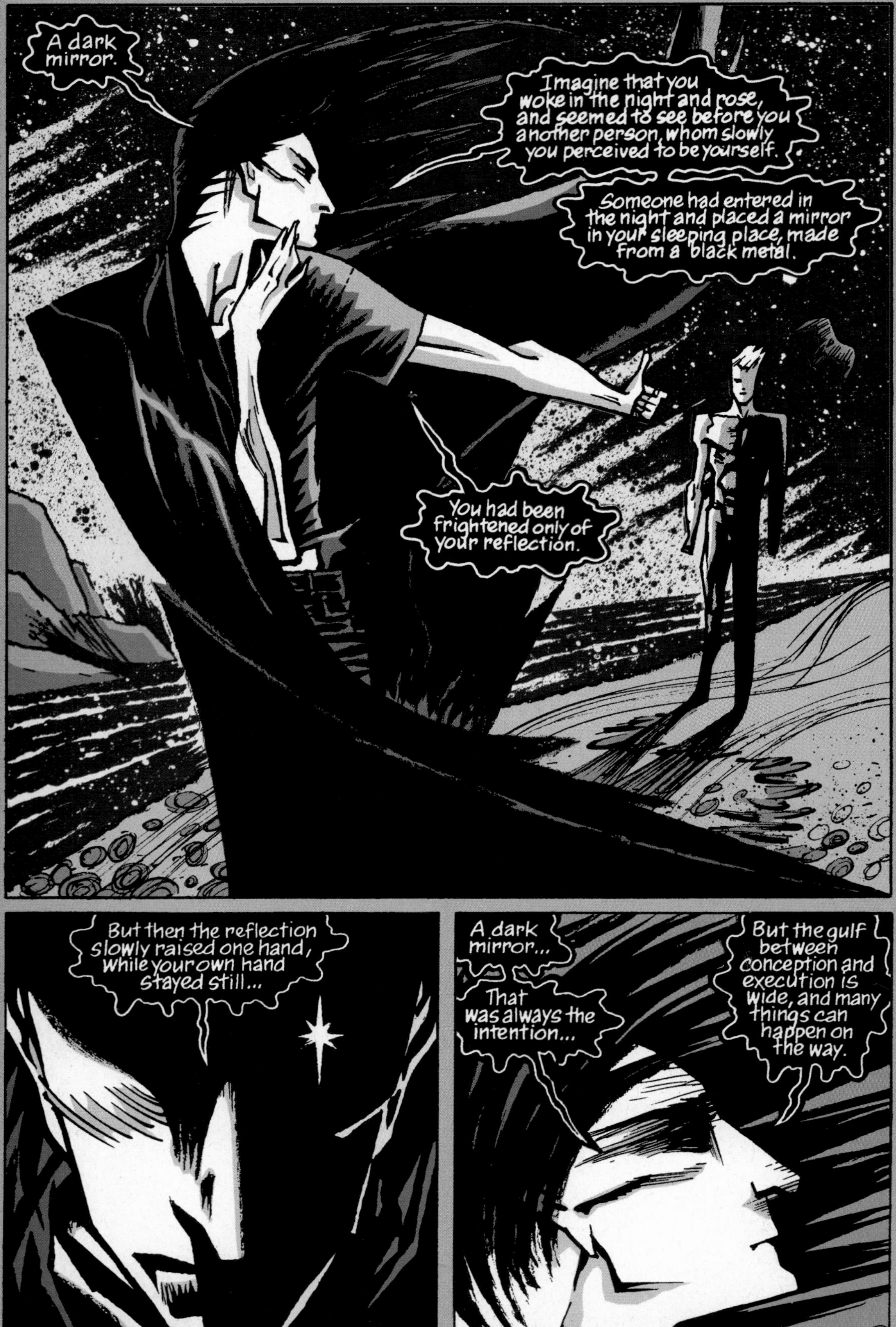
A dark mirror.
Imagine that you woke in the night and rose, and seemed to see before you another person, whom slowly you perceived to be yourself.
Someone had entered in the night and placed a mirror in your sleeping place, made from a black metal.
You had been frightened only of your reflection.
But then the reflection slowly raised one hand, while your own hand stayed still...
A dark mirror...
That was always the intention...
But the gulf between conception and execution is wide, and many things can happen on the way.

I DON'T THINK I EVER HEARD YOU *TALK* SO MUCH. NOT AT ONE TIME.

NO?

Walk with me, Matthew.

It is rare that I return to a previous theme...

AREN'T YOU WORRIED?

OF WHAT?

I DON'T KNOW. OF WHAT IT'S GOING TO *DO.* THE LAST CORINTHIAN TRIED TO KILL YOU.

The last Corinthian was a fool. This one will not be.

NO MORE OF THAT KILLING-PEOPLE-AND-EATING-THEIR-EYES SHIT?

The Corinthian was not intended to be a reassuring dream, Matthew.

SO WHY DID YOU DESTROY IT?

Sometimes dreams go bad, Matthew. I have known a few in my time.

Certain of them I removed from the body of the dreaming; others I uncreated.

BOSS?

Matthew?

WHEN I WAS IN THAT *CAR* WITH YOUR LITTLE SISTER, SHE SAID THERE'D BEEN ELEVEN OR TWELVE OTHER RAVENS. REMEMBER?

There have been rather more than that, Matthew.

AND SHE SAID THAT *ONE* OF THEM WENT BACK TO BEING A MAN AGAIN.

Aristeas of Marmora? Yes, briefly. It was what he thought he wanted. But it did not last.

Y'KNOW, I WAS ASKING EVE WHAT *HAPPENS* TO US RAVENS, IN THE END. WHEN WE'RE NOT IN THE DREAMING ANYMORE.

AND SHE WOULDN'T TELL ME, IF SHE KNEW.

15

Indeed?

UH-HUH.

That is as it should be, Matthew.

You may return to Eve's cave, Matthew. I shall send for you, if I have need of you.

BUT--

Go now.

KAAAAARK.

I FOUND HIM, EVE. WE TALKED SOME.

AND?

WE TALKED. THAT'S ALL. LISTEN, I DON'T WANT TO TALK ABOUT IT.

YOU'RE BROODING, LITTLE RAVEN.

I SAID I DON'T WANT TO TALK ABOUT IT.

HONESTLY.

MEN.

16

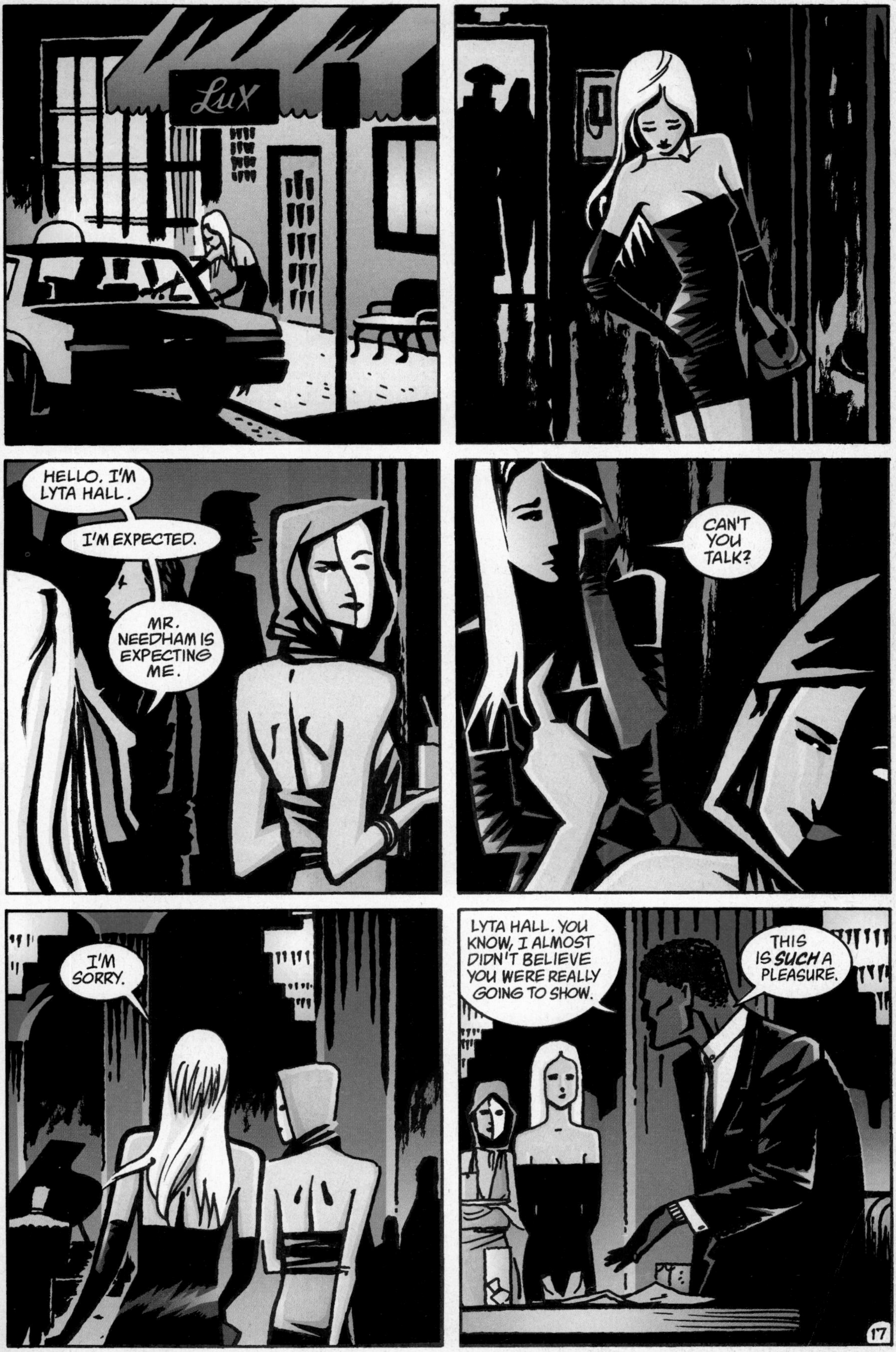

Lux
HELLO. I'M LYTA HALL.
I'M EXPECTED.
MR. NEEDHAM IS EXPECTING ME.
CAN'T YOU TALK?
I'M SORRY.
LYTA HALL. YOU KNOW, I ALMOST DIDN'T BELIEVE YOU WERE REALLY GOING TO SHOW.
THIS IS **SUCH** A PLEASURE.

HELLO, ERIC.

WELL, I'M **DELIGHTED** CARLA FINALLY CONVINCED YOU THAT WE SHOULD TALK FACE TO FACE.

PLEASE, TAKE A SEAT.

SO. HAVE YOU BEEN HERE BEFORE?

NO. I DON'T GET OUT MUCH.

WELL, *I* LIKE IT BECAUSE IT'S NOT AN L.A. PLACE. NO OFFENSE, BUT THERE'S SOMETHING *ABOUT* L.A. PLACES.

GOOD OLD LA-LA-LAND. PEOPLE WANT TO BE **SEEN** IN THIS TOWN.

Y'KNOW LUX'S HAS A NO PORTABLE PHONE POLICY. PRETTY **COOL,** HUH? DOESN'T MATTER IF YOU'RE EISNER OR OVITZ OR WHOEVER. NO PORTABLES. OR BEEPERS.

YOU'RE LOOKING TER**RIFIC.** YOU KNOW THAT?

UM. THANKS.

THAT **SONG** HE'S PLAYING. IT WAS MY LATE HUSBAND'S FAVORITE SONG.

♪ A ♫ CIGARETTE THAT BEARS LIPSTICK TRACES ... AN AIRLINE TICKET TO ROMANTIC ♪ PLACES... ♪

SOMETHING TO DRINK?

TOMATO JUICE, PLEASE.

STOLI AND CRANBERRY JUICE FOR ME, PLEASE. AND A VIRGIN MARY FOR THE LADY.

A *WHAT?*

IT'S A BLOODY MARY, JUST WITHOUT THE VODKA.

I THOUGHT YOU WERE GOING TO SAY WITHOUT THE BLOOD.

NO.

SO.

SO.

SO... SUPPOSING YOU TELL ME ALL ABOUT YOURSELF.

18

YOU KNOW ALL ABOUT ME, ERIC. YOU WOULDN'T BE TRYING TO *HIRE* ME IF YOU DIDN'T.

YOU NEVER SPOKE A TRUER WORD. I'VE GOT THE LYTA HALL DOSSIER IN MY BRIEFCASE.

SO WHAT EXACTLY IS THIS JOB OFFER ABOUT? WHAT KIND OF ASSISTANT DO YOU NEED?

WE'LL *COME* TO THAT, LYTA. THE NIGHT IS *YOUNG.* AND HERE ARE OUR DRINKS.

THE TWENTY'S ALL FOR YOU, GORGEOUS. SPEND IT ON SOMETHING *FUN*, OKAY?

COOL IDEA, HUH? SILENT WAITRESSES.

I THOUGHT SHE WAS ACTUALLY DUMB.

MAYBE. ANY-WAY IT GETS HER GOOD TIPS FROM ME. WHO WANTS TO HEAR WOMEN *TALK* ALL THE TIME?

WHAT...?

HEY--DON'T YOU GO PUTTING WORDS INTO MY MOUTH, LITTLE LADY. NOT *JUST* WOMEN. PEOPLE.

PEOPLE TALK *ALL* THE TIME. I MEAN, DON'T YOU JUST *HATE* A VERBOSE WAITER?

NOT REALLY.

CHEERS.

HERE'S TO BUSINESS. AND THE FUTURE.

CLINK!

SO. WHAT'S IN THE LYTA HALL DOSSIER?

YOU REALLY WANT TO KNOW?

WELL, YOU WERE BORN SOMETIME AROUND 1960. MOTHER WAS THE GREEK-BORN SUPERHEROINE WHO CALLED HERSELF THE FURY.

NO MENTION HERE OF WHO YOUR FATHER WAS.

AS AN INFANT YOU WERE ENTRUSTED TO A VIRGINIAN COUPLE, THE TREVORS.

THEY FORMALLY ADOPTED YOU ABOUT FIVE YEARS LATER, WHEN IT BECAME APPARENT THAT, WHEREVER YOUR MOTHER HAD GONE, SHE *WASN'T* COMING BACK.

HALL

19

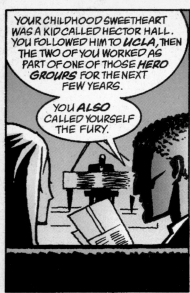

YOUR CHILDHOOD SWEETHEART WAS A KID CALLED HECTOR HALL. YOU FOLLOWED HIM TO *UCLA*, THEN THE TWO OF YOU WORKED AS PART OF ONE OF THOSE *HERO GROUPS* FOR THE NEXT FEW YEARS.

YOU *ALSO* CALLED YOURSELF THE FURY.

YOU WERE ENGAGED TO BE MARRIED.

HECTOR HALL *DIED* IN 1987, LEAVING YOU PREGNANT. YOU *MARRIED* HIM IN EARLY 1988. THAT'S KIND OF *STRANGE*, Y'KNOW?

YES.

THEN YOU *VANISHED* FOR A COUPLE OF YEARS. REAPPEARED A FEW YEARS BACK, *STILL* PREGNANT. NO MORE HECTOR. HAD A BABY--

DANIEL.

DANIEL. YES.

AND YOU'VE BEEN A *MOM* EVER SINCE.

YOU KNOW, THAT'S A PRETTY *AMAZING* LIFE STORY.

SOMEONE WHO'D TURN THEIR BACK ON STARDOM AND A VIRGINIA MANSION TO RAISE A BABY IN A TINY L.A. APARTMENT.

LISTEN. YOU *KNOW* THE MEDIA. YOU KNOW THE L.A. SOCIAL SCENE. YOU *LOOK* GOOD AND I WANT YOU WORKING FOR *ME*.

LIKE I SAID BEFORE. DOING EXACTLY *WHAT*?

WELL, OUR WEST COAST OPERATION IS JUST EXPANDING AND EXPANDING. MARKETING. INTERACTIVE MEDIA. PRODUCTION. MANAGEMENT. THE WHOLE *SHEBANG*.

I FIGURE YOU GET TO WRITE YOUR JOB DESCRIPTION. SEND IT TO ME. I'LL SIGN IT.

THEN YOU PICK A SALARY. TELL ME WHAT IT IS, AND I'LL INITIAL IT.

Lux MENU

YOU MAKE IT SOUND LIKE THE KIND OF DEAL I OUGHT TO SIGN IN *BLOOD*.

HA-HA-HA...

I...I DON'T KNOW. IT'S A *WONDERFUL-SOUNDING* OFFER.

BUT IT *WOULD* MEAN SPENDING TIME AWAY FROM DANIEL...

WELL, MAYBE A *LITTLE*. BUT IF YOU WANT AN IN-OFFICE CRECHE AND CAREGIVER, THAT COULD BE ARRANGED.

OKAY. LET'S HOLD OFF ON THE BUSINESS. *I'M* READY TO ORDER. ARE YOU READY TO ORDER?

20

HEY, *MAC.* WILL YOU PLAY "*MEMORIES*"? FOR MY GOOD LADY OVER THERE. FROM "*CATS*"? HER NAME'S VONDA.

Y'KNOW, "MIIIIDNIGHT, ALL ALONE ONNA PAAAAAVEMENT..." THAT ONE.

no.

no, I'M AFRAID NOT. IT IS A SONG I FIND *ENTIRELY* DEVOID OF INTEREST.

THE MELODY IS TRITE, WHILE THE AWKWARD PARAPHRASES OF LESSER ELIOT POEMS IN THE LYRICS ARE GRATING IN THE EXTREME.

HEY, BUD. HERE'S FIFTY DOLLARS SAYS YOU'LL PLAY IT. IT'S HER *BIRTHDAY* AND AFTER "*MEMORIES*", HOW ABOUT "*HAPPY BIRTHDAY TO VONDA*"?

I WILL NOT PLAY "*MEMORY*", AND I CANNOT BE BOTHERED TO LIE. VONDA'S BIRTHDAY WILL BE *FAR* FROM HAPPY.

"HOWEVER, I WILL PLAY SOMETHING APPROPRIATE ENOUGH, CONSIDERING HOW THIS EVENING WILL END FOR YOU BOTH."

HARVEY? IS HE GOING TO PLAY "*MEMORIES*"? WHAT DID HE *SAY*?

I, UH, WELL, I ASKED HIM...

THIS SONG IS FOR A YOUNG LADY NAMED VONDA WHO'S HAVING A BIRTHDAY TONIGHT.

I DREAMED LAST NIGHT I WAS ON THE BOAT TO HEAVEN, AND BY SOME CHANCE I HAD BROUGHT MY DICE ALONG...

21

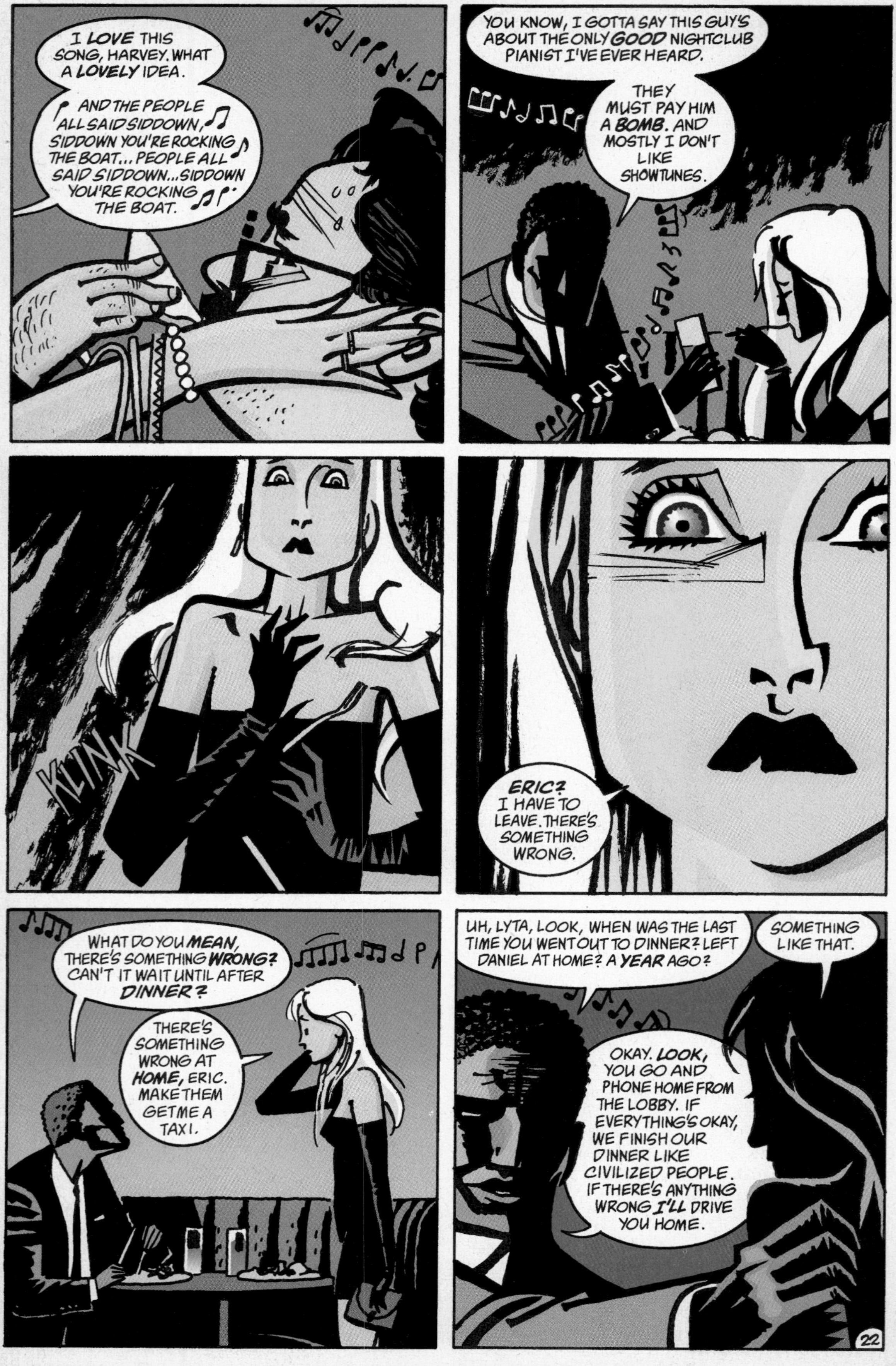
I LOVE THIS SONG, HARVEY. WHAT A LOVELY IDEA.
AND THE PEOPLE ALL SAID SIDDOWN, SIDDOWN YOU'RE ROCKING THE BOAT... PEOPLE ALL SAID SIDDOWN... SIDDOWN YOU'RE ROCKING THE BOAT.
YOU KNOW, I GOTTA SAY THIS GUY'S ABOUT THE ONLY GOOD NIGHTCLUB PIANIST I'VE EVER HEARD.
THEY MUST PAY HIM A BOMB. AND MOSTLY I DON'T LIKE SHOWTUNES.
KLINK
ERIC? I HAVE TO LEAVE. THERE'S SOMETHING WRONG.
WHAT DO YOU MEAN, THERE'S SOMETHING WRONG? CAN'T IT WAIT UNTIL AFTER DINNER?
THERE'S SOMETHING WRONG AT HOME, ERIC. MAKE THEM GET ME A TAXI.
UH, LYTA, LOOK, WHEN WAS THE LAST TIME YOU WENT OUT TO DINNER? LEFT DANIEL AT HOME? A YEAR AGO?
SOMETHING LIKE THAT.
OKAY. LOOK, YOU GO AND PHONE HOME FROM THE LOBBY. IF EVERYTHING'S OKAY, WE FINISH OUR DINNER LIKE CIVILIZED PEOPLE. IF THERE'S ANYTHING WRONG I'LL DRIVE YOU HOME.
22

THERE'S NO ANSWER.

DRIVE ME HOME.

NOW.

HERE YOU GO, HON. THIS SHOULD COVER IT, AND TAKE SOMETHING FOR YOURSELF OUT OF IT, OKAY?

COME. ON.

YEAH. I'M COMING. HAVE THEY BROUGHT THE CAR ROUND YET?

UH. UH.

LOOK, IT'S PROBABLY NOTHING. MAYBE THE BABYSITTER DIDN'T HEAR THE PHONE. SHE PROBABLY FELL ASLEEP OR SOMETHING.

THERE'S THE CAR.

CAN'T YOU GO ANY FASTER?

IT'S RAINING, LYTA. I'M GOING AS FAST AS I CAN. I TELL YOU, IF WE GOT STOPPED AND TICKETED, WE'D LOSE MORE TIME.

WHAT IS IT WITH THIS TOWN? A LITTLE RAIN COMES DOWN, NEXT THING YOU KNOW, EVERYBODY FORGETS HOW TO DRIVE.

LOOK AT THAT GUY. HE CAN'T BE GOING FASTER THAN 15 MILES AN HOUR. I MEAN, IT'S JUST A LITTLE WATER, YOU'D THINK IT WAS--

ERIC. SHUT THE F...

JUST DRIVE, OKAY?

23

SCREECH!

RATTLE RATTLE

ERIC? HE'S GONE.

DANIEL'S GONE.

THEY TOOK MY BABY.

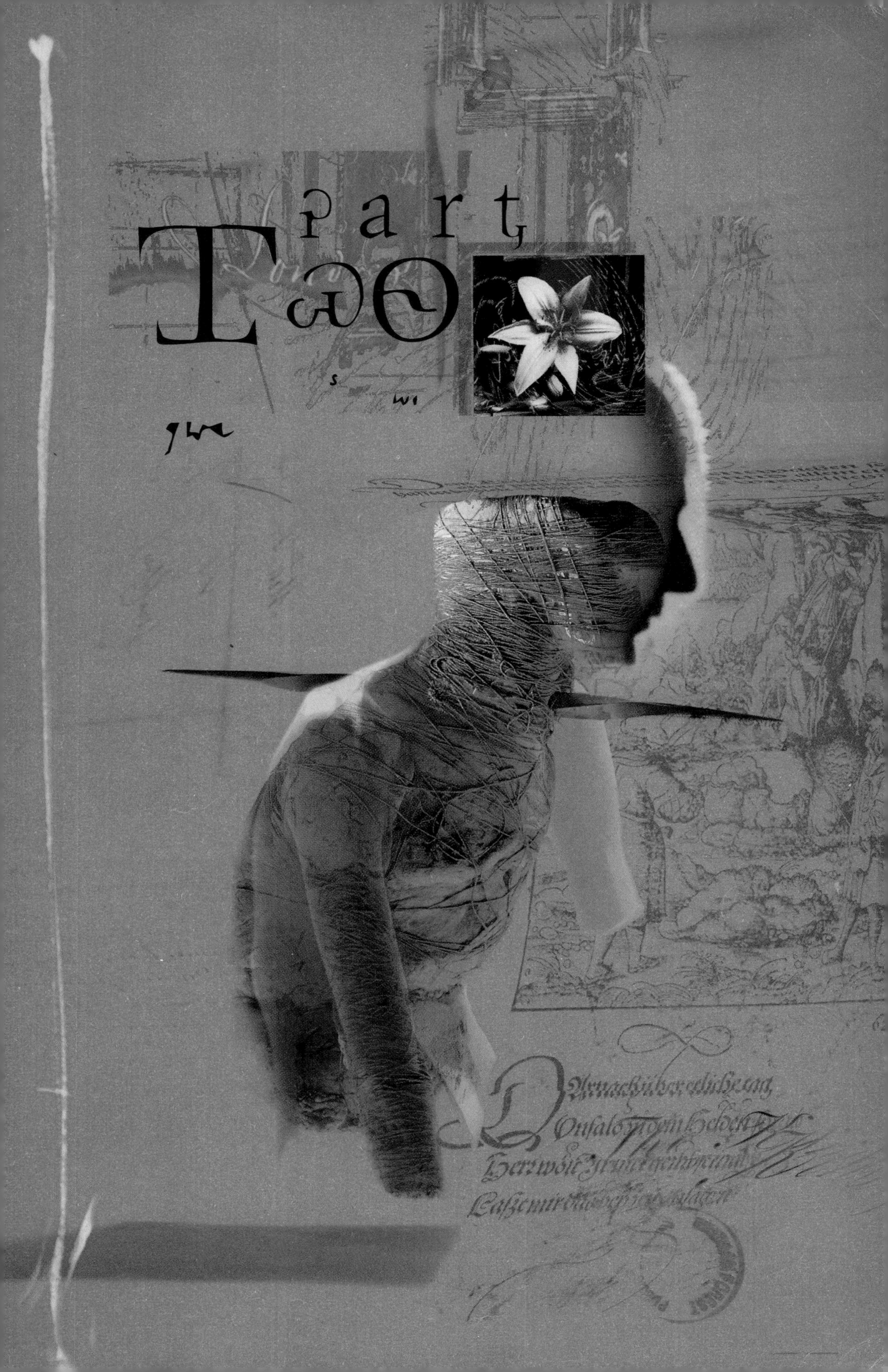
part
Two

WELL? HOW LONG IS IT GOING TO *TAKE?*

TRAGEDY STRUCK THIS EVENING FOR A TORRANCE COUPLE CELEBRATING A SPECIAL DAY.

LOOK, WE CALLED YOU ALMOST TWO *HOURS* AGO. I MEAN, THIS IS A *KIDNAPPING,* FOR CHRISSAKES.

HARVEY AND VONDA RAMSEY CLIMBED OVER *THIS* FENCE TO *THIS* LOCAL BEAUTY SPOT AND BOATING LAKE, WHERE THEY CLIMBED INTO ONE OF *THESE* LITTLE ROW BOATS.

I'M NOT CURSING AT *YOU,* OKAY, LADY. I'M JUST CURSING.

UH, H-HARVEY WAS SO HA-*HAPPY.* HE HAD THIS BOTTLE OF FRENCH CHAMPAGNE, AND HE SAID IT WAS TIME TO TOAST ME, AND HE STOOD UP AND I SAID HARVEY, DON'T STAND UP, BUT HE SAID, VONDA, HONEY, IT'S YOUR BIRTHDAY, AND HE...

FINE, IT'S NOT YOUR FAULT. BUT I HOPE *YOU* UNDERSTAND *MY* FRUSTRATION WITH--

IT WAS OUR TUH-TENTH WEDDING ANNIVERSARY NEXT WEEK.

I *TOLD* HIM. I *TOLD* HIM TO SIT DOWN. AND THEN HE, AHH, HE...

NO. *NO,* OF *COURSE* I DON'T *WANT* YOUR JOB.

I JUST WANT TO SEE SOME *COPS* HERE.

RIGHT. WELL, I DON'T LIKE *YOUR* ATTITUDE EITHER, SO THAT MAKES *TWO* OF US.

UH, TENTH WEDDING ANNIVERSARY? THAT'S *TIN,* ISN'T IT, MARY?

I THINK IT *IS,* RAY. ON A LIGHTER NOTE, TOMORROW IS THE FIRST DAY OF NATIONAL JAZZERCISE WEEK AND TO CELEBRATE...

COW.

SHE SAYS THEY'RE COMING. LYTA?

MM.

THEY'RE ON THEIR WAY.

LYTA?

LYTA, HONEY, THE *POLICE* ARE HERE TO SEE YOU.

MIZZ HALL?

I'M LIEUTENANT LUKE PINKERTON. I'M WITH THE *LA* POLICE DEPARTMENT. THIS IS MY PARTNER, GORDY FELLOWES...

MA'AM.

NOW, I UNDERSTAND THAT YOUR SON HAS BEEN ABDUCTED. THIS IS OBVIOUSLY A *VERY* TRAUMATIC TIME FOR YOU. WE DON'T WANT TO MAKE IT ANY HARDER.

DANIEL. HIS NAME IS DANIEL.

DANIEL. *RIGHT.* CAN YOU TELL US WHAT HAPPENED?

I WENT OUT THIS EVENING. LUX'S. IT'S A RESTAURANT. I GOT A BAD FEELING AND WANTED TO COME HOME. WHEN I GOT HERE MY SON HAD BEEN STOLEN.

THE BABYSITTER WAS ASLEEP ON THE FLOOR.

DO YOU HAVE ANY IDEA OF *ANY* PERSON WHO COULD HAVE BEEN RESPONSIBLE?

NO.

MA'AM, CAN WE TALK TO THE CHILD'S FATHER?

SURE. YOU GOT A OUIJA BOARD WITH YOU?

HE'S *DEAD?*

HE'S BEEN DEAD A LONG TIME.

I SEE. *I'M* SORRY. DO YOU HAVE ANY *ENEMIES?* IS THERE ANYONE WHO'S SHOWED ANY, UH, UNDUE *INTEREST* IN YOUR SON?

NO. NOBODY REAL.

YOUR *BABYSITTER.* YOU SAY SHE WAS ASLEEP?

LIKE A DEAD THING.

SHE USE *DRUGS?*

I WOULDN'T HAVE ENTRUSTED MY SON TO SOMEONE WHO DIDN'T SEEM VERY RESPONSIBLE.

SHE BABYSIT FOR YOU *OFTEN?*

LIEUTENANT PINKWATER--

PINKERTON. LIKE THE DETECTIVE AGENCY. PINKERTON.

2

LIEUTENANT PINKERTON, I'VE HARDLY BEEN OUT OF THE HOUSE IN THREE YEARS.

I ONLY WENT OUT THIS EVENING BECAUSE I'D BEEN OFFERED A JOB, AND MY FRIEND CARLA WANTED ME TO AT LEAST MEET THE GUY AND TALK ABOUT IT.

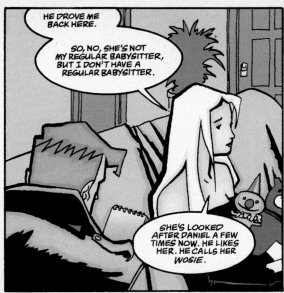

HE DROVE ME BACK HERE.

SO, NO, SHE'S NOT MY REGULAR BABYSITTER, BUT I DON'T HAVE A REGULAR BABYSITTER.

SHE'S LOOKED AFTER DANIEL A FEW TIMES NOW. HE LIKES HER. HE CALLS HER WOSIE.

DO YOU KNOW HOW... WHOEVER TOOK YOUR SON... GOT IN TO THE APARTMENT?

THE DOORS WERE LOCKED. THERE WAS A WINDOW OPEN IN MY BEDROOM. MAYBE THEY GOT OUT THROUGH THERE. I DON'T KNOW.

YEAH. WELL, IT'S A POSSIBILITY.

WE'LL TAKE A LOOK AROUND, NOW, IF YOU DON'T MIND. AND I'LL NEED TO TALK TO THE BABYSITTER.

SHE'S DOWNSTAIRS. THAT'S WHERE SHE LIVES.

SHE WANTED TO STAY UP HERE, BUT LYTA MADE HER GO HOME. THE POOR KID WAS REALLY UPSET.

MIZZ HALL? WE'RE TRYING TO HELP. YOU KNOW THAT?

YES. I DO.

WE CAN ONLY DO THAT IF YOU HELP US.

I AM HELPING YOU.

HEY! THIS OUTSIDE DOOR. ALL THE LOCKS HAVE BEEN MESSED UP.

MA'AM? I THOUGHT YOU SAID THE DOORS WERE LOCKED WHEN YOU GOT HERE.

THEY WERE.

WELL, THESE LOCKS ARE DESTROYED. IT LOOKS LIKE SOMEONE HIT THIS DOOR WITH A TRUCK.

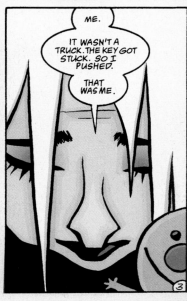

ME.

IT WASN'T A TRUCK. THE KEY GOT STUCK. SO I PUSHED.

THAT WAS ME.

3

THANKS FOR ALL YOUR HELP, LADY.

YEAH. WELL. NO PROBLEM.

LISTEN, YOUR FRIEND. IS SHE *OKAY*?

NO. OF *COURSE* SHE'S NOT OKAY. HER *SON'S* BEEN KIDNAPPED. SHE'S IN *SHOCK*.

BUT THAT'S NOT WHAT YOU *MEANT*, WAS IT. YOU MEANT, IS SHE CRAZY. RIGHT?

WELL....

YES, MA'AM.

WELL, LYTA'S MY BEST FRIEND. AND SHE REALLY *DID* FORCE THE DOOR OPEN.

SHE'S ...SHE'S VERY *STRONG*. WHEN SHE GETS UPSET. LIKE THE OLD *HULK* TV SHOW, Y'KNOW. "YOU WOULDN'T LIKE ME WHEN I GET ANGRY."

AND RIGHT NOW, SHE'S OBVIOUSLY *VERY* UPSET.

BUT SHE'LL BE FINE, WHEN SHE GETS *DANIEL* BACK.

YOU GOING TO *STAY* HERE WITH HER?

FOR THE NEXT FEW DAYS, SURE.

YOU'LL CALL US AS SOON AS YOU FIND ANYTHING?

OF COURSE.

LISTEN, MA'AM.

LET ME PUT THIS *BLUNT*LY. THERE'S NO POINT IN PESTERING US FOR INFORMATION. AS *SOON* AS WE KNOW ANYTHING WE'LL LET *YOU* KNOW.

WE'RE GOING TO WANT TO RETURN, TALK TO THE BABYSITTER, HAVE A LOOK AROUND IN THE DAYLIGHT, ALL THAT KIND OF THING.

WHAT IF THERE'S A RANSOM DEMAND? OR IF WE FIND OUT ANYTHING ON OUR OWN?

THEN YOU GET IN TOUCH WITH US IMMEDIATELY. YOU'VE GOT MY CARD?

YES.

AND MA'AM? TAKE CARE OF YOUR FRIEND.

I'LL TRY.

IT'S THE LEAST I CAN DO.

4

THE KINDLY ONES 2

HAIL!

HALT, STRANGER, AND ANNOUNCE YOURSELF.

CLURACAN OF FAERIE. AMBASSADOR-IN-EXTRAORDINARY TO HER MAJESTY, THE QUEEN OF THE SEELIE COURT.

AND YOU ARE HERE AS AN *ENVOY,* CLURACAN? WE WERE NOT NOTIFIED THAT WE SHOULD EXPECT YOU.

I AM HERE AS A PRIVATE INDIVIDUAL. I HAVE COME TO SEE MY SISTER, THE LADY NUALA, WHO RESIDES IN THIS REALM.

AH. WAIT THERE.

WE HAVE CONFERRED WITH OUR LORD. YOU ARE TO BE ADMITTED, AS A GUEST; UPON THE UNDERSTANDING THAT YOU ARE SOLELY AND WHOLLY RESPONSIBLE FOR YOUR ACTIONS.

BUT OF COURSE.

VERY WELL, CLURACAN. DISMOUNT AND ENTER. LEAVE YOUR HORSE HERE. IT WILL BE STABLED AND GROOMED.

FAIRY. KEEP TO THE PATH AND IT WILL TAKE YOU TO YOUR SISTER.

6

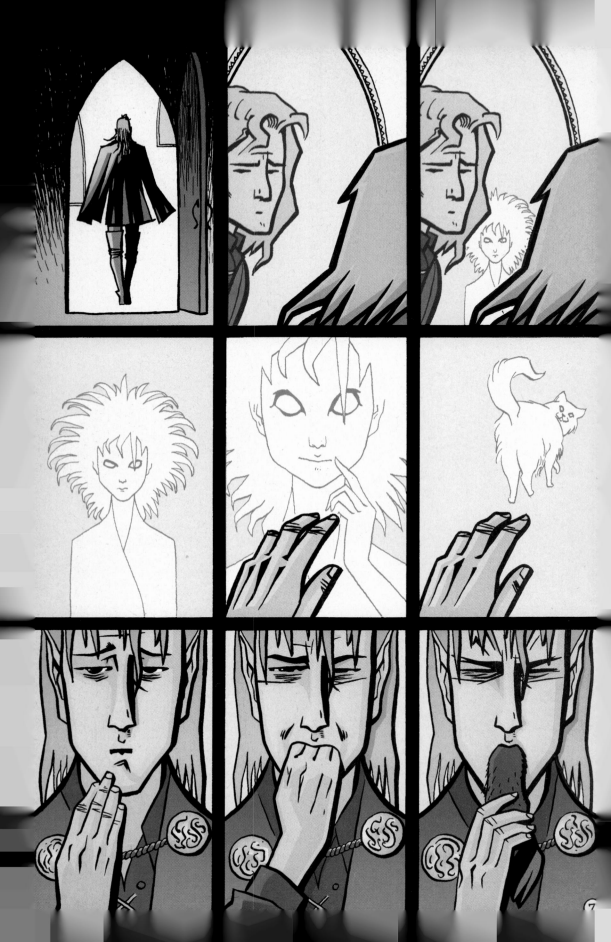

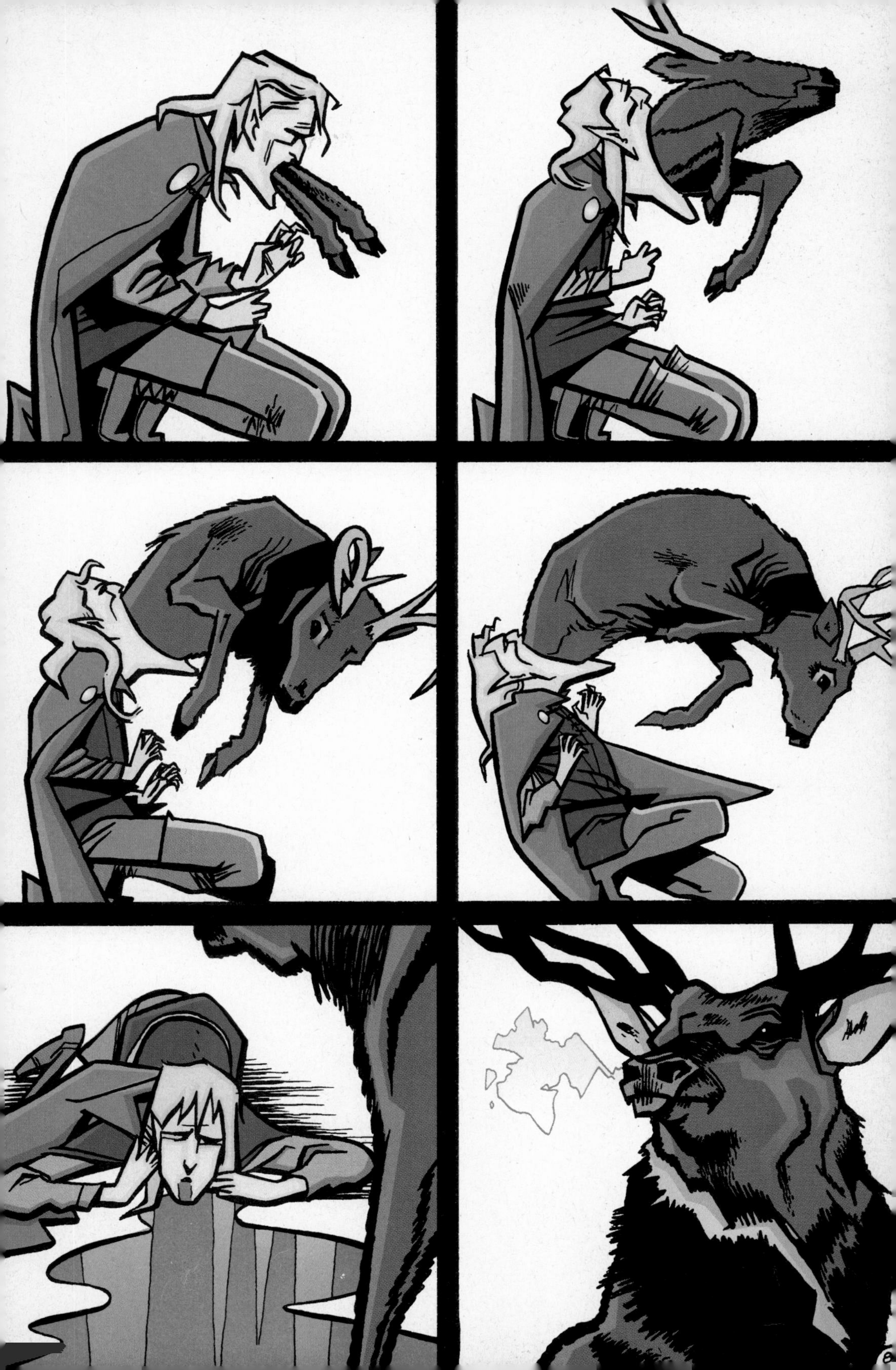

YOU ARE AN *IDIOT*. I DON'T *BELIEVE* IT.

YOU CAN JUST COUNT YOURSELF *LUCKY* THAT THE GRYPHON TOLD ME YOU WERE COMING, AND I RAN DOWN HERE TO *MEET* YOU.

HOW *COULD* YOU?

CLURACAN, HOW *COULD* YOU?

AND THAT *STAG*. DO YOU REALIZE WHAT YOU *DID* IN THERE? YOU COULD HAVE BEEN *KILLED*!

THAT WAS YOUR *NEMESIS*.

YOU'VE CREATED YOUR *NEMESIS*.

HOW *COULD* YOU?

YOU *HAVE* TO KEEP TO THE PROPER PATHS IN THIS PLACE. IT'S RAW DREAMSTUFF. IT'S *DANGEROUS*.

LET'S GO TO MY QUARTERS.

I...

I MEANT NO *HARM*. I WAS CURIOUS...

I...

I'M SORRY. *TRULY* SORRY. IT WAS A *MOST* STUPID THING TO DO.

OH, CLURACAN. I *AM* PLEASED TO SEE YOU. IT'S JUST I *WISH* YOU'D STOP AND THINK BEFORE YOU *DID* THINGS. YOU COULD HAVE GOTTEN YOURSELF INTO *SO* MUCH TROUBLE.

WELL, YOU SORT OF *HAVE* DONE, HAVEN'T YOU? WHAT ON *EARTH* POSSESSED YOU TO *RAISE* THE WILD HART?

9

I DIDN'T REALIZE.

THERE WAS SOMETHING IN MY THROAT. *TICKLING.* I HAD TO GET IT *OUT.*

HMPH. *AND* YOU'RE LATE.

LATE?

YOU SAID YOU WOULD COME AND *SEE* ME. *SOON,* YOU SAID. THAT WAS THREE *YEARS* AGO.

SIT DOWN OVER THERE.

AH. YES. I SUPPOSE I *AM* A LITTLE LATE. OUR QUEEN HAS KEPT ME BUSY.

WHO DID YOUR *DECORATING?*

THE LORD SHAPER GAVE ME THESE QUARTERS; HE HAD THE PALACE CREW MAKE THEM LOOK LIKE THIS. IT WAS *KIND* OF HIM.

WOULD YOU LIKE SOMETHING TO *EAT?* THERE ARE MANY FLOWERS HERE, AND FINE NECTARS TO DRINK.

I'LL TAKE *WINE,* IF YOU HAVE SOME, A RED.

MM. I *WISH* YOU WOULDN'T DRINK SO MUCH. I DON'T THINK IT'S *GOOD* FOR YOU. I'LL FIND SOME FOR YOU.

NUALA...

SOME MONTHS AGO I VISITED YOU IN MY DREAMS; YOU SENT LORD SHAPER TO FREE ME FROM SOME BOTHER I WAS IN.

REALLY? I...

ANYWAY. SHORTLY AFTER THAT, I FOUND MYSELF CAUGHT IN A...STORM.

I TOOK REFUGE IN THE *INN* AT THE END OF ALL WORLDS. IT'S ONE OF THE FOUR FREE HOUSES--

I HAVE *HEARD* OF THE PLACE.

AND I SAW CERTAIN *THINGS* THERE.

WHAT *KIND* OF THINGS?

10

I'D RATHER NOT *SAY*. I SAW CERTAIN THINGS, THROUGH A WINDOW, AND, WHEN THE STORM WAS OVER, I RETURNED HOME AND TOLD THEM TO OUR LADY, AND SHE...

WELL, SHE SENT ME *HERE.*

SHE SENT YOU? BUT YOU'RE NOT *HERE* AS AN *OFFICIAL* ENVOY--?

NO. I'M NOT. SHE SENT ME TO TALK TO YOU.

SHE SAYS IT'S TIME FOR YOU TO COME HOME.

OH.

POP!

≈SNIF≈

WON'T IT BE *WONDERFUL?*

IT WILL BE SO VERY FINE, WITH YOU ONCE MORE IN FAERIE. THE SEELIE COURT HAS DOZENS OF DELIGHTFUL NEW INTRIGUES FOR YOU TO CATCH UP ON.

AND YOU CAN BE BEAUTIFUL AGAIN.

YOU CAN BE THE ICE MAIDEN ONCE MORE. LA BELLE DAME SANS MERCI, EH?

HOW *MANY* YOUNG MEN KILLED THEMSELVES FOR LOVE OF YOU OVER THE YEARS, MY *SISTER?* HOW MANY SIMPLY PALED AND PINED AWAY FOR YOU?

THEY'LL BE DOING IT AGAIN. *DROVES* OF THEM. POSITIVE MULTITUDES. *HORDES.*

"O, NUALA, DO YOU BUT GLANCE IN MY GENERAL DIRECTION ELSE I MUST SURELY DIE."

I'VE NEVER HAD *YOUR* TALENT FOR ATTRACTING MEN. WHEN YOU HAVE YOUR *GLAMOUR* ON, OF COURSE. NOT *NOW.*

BUT AT LEAST *I'VE* KNOWN WHAT TO DO WITH THE ONES I *DID* GET.

WHAT DO I DO *NOW?*

WELL, YOU PROBABLY NEED TO PACK.

IT'S NOT THAT *EASY*, CLURACAN. YOU *GAVE* ME TO LORD SHAPER. WELL, OUR *LADY* DID. WELL, YOU *BOTH* DID.

I WAS A *PRESENT.* I WAS A *BRIBE.*

AND HE ACCEPTED ME.

HE'S *NOT* GOING TO JUST GIVE ME BACK BECAUSE YOU SAY TIME'S UP AND I WANT TO GO HOME.

I'LL *TELL* HIM THAT OUR QUEEN WON'T *MIND.* THEY'RE *OLD* FRIENDS-- MORE THAN *THAT*, PERHAPS, IF YOU LISTEN TO PALACE GOSSIP.

WE'LL ASK HIM TO SEND YOU BACK, AND HE'LL *WAVE US* ON OUR WAY.

AND WHILE WE'RE *AT IT*, I COULD ASK HIM TO DESTROY THE WILD HART.

YOU'RE THE ONLY ONE WHO CAN FIGHT THE HART, CLURACAN. AND IT'S *PROBABLY* NO LONGER EVEN IN THE *CASTLE.* PROBABLY NOT EVEN IN THE *DREAMING.*

I WISH YOU'D *THINK.*

≥SIGH≤

THE SHAPER *WON'T* LET ME GO. I *KNOW* HIM. HE'LL SAY *NO*, CLURACAN.

WELL THEN, LET'S GO AND ASK HIM.

12

EEEEEEE!

LYTA? *LYTA.* IT'S OKAY, HONEY. I'M HERE.

MMM. UHH. MMM.

LYTA?

WAKE *UP.* ARE YOU AWAKE? *LYTA?* I'M HERE. IT'S OKAY.

SHIT, GIRL. YOU'RE *SCARING* ME.

...CARLA?

YOU WERE SCREAMING. IN YOUR SLEEP.

I... I WAS?

UH-HUH.

YOU WANT TO *TELL* ME ABOUT IT?

I DON'T KNOW.

IT SEEMED SO REAL. IT SEEMED SO REAL.

WHAT DID?

I WOKE UP.

I KNOW THAT. *I* WOKE YOU--

NO. I MEAN, IN MY DREAM, I WOKE UP.

"I WOKE UP HEARING A NOISE. AND I SAT UP IN BED. IT WAS LIKE --

"I DON'T KNOW. WHEN YOU'RE DREAMING THERE ARE ALL THESE SENSES THAT YOU DON'T HAVE. YOU MIGHT SEE THINGS, HEAR THINGS, BUT YOU DON'T TOUCH, DON'T SMELL...

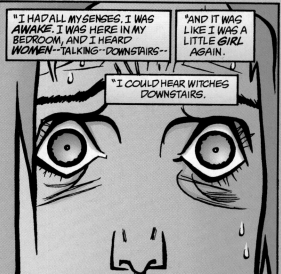

"I HAD ALL MY SENSES. I WAS *AWAKE.* I WAS HERE IN MY BEDROOM, AND I HEARD *WOMEN*--TALKING--DOWNSTAIRS--

"AND IT WAS LIKE I WAS A LITTLE *GIRL* AGAIN.

"I COULD HEAR WITCHES DOWNSTAIRS.

"*REAL WITCHES.* THE KINDS I WAS *SCARED* OF, WHEN I WAS A LITTLE GIRL. THERE WERE WITCHES WHO WOULD EAT YOUR *HEART.* LIKE HANSEL AND GRETEL. *THOSE* KINDS OF WITCHES.

"AND I WAS REALLY *SCARED.* BUT I HAD TO GET UP.

"SO I WENT TO THE DOOR. TO THE LIVING ROOM. BUT THERE *WASN'T* A LIVING ROOM ANYMORE. JUST STAIRS DOWN.

"I WAS SO SCARED.

"I WAS SO *DREAD-FULLY* SCARED."

ARE YOU *SURE* IT'S A FINGER? IT'S VERY *SMALL.*

IT WAS A VERY SMALL BABY.

DITCH-DELIVERED?

AND BIRTH-STRANGLED. *JUST* LIKE IT SAYS IN THE RECIPE.

14

AHH. *HERE* SHE IS. HERE'S THE LITTLE LADY NOW.

COME ON DOWN, MY DEARIE-DUCK.

WE'VE BEEN WAITING FOR YOU, GRANDDAUGHTER.

I DIDN'T KNOW THAT THERE WAS A DOWN-STAIRS, HERE.

THERE'S A DOWNSTAIRS IN EVERYBODY. THAT'S WHERE *WE* LIVE.

I'M DREAMING.

YOU'RE *NOT.*

ARE YOU GOING TO HURT ME?

HURT *YOU?* OF *COURSE* WE'RE GOING TO HURT YOU. EVERYBODY GETS HURT.

BUT WE'RE ALSO GOING TO *HELP* YOU, MY POPSY. YOUR BABBIE *HAS* BEEN STOLEN FROM YOU, AFTER ALL.

TOO *PROUD* TO HAVE A DAUGHTER, EH? *HAD* TO HAVE A SON.

DANIEL! WHERE IS HE? DID YOU THREE *TAKE* HIM?

I'LL THANK YOU NOT TO USE THAT TONE OF VOICE WITH *US,* YOUNG LADY.

YOUNG LADY? *ME?* JESUS. LIKE HOW OLD ARE *YOU,* BIMBO?

A LITTLE OLDER THAN MY TEETH AND AS OLD AS MY TONGUE.

I WASN'T TALKING TO *YOU.* I WAS TALKING TO *HER.*

YOU WERE TALKING TO *US,* GRANDDAUGHTER.

15

I'VE HAD **ENOUGH** OF HER. SHE'S **HAD** HER THREE QUESTIONS. SHE'S **WASTED** THEM. SHE HASN'T EVEN GOT HER MOTHER'S SPARK.

MY MOTHER? YOU KNEW MY MOTHER?

NOT TALKING TO **YOU** ANYMORE. WHERE'S THE TIGER'S CHAUDRON?

WHAT'S A CHAUDRON?

GUTS. ENTRAILS.

I THOUGHT IT WAS A COLOR. AH. **HERE** IT IS. BIT SMELLY, THOUGH.

HOLD ON. YOU **DIDN'T** ANSWER **ALL** MY QUESTIONS.

YOU **DIDN'T** TELL ME WHERE **DANIEL** IS. I ASKED YOU **THAT**.

THOSE WHO **ASK** DON'T **GET**.

AND THOSE WHO **DON'T** ASK DON'T **WANT**. HEE! HEE!

YOU'RE RIGHT. DANIEL'S BEEN **TAKEN** FROM YOU. YOU'VE MET ALREADY THOSE WHO TOOK HIM.

WHERE IS HE RIGHT NOW?

THEY'RE GOING TO PUT HIM IN THE FIRE, MY LITTLE DIDDLY-POUT.

WHAT?

CHOP CHOP CHOP CHOP CHOP

THAT'S A **LOT** MORE THAN THREE QUESTIONS. "**WHAT?**" INDEED. HERE -- HAVE A PORKIE PIE INSTEAD.

IT--IT'S COVERED IN **MUD**.

EVERYONE'S GOT TO EAT A PECK OF DIRT BEFORE THEY DIE.

GRANDDAUGHTER, WE **DO** WANT TO HELP YOU.

THIS WAS THE **FIRST** TIME. THERE WILL BE TWO MORE.

NOW, **POP** HER IN THE **POT**. LET'S SEE WHAT SHE'S MADE OF.

NOOOOO!

16

...IT WAS ONE OF THOSE MOMENTS THAT WENT ON FOREVER.

Y'KNOW, I COULD EVEN *SMELL* THE *STENCH* FROM THE CAULDRON. I COULD FEEL THE *HEAT.*

AND THEN -- *YOU* WERE HOLDING ME.

JESUS. WHAT A *NIGHT-MARE.* HERE.

CARLA. YOU *GOTTA* STOP MAKING ME COFFEE. IT'S NOT THAT I'M UNGRATEFUL, BUT I NEVER TAKE MORE THAN A COUPLA SIPS.

IT'S WHAT MY MOMMA USED TO DO. WHEN THERE WAS A CRISIS. SHE'D MAKE COFFEE.

AND THIS IS DEFINITELY A CRISIS.

WELL, NOW WE'VE GOT THOSE TWO REFUGEES FROM *DRAGNET* ON THE CASE, WITH THE MIGHT OF THE ENTIRE *LAPD* BEHIND THEM.

THEY SEEMED PRETTY COMPETENT.

THEY SEEMED LIKE *JERKS.*

LYTA. HONEY. I WONDER... MAYBE THOSE WITCHES IN YOUR NIGHTMARE WERE YOUR SUBCONSCIOUS, TRYING TO TELL YOU SOMETHING.

I DON'T *TRUST* DREAMS.

THEY *SAID* THEY *WEREN'T* DREAMS.

SO? DREAMS LIE.

AND DO YOU THINK *THIS* DREAM WAS LYING TO YOU?

CARLA, THEY SAID THEY'D COME AND *SEE* ME AGAIN. THEY SAID DANIEL WAS ON *FIRE.*

AND TO TELL YOU THE TRUTH, I DON'T KNOW *WHICH* SCARES ME MORE.

17

"WELL, WHAT DO WE DO *NOW*?"

"WE *TALK* TO HIM, I SUPPOSE."

"OF *COURSE* WE TALK TO HIM, SISTER. I WAS NOT PROPOSING TO WRITE HIM A *LETTER*. SO WHERE SHALL WE FIND YOUR *ERSTWHILE* LORD AND MASTER?"

I DON'T KNOW. I NEVER *HAD* TO SEE HIM BEFORE.

WELL, *SOMEBODY* MUST KNOW.

EXCUSE ME, MY FRIENDS?

YES?

WE NEED TO TALK TO THE LORD SHAPER.

TO LORRD MORRRPHEUS? RRRREALLY?

HOW DO WE GO ABOUT DOING THIS?

YOU'LL NEED TO SEEK AN AUDIENCE.

OH. HOW DO WE DO THAT?

I DON'T KNOW. DO YOU, MY *SWEET*?

NO, RUTHVEN. *WE'VE* NEVER SOUGHT ONE, YOU SEE.

HAVE YOU ASKED LUCIEN? HE MIGHT HAVE A BOOK ON PALACE PROTOCOL.

THANK YOU KINDLY. YOU'VE BOTH BEEN *MOST* HELPFUL.

AU RRREVOIR.

18

WE COULD **SUMMON** HIM.

I...I WOULD NOT...I...

HM. WHICH WAY IS THE THRONE ROOM?

ALONG THERE.

IT'S **CLOSED.** I'VE NEVER **SEEN** IT CLOSED BEFORE.

SO? WE CAN ALWAYS **KNOCK** ON IT.

I DON'T THINK HE'D **LIKE** THAT.

CLURACAN? LET US GO **BACK** TO MY QUARTERS. YOUR **OTHER** IDEA WAS **SO** GOOD. LET'S SEND HIM A FORMAL LETTER--

NONSENSE.

THDUD!

THDUD!

THDUD!

THDUD!

HOLA! LORD SHAPER?

IT IS **I,** THE CLURACAN, DUKE OF THE YARROW AND THE FLAY, FEORIN-CAPTAIN OF ALL THE GHOLES, ALSO ENVOY-IN-EXTRAORDINARY TO HER MAJESTY THE QUEEN OF FAERIE.

I AM HERE WITH MY SISTER, THE LADY NUALA, CURRENTLY IN YOUR SERVICE.

WE DESIRE AUDIENCE.

SEE? NOTHING *HAPPENED*. NOW--LET US RETURN TO MY QUARTERS AND--

OH. OH DEAR.

HE'S NOT HERE.

WE CAN *CALL* HIM.

MY LORD SHAPER? WE CRAVE AUDIENCE.

Indeed? Hello, Cluracan.

GOOD DAY, LORD SHAPER.

And to you, Duke of the Yarrow and the Flay, Feorin-Captain of all the Gholes, also envoy-in-extraordinary to Her Majesty the Queen of Faerie.

So. You seek an audience.

YES.

Why are you here, Cluracan?

I AM NOT HERE FOR MYSELF, SIRE, BUT FOR MY SISTER, THE LADY NUALA.

I see.

Your sister has served me well, Cluracan.

AS YOU SAID TO ME WHEN LAST WE SPOKE, SIRE, SHE HAS A GOOD HEART.

I said that to you, Cluracan?

YES, SIRE.

Well, it is a truth.

I am somewhat older than the fairy folk, Cluracan. But I have long had a fondness for them. You have entertained me.

Like me, your people live by strict rules, and binding traditions--although your ways are not my ways.

MY LORD, I HAVE COME TO ASK A FAVOR OF YOU. IT CONCERNS A GIFT.

A gift? Hmmm...

Fairy gifts traditionally are double-edged knives.

AND ARE YOUR OWN GIFTS ALWAYS WITHOUT CONSEQUENCE, SIRE?

You are a rogue, Cluracan. But you are an amusing rogue.

I notice you stepped off my path, when you came to this place.

I DID THAT THING, SIRE. I APOLOGIZE. IT WAS A MOST FOOLISH THING TO DO,

SIRE, I, UH, INADVERTENTLY... FREED AN... *ANIMAL* WHEN I DID THAT. I WAS WONDERING, IF YOU *RAN* INTO IT, IF IT'S NOT TOO MUCH TROUBLE, POSSIBLY YOU COULD...

Destroy your nemesis, *Cluracan?* No. It is no longer in the Dreaming; and it is not mine to destroy.

Is that the favor you wished to ask of me?

NO, SIRE. THE LADY NUALA. SHE WAS A GIFT TO YOU, FROM MY QUEEN.

I HAVE COME TO ASK IF SHE CAN RETURN TO FAERIE WITH ME...

AS *I* WAS THE ONE WHO GAVE HER TO YOU, I WAS THE ONE WHO FELT IT WAS TIME TO ASK YOU FOR HER BACK. SHE IS MUCH MISSED--HER CHEERY WAYS, HER WITTY JESTS... YOU KNOW HOW IT IS.

I see. And what does the lady Nuala say about all this?

SIR?

I--YOU'VE BEEN VERY *KIND*, SIR. FOR THE LAST THREE YEARS I -- SIR.

I AM *YOURS*. WHAT *YOU* WISH IS ALSO WHAT I WISH.

I see. And Cluracan, what does your Queen say?

SIRE, IT SHOULD BE UNDER-STOOD THAT I AM HERE AS A PRIVATE INDIVID-UAL, REPRESENTING ONLY MYSELF.

I AM NOT HERE TO SPEAK FOR MY QUEEN.

You try my patience, fairy. What does Titania say?

SPEAKING INFORMALLY, I CAN STATE THAT HER MAJESTY WOULD VIEW THE IDEA OF THE RETURN OF THE LADY NUALA WITH UNMIXED PLEASURE.

I see.

22

Hm. The palace staff are my responsibility, Cluracan.

YOU ARE RESPONSIBLE FOR *MANY* THINGS, SIRE.

Yes.

Very well. You may return to Faerie, Nuala.

Is there anything you wish to take with you?

WHAT?

Is there anything you wish to take away with you, Nuala?

N-NO.

Very well.

I would like to formally to thank you for your service, these last three years. Give me your pendant.

WHAT?

Your pendant.

HERE.

There. For your service. A gift. If in need, hold the stone with both hands, and call me. I will come to you; you may have one boon.

OH.

23

You desire more than that?

OH. NO. THANK YOU, SIR. THAT'S...

...VERY KIND.

Very well. This audience is at an end. Your horse, Cluracan, is fed and ready. Nuala, I have taken the liberty of furnishing you with a mare. Release her when you reach the borders of faerie.

Farewell.

WELL--THAT WAS EASY, WASN'T IT? I DIDN'T EXPECT IT WAS GOING TO BE THAT EASY. I HAD EXPECTED THAT HE WOULD AT LEAST DEMAND TRIBUTE OF SOME KIND.

WHAT DID HE SAY TO YOU ABOUT THE PENDANT? I COULDN'T HEAR HIM. OR UNDERSTAND HIM. OR SOMETHING.

NOTHING. HE JUST TOUCHED IT.

SO. NOW WE GO HOME.

ABOUT TIME, TOO.

NUALA?

NUALA, YOU'RE CRYING.

H-HE DIDN'T EVEN TRY TO FIGHT FOR ME, BROTHER.

HE DIDN'T CARE IF I STAYED OR I WENT.

EXACTLY.

AND I CANNOT TELL YOU HOW RELIEVED I AM. NOW: LET'S GO HOME.

part
Three

gwa tsi sv s

I THINK IT'S GOING TO BE BIGGER THAN I HAD PLANNED.

I DON'T MIND. AS BIG AS IT NEEDS TO BE.

YOU MAY WANT TO STAND BACK. THIS IS GOING TO BE HOT.

PROBABLY TIME TO HAUL THE BRAT IN, THEN...

≷ UHHHN... ≷

IT'S STUCK!

WHAT IF HE'S ESCAPED?

WHAT? BUT...

HO HO HOH! JUST PULLING YOUR LEG. IT'S COMING FINE.

DON'T DO THAT.

AS IF HE COULD GET AWAY. OR EVER THE SILVER CORD BE LOOSED, WE'LL BOTH BE UP TO OUR NECKS IN SHIT, EH?

WHOOMPH

I DID THAT ONCE. THEY MADE A SAGA ABOUT IT.

WHAT?

KEEP PULLING HIM IN, AND I'LL TELL YOU ABOUT IT. TRUE STORY.

MANY YEARS AGO I CONVINCED THOR OF THE AESIR THAT THE REASON FOR HIS IMPOTENCE WAS THAT HE WAS PREGNANT.

PREGNANT?

MM, HE'S NOT VERY BRIGHT.

AND I TOLD HIM TO LIE FACE DOWN AND NAKED ON HIS SLEEPING FURS UNTIL I CAME AND DELIVERED HIM OF CHILD.

HE *LISTENED* TO YOU?

I WAS DISGUISED AS A WANDERING PHYSICIAN. AND, AS I SAID, HE'S--

NOT VERY BRIGHT?

EXACTLY.

SO I FED HIM A GALLON OF CASTOR OIL, PAINTED HIS ARSE BLUE AND SHOVED A CORK IN HIS BUM-HOLE.

WHY?

BECAUSE IT AMUSED ME TO DO SO. I TOLD HIM IT WAS THE CURE FOR HIS CONDITION. THEN I WENT OFF TO SLEEP WITH HIS WIFE.

HOHOH!

SHE *WASN'T* MUCH OF A LAY. BUT IT AMUSED ME TO KNOW THAT IT WOULD DESTROY HIM IF EVER HE FOUND OUT.

SO THOR IS LYING FACE DOWN WITH A CORK UP HIS FUNDAMENT FOR A WEEK AND A DAY, WHILE HIS INSIDES CONTINUE TO RUMBLE THEIR COURSE.

AND *NOW* HE'S GOT A PAIN IN HIS GUT LIKE YOU WOULDN'T BELIEVE, AS THE PRESSURE CONTINUES TO BUILD...

I'D *TOLD* HIM HE MIGHT EXPERIENCE SOME PAIN. THAT IT WAS COMMON IN PREGNANCY.

SUDDENLY, INTO THE ROOM, THROUGH AN OPEN WINDOW, BOUNDS *RATATOSK,* THE SQUIRREL WHO LIVES IN THE BRANCHES OF THE WORLD TREE.

RATATOSK IS CURIOUS AS ANY LITTLE SQUIRREL.

AND HE CLIMBS ON TOP OF THOR'S STRAINING, SQUIRMING BUTTOCKS, AND HE-- PULLS *OUT* THE CORK.

≈*THRRRRRRPPPPPP!*≈ IT'S AN EXPLOSION-- EIGHT DAYS' WORTH OF OILED SHIT THUNDERS FORTH FROM THE FUNDAMENT OF THE LORD OF STORMS.

2

AND THE MIGHTY THOR SITS UP, AND LOOKS ROUND, AND SEES RATATOSK ON THE GROUND, STUNNED, GASSED, BEFOULED.

AND SLOWLY, WITH HANDS AS BIG AS HAM HOCKS, HE PICKS UP THE LITTLE ANIMAL, AND *STARES* AT IT.

AND THEN, WITH ONE PONDEROUS MOTION, HE *CLASPS* IT TO HIS BOSOM.

"YOU'RE UGLY," HE SAYS, "YOU'RE HAIRY, AND YOU'RE COVERED IN SHIT. BUT YOU'RE *MINE*, AND I *LOVE* YOU!"

EEEEEEHEEEHEHEHEHEHEHEHEHHHEEE! OHHH, THAT'S *RICH*, THAT IS...

"YOU'RE MINE AND I LOVE YOU."

HEEEEE!

THUP THUP THUP THUP

OOH...

UPS-A-DAISY. HERE HE COMES.

THERE YOU ARE, BOY. COME TO NUNCLE ROBIN.

WHAT'S HE GOT?

A FEATHER. LOOKS LIKE A PHOENIX'S.

THEY'RE *LUCKY.*

FOR WHOM?

3

GIVE HIM HERE.

THERE WE GO, DANNY-BOY. *WHAT* A LOVELY FEATHER WE'VE GOT.

YES, IT'S DEFINITELY FROM A PHOENIX.

See nibs.

NOW, YOUNG MAN-- ONTO THE NICE FIRE.

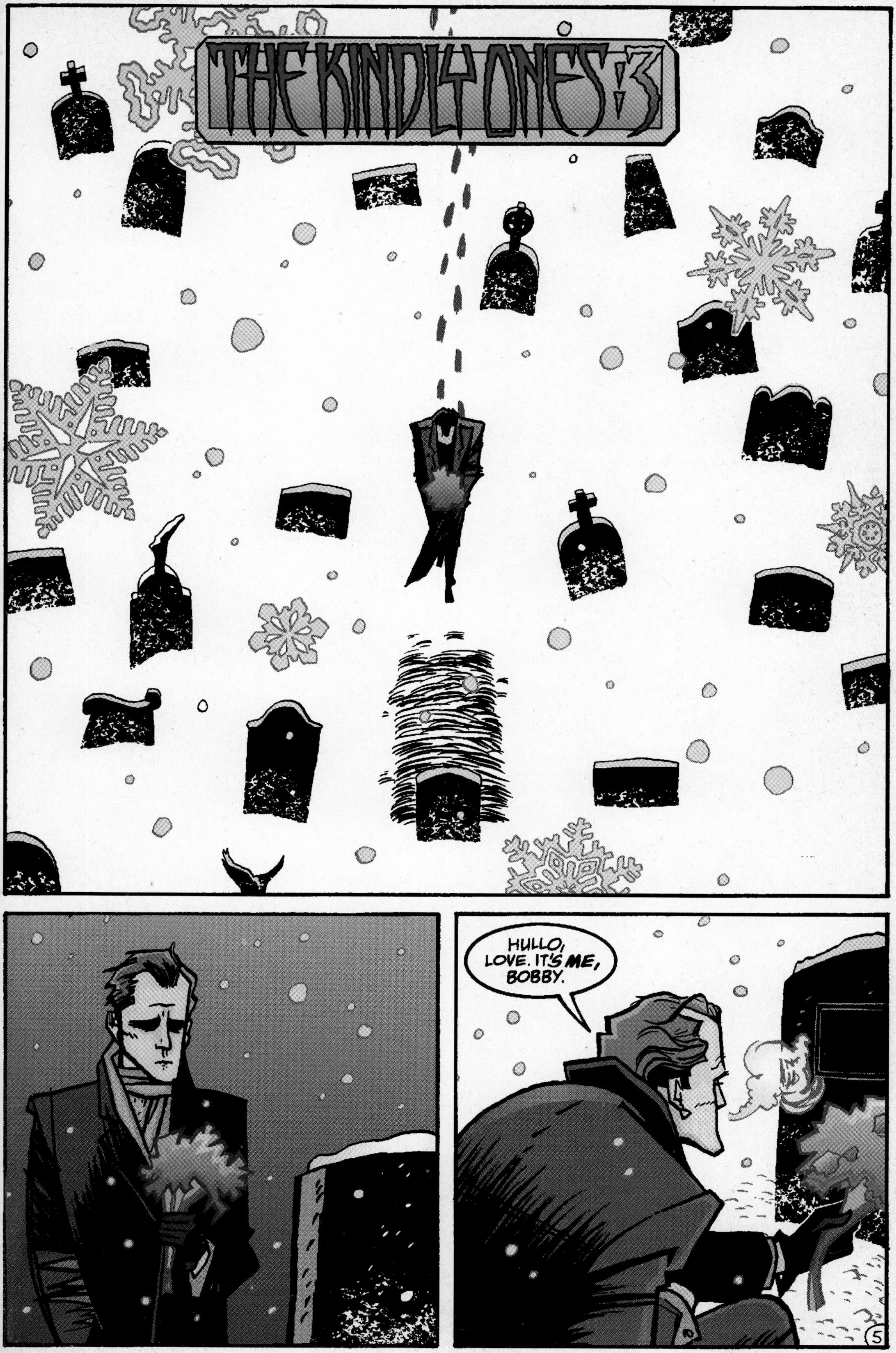
THE KINDLY ONES: 3
HULLO, LOVE. IT'S ME, BOBBY.
5

LET'S SEE. WHAT HAVE I GOT TO SAY?

WELL, *FIRST* OF ALL, I HOPE *THAT'LL* TEACH YOU TO LOOK BOTH WAYS BEFORE CROSSING THE STREET.

HAHHH...

OH *SHIT.*

I'M SORRY...

I *DO* THINK YOU'RE LISTENING TO ME, FROM SOMEWHERE.

I MEAN, I'VE SEEN TOO MUCH OVER THE YEARS TO BELIEVE THAT IT STARTS AND ENDS WITH BODIES.

THERE'S *SOMETHING* AROUND BEFORE BODIES START, SOMETHING AROUND *AFTER* THEY ROT.

BUGGERED IF I KNOW WHAT IT *IS,* THOUGH.

SOMEBODY ONCE TOLD ME YOU DON'T REALLY DIE UNTIL EVERYONE THAT YOU KNEW IS DEAD, TOO. THINK OF ALL THE PEOPLE I'M KEEPING ALIVE, EH?

≥sigh≤

I DON'T KNOW.

I DON'T REMEMBER WHAT YOU *SMELL* LIKE.

YOU'VE BEEN GONE TWO DAYS, AND I DON'T REMEMBER HOW YOU SMELLED. YOU DIDN'T SMELL LIKE ANYONE ELSE. I *LIKED* THE WAY YOU SMELLED.

I....

I MISS YOU A LOT.

6

BRRR.

LISTEN, AUDREY. THERE'S STUFF I NEVER TOLD YOU. I MEAN, THAT STUFF YOU WERE ASKING ME ABOUT. ABOUT MY FAMILY. ALL THAT STUFF.

I NEVER *WOULD* HAVE TOLD YOU, EITHER.

NOTHING PERSONAL.

IT'S JUST TOO EASY TO SEE MYSELF LOCKED AWAY WHILE A BUNCH OF NOBEL PRIZE WANNABES EXAMINE SLICES OF MY PANCREAS, AND TRY TO FIGURE OUT HOW I GOT TO BE SIX HUNDRED AND THIRTY YEARS OLD.

OR SIX HUNDRED AND THIRTY-FIVE. I DON'T KNOW.

AND THE TROUBLE IS, THERE'S NOTHING TO FIND OUT.

YOU KNOW HOW I GOT TO BE MY AGE?

I HAVEN'T *DIED*, YET. THAT'S HOW.

I EVEN *TOLD* YOU HOW NOT TO DIE. YOU THOUGHT I WAS JOKING. THERE'S NEVER BEEN A WOMAN BELIEVED ME YET...

OR A MAN, FOR THAT MATTER.

CHRIST. I'VE SEEN *SO* MANY PEOPLE DIE.

EVERYONE'S DIED. EVERYONE I'VE LOVED. MY WIVES. MY LOVES. MY CHILDREN.

YOU KNOW, THERE'S SOMETHING IT TOOK ME A COUPLE OF CENTURIES TO FIGURE OUT. I MEAN, THERE WAS A WHILE WHEN I THOUGHT THAT LIFE WAS ALL ABOUT FIGHTING AND EATING AND SEX.

MAINLY SEX. IT WAS NEVER *THAT* HARD TO DIP YOUR WICK. I MEAN, UNLESS YOU'RE A LEPER YOU CAN GET A MAID TO BED YOU, IF THAT'S WHAT YOU'RE AFTER.

BUT ONE DAY I REALIZED THAT IT WAS SORT OF EMPTY IF YOU WEREN'T WITH SOMEONE YOU WANTED TO SPEND SOME TIME WITH.

7

IT WASN'T THAT I DIDN'T GET *HORNY*. IT WAS THAT THERE DIDN'T SEEM MUCH *POINT*, IF IT WASN'T WITH SOMEONE I LOVED. LEANOR OR LISABET OR ANNE OR PEG...

YOU WAS THE FIRST WOMAN I'D BEEN WITH SINCE PEGGY DIED.

I *WISH* I COULD HAVE TOLD YOU ABOUT PEG. YOU'D'VE LIKED HER.

SHE DIED IN THE BLITZ. WE WERE TRAPPED IN A CELLAR. I HELD HER HAND, AS SHE STOPPED BREATHING...

AH, BUT THAT'S THE PAST, AND DONE WITH.

I THOUGHT WE'D HAVE LONGER.

IT NEVER GETS ANY EASIER. PEOPLE YOU LOVE NOT BEING THERE ANY MORE.

ANYWAY. THAT'S ALL THE STUFF I WANTED TO SAY.

I *MISS* YOU, AUDREY. I WISH I COULD REMEMBER WHAT YOU SMELLED LIKE.

HULLO YOU.

WHAT ARE YOU DOING HERE?

I came to talk with you, Hob Gadling.

YEAH? WELL, LET'S GET OUT OF THIS BLOODY SNOW, THEN. THERE'S A PUB OVER THE ROAD.

THE FAITH HOPE AND CHARITY

WHAT'LL YOU HAVE TO DRINK?

Dark mead, if you please.

IN THIS DAY AND AGE? MIGHT AS WELL ASK FOR SACK, OR HOT-SPICED MADEIRA.

I'M GOING TO HAVE A SCOTCH. YOU WANT ONE?

Whatever you think fit.

9

AN INTERJECTION: AT THIS TIME, CERTAIN OTHER THINGS WERE HAPPENING.

FOR EXAMPLE, IT WAS THEN THAT DESTINY FOUND HIMSELF TRAILING GHOST-BOOKS IN HIS WAKE.

IT WAS SHORTLY AFTER THAT DESTINY CAUGHT SIGHT OF HIMSELF, WHILE WANDERING THE GARDEN THAT WAS HIS REALM.

THIS WAS NO SURPRISE TO HIM; IT WAS WRITTEN IN HIS BOOK THAT HE WOULD SEE HIMSELF, BUT STILL, IT GAVE HIM A CHILL TO SEE HIM THERE.

IT WAS THEN THAT DESIRE CLOSED OFF ITS REALM. THE SILVER HEART IN ITS SIBLING'S GALLERIES WAS REPLACED BY A DARK VOID, SIGNIFYING DESIRE'S UNWILLINGNESS TO GIVE OR RECEIVE COMMUNICATION OF ANY KIND.

THE THRESHOLD, DESIRE'S HOME, A FLESH AND BLOOD CITADEL HIGHER THAN MOUNTAINS, CLOSED ITS EYES; AND DESIRE WANDERED THE PATHWAYS OF ITS BODY, IN THE DARKNESS, ALONE.

11

IT WAS THEN THAT DESPAIR, NOTICING THE MISSING HEART IN HER GALLERY, SAT MAKING SMALL NOISES IN THE MIRRORED MIST; HER RATS RAN OVER HER NAKED BODY, NIPPING AT HER FLESH TO ATTRACT HER ATTENTION.

IT WAS THEN THAT DELIRIUM NOTICED THAT SHE HAD ABSENT-MINDEDLY TRANSFORMED INTO A HUNDRED AND ELEVEN PERFECT, TINY MULTICOLORED FISH.

EACH FISH SANG A DIFFERENT SONG.

12

AND AS SHE PUT HERSELF BACK TOGETHER AGAIN, UNABLE FOR THE MOMENT TO REMEMBER WHETHER THE SILVER FLECKS WENT INTO THE BLUE EYE OR THE GREEN ONE, SHE DECIDED THAT A DOG WOULD BE A NICE THING TO HAVE.

AND THEN IT OCCURRED TO HER THAT THERE *HAD* BEEN A DOG AROUND AT *SOME* POINT, HADN'T THERE? A *NICE DOGGIE...*

AND SHE WENT OFF TO LOOK FOR IT, TRAILING OCCASIONAL FISH...

13

...WELL, IT'S HARD TO FORGET A DREAM THAT YOU WAKE UP FROM WITH HALF A BOTTLE OF HUNDRED-YEAR-OLD WINE YOU DIDN'T HAVE WHEN YOU WENT TO BED.

I DREAMED THAT YOU SAID YOU WERE OFF ON A JOURNEY, AND YOU MIGHT *MISS* OUR NEXT GET-TOGETHER.

YES. THE JOURNEY IN QUESTION WAS NOT ENTIRELY WITHOUT INCIDENT; HOWEVER, IT CONCLUDED IN A MORE-OR-LESS SATISFACTORY MANNER.

I...I WAS SORRY TO HEAR OF YOUR LOSS, HOB.

S'OKAY. PEOPLE DIE. WELL, *MOST* OF THEM.

NO, IT'S *NOT* OKAY. IT *STINKS.* LOOK. YOU'RE... I DUNNO, MAGIC OR SOMETHING. *YOU'VE* GOT POWERS AND STUFF, HAVEN'T YOU?

COULDN'T YOU BRING HER *BACK?*

OR COULD YOU GO BACK IN TIME AND MAKE HER STOP AND LOOK BEFORE SHE RAN ACROSS THE ROAD? COULD YOU MAKE THE BLOKE DRIVING THE VAN IN A LITTLE LESS OF A HURRY?

NO. I WILL NOT DO THESE THINGS.

WELL, WHAT *CAN* YOU DO, THEN?

I COULD MAKE IT THAT YOU DREAMED OF HER EACH NIGHT. BUT YOU WOULD NOT THANK ME FOR THAT.

NO, I WOULDN'T.

I REMEMBER ONCE I DREAMED THAT PEGGY DIED. AND I WOKE UP IN TEARS.

THEN I WOKE UP A BIT MORE, AND IT CAME TO ME IT WAS ONLY A SILLY DREAM.

AND I ROLLED OVER IN BED TO TELL PEG ABOUT IT, BUT SHE WASN'T THERE. AND THEN I WOKE UP PROPERLY, AND I REALIZED THAT SHE'D DIED A MONTH BEFORE.

DREAMS ARE TRICKY BUGGERS. YOU *CAN'T* TRUST THEM.

14

MAYBE YOU COULD TRACK DOWN THE BASTARD WHO WAS DRIVING THE VAN... JUST *HIT* HER AND DROVE OFF AS FAST AS HIS LITTLE WHEELS COULD CARRY HIM.

And what should I do with him, when I find him?

WELL, IN THE *OLD* DAYS WE'D BEGIN BY CUTTING OFF HIS *EARS* AND MAKING HIM EAT THEM. NOW?

I DON'T KNOW. SOMETHING TO TEACH HIM A LESSON.

I do not recommend revenge. It tends to have repercussions.

I KNOW.

I SUPPOSE I JUST WANT HIM TO KNOW WHO HE *KILLED*. WHAT AUDREY *MEANT* TO ME. WHY SHE WAS A GOOD PERSON. WHY SHE MADE ME *HAPPY* WHEN SHE *SMILED*.

Very well. It is done.

I should not have come here.

YOU'RE *GOING*? ALREADY?

LISTEN, I'M PLEASED YOU CAME, BUT...

ARE YOU IN TROUBLE?

NO.

THEN WHAT'S *WRONG*?

There is nothing wrong.

15

HOY!

LOOK. I SHOULDN'T SAY THIS. IT'S NOT MY PLACE--

I'VE BEEN AROUND A BIT. NOT AS LONG AS YOU, OBVIOUSLY. BUT IF THERE'S ONE THING I'VE LEARNED TO PICK UP ON, IT'S THE SMELL OF DEATH. I MEAN, IT'S ALMOST LIKE A REAL SMELL.

YOU SNIFF IT ON A BLOKE AND TWO WEEKS LATER HE GETS HIS THROAT CUT IN AN ALLEY.

AND MATEY, YOU STINK OF IT. I WORRY. YOU TAKE CARE OF YOURSELF.

Thank you, Hob. I shall.

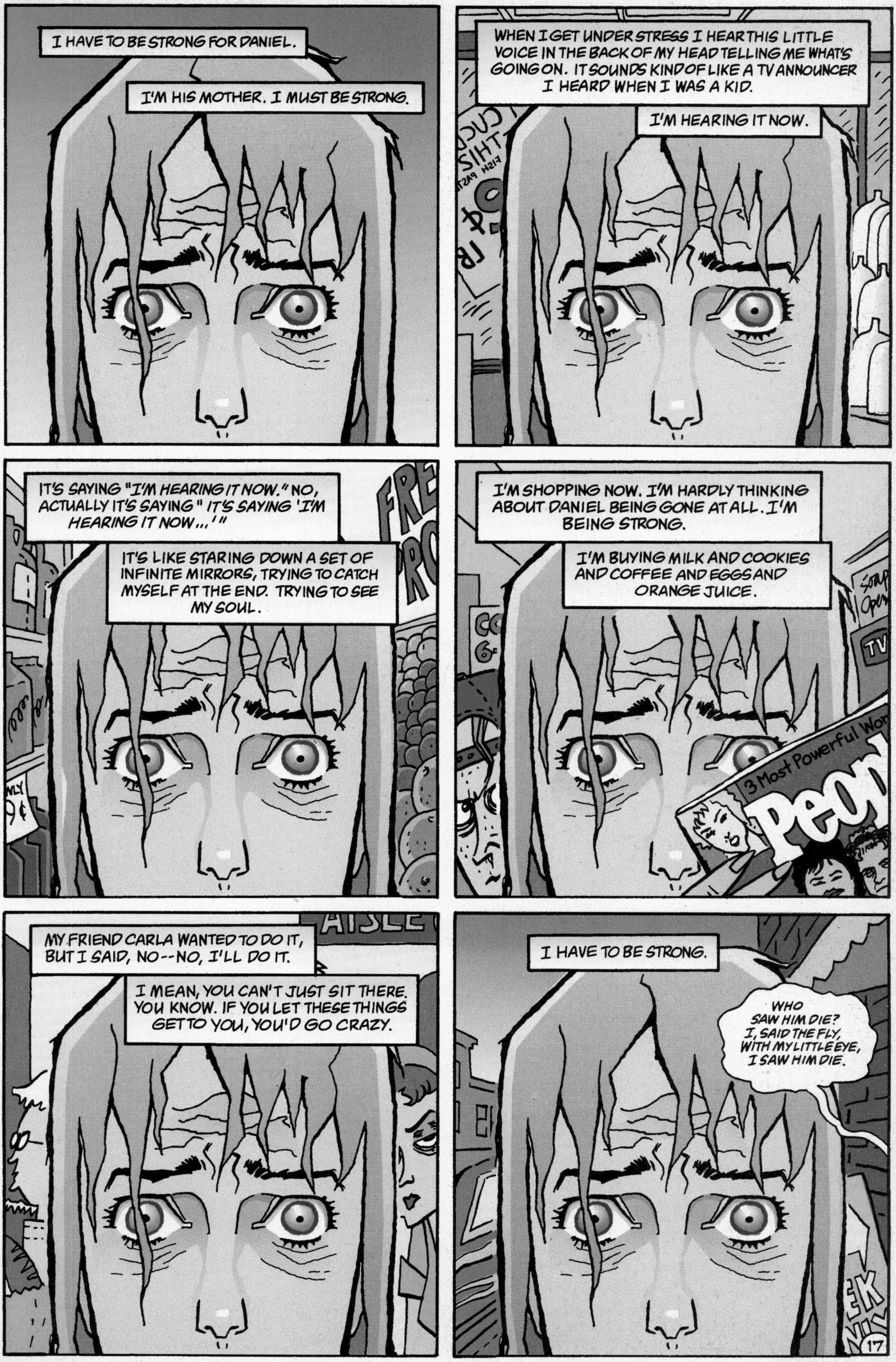
I HAVE TO BE STRONG FOR DANIEL.
I'M HIS MOTHER. I MUST BE STRONG.
WHEN I GET UNDER STRESS I HEAR THIS LITTLE VOICE IN THE BACK OF MY HEAD TELLING ME WHAT'S GOING ON. IT SOUNDS KIND OF LIKE A TV ANNOUNCER I HEARD WHEN I WAS A KID.
I'M HEARING IT NOW.
IT'S SAYING "I'M HEARING IT NOW." NO, ACTUALLY IT'S SAYING " IT'S SAYING 'I'M HEARING IT NOW...' "
IT'S LIKE STARING DOWN A SET OF INFINITE MIRRORS, TRYING TO CATCH MYSELF AT THE END. TRYING TO SEE MY SOUL.
I'M SHOPPING NOW. I'M HARDLY THINKING ABOUT DANIEL BEING GONE AT ALL. I'M BEING STRONG.
I'M BUYING MILK AND COOKIES AND COFFEE AND EGGS AND ORANGE JUICE.
3 Most Powerful Wom
Peop
MY FRIEND CARLA WANTED TO DO IT, BUT I SAID, NO--NO, I'LL DO IT.
I MEAN, YOU CAN'T JUST SIT THERE. YOU KNOW. IF YOU LET THESE THINGS GET TO YOU, YOU'D GO CRAZY.
AISLE
I HAVE TO BE STRONG.
WHO SAW HIM DIE? I, SAID THE FLY, WITH MY LITTLE EYE, I SAW HIM DIE.

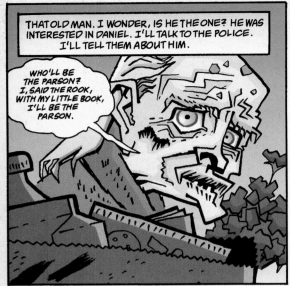

THAT OLD MAN. I WONDER, IS HE THE ONE? HE WAS INTERESTED IN DANIEL. I'LL TALK TO THE POLICE. I'LL TELL THEM ABOUT HIM.

WHO'LL BE THE PARSON? I, SAID THE ROOK, WITH MY LITTLE BOOK, I'LL BE THE PARSON.

NOW I'M HOME AGAIN.

NOW ERIC'S COME OVER TO SEE HOW I'M DOING.

HE TELLS ME THAT OF COURSE THE JOB OFFER'S STILL OPEN, BUT HE'LL WAIT UNTIL I'M FEELING BETTER AND OF COURSE UNTIL THEY FIND DANIEL BEFORE PUSHING IT FURTHER.

HE TELLS ME THAT I'M BEING STRONG.

I TELL HIM I'M BEING STRONG FOR DANIEL.

HE ASKS ME IF I'VE THOUGHT ABOUT HAVING A MAN AROUND. HE TELLS ME I'M A VERY ATTRACTIVE WOMAN, AND THAT IF I NEED A SHOULDER TO CRY ON IN MY TIME OF TROUBLE, IF I NEED SOMEONE TO TURN TO, WELL, HE'D BE PROUD TO BE THERE FOR ME.

HE TOUCHES MY NECK AND I DON'T WANT HIM TOUCHING MY NECK SO I MOVE HIS ARM AWAY AND THERE'S A CRUNCHING NOISE, AND HE STARTS SAYING I'VE BROKEN HIS ARMBONE AND HE WINDS UP GOING OFF IN AN AMBULANCE.

18

THE BONES IN THE ARM ARE CALLED THE ULNA, THE RADIUS AND THE HUMERUS.

THEN CARLA COMES BACK AND WE HAVE A SORT OF DISCUSSION ABOUT THINGS, AND SHE DECIDES NOT TO STAY ANOTHER NIGHT AND I SAY THAT'S FINE BECAUSE I CAN MANAGE ON MY OWN.

I DON'T GO TO SLEEP THAT NIGHT. I STAY UP ALL NIGHT AND WALK AROUND.

LAST NIGHT I GOT MAYBE AN HOUR OF SLEEP.

THERE WAS A --

(DREAM. MAYBE. A DREAM. A BAD DREAM. JUST A DREAM.)

I THINK ABOUT MY MOTHER, AND I THINK ABOUT MY SON, AND I START AT EVERY NOISE, AND EVERY TIME A CAR COMES DOWN THE STREET I'M SURE IT'S THE POLICE, BRINGING DANIEL BACK TO ME.

AND EVERY TIME THE CAR JUST KEEPS ON GOING AND I JUST WANT TO BREAK DOWN AND CRY BUT I DON'T BECAUSE I HAVE TO BE STRONG FOR DANIEL.

I MUST BE STRONG FOR DANIEL.

19

I WISH I SMOKED CIGARETTES. IT WOULD GIVE ME SOMETHING TO DO. I READ *PEOPLE* MAGAZINE TWICE ALREADY.

I'M NOT HUNGRY, THOUGH.

AND THERE'S NOTHING ON *TV* AT 4:00 AM BUT HOME SHOPPING CHANNELS AND TWILIGHT ZONE RERUNS AND I JUST DON'T HAVE THE ATTENTION SPAN SO I GO BACK TO THE WINDOW ONCE MORE AND WAIT.

AND FINALLY AFTER A NIGHT THAT LASTS FOREVER I WATCH THE PURPLE DARKNESS FADE INTO TWILIGHT AND THE EASTERN SKY SWIM WITH BLOOD AND SALMON.

RED SKY IN THE MORNING, SAILORS' WARNING...

AND THE BLOOD FADES INTO BLUE AND SOON IT'S STARTING TO GET HOT, AND IT'S A PRETTY, CLEAR DAY BECAUSE THE RAIN CLEANED THE SMOG OUT OF THE AIR ...

AND I READ SOMEWHERE THAT YOU CAN GO CRAZY IF YOU DON'T GET ANY SLEEP.

BUT I'M DOING FINE FEELING JUST FINE AND EVERYTHING'S CLEAR AS CRYSTAL.

I'M NOT EVEN HUNGRY.

AND THE ROAR OF CARS GETS LOUD AND STEADY ENOUGH THAT I CAN'T TELL THE SOUNDS OF INDIVIDUAL CARS ANYMORE SO IN THE END THE SOUND OF THE DOORBELL TAKES ME BY SURPRISE.

WATCH ME. THIS IS ME GOING TO THE DOOR, JUST LIKE I'VE DONE THOUSANDS AND THOUSANDS OF TIMES IN THE PAST AND NONE OF THOSE TIMES WAS IMPORTANT I MEAN NOT ONE OF THOSE TIMES WAS IMPORTANT, I CAN'T EVEN REMEMBER THEM AS INDIVIDUAL TIMES, WHO REMEMBERS WALKING TO THE DOOR...?

AND THEN I OPEN THE DOOR.

MA'AM?

DETECTIVE PINKERTON. DETECTIVE FELLOWES.

THAT'S RIGHT, MA'AM.

IS THERE ... IS THERE NEWS?

I'M AFRAID SO, MA'AM. WE'D BETTER COME INSIDE.

NO. TELL ME. NOW.

DANIEL?

WE RECOVERED A BODY, MA'AM.

LAST NIGHT.

IT'S ... IT'S KIND OF BADLY BURNED.

2

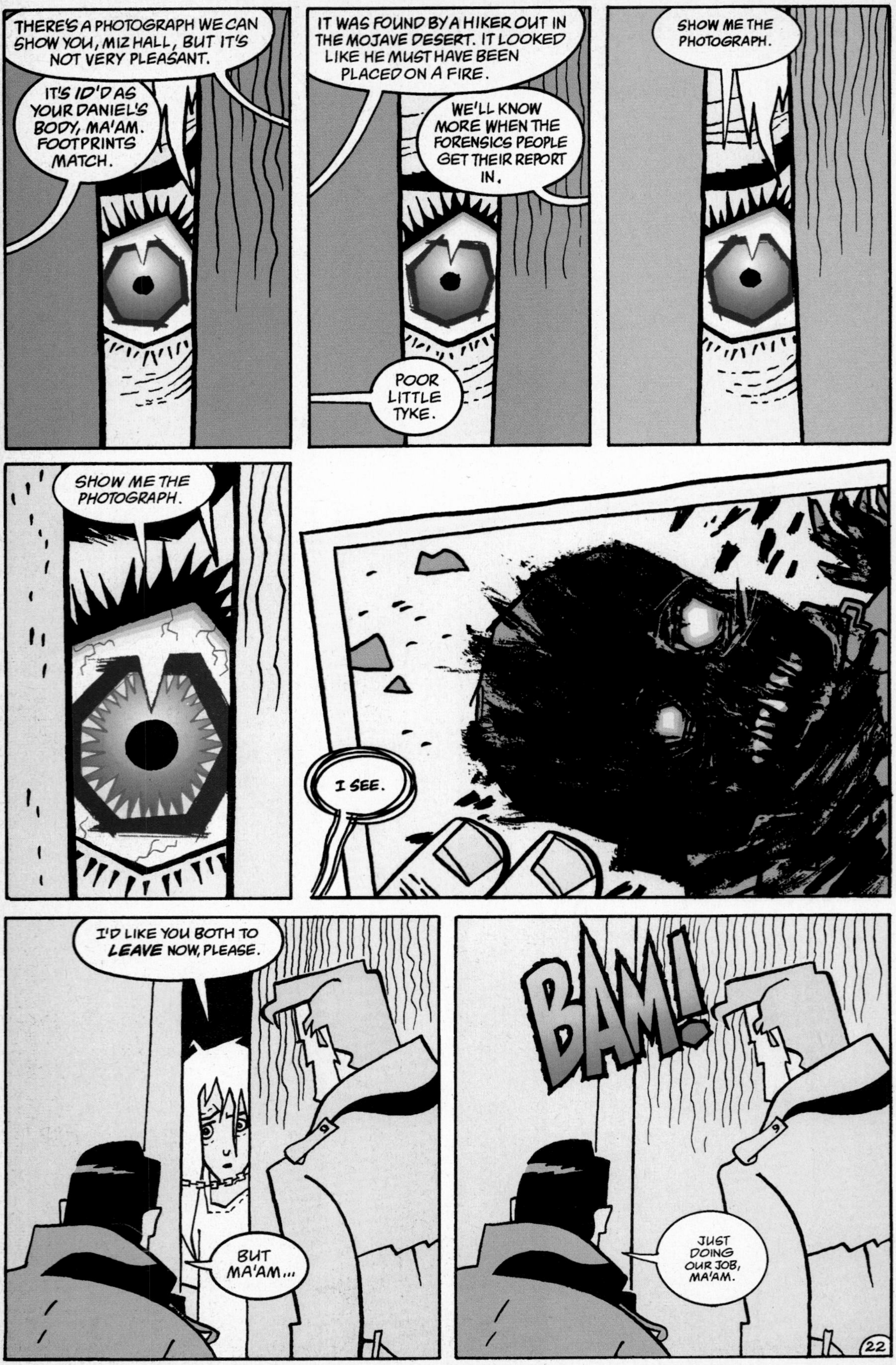
THERE'S A PHOTOGRAPH WE CAN SHOW YOU, MIZ HALL, BUT IT'S NOT VERY PLEASANT.
IT'S *ID'D* AS YOUR DANIEL'S BODY, MA'AM. FOOTPRINTS MATCH.
IT WAS FOUND BY A HIKER OUT IN THE MOJAVE DESERT. IT LOOKED LIKE HE MUST HAVE BEEN PLACED ON A FIRE.
WE'LL KNOW MORE WHEN THE FORENSICS PEOPLE GET THEIR REPORT IN.
POOR LITTLE TYKE.
SHOW ME THE PHOTOGRAPH.
SHOW ME THE PHOTOGRAPH.
I SEE.
I'D LIKE YOU BOTH TO *LEAVE* NOW, PLEASE.
BUT MA'AM...
BAM!
JUST DOING OUR JOB, MA'AM.

THIS IS ME WALKING INTO THE FAMILY ROOM.

THIS IS ME JUST STANDING HERE LISTENING TO THE VOICES IN MY HEAD. ONE OF THEM'S SAYING "*THIS IS ME JUST STANDING HERE...*"

AND THE OTHER ONE'S GOING "*EEEEEEE...*" IN ONE LONG CEASELESS SCREAM.

AND THE LAST ONE DOESN'T SAY ANYTHING AT ALL.

I CLOSE MY EYES TO TRY TO ESCAPE FROM THE IMAGE, TELLING MYSELF THAT IMAGES CAN LIE.

BUT OTHER PICTURES WAIT FOR ME.

YOU KILLED HECTOR, YOU DESTROYED OUR HOME.

YOU'VE RUINED MY LIFE.

YOU CALL THAT *NOTHING?*

Exactly. Nothing.

The child you have carried so long in dreams. That child is mine.

Take good care of it. One day I will come for it.

BUT, BUT, YOU *CAN'T,* MY BABY...

I will see you again, Hippolyta.

Until then, fare well.

23

Calm yourself, Hippolyta. You have nothing to fear from me today.

I have come to see your son. That is all.

I HAVE TO BE STRONG.

YOU TAKE MY CHILD OVER MY DEAD BODY, YOU SPOOKY BASTARD.

OVER MY DEAD BODY.

I MUST BE STRONG.

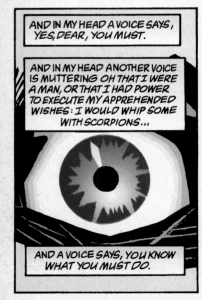

AND IN MY HEAD A VOICE SAYS, YES, DEAR, YOU MUST.

AND IN MY HEAD ANOTHER VOICE IS MUTTERING OH THAT I WERE A MAN, OR THAT I HAD POWER TO EXECUTE MY APPREHENDED WISHES: I WOULD WHIP SOME WITH SCORPIONS...

AND A VOICE SAYS, YOU KNOW WHAT YOU MUST DO.

AND IT'S TRUE.

I KNOW EXACTLY WHAT I MUST DO.

Part Four

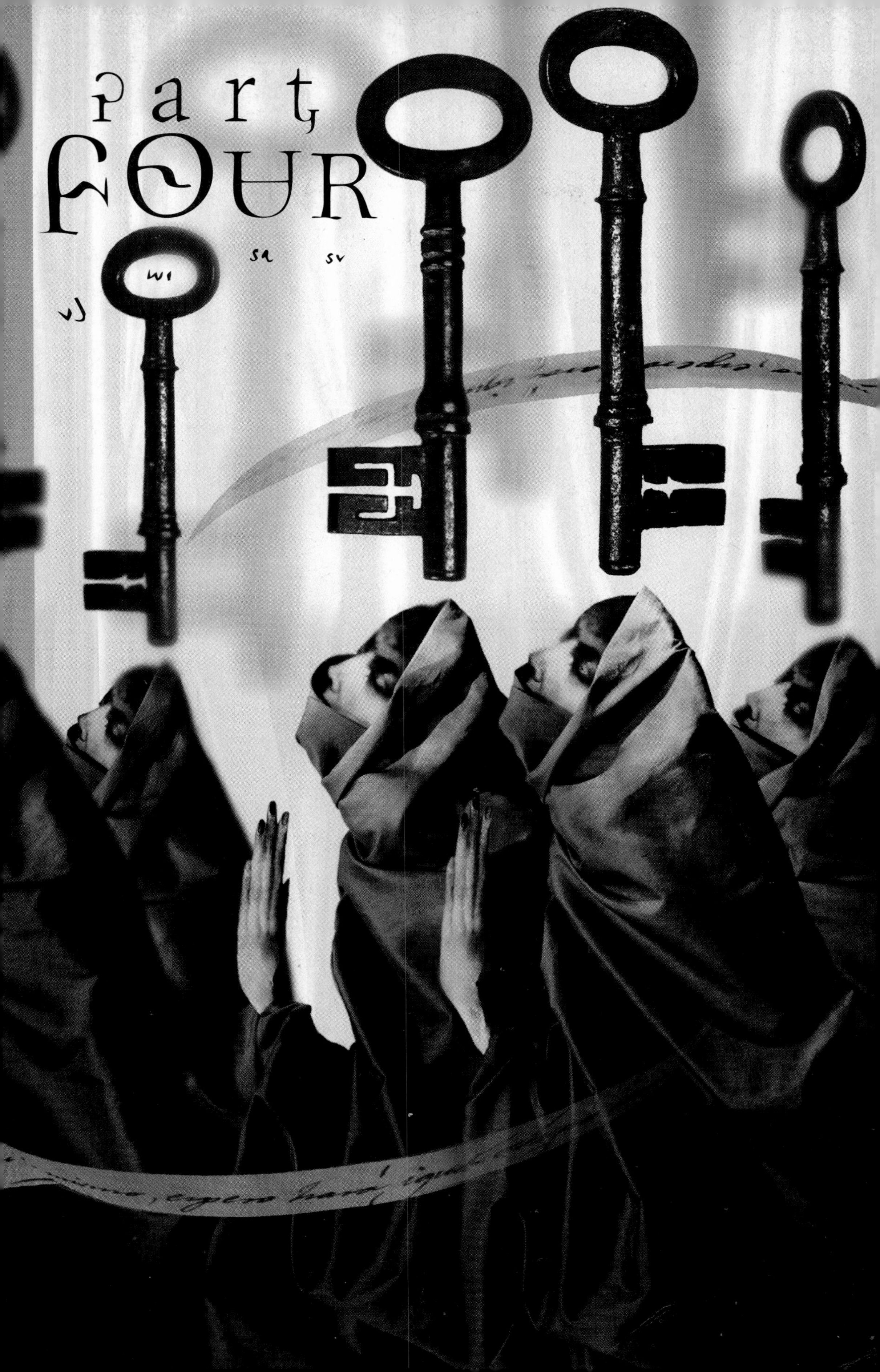

I wish I could be certain that I was doing the right thing.

Hello. Might I talk to the owner?

Look, I know this is the right place.

My people. They told me this was where I should come in order to talk to him.

I've come rather a long way.

I seek the Star of the Morning. Do you understand me?

Thank you.

REMIEL.

ISN'T IT A LITTLE EARLY IN THE DAY TO BE PAYING SOCIAL CALLS?

The early bird catches the worm, Star of Morning.

The, um, worm that dieth not, in this case. Eh? Haha...

HOW REMARKABLY FUNNY, REMIEL. NOT ACTUALLY *ORIGINAL* THOUGH, OF COURSE.

SO, YOU'RE IN CHARGE DOWN IN MY OLD HAUNTS, EH? I WONDER WHO THE GREAT-AND-POWERFUL HAS SET OVER THOSE WHO RISE, IN YOUR ABSENCE.

I-- I am not in *sole* charge, Morningstar. I rule in tandem with the angel Duma.

MY MISTAKE. OF *COURSE* YOU DO. AND I'M SURE YOU JUST CAN'T *SHUT DUMA UP*. IT MUST BE JUST BRIMMING OVER WITH CO-MONARCH-ICAL ADVICE.

Duma is still silent.

JUST SITS THERE AND PLAYS WITH MY OLD FRONT-DOOR KEY, AND *WATCHES* YOU, EH?

AND NEVER SAYS A THING. I BET THAT DRIVES YOU *QUITE* MAD.

2

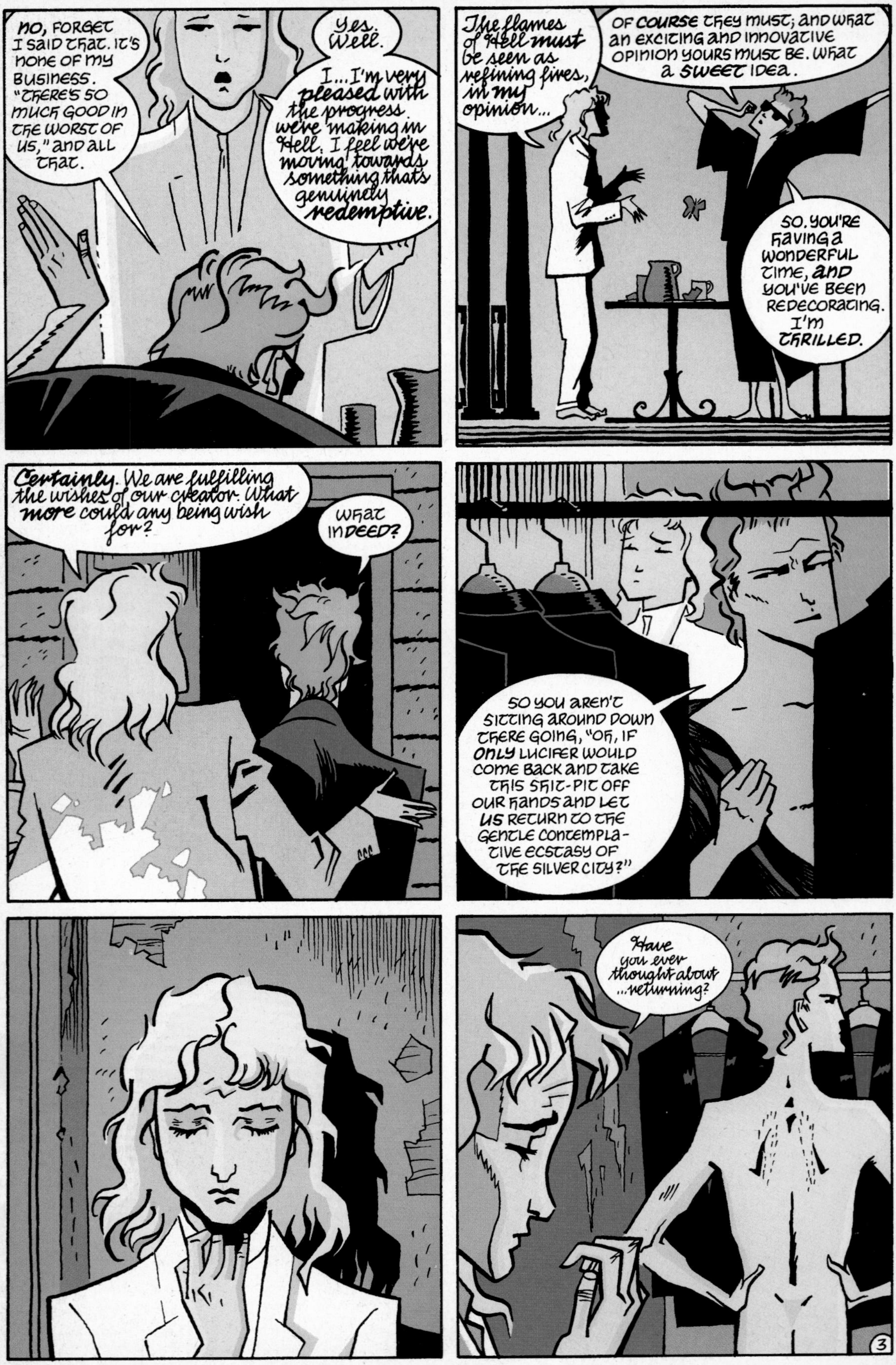
NO, FORGET I SAID THAT. IT'S NONE OF MY BUSINESS. "THERE'S SO MUCH GOOD IN THE WORST OF US," AND ALL THAT.
Yes. Well.
I... I'm very pleased with the progress we're making in Hell. I feel we're moving towards something that's genuinely redemptive.
The flames of Hell must be seen as refining fires, in my opinion...
OF COURSE THEY MUST; AND WHAT AN EXCITING AND INNOVATIVE OPINION YOURS MUST BE. WHAT A SWEET IDEA.
SO, YOU'RE HAVING A WONDERFUL TIME, AND YOU'VE BEEN REDECORATING. I'M THRILLED.
Certainly. We are fulfilling the wishes of our creator. What more could any being wish for?
WHAT INDEED?
SO YOU AREN'T SITTING AROUND DOWN THERE GOING, "OH, IF ONLY LUCIFER WOULD COME BACK AND TAKE THIS SHIT-PIT OFF OUR HANDS AND LET US RETURN TO THE GENTLE CONTEMPLATIVE ECSTASY OF THE SILVER CITY?"
Have you ever thought about ...returning?

AHAHAHAHAHAH!

NO.

BEEN THERE, REMIEL. *DONE* THAT. WORE THE TEE SHIRT, ATE THE BURGER, BOUGHT THE ORIGINAL CAST ALBUM, CHOREOGRAPHED THE LEGIONS OF THE DAMNED AND ORCHESTRATED THE SCREAMING...

Now, now Morningstar. Really? Be honest.

HONESTY IS A SOMEWHAT OVERRATED VIRTUE, REMIEL.

HONESTY, FOR EXAMPLE, WOULD *COMPEL* ME TO ADMIT THAT I HAVE NEVER LIKED YOU. EVEN WHEN I WAS AN ANGEL. I DIDN'T LIKE YOU. ALSO, I NEVER *RESPECTED* YOU.

YOU DIDN'T JOIN THE REBELLION, NOT BECAUSE YOU FELT I WAS WRONG, BUT BECAUSE YOU WERE TOO DAMNED SCARED.

WHAT WOULD YOU HAVE DONE, HAD I WON? TOLD ME THAT YOU'D ALWAYS SUPPORTED ME IDEOLOGICALLY? THAT YOU WERE SECRETLY CHEERING ME ON THE WHOLE TIME?

4

TELL ME, REMIEL... WHAT DID YOU DO WHEN THE ORDER CAME FOR YOU TO SPREAD YOUR WINGS AND REIGN IN HELL? DID YOU WHIMPER? DID YOU WAIL?

SOMEHOW, I CONFESS I FIND MYSELF CERTAIN THAT DUMA WAS THE ONE ACTUALLY TO TAKE THE KEY.

DUMA ALWAYS STRUCK ME AS HAVING SOME BACKBONE...

REMIEL...

YOU KNOW, WHEN I GAVE UP HELL, I GAVE UP NONE OF MY POWERS, NONE OF MY SKILLS.

I WAS THE CAPTAIN OF THE HOST OF HEAVEN. LATER, I WAS THE ADVERSARY.

NOW AT PRESENT, IT IS TRUE, I AM A SIMPLE, PRIVATE INDIVIDUAL.

BUT IF I COULD WIPE OUT YOUR EXISTENCE WITH AS FEW CONSEQUENCES AS I WIPED YOUR SPITTLE FROM MY FACE...

YOU WOULD NO LONGER EXIST.

I COULD DO IT.

I CHOOSE NOT TO.

GO NOW. I WILL TALK TO YOU NO FURTHER.

5

Well, *that* was a complete and entire failure. We didn't even *begin* to talk about the Dream King situation.

The Morningstar made me so... *angry*, Duma. I couldn't talk to him further. I thought it wiser simply to walk away.

And if *you* want to deal with him... *You* can damned well talk to him.

6

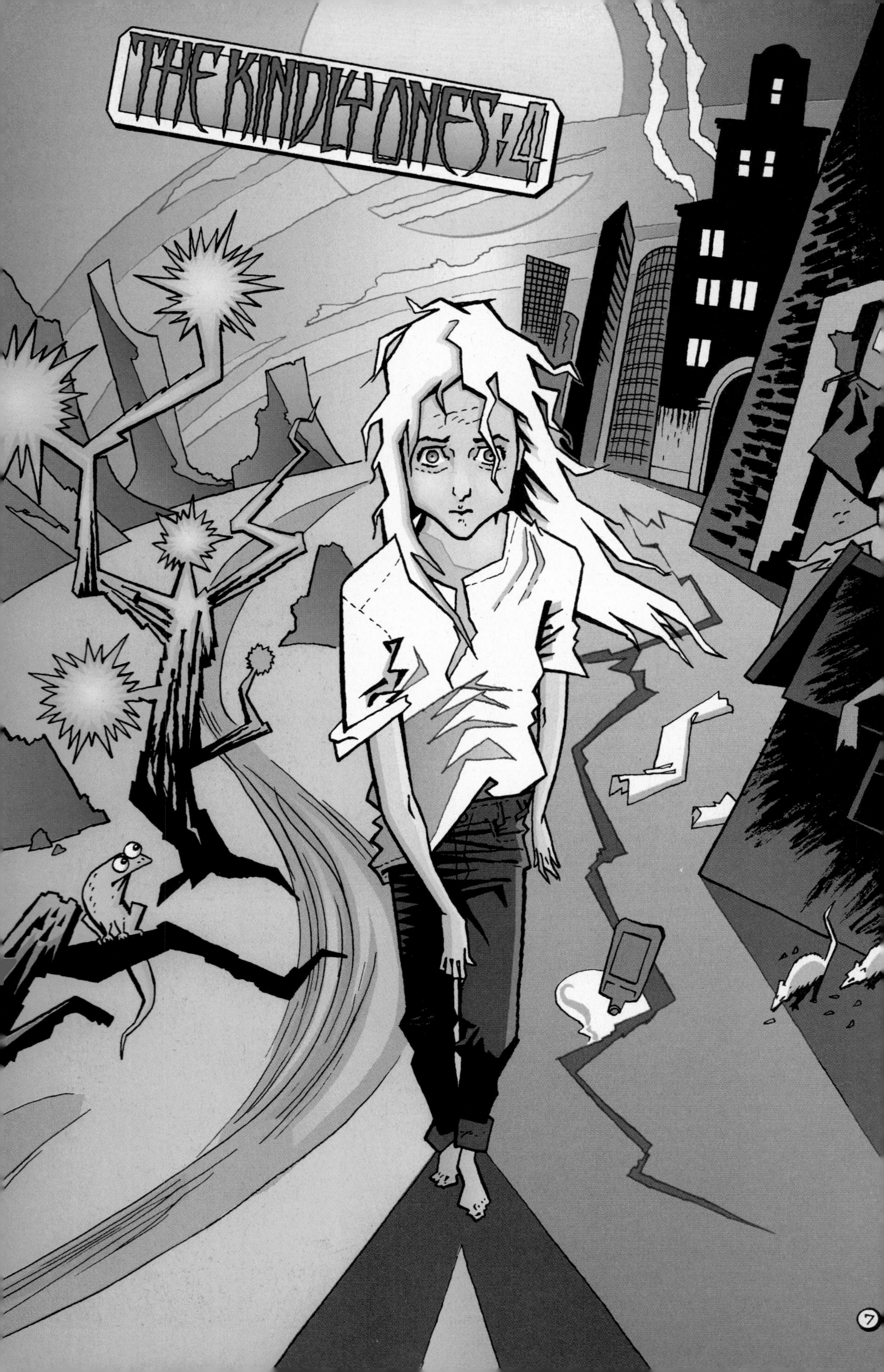
THE KINDLY ONES:4

HOLA! HOW NOW, LASS, AND WHAT WOULD YOU BE QUESTING AFTER, IN THIS FORSAKEN LAND?

I'M GOING TO FIND REVENGE. DO YOU KNOW WHERE IT IS?

AHA! POWERFUL LONG WAY, OR SO I'M TOLD. OVER THAT HILL, PERHAPS? AND WHY WOULD YOU BE A-SEEKING REVENGE, LADY?

MY SON IS DEAD.

ALAS! AND WHAT MANNER OF REVENGE WOULD YOU BE SEEKING?

MY MOTHER WAS BLESSED BY THE THREE LADIES WITH THE SCORPION WHIPS. THE FURIES--

HUSH! YOU MUSTN'T TALK ABOUT THEM LIKE THAT.

WHY NOT?

ZOUNDS! BECAUSE THEY DON'T LIKE IT, I SUPPOSE. WOULD YOU?

I DON'T KNOW. I DON'T THINK SO.

DO YOU WANT TO COME WITH ME?

NAY! I CANNOT. MY TRUE LOVE'S IMPRISONED IN A HIGH TOWER, AND I HAVE TO SET HIM FREE.

THAT'S TERRIBLE.

AYE! BUT NOT HOPELESS. I'VE A BRASS FISH THAT WILL SING HIS GUARDS TO SLEEP,

AN ACORN THAT WILL GROW A LADDER IN A MOMENT, IF I PLANT IT AND WATER IT WITH MY OWN TEARS,

A COMB THAT WILL TURN INTO A FOREST IF THEY PURSUE US.

ACH! BUT HERE, LASS, TAKE THIS COIN.

IT COULD BRING YOU GOOD LUCK.

8

WHERE ART Y'GOING OF, LI'L LADY?

I'M GOING TO FIND MY REVENGE. I'M GOING TO LOOK IN A CAVE FOR THE, UM, THE FURIES...

UH-UH-UH-UH-*UH*! MUSTN'T *NEVER* CALL THEM THAT. *BAD* IDEA.

EVEN THE GODS'RE SCARED OF THEM, Y'KNOW.

REALLY?

A'COURSE. THEY WERE AROUND BE*FORE* THE GODS, Y'SEE. THE OLD REVENGERS. YOU'LL NEED TO CROSS THAT FOREST AND KEEP WALKING.

DO YOU WANT TO COME WITH ME?

CAN'T, MY DUCKLING. HAVE TO STAY HERE. I'M UNDER AN ENCHANTMENT. HAVE TO WAIT HERE UNTIL THE SEVENTH SON OF A SEVENTH SON COMES BY, CARRYING A WHITE ROSE AND A GOLDEN WHISTLE.

ONLY *THEN* WILL I RETURN TO MY TRUE FORM, TO BE REUNITED WITH MY SEVEN POOR SONS, AND MY FAITHLESS HUSBAND THE KING.

OH, YOU *POOR* THING. WELL, I HOPE ONE TURNS UP *SOON*.

PUSH BUTTON TO CROSS

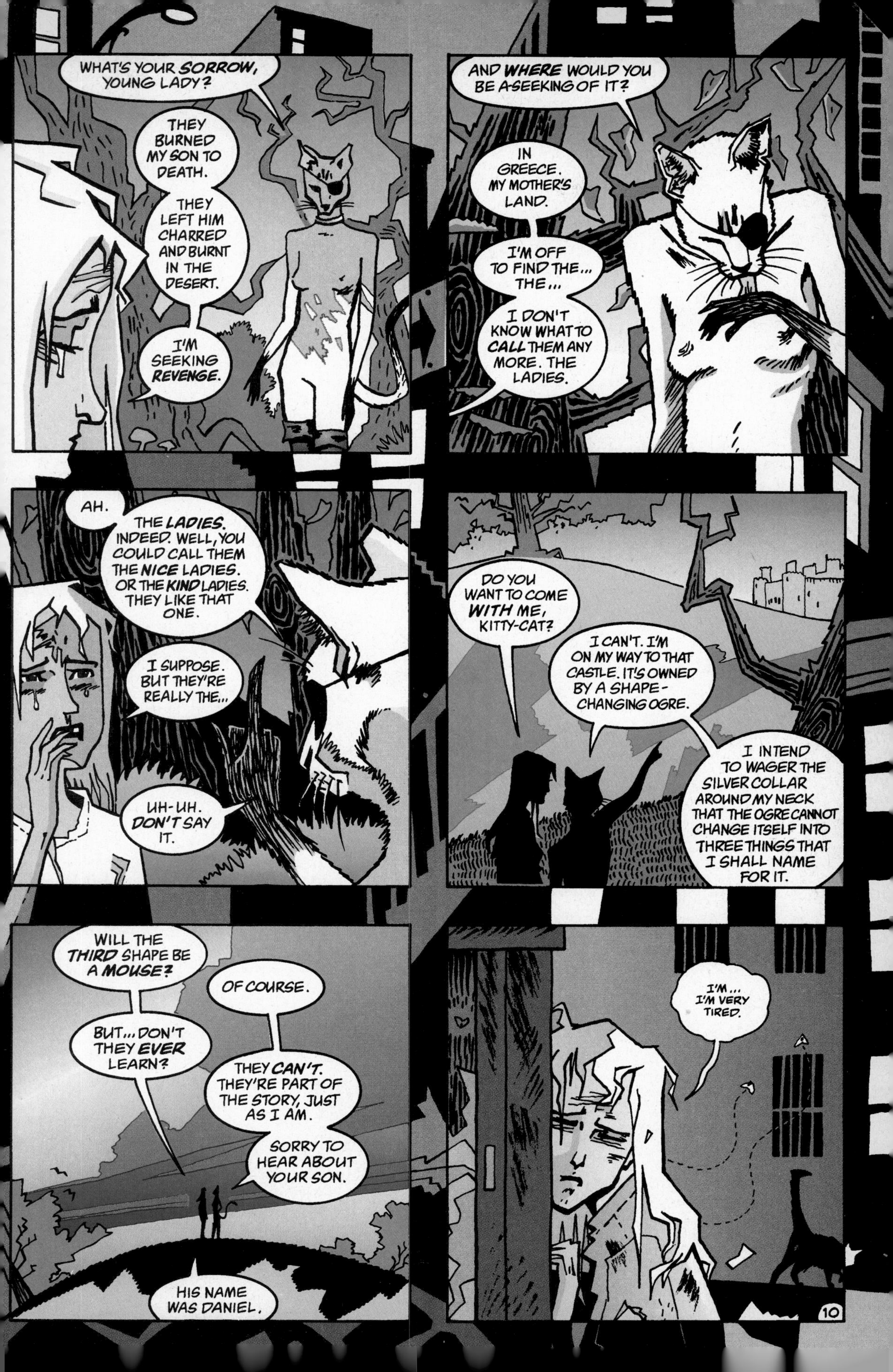
WHAT'S YOUR SORROW, YOUNG LADY?
THEY BURNED MY SON TO DEATH.
THEY LEFT HIM CHARRED AND BURNT IN THE DESERT.
I'M SEEKING REVENGE.
AND WHERE WOULD YOU BE A-SEEKING OF IT?
IN GREECE. MY MOTHER'S LAND.
I'M OFF TO FIND THE... THE...
I DON'T KNOW WHAT TO CALL THEM ANY MORE. THE LADIES.
AH.
THE LADIES. INDEED. WELL, YOU COULD CALL THEM THE NICE LADIES. OR THE KIND LADIES. THEY LIKE THAT ONE.
I SUPPOSE. BUT THEY'RE REALLY THE...
UH-UH. DON'T SAY IT.
DO YOU WANT TO COME WITH ME, KITTY-CAT?
I CAN'T. I'M ON MY WAY TO THAT CASTLE. IT'S OWNED BY A SHAPE-CHANGING OGRE.
I INTEND TO WAGER THE SILVER COLLAR AROUND MY NECK THAT THE OGRE CANNOT CHANGE ITSELF INTO THREE THINGS THAT I SHALL NAME FOR IT.
WILL THE THIRD SHAPE BE A MOUSE?
OF COURSE.
BUT... DON'T THEY EVER LEARN?
THEY CAN'T. THEY'RE PART OF THE STORY, JUST AS I AM.
SORRY TO HEAR ABOUT YOUR SON.
HIS NAME WAS DANIEL.
I'M... I'M VERY TIRED.
10

UH.

UH. UH. UHHHH.

I LOVE YOU. *GOD* I LOVE YOU, YOU BASTARD.

UHHHHH. *JESUS.* OHH YES. *AHHHAAH.*

OHHHHHHHHHH YEHHHHSSSSS...

MMMMM.

HEY.

OKAY. YOU. DON'T THINK I DON'T *SEE* YOU UP THERE.

WHAT THE *HELL* DO YOU THINK YOU'RE *DOING?*

GODDAMN PERVERT.

OHH I UHHH. *UHH.* MM. HM. AH.

I WAS. UHH. *I.* UHH. WUHWUH*WELL.* FUH*FUNNY* YUH*YOU* SHOULD *ASK,* UM, BUH-BUH*BUT* I WAS, *UM,* UP *HERE,* UHH, WUH*WELL,* BECAUSE, UM.

I'M NOT. RUH*REALLY.* *HERE.* UH.

YOU WERE *WATCHING* ME.

YOU WERE WATCHING ME WHILE I WAS--

OH, JESUS *CHRIST!*

BANG! BANG! BANG!

11

BDAM! BDAM! BDAM!

HI, ROSE.

OH I UH...

I'M *CARLA*. LYTA'S FRIEND. FROM UPSTAIRS. REMEMBER?

OH. SURE. HI...

JEEZ. I WAS HAVING THIS DREAM LIKE YOU WOULDN'T *BELIEVE.* I MEAN, A REAL Y'KNOW, *WEIRDY.* STARTED OUT HORNY AS HELL. ONE OF THOSE. I WAS WITH MY EX.

WE WERE SCREWING LIKE WEASELS IN HEAT.

AND THEN I REALIZED THERE WAS THIS FAT GUY UP ON THE WARDROBE. HE WAS PEEKING AT ME. I JUST FELT SO *BETRAYED.*

IT WAS JUST A *DREAM.*

I KNOW.

WELL, I HOPE HIS *EYES* FALL OUT. PEEPING IN MY FUCKING DREAM LIKE THAT.

I COULD HAVE *DIED.*

LISTEN, ROSE, HAVE YOU SEEN ANYTHING OF LYTA SINCE YESTERDAY?

I DON'T KNOW WHERE SHE IS.

I THOUGHT YOU WERE *STAYING* WITH HER.

YEAH, WELL, WE HAD A KIND OF *ARGUMENT* LAST NIGHT AND I JUST THOUGHT TO *HELL* WITH IT. I OWED MYSELF A NIGHT OF REAL SLEEP, AND SHE WAS ACTING SO *CRAZY.*

12

AND THEN TODAY I THOUGHT, *GIRL*, IF *YOUR* KID WAS STOLEN, *YOU'D* BE NUTS *TOO*. AND SHE'S YOUR *FRIEND*. YOU GET *STRAIGHT* BACK UP THERE THIS MINUTE AND YOU DO WHATEVER HAS TO BE DONE TO MAKE THINGS *RIGHT*.

BUT SHE'S NOT *UP* THERE.

IS THERE ANY NEWS OF THE KID YET?

UH-UH.

JESUS.

I KEEP THINKING IT'S MY RESPONSI*BIL*ITY. IF I HADN'T FALLEN ASLEEP LIKE THAT. I WAS MEANT TO BE LOOKING *AFTER* DANNY...

IT WASN'T YOUR *FAULT*.

I DIDN'T *SAY* IT WAS MY FAULT. I SAID IT WAS MY RESPONSIBILITY. I *KNOW* THE DIFFERENCE. YOU WANT *COFFEE*?

GOD, YES.

SO, WHAT DID THE COPS SAY?

WHAT DID *WHAT* COPS SAY?

YOU KNOW. FRIDAY AND GANNON. WHATEVER THEIR NAMES ARE. DIDN'T THEY TAKE A *STATEMENT* FROM YOU? THEY SAID THEY WERE GOING TO. WANTED TO KNOW ALL ABOUT YOU.

NOBODY'S SPOKEN TO ME.

THEY WANTED TO KNOW IF YOU WERE DOING ANY DRUGS.

I FELL *ASLEEP*. THAT WAS ALL. I'VE NEVER FALLEN ASLEEP LIKE THAT...

I JUST DON'T *REMEMBER* ANYTHING. I PUT HIM TO BED, SAT DOWN, THEN LYTA WAS SHAKING ME AWAKE AND SAYING DANIEL WAS GONE.

LOOK, KID. YOU MUSTN'T JUST--

I'M *NOT* A KID, CARLA. I'M *25*, FOR CHRISSAKES. NEARLY *26*. I JUST LOOK YOUNGER THAN I AM, IS ALL. WANNA SEE MY DRIVER'S LICENSE?

25? WOW. SO WHAT'S YOUR *SECRET*, ROSE WALKER?

13

WHAT'S MY SECRET? HEY, I'VE GOT A MILLION OF 'EM.

HASN'T *EVERYBODY*?

YOU MIND IF I PUT ON THE *TV*? I GOTTA SET THE VCR--IT'S A ROSEANNE RERUN IN A COUPLE OF MINUTES. I'M TRYING TO TAPE 'EM FOR SOMETHING I'M WRITING.

GO FOR IT.

I'M COLLECTING THEM. AND THE ADDAMS FAMILY. AND BEWITCHED.

I WENT UP THERE, YOU KNOW. THE DAY AFTER. I TRIED TO SAY HOW *SORRY* I WAS, HOW *BAD* I FELT. IT WAS LIKE SHE HARDLY EVEN KNEW I WAS THERE.

ROS

SHE'S... *LISTEN*, YOU DON'T GO THROUGH WHAT SHE'S BEEN THROUGH WITHOUT GETTING KIND OF WEIRD.

I DON'T KNOW. I'VE KNOWN PEOPLE GO THROUGH *PRETTY* WEIRD THINGS AND COME OUT THE OTHER SIDE. REMIND ME TO TELL YOU ABOUT MY FAMILY TREE SOME TIME.

CLIK

DON'T GET ME STARTED ON *FAMILIES*. MY COUSIN ERIC,...OYYY.

SAY, YOU'RE REALLY, TRULY 25? I FIGURED YOU WERE STILL AT SCHOOL. I CAN'T REALLY BELIEVE IT.

I'M NOT IN SCHOOL. I'M REALLY ONLY IN *LA* TO SPEND TIME WITH A SICK OLD FRIEND.

HEY, *LOOK!* WITH MONTEL. IT'S VIXEN LaBITCH, SHE IS SOOOO FUNNY. YOU EVER *SEEN* HER?

...PRANCING AROUND TELLING US THAT THE KID WAS NOT HIS SON. WELL, OBVIOUSLY-- IT WAS HIS BOY-FRIEND. AND BEAT IT?...

I'VE SEEN VIXEN'S ACT. I'M *NOT* A FAN.

SO. HOW SICK'S YOUR *FRIEND*?

PRETTY TERMINAL.

I'M SORRY.

ME *TOO*.

14

ROSE. LOOK, IF IT ISN'T A DUMB QUESTION, BUT WHAT DO YOU *DO?* I MEAN, YOU GOT A JOB OR SOMETHING?

NO. NOT A REAL JOB. MY FAMILY'S...WELL, MY MOM, REALLY--THERE'S AN AWFUL LOT OF MONEY. IT WAS INHERITED. FROM MY GRANDMOTHER.

I'M DOING SOME WRITING.

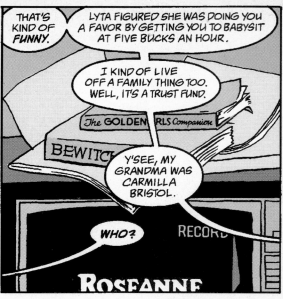

THAT'S KIND OF *FUNNY.*

LYTA FIGURED SHE WAS DOING YOU A FAVOR BY GETTING YOU TO BABYSIT AT FIVE BUCKS AN HOUR.

I KIND OF LIVE OFF A FAMILY THING TOO. WELL, IT'S A TRUST FUND.

The GOLDEN GIRLS Companion

BEWITCH

Y'SEE, MY GRANDMA WAS CARMILLA BRISTOL.

WHO?

RECORD

ROSEANNE

CARMILLA *BRISTOL.*

SHE PLAYED, LIKE, EVERY BLACK LADIES' MAID IN EVERY CRAPPY HOLLYWOOD FILM MADE BETWEEN 1925 AND 1950. *"NOW DERE, MISSY, YOU HUSH UP WID YO' CRYIN'."*

SHE DIDN'T GET TO DEMONSTRATE MUCH DRAMATIC RANGE, BUT SHE HAD A GREAT EYE FOR A LAND DEAL.

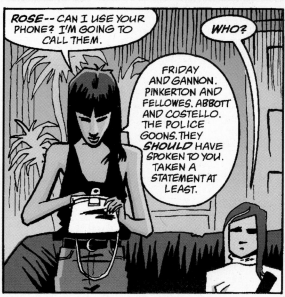

ROSE-- CAN I USE YOUR PHONE? I'M GOING TO CALL THEM.

WHO?

FRIDAY AND GANNON. PINKERTON AND FELLOWES. ABBOTT AND COSTELLO. THE POLICE GOONS. THEY *SHOULD* HAVE SPOKEN TO YOU. TAKEN A STATEMENT AT LEAST.

THAT'S *FUNNY.* I COULDA *SWORN...*

WHAT'S THE MATTER?

THEY GAVE ME THE WRONG CARD.

DOESN'T IT HAVE THEIR PHONE NUMBER ON IT?

IT DOESN'T HAVE *ANYTHING* ON IT.

LOOK, I'LL GIVE YOU *MY* NUMBER. IF THE POLICE COME BY, OR IF LYTA SHOWS UP, YOU *CALL* ME, OKAY?

OF COURSE.

I JUST HOPE SHE HASN'T DONE ANYTHING *STUPID.*

15

HELLO?

IS ANYONE *HERE?*

HELLO?

HELLO?

I'VE BEEN TRAVELLING FOR A WHILE. I WONDERED IF I COULD HAVE SOME WATER, OR SOME FOOD. MAYBE SOMEWHERE TO SLEEP TONIGHT?

HEL*LO?*

COME IN, SISTER. OF COURSE. COME IN.

HELLO.

ASK HER WHAT SHE'S HERE AFTER.

AS IF I'D NEVER THINK OF IT ON MY OWN. I WAS GOING TO ASK HER. JUST *ABOUT* TO.

WELL, GO ON. *ASK HER.*

WHAT ARE YOU LOOKING FOR, GIRL?

I'M LOOKING FOR REVENGE. SOMEONE STOLE MY SON, AND KILLED HIM.

I WILL HAVE VENGEANCE.

I'M SEEKING THE FU-- THE KIND LADIES.

OUR SISTER DIED. BUT WE NEVER TOOK REVENGE.

WE KNEW THERE'D BE TROUBLE ONE DAY, HER BEING MORTAL. IT'S NOT AS IF WE NEVER SAID ANYTHING.

WE STILL MISS HER. WE STILL MOURN.

I'M SORRY.

I AM STHENO, DEARIE. THIS IS EURYALE.

HELLO. I'M LYTA.

YOU'RE WELCOME TO STAY FOR A NIGHT, AND A DAY, AND ANOTHER NIGHT.

BUT WE DON'T HAVE **ANY** FOOD HERE.

WE **HAD** FOOD, WHEN OUR SISTER WAS WITH US.

BUT AFTER SHE WENT AWAY, IT WENT **FOUL** AND BRED **FLIES**, AND THEN IT BECAME DUST.

THERE'S **WATER**. PROPER WATER. ALL THE WATER YOU CAN DRINK, AND **MORE**.

THESE ARE LOVELY STATUES.

DID YOU CARVE THEM YOURSELVES?

OH, PLEASE.

WOULD **YOU** LIKE TO BE OUR SISTER?

SORRY?

HE CUT OFF HER **HEAD**. HE WAS A **STRANGER**. WE WANTED TO BURY IT WITH HER, BUT HE CARRIED IT OFF WITH HIM.

THERE **SHOULD** BE THREE OF US. YOU COULD BE THE MORTAL ONE.

DON'T CONFUSE THE POOR LOVE, EURYALE.

THERE ARE **APPLES** FOR YOUR SUPPER AT THE BOTTOM OF THE GARDEN. YOU'LL HAVE TO GET 'EM ON YOUR OWN. **WE** CAN'T GO WITH YOU -- IT'S NOT **OUR** GARDEN.

WOULD YOU LIKE AN **APPLE**?

SURE.

"IF YOU SEE AEGLE, ERYTHIA, AND ARETHUSA, BE NICE TO THEM. IT'S **THEIR** GARDEN."

"THE TREE IS AT THE TOP OF THE HILL."

17

EAT THAT APPLE--LOSE SOME OF YOUR MORTALITY--BIT OF A WARNING--WORD TO THE WISE.

WHO--WHO ARE *YOU?*

ARE YOU... *SATAN?*

NOT BLOODY LIKELY--NAME OF *GERYON*--YOU ARE?

I'M LYTA. HIPPOLYTA HALL.

HIPPOLYTA--ALSO ANTIOPE, QUEEN OF AMAZONS, GIVEN IN MARRIAGE BY HERCULES TO THESEUS.

HALL--A CORRIDOR. PLACE BETWEEN PLACES.

LYTA--LESS DARK. YES?

I SUPPOSE. IT'S JUST A *NAME.*

ARE *THESE* THE APPLES FROM THE *BIBLE?*

THESE? NOT A *BIT*--QUITE USELESS FOR KNOWLEDGE OF GOOD AND EVIL--MORE LIKE THE OTHER TREE--*YOU* KNOW.

UH. NO.

QUESTION: WHY *DID* HE THROW THEM OUT?

WHO? WHAT?

NICE COUPLE--FIG LEAVES--ADAM, EVE.

OH. YES. I SEE.

WHY DID GOD EXPEL THEM FROM THE GARDEN OF EDEN? BECAUSE THEY DISO*BEYED* HIM, I SUPPOSE.

NOT A BIT.

SCARED THEY WOULD FIND THE TREE OF LIFE NEXT, "AND EAT, AND LIVE FOR EVER." --GENESIS THREE, TWENTY-TWO.

TAKE APPLES, BY ALL MEANS--I'M GUARDIAN--TO BE HONEST, DON'T GIVE A TOSS *WHO* HAS THEM--NO ONE EVER COMES HERE.

JUST ROT ON THE GROUND--*WORMS* GET THEM--*PITY.*

18

WORD TO THE WISE.

LADIES WHO **SENT** YOU DOWN HERE -- EURYALE -- STHENO -- STILL MISS THEIR SISTER, IF YOU GET MY DRIFT.

SLEEP IN THEIR HOUSE -- EAT THIS FOOD...

WELL -- WOULDN'T RECOMMEND IT, **THAT'S** ALL.

NOT RECOMMENDED -- THERE.

WORD TO THE WISE.

PAPER ONLY

≥CHOMP≤

19

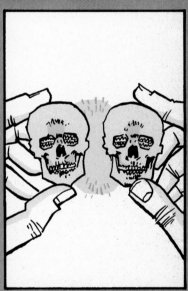

Storms are coming.

20

HEY MATTHEW.

MERV. WHAT'S NEW?

SAME OLD SAME OLD. I'M ONE MAN SHORT ONNA CLEANING DETAIL, LIKE I AIN'T GOT *ENOUGH* TA WORRY ABOUT.

≳phhhhht!≲

YOU KNOW *ABUDAH?*

HI ABUDAH.

AYUH.

SO WHO'RE YOU MISSING?

YOU DIDN'T *HEAR* YET? THE *ELF.* THE BOSS SENT HER HOME.

NUALA'S GONE? PITY.

PITY? WHY?

PHOOT!

I DON'T KNOW. IT WASN'T EVEN AS IF I *KNEW* HER THAT WELL.

BUT WITH *HER* GONE, THE CASTLE FEELS LIKE A.... I DON'T KNOW.... A BOY'S CLUB.

SO? WHAT'S SO BAD ABOUT THAT?

HELLO MATTHEW, MERVYN, ABUDAH.

AYUH.

HEEEY, LOOSH. KEEPIN' OUTTA TROUBLE?

TOLERABLY SO, THANK YOU, MERVYN. YOURSELF?

I'M ACES. HEY, I WAS JUS' TELLIN' *MATTY* HERE THAT THE ELF HAD HIGHTAILED IT, AN' HE WAS *BITCHIN'* AND *MOANIN'.*

I AGREE WITH MATTHEW.

I PARTICULARLY MISS HER LITTLE *SONGS.* YOU COULD HEAR THEM-- DISTANTLY-- ALL THE WAY DOWN THE CORRIDOR.

I RATHER ENJOYED THEM. QUITE A LOT, IN FACT.

21

WELL, I THINK YOU'RE *ALL* CRAZY. DAMES. WHO NEEDS 'EM?

MERV, YOU SAY SOME *AMAZINGLY* DUMB THINGS SOMETIMES.

NAH. I JUST CALL 'EM LIKE I SEE 'EM.

F'REXAMPLE, SAW THE FASHION THING, COUPLA DAYS BACK, WEARING A DRESS THAT LEFT ABSITIVELY *NUTHIN'* TO THE IMAGINATION. WOULDN'T CATCH *ME* DRESSIN' LIKE THAT.

AYUH.

NOPE. THEY AREN'T *LIKE* US.

WELL, THEY AREN'T LIKE *YOU.*

BRR. IT'S *SO* COLD...

YOU'RE TELLING *ME.*

OF COURSE, TALL, PALE AND INTERESTIN' STILL EXPECTS SOME OF US TO HAUL VOLCANOES ABOUT IN THIS KINDA WEATHER.

SO WHAT *I* WANT TO KNOW IS, WHAT CRAWLED UP *HIS* BUTT AND DIED?

I DO NOT BELIEVE THAT OUR LORD IS UNUSUALLY DISTURBED ABOUT ANYTHING IN PARTICULAR, MERVYN.

NO?

THEN WHAT'S THIS *WEATHER* ALL ABOUT THEN?

I TELL YA, I'VE *NEVER* KNOWN IT LIKE THIS.

UH, MERV...

FIRST YOU GET THE WINDS. *THEN* THE COLD. AND THEN THE SKY JUST KINDA *SPITS,* LIKE IT'S GOING TO RAIN, AND IT *DOESN'T* RAIN. AND THE *CLOUDS* ARE BLACK, AND THEY DON'T STORM, AND THEY DON'T *RAIN,* AND THEY DON'T *GO AWAY.*

MERV!

YOU ASK *ME,* HE'S HEADING FOR *BIG* TROUBLE. YA GOTTA *LOVE* HIM, SURE, BUT THE GUY'S A COMPLETE--

MERVYN!

22

A complete what, Mervyn?

A, UH. JUST A... COMPLETE, BOSS.

Completeness is a virtue, Mervyn, is it not?

HHEEEEH. WHATEVER.

BOSS.

Matthew. If I might intrude? I have need of you and Lucien.

UH. YES. SURE, BOSS.

Mervyn, Abudah. It was good to see you both.

UM. OUTTA HERE. NO REST FOR THE WICKED. MOHAMMED AIN'T GONNA COME TO THE MOUNTAIN, ALL THAT.

AYUH.

AAAARK! YOU MUSTN'T BE TOO HARD ON HIM.

WELL, FOR THE STUFF HE SAYS ABOUT YOU, HE CAN BE SORT OF OFFENSIVE...

Hard on him, Matthew?

It has always been the prerogative of children and half-wits to point out that the emperor has no clothes.

But the half-wit remains a half-wit, and the emperor remains an emperor.

HE'S A VERY CONSCIENTIOUS WORKER. I THINK IT'S JUST THE WEATHER THAT HAS HIM ON EDGE, LORD.

It has us all on edge, Lucien.

BUT, BOSS, I THOUGHT YOU MADE THE WEATHER HERE. I THOUGHT YOU MADE EVERY-THING HERE.

This place is an aspect of part of me, Matthew. That is true.

However, I am also, to some extent, an aspect of this place. That should not be forgotten.

IF YOU SAY SO, BOSS.

Do you follow me, Matthew?

'FRAID YOU LOST ME A COUPLA MILES BACK, BOSS.

23

It is nearly completed. What do you think?
IT LOOKS...LIKE THE LAST ONE DID. IT LOOKS--OKAY.
Yes.
Now: Live.
THANK YOU, MY LORD. IT IS GOOD TO LIVE ONCE MORE.
I AWAIT YOUR COMMAND.

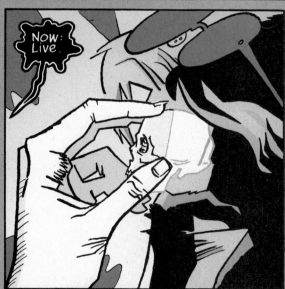

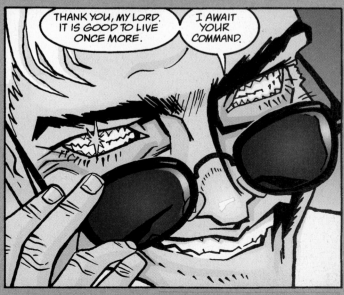

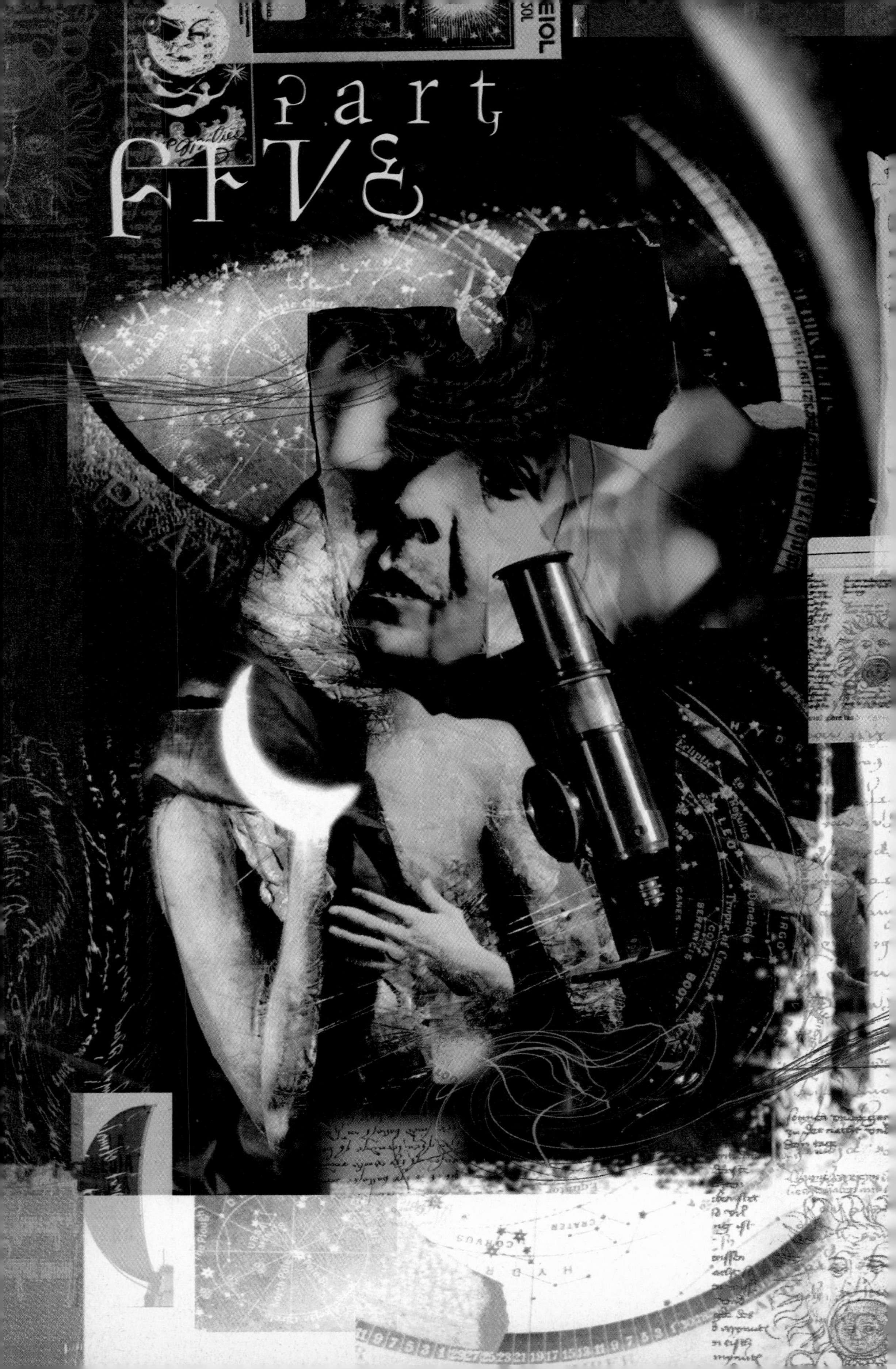
part
FIVE

IT'S HAPPENING. VERY SLOWLY. BUT IT'S HAPPENING.

IT ALWAYS TAKES LONGER THAN YOU THINK, DOESN'T IT?

LOOK AT HER HAIR.

SHE'S VERY BEAUTIFUL, STHENO, ISN'T SHE?

DO YOU THINK SHE'S GOING TO BE OUR SISTER?

WE CAN PRAY.

THE GODS WE PRAYED TO WHEN WE WERE YOUNG USED UP THEIR TIME SO LONG AGO. THEY CANNOT ANSWER ANYMORE.

THEY NEVER LIKED US, DID THEY?

GODS DON'T "LIKE". THEY LOVE AND THEY HATE AND THEY IGNORE...

IF THEY LIKED US THEY WOULDN'T HAVE LET THAT YOUNG MAN DECAPITATE OUR DARLING...

IT WAS GOOD TO BE THREE. I HAVEN'T FORGOTTEN...

TWOS DON'T WORK. TWOS HURT AND CRUMBLE. TWOS FALL INTO ONES, AND THEN INTO DUST AND NOTHINGS.

WE'RE STILL HERE.

THAT'S BECAUSE WE HAVEN'T GIVEN UP HOPE OF BEING A THREE AGAIN. I HOPE IT IS HER.

SHE'S VERY LOVELY.

GOOD MORNING SISTER LYTA. DID YOU SLEEP WELL?

I...I'M NOT YOUR SISTER.

YOU CAN BE IF YOU LIKE.

NO. I *DIDN'T* SLEEP WELL. I DREAMED OF MY HUSBAND, AND I DREAMED OF MY SON.

DID YOU DREAM OF YOUR FATHER?

I NEVER *KNEW* MY FATHER.

AH. PROBABLY A GOD. THEY NEVER SEEMED TO CARE WHERE THEY SPURT THEIR SEED. NOT KEEN ON THEIR RESPONSIBILITIES AS FATHERS, GODS.

I FEEL VERY STRANGE.

HERE. HAVE SOME WATER.

MY *HAIR*. THERE ARE SNAKES IN MY HAIR.

ONLY A FEW NOW. BUT THERE WILL BE MORE, THE LONGER YOU STAY HERE.

SOON YOU'LL BE JUST LIKE MEDUSA.

SNAKES.

SHE WAS YOUR SISTER?

SHE WAS SPECIAL. SHE'S *STILL* IN OUR HEARTS.

2

I ... I DON'T **WANT** TO BE LIKE YOU TWO.

AH. BUT YOU COULD BE SO MUCH WORSE.

I DON'T **NEED** GORGONS. I NEED VENGEANCE...

YOU MUST HAVE NEEDED US A **LITTLE**, OR YOU WOULDN'T HAVE COME HERE.

WE'RE NOT OFFENDED, DEAR. NOT REALLY. WE REALLY LIKE HAVING THE COMPANY. BUT YOU MIGHT WANT TO RECONSIDER.

IF YOU GO LOOKING FOR THE LADIES... WELL, I DON'T KNOW THAT THAT'S SUCH A GOOD IDEA. YOU MIGHT FIND THEM.

ARE YOU SURE YOU WON'T STAY?

HE KILLED MY HUSBAND. HE KILLED MY SON.

I WILL NOT STAY.

AND I WILL HAVE REVENGE.

CAN I HAVE MORE WATER, PLEASE?

MY HAIR DRANK MOST OF IT.

ROSE WALKER'S JOURNAL:

I've been making a list of the things they don't teach you at school.

They don't teach you how to love somebody. They don't teach you how to be famous. They don't teach you how to be rich, or how to be poor.

They don't teach you how to walk away from someone you don't love any longer. They don't teach you how to know what's going on in someone else's mind.

They don't teach you what to say to someone who's dying.

They don't teach you anything worth knowing.

Sometimes I feel. Shit. I don't know. Hollow.

Mostly when I don't feel what I ought to feel, inside.

I've got a friend who's dying from AIDS. How does that make me feel?

Empty. That's all. Just empty.

④

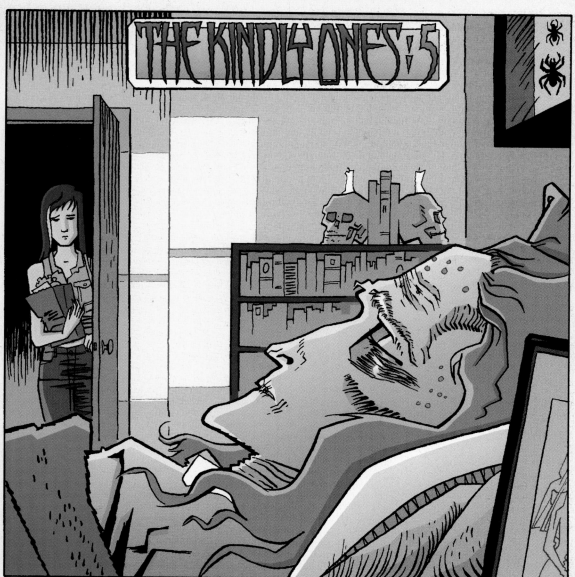

THE KINDLY ONES:5

HI, ZELDA. IT'S ME. IT'S ROSE.

ROSE?

THAT'S RIGHT.

HOW YOU DOING TODAY?

A BB--

BIT WEAK. A BIT CRAZY FOR A WHILE. I CAN'T SWALLOW PROPERLY. THREW UP ALL MY PILLS AGAIN...

AND I'M SO HHH--

HHORNY I COULD GC--

REAM...

WELL, HANG IN THERE.

DD-- DID I EVER TELL YOU THE STORY ABOUT THE FOOTSTEPS IN THE SAND AND THERE ARE TWO SETS OF FOOTSTEPS TOGETHER, BECAUSE SOME OF THEM ARE GGGGG--

GOD'S EXCEPT THERE AREN'T ALWAYS TWO OF THEM. AND THE WOMAN SAYS TO GOD, WHERE WERE YOU WHEN I WAS IN TROUBLE? AND HE SAYS, THAT WAS ME CARRYING YOU...

YOU TOLD ME. IT'S A VERY *PRETTY* STORY.

5

WHATEVER, ROSIE, THESE DAYS I JUST FEEL LIKE GOD'S DDDDDD--

DUMPED ME DOWN ON THE SAND.

DO YOU BBBBB--

BELIEVE IN GOD?

CHANTAL DIDN'T BBB--

BELIEVE IN GOD. SHE LOVED SPIDERS AND SKULLS AND GRAVEYARDS FOR THEMSELVES. I LOVED THEM BECAUSE THEY SHOWED TTTTT--TT--

TTTRANSIENCE.

I BELIEVE IN *LOTS* OF THINGS.

YOU'RE SMILING.

WHUWHAT ARE YOU SMILING AT?

I DON'T KNOW. BECAUSE YOU NEVER USED TO *SPEAK*, I SUPPOSE. CHANTAL DID ALL THE SPEAKING FOR BOTH OF YOU.

BBBB--

BECAUSE I SSSSSSS--

SSTTTTT--

AND I'M SITTIN' THERE NOT SAYING "STAMMER," BECAUSE THE LAST TIME I FINISHED ONE OF HER SENTENCES SHE STARTED TO CRY AND WOULDN'T TALK AGAIN FOR AN HOUR.

S-*STUTTERED.*

I THOUGHT SKULLS WERE A WAY OF TTT--

TOUCHING FOREVER.

CAN YOU SEE MY SKULL YET?

YOU'RE GETTING PRETTY SKINNY, ZELDA, BUT NOT YET.

6

I *WISH* I WAS STILL BBB— BEAUTIFUL, ROSE. AND I'M SO HORNY. THEY DON'T TELL YOU THAT IN THE...

LITERATURE. IT'S LIKE MY BODY KNOWS IT'S DYING, AND IT'S SSSS—

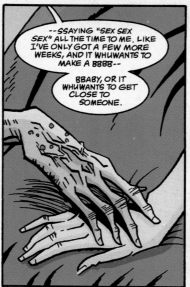

—SSAYING "SEX SEX SEX" ALL THE TIME TO ME. LIKE I'VE ONLY GOT A FEW MORE WEEKS, AND IT WHUWANTS TO MAKE A BBBB—

BBABY, OR IT WHUWANTS TO GET CLOSE TO SOMEONE.

WE'VE BEEN OVER THIS A *DOZEN* TIMES, ZELDA. I'M HAPPY TO COME DOWN AND SEE YOU EVERY DAY. I'M HAPPY TO PICK UP YOUR BILLS.

THAT'S WHERE IT STOPS.

WHAT?

NOTHING.

I'LL BE *DEAD* SOON.

I KNOW.

IT'S MY BBB—

BIRTHDAY NEXT WEEK.

YOU *TOLD* ME.

I'LL BE THIRTY.

ROSIE?

YES.

WHY ARE YOU DOING THIS?

WHAT?

VVVV—

VISITING ME EVERY DAY. PPPPPP—

PAYING ALL MY MEDICAL BILLS. YOU HARDLY EVEN KNEW ME. *WHY?*

BECAUSE I *CAN*, I SUPPOSE.

IT'S A VIGIL. THAT'S WHAT IT IS. IT'S A VIGIL.

7

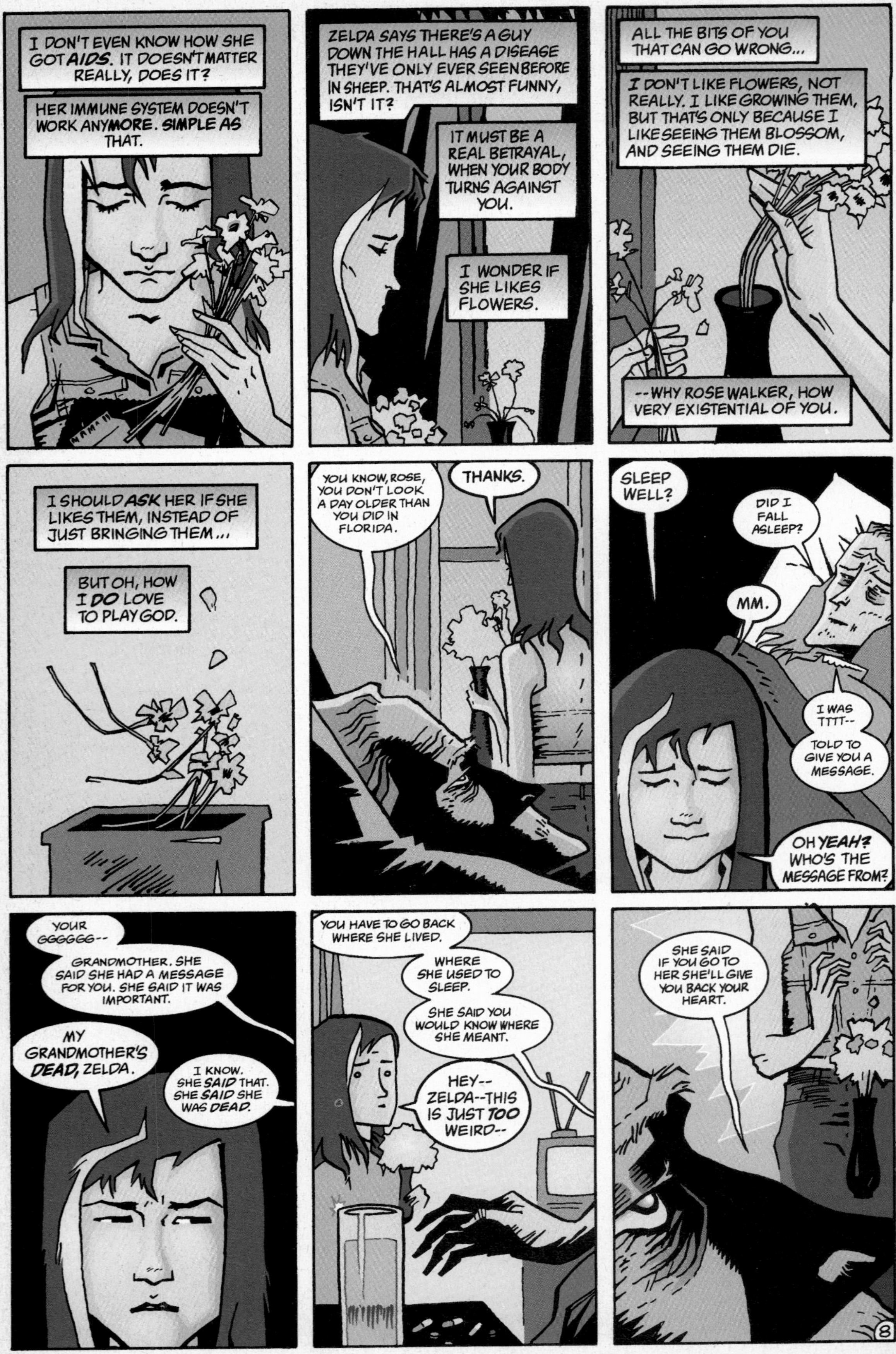

I DON'T EVEN KNOW HOW SHE GOT AIDS. IT DOESN'T MATTER REALLY, DOES IT?
HER IMMUNE SYSTEM DOESN'T WORK ANYMORE. SIMPLE AS THAT.
ZELDA SAYS THERE'S A GUY DOWN THE HALL HAS A DISEASE THEY'VE ONLY EVER SEEN BEFORE IN SHEEP. THAT'S ALMOST FUNNY, ISN'T IT?
IT MUST BE A REAL BETRAYAL, WHEN YOUR BODY TURNS AGAINST YOU.
I WONDER IF SHE LIKES FLOWERS.
ALL THE BITS OF YOU THAT CAN GO WRONG...
I DON'T LIKE FLOWERS, NOT REALLY. I LIKE GROWING THEM, BUT THAT'S ONLY BECAUSE I LIKE SEEING THEM BLOSSOM, AND SEEING THEM DIE.
--WHY ROSE WALKER, HOW VERY EXISTENTIAL OF YOU.
I SHOULD ASK HER IF SHE LIKES THEM, INSTEAD OF JUST BRINGING THEM...
BUT OH, HOW I DO LOVE TO PLAY GOD.
YOU KNOW, ROSE, YOU DON'T LOOK A DAY OLDER THAN YOU DID IN FLORIDA.
THANKS.
SLEEP WELL?
DID I FALL ASLEEP?
MM.
I WAS TTTT--
TOLD TO GIVE YOU A MESSAGE.
OH YEAH? WHO'S THE MESSAGE FROM?
YOUR GGGGGG--
GRANDMOTHER. SHE SAID SHE HAD A MESSAGE FOR YOU. SHE SAID IT WAS IMPORTANT.
MY GRANDMOTHER'S DEAD, ZELDA.
I KNOW. SHE SAID THAT. SHE SAID SHE WAS DEAD.
YOU HAVE TO GO BACK WHERE SHE LIVED.
WHERE SHE USED TO SLEEP.
SHE SAID YOU WOULD KNOW WHERE SHE MEANT.
HEY--ZELDA--THIS IS JUST TOO WEIRD--
SHE SAID IF YOU GO TO HER SHE'LL GIVE YOU BACK YOUR HEART.

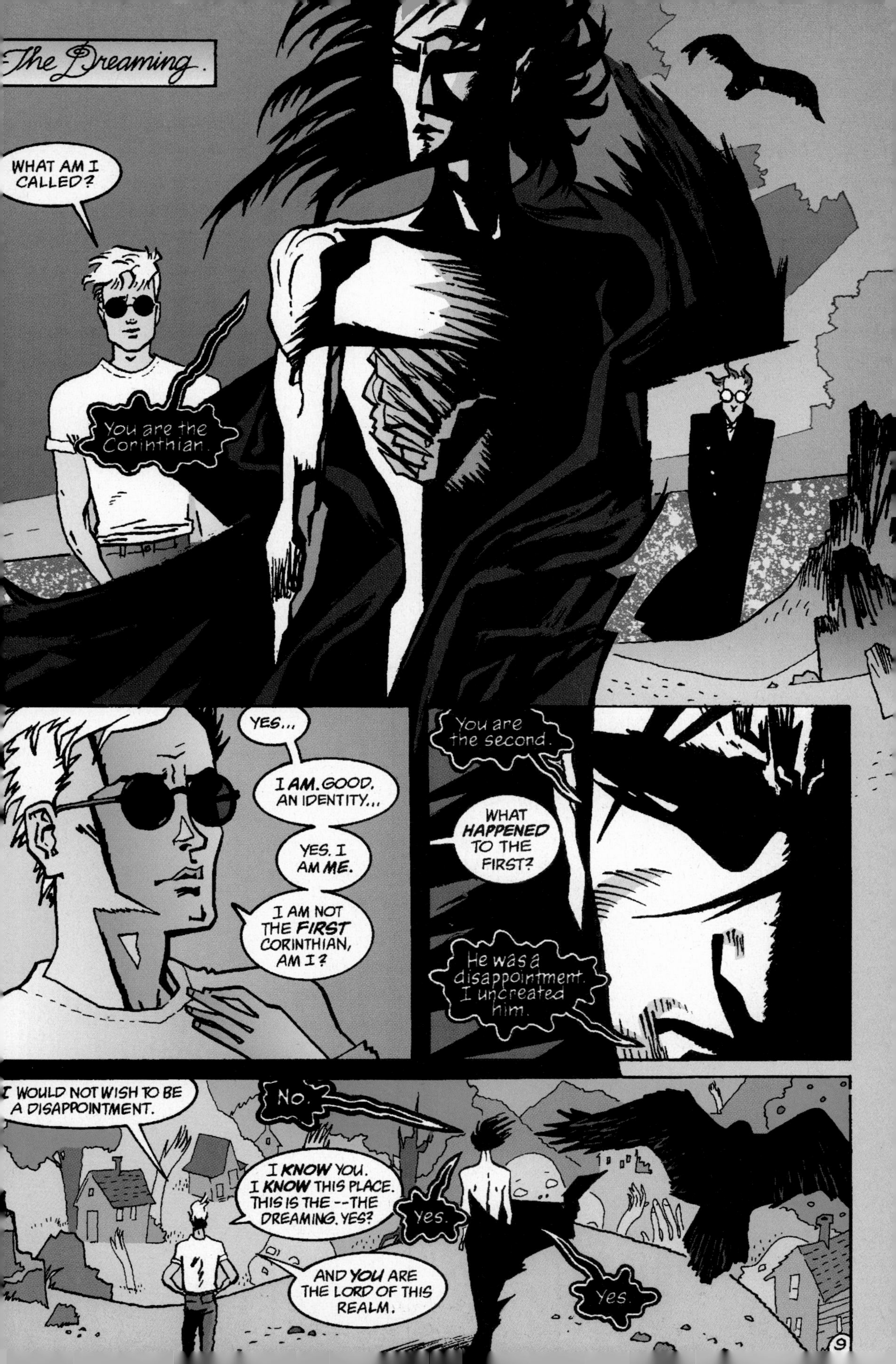
The Dreaming.
WHAT AM I CALLED?
You are the Corinthian.
YES...
I AM. GOOD. AN IDENTITY...
YES. I AM ME.
I AM NOT THE FIRST CORINTHIAN, AM I?
You are the second.
WHAT HAPPENED TO THE FIRST?
He was a disappointment. I uncreated him.
I WOULD NOT WISH TO BE A DISAPPOINTMENT.
No.
I KNOW YOU. I KNOW THIS PLACE. THIS IS THE --THE DREAMING. YES?
Yes.
AND YOU ARE THE LORD OF THIS REALM.
Yes.
9

AND **THIS** IS THE RAVEN... JESSAMY?

This is the Raven Matthew. The Raven Jessamy has not been with us for some time.

MATTHEW. YOU HAVE BEAUTIFUL EYES, MATTHEW.

I WAS... WALKING THE WAKING WORLD, TEACHING THEM THINGS.

YES.

I REMEMBER. IN TINY FRAGMENTS, I REMEMBER.

WHY DO I REMEMBER?

Because there is a fragment of the first Corinthian in your essence. I saved a little of him.

WHAT...

WHAT SHALL I DO? WHAT SHALL I MAKE? WHAT SHALL I BE?

Eventually, many things.

For now...

You will run an errand for me. There is a task to be done.

Matthew will go with you.

I'LL WHAT?

You will accompany him, Matthew.

BUT-BOSS- I DON'T **LIKE** HIM.

I did not ask you to like him. I told you to accompany him.

WHY DON'T YOU LIKE ME?

10

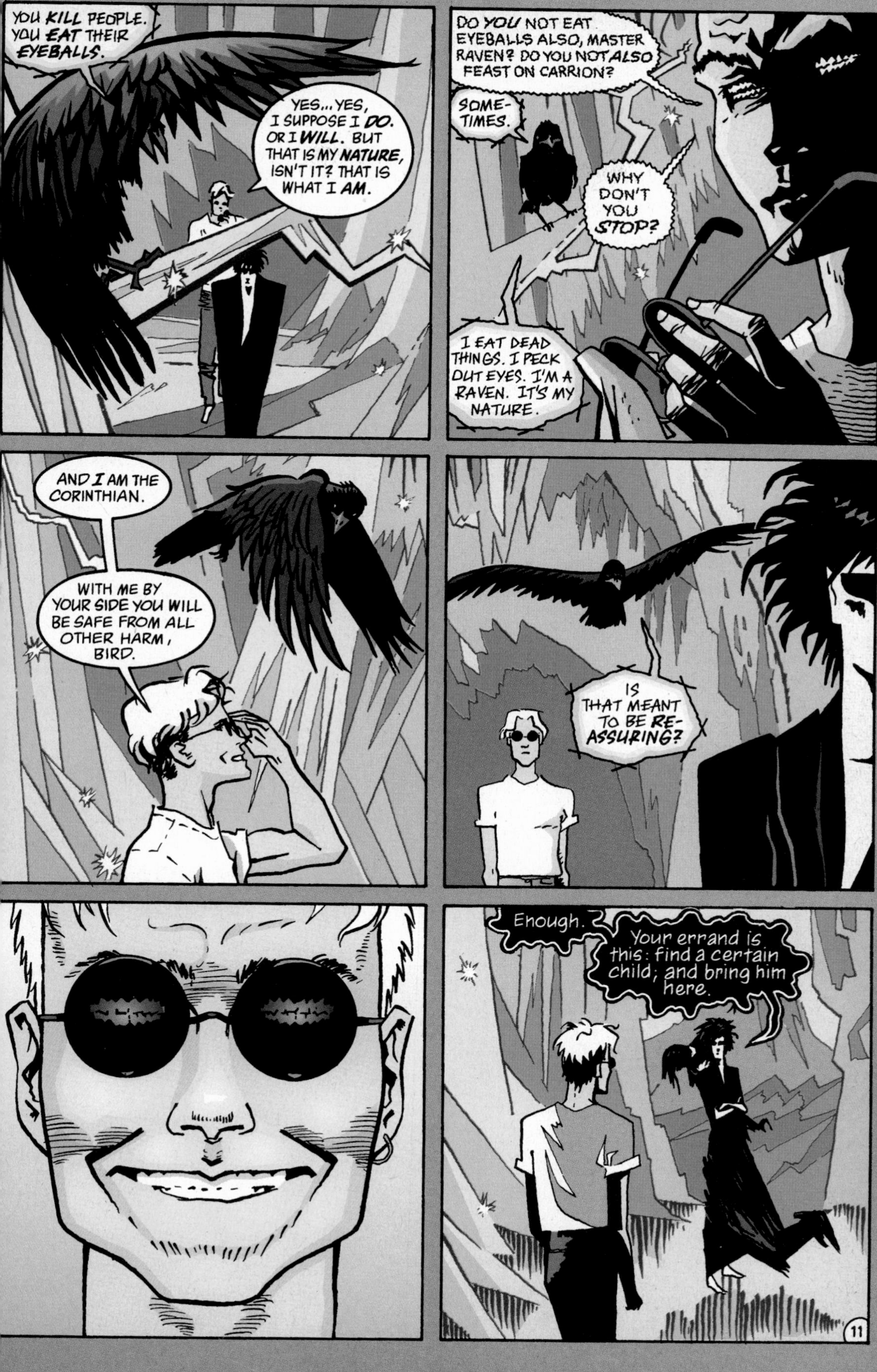
YOU KILL PEOPLE. YOU EAT THEIR EYEBALLS.
YES... YES, I SUPPOSE I DO. OR I WILL. BUT THAT IS MY NATURE, ISN'T IT? THAT IS WHAT I AM.
DO YOU NOT EAT EYEBALLS ALSO, MASTER RAVEN? DO YOU NOT ALSO FEAST ON CARRION?
SOME-TIMES.
WHY DON'T YOU STOP?
I EAT DEAD THINGS. I PECK OUT EYES. I'M A RAVEN. IT'S MY NATURE.
AND I AM THE CORINTHIAN.
WITH ME BY YOUR SIDE YOU WILL BE SAFE FROM ALL OTHER HARM, BIRD.
IS THAT MEANT TO BE RE-ASSURING?
Enough.
Your errand is this: find a certain child; and bring him here.

Faerie

"WELCOME HOME, DEAR, DEAR NUALA. WELCOME BACK."

"THANK YOU, MY LADY."

I TRUST YOU DID NOT THINK YOUR EXILE WOULD BE PERMANENT, NUALA, MY SWEET. IT WAS FITTING FOR ITS TIME, BUT I ASSURE YOU THAT *NO ONE* HERE IS MORE PLEASED TO SEE YOU BACK THAN I.

THANK YOU, YOUR MAJESTY.

HMM. VERY *PRETTY*. THAT'S *NEW*, ISN'T IT?

YES...MY LADY.

SO. HOW WAS HE?

WHO, MY LADY?

THE LORD SHAPER, NUALA. IN WHOM ELSE'S REALM MIGHT YOU HAVE SPENT THE LAST THREE YEARS?

OH. HIM. HE WAS PERFECTLY TOLERABLE.

DID HE EVER SPEAK OF ME?

OF *YOU*, MY LADY?

YES. OF ME.

HE *MIGHT* HAVE DONE, MY LADY. I REALLY COULD NOT SAY.

NO?

I WAS *RARELY* PRIVY TO THE LORD SHAPER'S CONVERSATION, MY LADY. HE KEEPS HIS OWN COUNSEL.

12

DID HE HAPPEN TO GIVE YOU ANY *MESSAGES* FOR ME?

NOT ONE, MY LADY.

IS THAT YOUR *OLD* FACE, DEAR? IT SEEMS, IF YOU'LL PARDON MY SAYING SO, A LITTLE LESS *GLAMOROUS* THAN I REMEMBER.

AND YOU MIGHT LOOK BETTER WITH A FEW MORE *CURVES.*

THIS GLAMOUR MAY HAVE CHANGED A *LITTLE,* MY LADY. BUT I SEEM AS I FEEL *COMFORTABLE* SEEMING.

THAT REALLY IS A *LOVELY* LITTLE BAUBLE...

IS IT?

IF I WERE TO *ASK* YOU FOR IT, WHAT WOULD YOU SAY?

I WOULD BE FORCED TO ADMIT THAT IT WAS A *GIFT,* MILADY, AND NOT IN MY POWER TO GIVE. *IF,* OF COURSE, YOU WERE TO ASK.

THIS *BORES* ME. FAREWELL.

ONE *HAD* HOPED THAT HER TIME IN THE DREAMING MIGHT HAVE TAUGHT HER BETTER *MANNERS.*

MAJESTY.

13

I dreamed of kittens who were born to neutered puss, then dreamed about a body buried in the corn--

--be sure your sins will find you out.

AWAY! FOOLISH LITTLE BOGGART.

But I've three more verses, and an *envoi* and I must tell them to only you, lady.

ENOUGH, AND AWAY, I SAY.

SO, I COULD CALL YOU, I COULD ALWAYS CALL. AND IF I *DID* GIVE IN AND CALL, WHAT THEN?

YOU'D BOLT TOWARD THAT BITCH AND KISS HER HAND, THEN BOW TOO DEEP, AND WALK, OR MINUET...

HOW FITTING THAT LORD AUBERON IS HORN'D.

BUT I CAN CALL YOU. I CAN ALWAYS CALL.

14

YOU KNOW, THERE'S A THREE-HEADED SNAKE OUT IN THE GARDEN. I DON'T THINK IT TRUSTS YOU TWO. IT WAS RUDE ABOUT YOU.

WELL, THEN THE NEXT TIME WE SEE IT WE'LL GLARE AT IT.

CUT IT DEAD.

AHH...

WHERE DID YOU GO?

WE WERE HERE. WE'RE ALWAYS HERE.

WE'LL MISS YOU.

WE GIVE YOU GIFTS, AS YOU LEAVE. WE GIVE YOU CLAWS OF BRASS. WE GIVE YOU THE NIMBIC GLIMMERING.

IF YOU HAD STAYED WITH US, WE COULD HAVE GIVEN YOU LIFE UNTIL DEATH.

DON'T I GET THAT ANYWAY?

THAT'S WHAT WE LIKED ABOUT YOU.

YOU WERE SO FUNNY.

15

"TO BE TOTALLY HONEST, *NO*, I *DON'T* UNDERSTAND YOU.

"COULD YOU START AGAIN AT THE BEGINNING?"

SURE. I'VE GOT A FRIEND NAMED LYTA HALL. *RIGHT?* SHE'S GOT A KID NAMED DANIEL--HE'S TWO, THREE YEARS OLD. *OKAY?*

THREE NIGHTS AGO, LYTA WENT OUT FOR THE EVENING. WHEN SHE CAME BACK, HER SON WAS GONE, *RIGHT?*

WE CALLED THE POLICE, AND EVENTUALLY YOUR DETECTIVES FELLOWES AND PINKERTON SHOWED UP AND TOOK OUR STATEMENT. YOU WITH ME *SO FAR?*

UH-HUH.

THEY *SAID* THEY'D BE TALKING TO ROSE DOWN- STAIRS, TOO, BUT THEY NEVER *DID*, YEAH? I MEAN, SHE *TOLD* ME THAT.

NOW, LYTA'S NOT REALLY VERY *WELL- BALANCED.* SHE USED TO DRESS UP IN *COSTUMES*, Y'KNOW? THEN SHE GOT MARRIED, AND PREGNANT, AND SHE *VANISHED* FOR A FEW YEARS.

WHEN SHE GOT BACK SHE WAS *STILL* PREGNANT, AND IT WAS LIKE, HER *MIND* WASN'T QUITE THE SAME.

SHE HASN'T REALLY BEEN OUT OF THE HOUSE IN YEARS. SINCE DANIEL WAS *BORN*. AND NOW SHE'S VANISHED AND I'M *REALLY* WORRIED.

THESE DETECTIVES. WHAT DID THEY *LOOK* LIKE?

PINKERTON'S A TALL, SKINNY WHITE GUY WITH RED HAIR, FELLOWES IS A REALLY SHORT WHITE GUY WITH DARK HAIR.

MM. DOESN'T RING ANY BELLS.

WELL, MAYBE THEY WERE FROM ANOTHER *PRECINCT*, OR SOMETHING. AND WHAT ABOUT FINDING *LYTA?* WHAT ABOUT *DANIEL?*

WE'LL MAKE OUR OWN ENQUIRIES.

THANKS FOR STOPPING BY.

LOOK--THEY GAVE ME *THIS*.

YEAH?

I'M *SURE* IT HAD A NAME AND A PHONE NUMBER ON IT WHEN THEY *GAVE* IT TO ME. MAYBE IT WAS WRITTEN IN DISAPPEARING INK. AND YOU COULD CHECK IT FOR *FINGERPRINTS*.

I'M SOUNDING LIKE A CRAZY PERSON NOW, AREN'T I?

THANKS AGAIN. WE'LL GET *BACK* TO YOU.

HEY! I *KNOW* YOU! MISSY! DON'T I *KNOW* YOU?

JUST LEAVE ME THE HELL ALONE.

HEY, YOU LEAVE THE PEOPLE BE, NOW.

HEY! MISSY! YOUR *FRIEND?* THE *MEAN* ONE? I *SEEN* HER. SHE'S GOT SNAKES IN HER HAIR.

AND SHE'S *NOT* ALONE IN HER HEAD ANYMORE.

HEY!

AREN'T YOU LISTENING? I SAID TO KEEP IT *DOWN*.

17

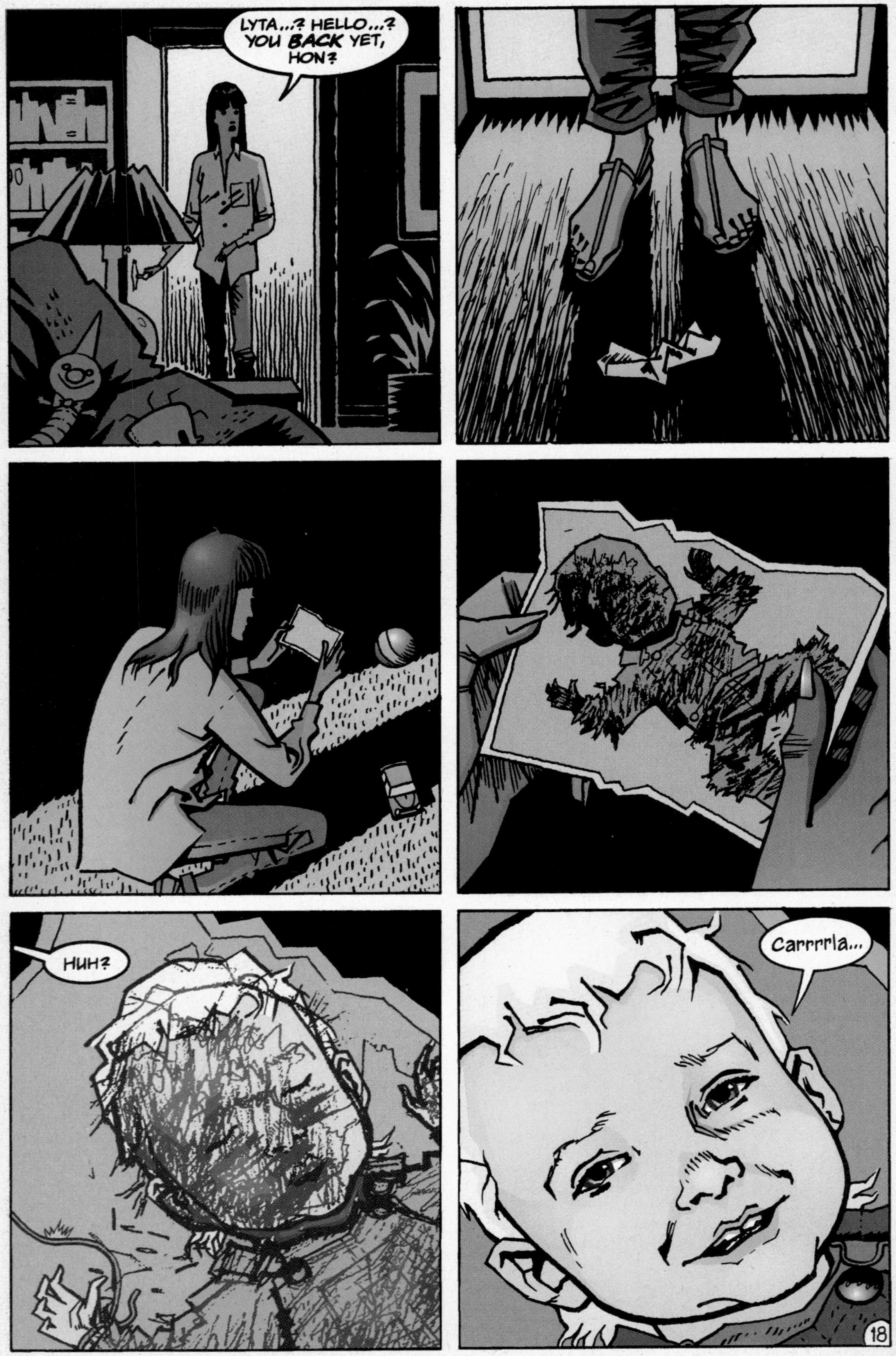
LYTA...? HELLO...? YOU BACK YET, HON?
HUH?
Carrrrla...
18

WHAT THE F...

AH.

AAAAH!

OWWW...

YOU OKAY? I HEARD THE NOISE UP HERE. I THOUGHT MAYBE LYTA WAS BACK.

WHAT'S THAT SMELL?

ROAST ME. I WAS HOLDING THIS PHOTOGRAPH AND...

OWWWWW...

DO PHOTOGRAPHS SPONTANEOUSLY COMBUST?

I DON'T KNOW. I THOUGHT THAT WAS ONLY PEOPLE.

LOOK, LYTA HAS A PRETTY EXTENSIVE FIRST-AID KIT IN THE BATHROOM. CAN YOU BRING ME SOME BURN OINTMENT, AND SOME GAUZE BANDAGES?

SURE. IN THE BATHROOM. RIGHT.

19

YOU WEREN'T *KIDDING* ABOUT THE FIRST-AID KIT. IT'S LIKE A MINI-HOSPITAL IN HERE.

YEAH, WELL. LYTA WAS ALWAYS SCARED THAT DANIEL WOULD HURT HIMSELF AND SHE WOULDN'T BE ABLE TO *DO* ANYTHING ABOUT IT.

THAT'S A REALLY NASTY *BURN.* YOU REALLY OUGHT TO SEE A DOCTOR.

I *WILL.*

SAY... *ROSE?* DO YOU BELIEVE IN MAGIC?

NOT REALLY, *NO.* BUT THAT'S *NOT* WHAT YOU'RE ASKING ME.

IT'S *NOT?*

NOPE.

WHAT YOU'RE ASKING ME IS, DO I BELIEVE IN *WEIRD SHIT?* AND THE ANSWER IS *YES.* OF *COURSE* I DO. I'D HAVE TO BE *CRAZY* NOT TO. I'VE HAD A *WEIRD SHIT LIFE.*

WEIRD SHIT. THAT'S A GOOD WAY OF PUTTING IT.

LOOK, I WAS *WONDERING,* IF YOU'RE NOT BUSY TOMORROW, COULD WE GET TOGETHER? I WANT TO TALK SOME MORE ABOUT THIS STUFF.

NOT TOMORROW. MAYBE *NEXT* WEEK. I'M GOING TO ENGLAND FOR A FEW DAYS. I JUST BOUGHT MY TICKET. I LEAVE TONIGHT.

FAMILY PROBLEM?

IN A MANNER OF SPEAKING. I GOT THIS MESSAGE THAT MY GRANDMOTHER NEEDS TO TELL ME SOMETHING.

DOESN'T SHE BELIEVE IN THE *TELEPHONE?*

NOT ANYMORE; SHE'S BEEN *DEAD* FOR FOUR YEARS.

HUH?

LIKE I SAID: *WEIRD SHIT.* YOU THINK YOU'RE THE ONLY ONE?

20

HELLO...

HELLO. WHO *ARE* YOU?

TAKE A MOMENT TO REFLECT.

I DON'T KNOW. I REALLY *DON'T*.

I WAS SUCH A *TOGETHER* PERSON. AND I DIDN'T *MAKE* DECISIONS.

AND HOW DID YOU GET HERE FROM THERE, MRS. HALL?

I MEAN, I NEVER *DID* ANYTHING IN MY WHOLE LIFE THAT WASN'T SOMEONE ELSE'S IDEA.

LIKE A GIRL IN A MIRROR.

LIKE I WAS *WATCHING*, SITTING, BRUSHING MY HAIR, WHILE MY LIFE WENT BY ON THE GLASS. WHEN MY *MOTHER* DESERTED ME. WHEN *HECTOR* DIED. WHEN HECTOR DIED *AGAIN*.

IT'S LIKE HOW MANY TIMES CAN LIFE HIT YOU?

WHEN DO THE BLOWS START TO HURT?

WHEN DO YOU JUST ...*STOP*?

WHEN DANIEL WAS KILLED, IT WAS LIKE THE MIRROR WAS *BROKEN*.

THERE WERE ONLY *TWO* THINGS I *COULD* HAVE DONE. AND ONE OF THEM WOULD HAVE BEEN JUST TO LIE DOWN AND NEVER GET UP AGAIN.

ACTUALLY, THAT'S A *VERY GOOD* POINT. YOU'RE NOT REALLY STOPPING, OF COURSE, DEAR. RIGHT NOW, YOU'RE JUST SORTING EVERYTHING OUT. THROUGH THE LOOKING GLASS, AS IT WERE.

PRIOR TO DOING SOMETHING YOU CAN'T *POSSIBLY DO*.

NOT A *HOPE*, MY DEARIE. *DOOMED* TO FAIL.

ON YOUR *OWN*...

EX*CUSE* ME. BUT WHICH ONE OF US AM *I*?

NO. IT DOESN'T MATTER.

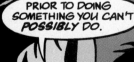

DOES IT *MATTER*?

NICE EVENING.

YOU KNOW, WHERE *I* COME FROM, WE GET SIX MONTHS OF SNOW AND ICE, SIX MONTHS OF MUD AND MOSQUITOS. IN MIDWINTER THE SUN RISES AT NOON, SETS AN HOUR OR SO LATER. THERE'S NEVER ANY CERTAINTY THAT THE SUN WILL *EVER* COME BACK.

SOMEONE COULD JUST STICK A SHARPENED SPRIG OF MISTLETOE THROUGH ITS HEART AND, WELL, *GAME OVER.* WINTER DARKNESS FOREVER.

WHO *ARE* YOU? YOU AREN'T A COP.

WHERE'S *LYTA?*

WHAT THE HELL IS GOING *ON?*

WELL, IF YOU GET IN THE CAR, I'LL TELL YOU.

STRAP YOURSELF IN. THEN TOSS THE KEYS INTO THE BACK. YOU CAN GO FIND THEM WHEN WE'RE DONE TALKING.

YOU *GOT* THAT?

UH-HUH.

22

YOU'RE **NOT** A COP. WHO THE FUCK **ARE** YOU?

MERELY ONE WHO REGRETS THE ABANDONMENT OF THEOLOGY, IN THESE STRANGE WARM TIMES.

MISTER PINKERTON. UH, LUKE ... WHY DON'T YOU PUT THE **GUN** AWAY?

BECAUSE I'M NOT **HOLDING** A GUN.

UH. RIGHT. *FINE.* WHATEVER YOU SAY.

AREN'T I **SLY**? IT WAS A **CIGARETTE** ALL THE TIME.

THERE'S A **THEORY** THAT FOR A HUMAN TO BE KILLED BY A GOD IS THE BEST THING THAT COULD POSSIBLY HAPPEN TO THE HUMAN UNDER DISCUSSION.

IT ELIMINATES ALL QUESTIONS OF BELIEF, WHILE MANIFESTLY PLACING A HUMAN LIFE AT THE SERVICE OF A HIGHER POWER. WHERE DO **YOU** STAND ON THIS THEORY?

I--I DON'T BELIEVE IN GOD.

YOU DON'T **HAVE** TO BELIEVE IN GOD. BUT WHAT ABOUT GODS? EH? THE **PLURALITY** OF POWERS AND DOMINIONS. THE LORDS AND LADIES OF FIELD AND THORN, OF ASPHALT AND SEWER, GODS OF TELEPHONE AND WHORE, GODS OF HOSPITAL AND CAR-CRASH?

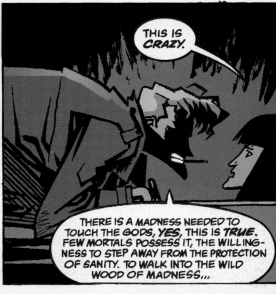

THIS IS **CRAZY.**

THERE IS A MADNESS NEEDED TO TOUCH THE GODS, **YES**, THIS IS **TRUE.** FEW MORTALS POSSESS IT, THE WILLING- NESS TO STEP AWAY FROM THE PROTECTION OF SANITY. TO WALK INTO THE WILD WOOD OF MADNESS...

23

MISTER PINKERTON. WHATEVER YOUR NAME IS. *PLEASE.* STOP THIS.

HOW ABOUT A KISS? *NO?* I COULD TAKE IT, IF I WANTED.

YOU KNOW WHAT *STICKS* PEOPLE TO SOMETHING? THE DESIRE TO KNOW HOW IT'S ALL GOING TO END. IT'S LIKE GLUE.

AND *DO YOU* KNOW *YOUR* TRAGEDY, CARLA?

UH-UH.

IT'S THAT, FOR *ALL YOUR* GOODWILL, FOR ALL YOUR WILLINGNESS TO HELP, YOU NEVER KNEW WHAT *ANY* OF THIS WAS ALL ABOUT. WHAT WAS GOING ON.

YOU DON'T KNOW HOW IT ENDS.

AND YOU'LL *NEVER* GET TO FIND OUT.

STAY THERE. YOU CAN'T MOVE, CAN YOU?

NO. I CAN'T.

WHO ARE YOU?

I AM THE MOTHER TO ODIN'S STALLION, SLEIPNIR. I AM THE FATHER OF FENRIR SUN-EATER, AND OF HEL HALF-ROTTED AND OF JORMUNGUND THE WORLD-SERPENT.

I AM LOKI SCAR-LIP, LOKI SKYWALKER, LOKI GIANT'S CHILD, LOKI LIE-SMITH.

I AM *LOKI*, WHO IS FIRE AND WIT AND HATE.

I AM LOKI.

AND I WILL BE UNDER AN OBLIGATION TO NO ONE.

part
Six

PRESSURE IN MY EARS WOKE ME UP WHEN WE WERE COMING IN FOR A LANDING.

I WOKE UP IN PAIN, DISORIENTED.

I HELD MY NOSTRILS SHUT WITH MY FINGERS, BLEW HARD UNTIL MY EARS POPPED OUT AND THE PAIN STARTED TO GO AWAY.

SOMEHOW, WHEN I WOKE, I WAS EXPECTING TO SEE MY MOM IN THE SEAT BY THE WINDOW.

I WAS GOING TO TELL HER THE DREAM I JUST HAD. IT WAS ABOUT THE OLD DAYS IN FLORIDA WITH HAL AND CHANTAL AND GILBERT AND EVERYONE.

INSTEAD OF MOM, THERE'S A GUY BY THE WINDOW AS BIG AS GILBERT WAS.

GILBERT SMELLED LIKE CINNAMON AND LICORICE. A LITTLE LIKE THANKSGIVING, OR CHRISTMAS. THIS GUY SMELLS SOUR AND UNWASHED.

HE'S SITTING READING THE SAME LITTLE PORN MAG HE PULLED OUT OF HIS BAG WHEN WE TOOK OFF.

HOW DO YOU READ THE SAME PORN MAG FOR TWELVE HOURS?

HE DOESN'T EVEN LOOK OUT OF THE WINDOW AS WE COME DOWN.

CREEP.

GATWICK AIRPORT HASN'T CHANGED FROM HOW I REMEMBER. THIS TIME I GET GRABBED BY A CUSTOMS GUY. HE'S GOING THROUGH MY VALISE WHEN I SMELL THE SAME SOUR SMELL AGAIN.

THE CREEP'S TRUNDLING HIS TROLLEY PAST ME. I REALIZE HE'S SEEN MY MAYBE-I'LL-GET-LUCKY LACY PANTIES. AND I FEEL SUDDENLY KIND OF EXPOSED AND STUPID.

HEY. YOU LOOKING FOR ME?

MISS WALKER?

WALKER

THAT'S ME. BUT I WAS EXPECTING MISTER HOLDAWAY.

THAT'S ME.

UH-UH. I MET MISTER HOLDAWAY, FOUR, FIVE YEARS BACK.

I'M JACK HOLDAWAY. YOU MET MY UNCLE. HE PASSED ON A FEW YEARS AGO, I'M AFRAID. DICKY HEART.

I'M SORRY.

WELL, HE HAD A GOOD INNINGS. COME ON, THE CAR'S IN THE CAR PARK. I'LL TAKE YOUR SUITCASE.

I'D BEEN LOOKING FORWARD TO RIDING IN MISTER HOLDAWAY'S BIG OLD JAGUAR AGAIN. I COULD SMELL THE LEATHER IN MY MEMORY.

INSTEAD JACK'S DRIVING SOMETHING ROUGHLY THE SIZE OF A BATHTUB.

IT IS, HE TELLS ME PROUDLY, A RESTORED AUSTIN SOMETHING-OR-OTHER.

WE SPEND HALF AN HOUR DRIVING THROUGH THE SUSSEX COUNTRYSIDE. IT SEEMS PRETTIER THAN I REMEMBER IT : OR PERHAPS MY TASTES ARE CHANGING.

I STAY AWAKE THE WHOLE WAY, THIS TIME, WHILE JACK DOES THE CONVERSATION THING THAT THE ENGLISH DO SO WELL, WHERE THEY CAN TALK FOREVER AND NEVER TELL YOU A THING.

2

SO, DO YOU, UM. KNOW HOW LONG YOU'RE GOING TO BE HERE?

NO. I JUST WANT TO WANDER AROUND. TALK TO PEOPLE.

THIS WAS WHERE MY GRANDMOTHER SPENT MOST OF HER *LIFE*, YOU KNOW.

WELL, YES. UNCLE JACK TOLD ME A LITTLE BIT ABOUT IT. FUNNY BUSINESS. SLEEPING YOUR LIFE AWAY.

LIKE THAT ROBIN WILLIAMS FILM.

WELL, I'LL INTRODUCE YOU TO THE DUTY NURSE, AND THEN, IF YOU DON'T NEED ME TO HANG AROUND, I'LL TAKE THE CAR INTO WYCH CROSS AND GET YOU ALL BOOKED INTO THE HOTEL.

I PICKED THE *WHITE HART INN*. IT'S MEANT TO BE VERY NICE.

I CAN DROP OFF YOUR SUITCASE, TOO.

THANKS.

③

KNOCKETY KNOCK. HULLO. ANYBODY HOME?

PAUL! GOOD LORD-- PAUL McGUIRE. HOW ON EARTH *ARE* YOU?

HELLO, YOUNG JACK.

ROSE, THIS IS PAUL McGUIRE. HE ACTUALLY *OWNS* THIS NURSING HOME. PAUL, THIS IS ROSE WALKER, A HOLDAWAYS CLIENT.

ROSE, THIS IS THE DUTY NURSE, MRS., UM ...

SHORE. MRS. SHORE. PLEASURE, DEAR. *TEA?* I'VE GOT COFFEE, TOO.

NO. NO, THANK YOU.

JACK'S A FRIGHTFUL LIAR. I'M MERELY REPRESENTING ONE OF THE INVESTORS. DO YOU HAVE A *RELATIVE* HERE, MISS WALKER?

NOT ANYMORE. MY GRANDMOTHER WAS HERE, SOME YEARS BACK.

SHE WAS ASLEEP HERE.

NOW, *YOU'RE* NOT ENGLISH, ARE YOU? HOW DO YOU KNOW YOUNG HOLDAWAY?

HIS COMPANY ARE MY FAMILY'S ENGLISH LAWYERS. THEY'VE WORKED FOR US FOR LIKE, A ZILLION YEARS.

SINCE THE '45 REBELLION, I WAS TOLD.

SO I FAXED HIS OFFICE AND TOLD THEM I WAS COMING TO ENGLAND. I'M A *WRITER.* I'M WRITING A BOOK ABOUT MY GRAND-MOTHER. I WANTED TO GET A *SENSE* OF THE PLACE WHERE SHE LEFT HER LIFE. *SPENT* HER LIFE.

YOU SAID SHE WAS *ASLEEP* HERE?

SHE WAS *SICK.* HER NAME WAS UNITY KINKAID.

UNITY KINKAID? THE *NAME'S* FAMILIAR ...

YOU REMEMBER, MISTER McGUIRE. THE SLEEPING BEAUTY.

4

OF *COURSE*. OUR LONGEST RESIDENT. THE *MIRACLE* CURE. I MET HER, ONCE, TOWARD THE END. AFTER SHE HAD WOKEN UP.

VERY *VITAL* WOMAN. VERY YOUNG IN THE HEART.

I'M AFRAID THAT AT THE TIME I FOUND IT DIFFICULT TO APPRECIATE THE *IRONY*.

WELL, I *MUSTN'T* KEEP YOU. FEEL FREE TO POTTER AROUND AS MUCH AS YOU LIKE.

JACK, *GOOD* SEEING YOU. YOU SHOULD COME DOWN TO THE GATEHOUSE SOME TIME.

GOODBYE, MISS WALKER.

NURSE, I'M GOING TO HAND ROSE OVER TO YOU. I'LL COME BACK AND PICK HER UP IN, WHAT, A COUPLE OF HOURS, ROSE?

THREE.

THREE HOURS IT IS, I'LL HAVE YOU ALL CHECKED IN AND EVERYTHING.

RIGHT, LOVE. WHAT CAN I *DO* FOR YOU?

I'D REALLY LIKE TO SEE MY GRANDMOTHER'S OLD ROOM, I THINK. WHERE SHE SLEPT.

VERY GOOD. DO YOU REMEMBER WHICH *ROOM* IT WAS?

I COULD PROBABLY LOOK IT UP, IF YOU CAN'T.

I'M NOT SURE I COULD *FORGET* IT. UP THE STAIRS, AND DOWN THE HALL TO THE END.

THERE'S NO ONE IN THERE JUST NOW. CAN YOU SEE YOURSELF UP? ONLY THERE'S REALLY ONLY *ME* RIGHT NOW, AND I CAN'T BE DOING WITH ALL THE STAIRS IF SOMEONE NEEDS ME.

NO, SURE. *FINE*. WHATEVER.

UH, HELLO? IS THERE ANYBODY HERE?

6

TCH.

THAT'S THE *BROOM* CUPBOARD IN THERE, LOVE. *WHAT* YOU DOIN' IN THERE?

JUST LOOKING.

WHAT ARE *YOU* THEN? SOMEBODY'S GRAND-DAUGHTER? SOMEBODY'S *NIECE*? ARE YOU VISITIN'? OR ARE YOU WITH THE HOME?

YOU CAN *TELL ME OFF* IF I'M ASKING TOO MANY QUESTIONS. BUT IT'S NOT *OFTEN* THERE'S A LASSIE IN THE BROOM CUPBOARD.

WELL, IT'S KIND OF A LONG STORY.

WELL, WE'VE *ALL* GOT TIME HERE, MY PET. I'M GOING DOWN TO THE DAY ROOM.

YOU COMIN'?

YES. I SUPPOSE I AM.

AND I *HOPE* I'M NOT BEING TOO BOLD, BUT DID I HEAR YOU ASKIN' IF THERE WAS ANYONE IN THE BROOM CUPBOARD?

YES.

WERE YOU EX*PEC*TIN' SOMEONE? IN THE BROOM CUPBOARD?

NOT REALLY.

THANK YOU, DEAR. WHERE ARE YOU FROM? SOUNDS LIKE YOU'RE A BIT OF A YANKEE DOODLE DANDY TO ME.

YES. I'M FROM AMERICA.

I HAD A *BOY*FRIEND FROM AMERICA. YOU'D NOT THINK IT TO LOOK AT ME NOW, BUT I *DID*.

7

OVER IN THE **WAR**, HE WAS. AND HE WAS BLACK AS THE ACE OF SPADES. HE WAS **LOVELY**. I HAD A LITTLE **GIRL**, TOO. BUT MY MOTHER MADE ME PUT HER OUT FOR ADOPTION. I WAS HOPIN' NO ONE WOULD WANT HER, BEING HALF DARKIE, AND SO I'D GET TO **KEEP** HER.

BUT THEY **DID** AND I **COULDN'T**.

EVEN THE OLDEST STORIES ARE NEW TO **SOMEBODY**...

YOU'RE NOT TELLING **THAT** OLD STORY AGAIN?

WE BETTER INTRODUCE OUR-SELVES, DEARIE. **I'M** AMELIA CRUPP, **THIS** IS MAGDA TREADGOLD, AND THIS IS,...I CAN'T SAY YOUR LAST NAME, DEARIE.

THEY **NEVER** GET MY NAME RIGHT. CALL ME HELENA, MY DEAR.

I'M ROSE. ROSE WALKER. MY GRANDMOTHER WAS UNITY KINKAID. SHE WAS **HERE**, UNTIL A FEW YEARS AGO.

SLEEPING BEAUTY, YES?

THAT WAS HER.

I REMEMBER **HER**. THEY WOULD WHEEL HER OUT INTO THE SUN, OR DOWN **HERE** WHEN IT WAS COLD. SHE WAS FAST ASLEEP...

THIS IS WHERE **WE** SIT. IN THE EVENING WE WATCH TELLY. IN THE AFTER-NOON, TOO, ONCE BLOCKBUSTER COMES ON. 'I'LL HAVE A P, BOB...'

HEHEHEH...

WE PLAY A LITTLE DRAUGHTS. **AND** SNAKES AND LADDERS. WE **USED** TO PLAY **BRIDGE** UNTIL MRS. SMALL HAD HER STROKE.

YOU DON'T PLAY BRIDGE, DO YOU?

NO.

PITY. WE ALSO TELL STORIES. THINGS WE DID AND THINGS WE HEARD. STUFF FROM WHEN WE WAS LITTLE. YOU SHOULD SIT **DOWN**, LOVEY. TAKE THE WEIGHT OFF YOUR LEGS.

IT'S **FUNNY** WHAT YOU REMEMBER...

NOT FUNNY HA-HA, THE **OTHER** FUNNY.

8

ME, I COULDN'T TELL YOU WHAT I DID YESTERDAY. MY DAUGHTER, SHE CAME OUT OVER WHITSUN, WITH HER CHILDREN, I COULDN'T REMEMBER THEIR *NAMES*.

BUT I REMEMBER MY *CHILDHOOD* SO CLEARLY. I REMEMBER THE NAMES OF THE GIRL I SHARED A DESK WITH, IN THORNTON ROAD PRIMARY SCHOOL. PRUNELLA WIPER, IT WAS. *SUCH* A FUNNY NAME.

I REMEMBER ALL OUR SKIPPING RHYMES, CLEAR AS DAY. MY MOTHER SAID, I NEVER SHOULD, PLAY WITH A GYPSY IN THE WOOD...

I REMEMBER *SO* MANY THINGS.

MY MAM, SHE WAS AN OLD *HARPY*, SHE WAS. BUT WHEN YOU GOT HER TO TALKING, SHE COULD TELL *SUCH* STORIES.

I NEVER KNEW WHERE SHE *GOT* THEM FROM. SHE COULDN'T READ MUCH. SOME SHE MUST'VE MADE UP, SOME SHE MUST'VE HEARD.

SHE TOLD US THAT ONE ABOUT THE SLEEPING BEAUTY IN THE WOOD, ONLY SHE *DIDN'T* TELL IT LIKE THEY DO ON THE TELLY. HE DIDN'T WAKE HER WITH A *KISS*.

IT WAS *MORE* THAN *KISS* HER HE DID, TO HEAR MY MAM TELL IT, AND EVEN *THAT* DIDN'T WAKE HER. SHE SLEPT UNTIL SHE GAVE BIRTH TO TWINS...

AND THEY CRAWLED UP HER BODY, SEEKING MILK TO SUCK, AND ONE OF THEM SUCKED THE POISONED NEEDLE FROM HER FINGER. YES?

WHY, *YES*. THAT WAS HOW ME MAM TOLD IT.

IT'S AN *EARLY* FORM OF THE STORY, BEFORE THEY STARTED TIDYING IT UP. I USED TO HAVE A *FRIEND* WHO'D TELL ME SOME OF THE ORIGINAL STORIES.

THERE, AND YOU *SEE?* I THOUGHT ME MAM JUST MADE IT WORSE TO SCARE US.

THE STORY SHE USED TO TELL US THAT I COULD *NEVER* GET OUT OF MY HEAD, SHE CALLED THE FLYING CHILDREN. HAVE YOU HEARD *THAT* ONE, DEAR?

I DON'T *THINK* SO.

STORIES, MAGDA. *ALWAYS* YOU TELL STORIES.

WELL, IT'S NOT LIKE ANYONE'S GOING TO TAKE ME *DANCING*.

IT'S A *BAD* THING WHEN YOU GET SO OLD. A BODY SHOULDN'T GET OLD.

IN*SIDE* I'M NOT OLD. BUT I COULDN'T DANCE NOW, NOT EVEN IF I WAS *ASKED*...

THE STORY ABOUT THE CHILDREN WHO FLEW AWAY?

OF COURSE, PRETTY. I WAS JUST *GETTING* TO THAT...

9

Well, the way me mam told it, there was a man who loved the ladies. He was always carrying on with one pretty face after another. Loved 'em, and forgot 'em as he went from town to town.

So one day he spied a gal washing herself in the river, mother-naked and all in her birthday suit. So he hides her clothes. And when she comes out of the river, she sees him.

He says he'll give her back her clothes if she'll be his lady-love, but she won't be his lady unless he swears he'll make her his wife --- and in the first church they come to, at that.

I swear if I set foot in a church, it'll be to marry you, he said (and the devil he'd step into a church ever again, he swore under his breath).

And what'll you swear, she asks, if you break the vow?

*I*f I don't marry you, he said, may that worms shall eat me (for they'll do that anyway, he thought, when my time's over and up), and if I don't marry you, I wish our children might grow wings and fly away (and no great matter if they do, he thought).

So they kissed then and there, and did other things besides, and when they were all done, he gave her her clothes back, and she followed him down the road.

They passed the first church. Let's get married here, she says. Oh, he says, we can't get married here, for the vicar's a sick man, and besides, he's off a-hunting.

She said nothing but she looked at him as if her heart would break.

When they came to the next church, her belly was already beginning to swell.

Let's be married here, she says.

I'm not going into that church, he says, for the vicar's a drunkard, and no better than he should be, and the sexton's no partic'lar friend of mine, neither.

But you SWORE, she said.

I'm not going in the church, he tells her, and he knocks her down.

Her face is bleeding when she gets up.

So THAT'S how it is, she says.

That's how it is, he tells her.

⑪

Well, she says, my belly's big with child. And I want to stop for a while. I can't keep on the road. Isn't there a place where I can rest?

So he has her stop there and sit, at the side of the road, and he goes on ahead.

He gets to a cottage, and he goes into the cottage, for the door's just on the latch, not locked, and in the cottage he sees an old woman fast asleep on the bed.

Now, sometimes the way me mam would tell it, the woman was a witch, and sometimes when she told it, she wasn't. But whichever, she was old and weak, and he held her mouth shut, and held his fingers over her nose until she couldn't breathe no more, and he took her out the back, and buried her in the midden heap.

He went back to his wife, and he says It's a good thing we passed by here, as my old aunt has just died and left us her cottage.

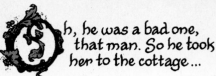

Oh, he was a bad one, that man. So he took her to the cottage...

‖ He was a man. They're all bad.

Not my Danny, he wasn't, God rest him.

‖ So he took her to the cottage...?

Yes, dear, and there he left her. He'd come back every few weeks to make sure she was still there, and to see his children, for she had three lovely girls over the next few years. But he was only home for a day here or there, and then he'd be off tomcatting over the whole countryside again.

It was a deserted part of the country, but there were vegetables in the garden, and now and then he'd bring her back a hen or a pig, so she never starved, and neither did the children.

Only, one day he comes home, and the children are nowhere to be seen. And the little girls are the apples of his eye...

(13)

Where are the children? He asks his wife.   Gathering berries, she says.

In the spring? He says. (There aren't any berries in the spring, dear.
I don't know if they have spring where you come from.)
But she says nothing, and the children don't come home.

So when night comes, he says to her Where's the children? Off fishing, she tells him.

The baby too? he asks her. But she pretended she couldn't hear him.

In the morning he woke her up: Where are the children? WHERE ARE MY GIRLS?
They've flown away, she told him.

Flown away? He shakes her to make her tell him the truth, but she won't change her tale.

So he fetches the axe in from outside, and he chops her up into bits.

There's a noise from outside, so he pushes the lumps and limbs and lights of her under
their bed.
And it's his daughters, the oldest, the middle, and the little wee baby,
coming down from the sky, each on wings.
They come inside the cottage.

here's our mam? they asked him.

She's out, picking berries, he tells them.

And what's all this blood on your hands and on the floor?

I was killing a pig, he says.

But the youngest girl she looks under the bed, and she sees her mother's dead face, staring out at them.

And they let out a wail deep and long and sad. Then they fell on him, all three of them, teeth and claw, and they killed him. They left his body there on the floor.

And they flew off into the sky, and nobody saw them again.

And as soon as he was sure that he was dead, he got up and shook himself, and looked around, and there waiting for him on the bed was his wife, with long claws out, and her eyes blazing like a green cat ready to spring.

And naturally the man got up and ran away, but he could feel her cold breath on the back of his neck.

nd he called out to the thunder, *Strike me dead,* but the thunder wouldn't, for he was dead already.

And he ran to the fire, and begged the fire to burn him up.

But the fire couldn't burn him, for the chill of death put it out...

And he threw himself in the water, and he screamed, *Drown me blue,* but the water wouldn't, for the death-color was coming into his face already, and the water tossed him out.

And last of all, he throws himself onto the ground, onto the midden-heap, and prays for the worms to come and eat him, so he could rest in his grave, and be quit of the woman.

He puts out one hand and he finds himself touching the skeleton hand of the old woman he'd killed for the cottage.

And he lies on the mud, his hand holding tight to that skeleton hand, waiting for his wife...

nd by and by along crept a great worm, and a strange thing it was, with his wife's face on the end of its long slimy body, and it crept up beside him and over him and all around him, and it druv all the other worms away. Her teeth were sharp and long.

And she wrapped her slimy worm body around his, and she whispered his name into his ear.

And he screams, Kill me, for god's sake, just get it over with. But she licks her lips with a long worm tongue, and she shakes her head.

A meal this good must never be hurried, she says. Just hold still, boy, and let me enjoy myself.

And she takes her first, gentle bite from his cheek with her sharp sharp teeth...

And that's the story, as my mother used to tell it.

THAT'S A STRANGE STORY.

IT'S HORRID.

I ALWAYS WONDERED WHAT HAPPENED TO THE *CHILDREN*, AFTER THEY FLEW AWAY...

THEY'RE JUST *MADE-UP* PEOPLE. THEY DIDN'T REALLY EXIST.

THAT DOESN'T MEAN THEY DON'T HAVE *STORIES*.

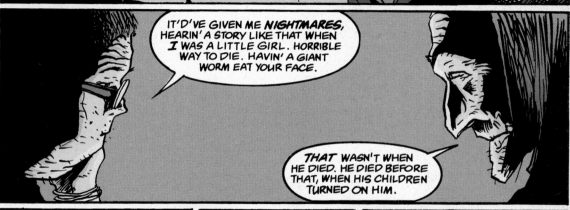

IT'D'VE GIVEN ME *NIGHTMARES*, HEARIN' A STORY LIKE THAT WHEN *I* WAS A LITTLE GIRL. HORRIBLE WAY TO DIE. HAVIN' A GIANT WORM EAT YOUR FACE.

THAT WASN'T WHEN HE DIED. HE DIED BEFORE THAT, WHEN HIS CHILDREN TURNED ON HIM.

ALL DEATHS ARE HORRIBLE.

MY DANNY-- HE WAS THE AMERICAN I WAS TELLING YOU ABOUT, ROSE -- HE DIED THE DAY *PEACE* BROKE OUT. RIDIN' IN A JEEP, CELEBRATIN' THE END OF THE WAR.

HE WAS LEANIN' OUT THE SIDE, AND THE DRIVER WENT TOO CLOSE TO A BRIDGE. IN PARIS. CUT DANNY'S HEAD CLEAN OFF. *BOMP.*

I LIKE TO THINK HE *WOULD'VE* MARRIED ME.

PROBABLY *WOULDN'T'VE*, THOUGH.

HE DESERVED IT. IT WAS AN ACT OF REVENGE. HE HAD KILLED AND LIED.

DANNY? HE WAS A SOLDIER. THAT'S THEIR *JOB.* KILLIN'. AND I DON'T THINK HE REALLY *LIED.* HE JUST SAID THINGS THAT WEREN'T *TRUE.* WELL, *YOU* KNOW MEN. THEY ALL DO THAT. THEY *HAVE* TO.

18

THE MAN IN THE STORY. HE DESERVED IT.

ACTS OF REVENGE ARE SANCTIFIED.

I HAVE ALSO DONE IT. I SPENT TWO DECADES LOOKING FOR THE MAN WHO HAD KILLED A PERSON I LOVED. I HOUNDED HIM FOR YEAR AFTER YEAR AFTER YEAR, ACROSS THE WORLD...

I FOUND HIM, AT THE LAST, IN BRIGHTON, IN ENGLAND IN THE WINTER: A GRAY, SAD TOWN. IT IS A COLD PLACE, ENGLAND.

REALLY? WHAT DID YOU DO WHEN YOU FOUND HIM?

EVENTUALLY, I KILLED HIM. FIRST, THOUGH, I DESTROYED HIS LIFE.

YOU'RE KIDDING, RIGHT?

JOKING WITH YOU? OF COURSE: IF I HAD REALLY KILLED A MAN, WOULD I TELL ANYONE?

WELL, YEAH, EXACTLY WHAT I THOUGHT.

YOU ARE SO WISE, GIRL.

AFTER MY TASK WAS OVER THE LIFE WENT OUT OF ME, AND I CAME HERE.

DID YOU KNOW MY GRANDMOTHER?

DID YOU EVER TALK TO HER?

I REMEMBER HER. SHE WAS ASLEEP.

A WOMAN SHOULDN'T HAVE TO SLEEP HER LIFE AWAY. WOMEN AREN'T ABOUT DREAMING. WE'RE ABOUT THE REAL WORLD.

EVEN YOUR GRANDMA WOKE BEFORE SHE DIED.

WOMEN ARE ABOUT WAKING, ROSE.

AS MOTHERS WE WAKE THEM FROM NOTHINGNESS TO EXISTENCE.

AS MAIDENS WE WAKE THEM TO THE JOYS AND MISERIES OF ADULTHOOD, WAKE THEM TO THE WORLDS OF LUST AND RESPONSIBILITY.

AND WHEN THEIR TIME'S UP, IT'S ALWAYS US HAS TO WASH THEM FOR THE LAST TIME, AND WE LAY THEM OUT FOR THE WAKE.

19

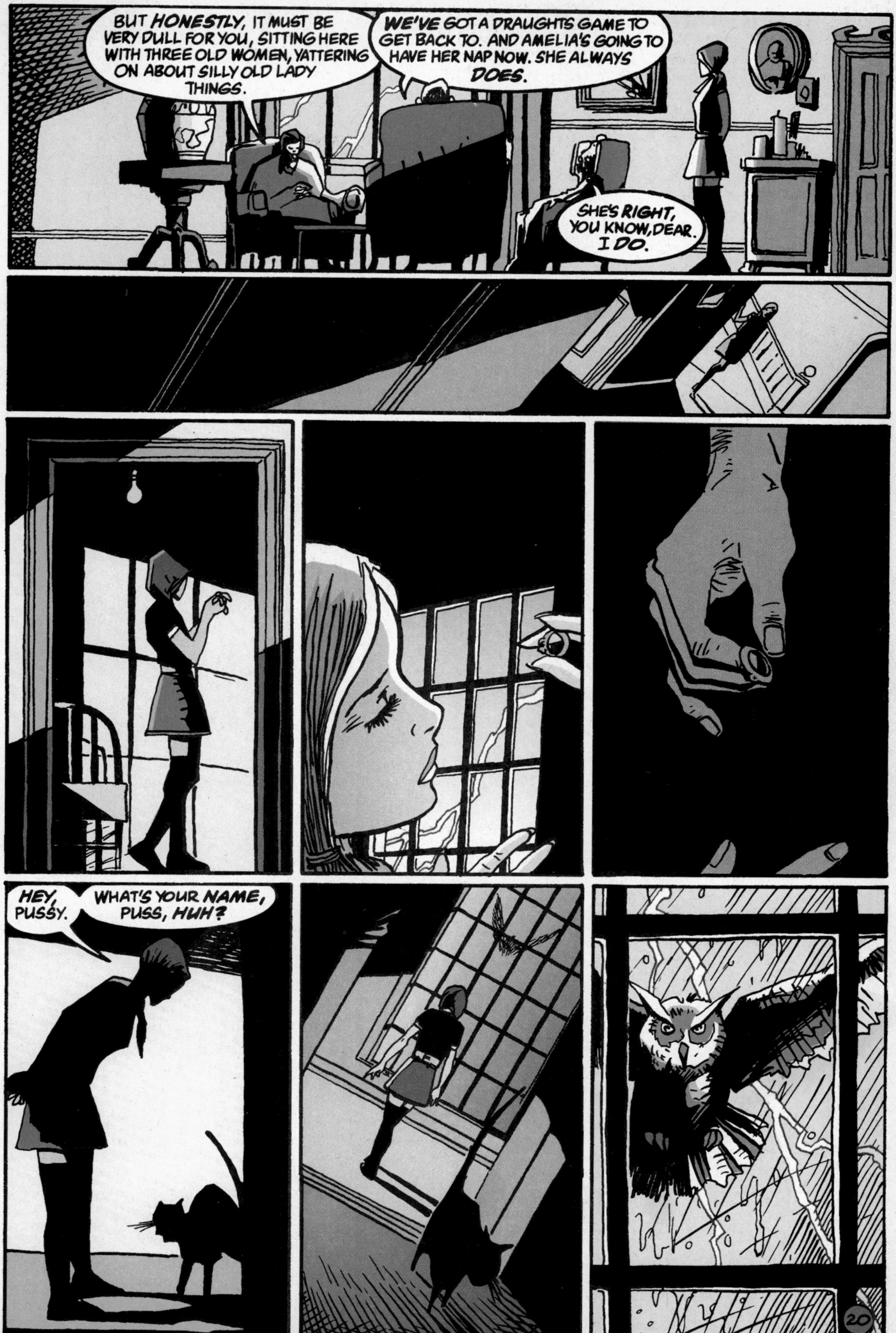
BUT HONESTLY, IT MUST BE VERY DULL FOR YOU, SITTING HERE WITH THREE OLD WOMEN, YATTERING ON ABOUT SILLY OLD LADY THINGS.
WE'VE GOT A DRAUGHTS GAME TO GET BACK TO. AND AMELIA'S GOING TO HAVE HER NAP NOW. SHE ALWAYS DOES.
SHE'S RIGHT, YOU KNOW, DEAR. I DO.
HEY, PUSSY.
WHAT'S YOUR NAME, PUSS, HUH?

WOW. DID YOU SEE *THAT*?

THE BIRD? YES. VERY IMPRESSIVE.

IT WAS AN *OWL*. YOU DON'T NORMALLY SEE THEM OUT IN THE DAYTIME.

MUST BE THE *STORM*. CONFUSED IT. SILLY BIRD.

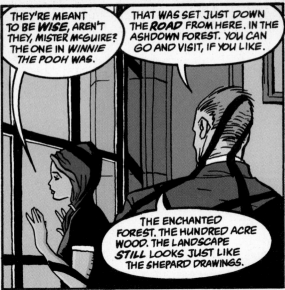

THEY'RE MEANT TO BE *WISE*, AREN'T THEY, MISTER MCGUIRE? THE ONE IN *WINNIE THE POOH* WAS.

THAT WAS SET JUST DOWN THE *ROAD* FROM HERE. IN THE ASHDOWN FOREST. YOU CAN GO AND VISIT, IF YOU LIKE.

THE ENCHANTED FOREST. THE HUNDRED ACRE WOOD. THE LANDSCAPE *STILL* LOOKS JUST LIKE THE SHEPARD DRAWINGS.

I ALWAYS THOUGHT THAT THE WHOLE THING WAS MADE *UP*.

OH NO.

THE *ORIGINAL* PIGLET TOY WAS LOST IN THE ASHDOWN FOREST BY CHRISTOPHER ROBIN MILNE. MY MOTHER USED TO TAKE ME FOR WALKS IN THE FOREST AS A BOY, AND WE'D LOOK FOR PIGLET.

I WISH *I'D* DONE SOMETHING LIKE THAT. AS A KID. ALL THE DREAMS YOU HAVE. 'LOOKING FOR PIGLET...'

IT DOESN'T *MATTER* THAT YOU NEVER FIND IT. IT'S THE *DREAMS* THAT KEEP YOU GOING.

I SUPPOSE THE POINT YOU GROW UP IS THE POINT YOU LET THE DREAMS *GO*.

PERHAPS.

DID YOU FIND WHAT YOU WERE LOOKING FOR HERE?

NO. NOT REALLY.

COME DOWN HERE.

THERE'S SOMETHING I WANT TO *SHOW* YOU.

YOU'RE NOT *SOME* KIND OF PERVERT, ARE YOU?

21

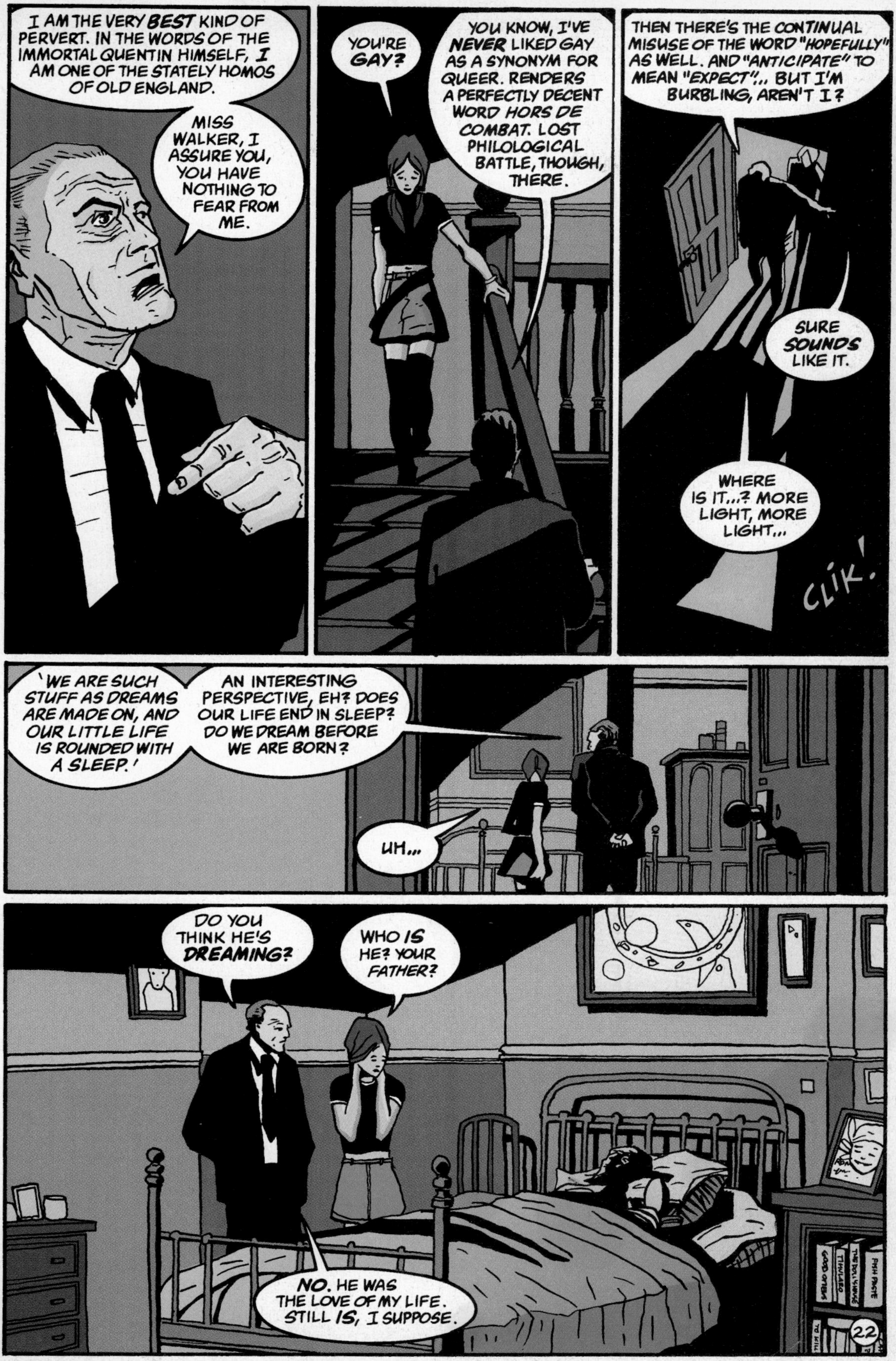
I AM THE VERY BEST KIND OF PERVERT. IN THE WORDS OF THE IMMORTAL QUENTIN HIMSELF, I AM ONE OF THE STATELY HOMOS OF OLD ENGLAND.
MISS WALKER, I ASSURE YOU, YOU HAVE NOTHING TO FEAR FROM ME.
YOU'RE GAY?
YOU KNOW, I'VE NEVER LIKED GAY AS A SYNONYM FOR QUEER. RENDERS A PERFECTLY DECENT WORD HORS DE COMBAT. LOST PHILOLOGICAL BATTLE, THOUGH, THERE.
THEN THERE'S THE CONTINUAL MISUSE OF THE WORD "HOPEFULLY" AS WELL. AND "ANTICIPATE" TO MEAN "EXPECT"... BUT I'M BURBLING, AREN'T I?
SURE SOUNDS LIKE IT.
WHERE IS IT...? MORE LIGHT, MORE LIGHT...
CLIK!
'WE ARE SUCH STUFF AS DREAMS ARE MADE ON, AND OUR LITTLE LIFE IS ROUNDED WITH A SLEEP.'
AN INTERESTING PERSPECTIVE, EH? DOES OUR LIFE END IN SLEEP? DO WE DREAM BEFORE WE ARE BORN?
UH...
DO YOU THINK HE'S DREAMING?
WHO IS HE? YOUR FATHER?
NO. HE WAS THE LOVE OF MY LIFE. STILL IS, I SUPPOSE.
22

HE WAS A MAGICIAN WITH *NO* TALENT FOR MAGIC. THEY SAY HIS *FATHER* COULD SUMMON THE FOUR WINDS TO ATTEND HIM. BLACK-MAILED PRINCES *AND* PRIME MINISTERS.

ALEX *TOLD* ME THAT THAT OLD FRAUD CROWLEY HIMSELF CON-CEDED THAT ALEX'S FATHER WAS BY FAR THE GREATER OF THE TWO. DOESN'T SOUND LIKELY...

ALEX WAS NO MAGICIAN. BUT HIS FATHER LEFT HIM AN OBLIGATION, YOU SEE, ROSE.

HE WOULD HAVE MADE A FINE STOCKBROKER, OR HEADMASTER. A REVIEWER PERHAPS, FOR ONE OF THE QUALITY PAPERS. HIS CRITICAL WRITINGS WERE NOT WITHOUT INTEREST.

HE'S BEEN ASLEEP FOR OVER FIVE YEARS. I JUST HOPE HIS DREAMS ARE *PLEASANT* ONES.

DO YOU THINK THEY ARE?

NO. NOT REALLY.

BRR. WHEN IT STARTS TO COME DOWN LIKE THIS, YOU THINK IT COULD RAIN FOREVER.

WASH THE WHOLE WORLD AWAY.

YOUR... UH, YOUR GRANDMOTHER WOKE ON SEPTEMBER THE 14th, 1988.

SOMETHING LIKE THAT. HOW DO YOU KNOW?

THAT WAS WHEN ALEX FELL ASLEEP. IRONY, EH?

RODDY YOUR SLAVE IN LOVE Ethel

I SUPPOSE.

I COME IN HERE EVERY *DAY* FOR AN HOUR OR TWO. SOMETIMES LONGER.

I JUST SIT HERE. HOPING HE'LL WAKE UP.

THAT'S GOOD IF MY GRANDMOTHER WOKE UP, I'M *SURE* YOUR ALEX WILL TOO.

NEVER LET GO OF YOUR DREAMS, EH?

EXACTLY.

23

MISS WALKER? SORRY TO INTRUDE. MISTER HOLDAWAY'S DOWNSTAIRS. HE SAYS WHENEVER YOU'RE READY.

CAN YOU TELL HIM I'LL BE RIGHT DOWN?

OF COURSE, DEAR.

WELL, VERY NICE TO MEET YOU, MISS WALKER.

YES. YOU TOO.

I DON'T KNOW HOW LONG YOU'LL BE HERE, BUT FEEL FREE TO COME DOWN TO THE GATEHOUSE AND SAY HELLO. ANY TIME AFTER FIVE.

IF YOU'RE INTO EERIE, EMPTY OLD MANOR HOUSES, WE CAN WALK UP TO THE HOUSE, AND I'LL SHOW YOU AROUND. TOO MUCH FOR ME TO KEEP UP. WE'RE NONE OF US AS YOUNG AS WE WERE.

I AM.

SORRY?

SURE. SOUNDS LIKE FUN!

HERE YOU GO, ALEX. FOR LUCK. IT WAS MY GRAND-MOTHER'S.

THE SINS OF THE FATHERS, EH, OLD FELLOW?

THE SINS OF THE FATHERS...

part SEVEN

tse   s   tse

I NEVER THOUGHT I WOULD EVER GET TO THIS PLACE.

DESTINATIONS ARE OFTEN A SURPRISE TO THE DESTINED.

YOU *SURE* THIS IS THE PLACE YOU ARE GOING? A NICE LADY LIKE YOU?

YES, THANK YOU. PLEASE WAIT HERE UNTIL I RETURN. I'LL PAY YOU FOR THE WAITING TIME.

NOT A PLACE *I* PLAN TO HANG AROUND, I AM AFRAID.

NOT A GOOD PLACE. ON A BETTER NIGHT I WOULD NOT HAVE *COME* HERE. DO YOU *KNOW* HOW MANY TAXI-DRIVERS BEEN *KILLED* IN *LA* THIS YEAR?

SEE *THIS?* IT'S A HUNDRED DOLLAR BILL. I'M GIVING YOU HALF OF IT. *IF* YOU'RE STILL HERE WHEN I GET BACK, I SHALL GIVE YOU THE OTHER HALF.

OKAY, LADY. I SHALL BE HERE, UNLESS THERE BE *GUNS.* IF THERE BE GUNS, I WILL BE GONE.

EXCUSE ME... I'M LOOKING FOR A *WOMAN*.

YOU SEE, BY THE MOTEL DOOR OVER THERE? THAT'S ANNIE. SHE'S CHEAP AND PRETTY CLEAN, AND SHE'S GOT A BAD HABIT TO FEED, SO SHE'S NOT EVEN THAT PARTICULAR.

I'M LOOKING FOR A PARTICULAR WOMAN. SHE'S GOT BLONDE HAIR. QUITE THIN, I BELIEVE SHE'S VERY *STRONG*.

HER? *JEEZ.* SHE'S ASLEEP OVER BY THE WALL.

JERRY TRIED TO COP A FEEL. SHE NEARLY BROKE HIS JAW. *BAM*-- JUST KNOCKED HIM DOWN, WENT BACK TO SLEEP.

HEY. BITCH WUZ ASLEEP. WHUZZA FUGGEN *PROBLEM*, HUH? *I* DIN' HURT HER. BITCH NEAR *KILLED* ME.

WHERE IS SHE NOW?

STILL THERE. BY TH' WALL. AIN'T NOBODY GON' BOTHER HER. SOME DAYS A MAN CAN'T WIN FOR LOSIN'.

2

HIPPOLYTA? HELLO? CAN YOU *HEAR* ME? I'M CALLED LARISSA.

YOU HAVE TO COME WITH ME, NOW.

3

OH YES... WHITE BIRD... LITTLE WHITE BIRD...

LITTLE BIRD. I SHALL FOLLOW YOU.

TAKE ME TO THE LADIES, TO THE KIND AND GENTLE LADIES.

WHAT DID SHE JUST SAY?

I DON'T KNOW. SHE'S A BIT MIXED-UP RIGHT NOW. JUST HELP ME GET HER IN THE CAR.

HERE'S THE REST OF YOUR HUNDRED.

GREAT. THE WAY YOUR FRIEND STINKS, IT WILL COST ME THAT TO CLEAN MY TAXI.

NONSENSE. NOW, THE CORNER OF SWEETZER AND MELROSE.

YOU GOT ANY IDEAS WHAT THAT WUZ ALL ABOUT?

UH-HUH. I THINK THE ONE WHO BROKE JERRY'S FACE, SHE WAS LIKE, A ROBOT SPACE ALIEN.

AN' THE OTHER ONE, SHE WAS MEBBE FBI OR SOMEP'N.

AN' THAT TAXI WASN'T NO TAXI. IT WAS A CAMOUFLAGED GUV'MINT SPACE-SHIP.

YOU BELIEVE ANY A' THAT SHIT COMIN' OUTTA YOUR MOUTH?

HELL, NO.

4

TELL YOUR MASTER, THE DREAM-WEAVER, THAT THERE IS ONE HERE TO TALK WITH HIM.

TELL HIM TO COME OUT OF HIS HALL, AND TALK TO ME.

AND WHO ARE YOU, THEN, TO DEMAND ENTRY?

I DO *NOT* DEMAND ENTRY. I DO NOT *ENTER* THE HOUSES OF MY ENEMIES. I DEMAND ONLY THAT YOUR MASTER COME OUT AND TALK.

AS FOR WHO I AM?

I AM CALLED GRIM, THE DEATH-BLINDER, THE HIGH ONE, THE GALLOWS-GOD.

I AM CALLED GONDLIR THE WAND-BEARER, AND I AM GRIMNIR THE HOODED ONE, THE TERRIBLE, THE WAKEFUL. YOU KNOW ME: I AM ODIN, BOR'S SON.

AND YOUR MASTER HAS DONE ME A GREAT WRONG.

5

≷KOFF≷
≷HRRACK≷   ≷KOFF≷

≷HHROUGHH!≷

Greetings,
Lord Odin.

You are
Welcome
here.

AYE, **GREETINGS**, DREAM-WEAVER, HEARTH'S-BETRAYER. I COUNTED YOU AS FRIEND ONCE, BUT CAN COUNT YOU SO NO MORE.

I SHALL STATE MY GRIEVANCE. **LISTEN**: THE AESIR BOUND MY BLOOD-BROTHER LOKI, LONG AGO. BOUND HIM WITH THE ENTRAILS OF HIS SON, BOUND HIM FAR BENEATH THE EARTH.

"WISE SKADI SET A SNAKE ABOVE HIS HEAD TO DRIP ITS BURNING POISON INTO LOKI'S FACE, THAT HE COULD NEITHER THINK NOR TALK HIS WAY OUT OF HIS PRISON.

"HE WAS TOO CLEVER, TOO WILY, TOO MALEVOLENT TO BE FREE."

6

STILL, AS YOU KNOW, I FREED HIM, SOME YEARS AGO, FOR BUT A SHORT TIME...

I HAD *THOUGHT* THAT I HAD RETURNED LOKI TO HIS PLACE BENEATH THE WORLD; BUT I WAS *WRONG*. IT IS MERELY A DREAM-THING THAT SCREAMS AND CURSES; A WISP, A FIGMENT, THAT WRITHES IN PAIN.

LOKI IS FREE IN THE WORLD ONCE MORE. HE MUST HAVE BEEN FREE FOR SOME *YEARS* NOW.

AHHH...

THIS IS *YOUR* DOING, WEAVER, IS IT NOT?

Yes. I am afraid that it is.

He had already escaped you, and had bound another beneath the earth, when I discovered him. I freed that other, and placed a dream there in its place.

WHAT DID YOU *WANT*, EH? A FAVOR FROM LOKI? TO PLACE HIM IN YOUR DEBT? TO USE HIM AS YOUR AGENT, IN SOME HUMAN DEAL OR OTHER?

Something like that.

YOU'RE A *FOOL*, WEAVER. LOKI HAS NO SENSE OF GRATITUDE. IT BURNS AND GALLS AND ACHES HIM TO BE BEHOLDEN.

HE IS A SERPENT, WHO MUST BITE YOUR HAND EVEN AS YOU SAVE HIM FROM A HUNTER.

LOKI CANNOT HELP STRIKING THE HAND THAT AIDS HIM, STRIKING WITH MALICE AND SLOW POISON. THAT IS WHAT HE *IS*. THAT IS WHAT HE *DOES*.

I HAVE HEARD STRANGE RUMORS ABOUT YOU, DREAM-WEAVER. HUGINN AND MUNINN TELL ME WHAT THEY SEE AND HEAR, AS THEY TRAVEL THE MIDDLE WORLD.

THEY ALSO SAY THE RAVEN HOST WILL BE COMING TO THE DREAMING, SOON ENOUGH. RAVENS *KNOW* THESE THINGS, IT SEEMS.

7

I hear rumors too, Odin One-eye. But only a fool listens to rumors.

ONLY A FOOL *IGNORES* THEM.

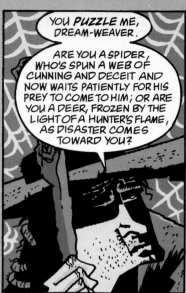

YOU *PUZZLE* ME, DREAM-WEAVER.

ARE YOU A SPIDER, WHO'S SPUN A WEB OF CUNNING AND DECEIT AND NOW WAITS PATIENTLY FOR HIS PREY TO COME TO HIM; OR ARE YOU A DEER, FROZEN BY THE LIGHT OF A HUNTER'S FLAME, AS DISASTER COMES TOWARD YOU?

You have known me for some time, old god. Which would you say I am?

YOU'RE A *DEEP* ONE. BUT *HOW* DEEP? WHAT'S *ILLUSION?* *THAT'S* THE QUESTION... AND THIS IS A BAD PLACE TO TALK OF ILLUSION...

AHH. KOFF... ≳KHAKOFF!≲

IN TRUTH, THERE'S NO *REAL* ENMITY BETWEEN US. WERE I TO DECLARE A BLOOD-FEUD WITH EVERY BEING EVER FOOLED BY LOKI, I COULD BEGIN BY KILLING MYSELF...

...AND CONTINUE THE SLAUGHTER UNTIL THERE WERE NEITHER GOD NOR DWARF NOR GIANT LEFT.

IT IS, AFTER ALL, WHAT HE *DOES.*

BUT I *AM* DISAPPOINTED. SOMEHOW, I EXPECTED *MORE* FROM YOU, DREAM-WEAVER.

And, for my part, I am sorry to have disappointed you, Odin Battle-king.

⑧

SO. UM. WELL, THERE WAS THIS DOGGY. HE WAS A VERY CLEVER DOGGY. HE SAID THINGS LIKE... LIKE...

"I WOULD FEEL INFINITELY MORE COMFORTABLE IN YOUR PRESENCE IF YOU WOULD AGREE TO TREAT GRAVITY AS A LAW, RATHER THAN ONE OF A NUMBER OF SUGGESTED OPTIONS."

HE SAID THAT. I ONLY REMEMBERED IT. IN MY HEAD.

AND I PROMISED OUR BROTHER I'D LOOK AFTER HIM. NOT TO MENTION THE OTHER WAY AROUND.

ONLY. THEN WHEN IT OCCURRED TO ME THAT I WAS BEING ALL FISHIES, AND I DIDN'T KNOW WHERE TO START, AND I LOOKED ALL UP AND DOWN AND THROUGH AND ROUND MY REALM AND EVEN IN THE PIGPOND, BUT HE WASN'T ANYWHERE.

SO I THOUGHT, I SHOULD HAVE ANOTHER QUEST TO FIND HIM. LAST TIME I HAD A QUEST TO FIND SOMEONE I DID REALLY WELL. AND YOU TOLD US WHERE TO GO, IN THE END. AND YOU WERE RIGHT, TOO.

...I THOUGHT... I SHOULD ASK YOU FIRST.

THAT'S RIGHT, ISN'T IT?

I MEAN, IT IS... I THINK. EXCEPT FOR THE BIT ABOUT THE PIGPOND. I MADE THAT UP.

UM. THE LAST TIME I SAW YOU I GOT KIND OF MAD AT YOU, BUT I FIGURED THAT IF I DIDN'T MENTION IT YOU'D PROBABLY HAVE FORGOTTEN ALL ABOUT IT BY NOW, LIKE I HAVE, SO THAT'S OKAY.

9

I BEAR NO GRUDGES. I SEE THINGS AS THEY ARE: HOW THEN CAN I BEAR A GRUDGE?

BUT... MY SISTER. YOU MUST UNDERSTAND: EVENTS DO NOT OCCUR APART AND SINGLY. AND ANYTHING WORTH THE HUNTING HAS A COST.

IF I DON'T FIND THE DOGGY HE'LL BE SAAAD. HE'S PROBABLY GOING "I SHOULDN'T HAVE TAKEN MY EYES OFF HER AT THE 'IT'S A SMALL WORLD AFTER ALL' PLACE BOAT RIDE" EVEN RIGHT NOW.

AND I MUST HUG HIM TIGHTLY AS ANYTHING, AND I MUST SAY SORRY, AND TELL HIM I WON'T EVER LEAVE HIM EVER EVER AGAIN.

MY SISTER. YOU HAVE COME TO ME FOR ADVICE. AND I CAN GIVE YOU ADVICE: IF YOU LOOK FOR YOUR DOG, YOU SHALL FIND IT. BUT IF YOU FIND YOUR DOG, YOU SHALL FIND OTHER THINGS, ALSO. THE CHOICE IS YOURS.

DO YOU UNDERSTAND ME?

LOOK AT DREAM.

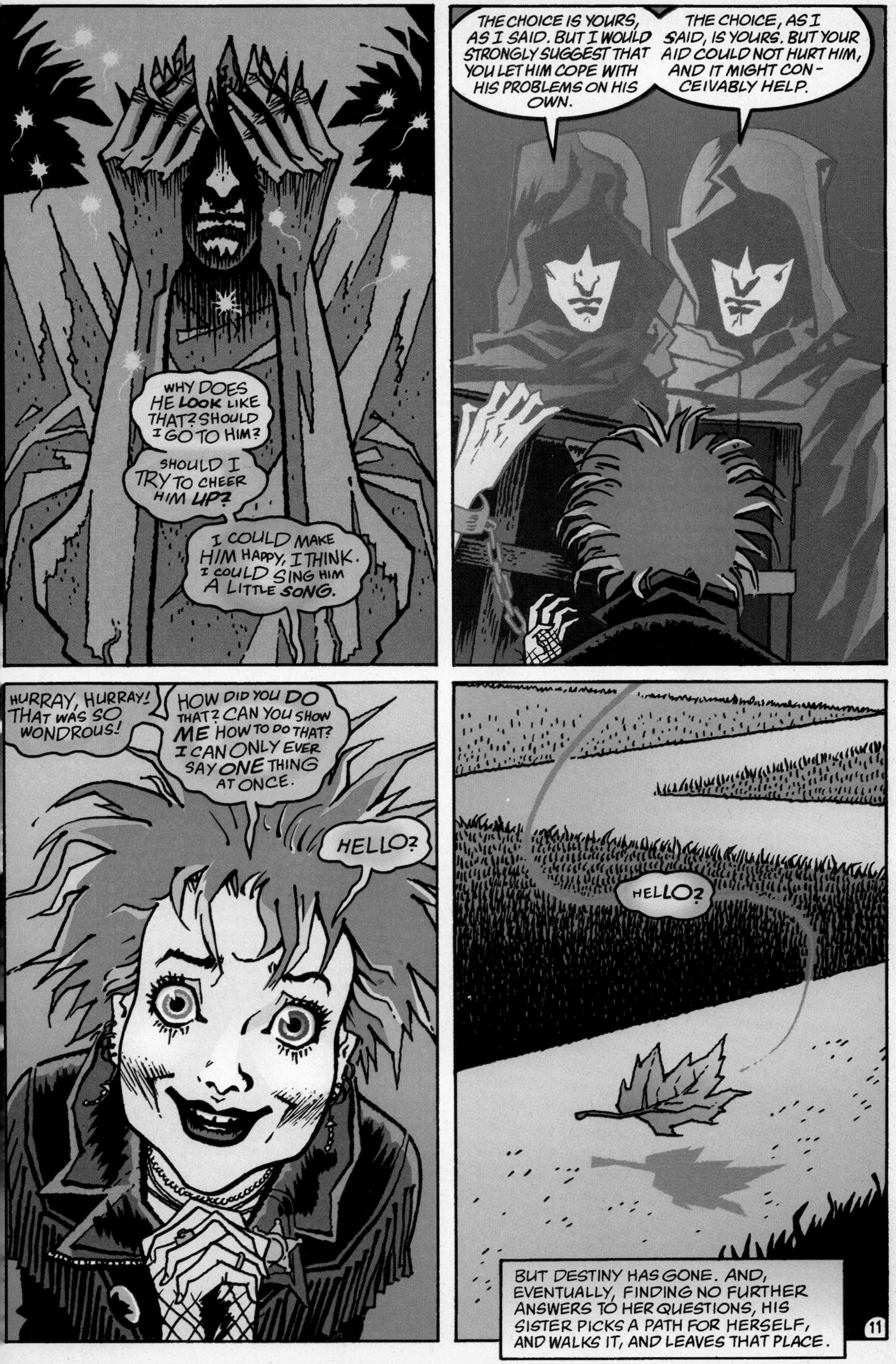
WHY DOES HE LOOK LIKE THAT? SHOULD I GO TO HIM?
SHOULD I TRY TO CHEER HIM UP?
I COULD MAKE HIM HAPPY, I THINK. I COULD SING HIM A LITTLE SONG.
THE CHOICE IS YOURS, AS I SAID. BUT I WOULD STRONGLY SUGGEST THAT YOU LET HIM COPE WITH HIS PROBLEMS ON HIS OWN.
THE CHOICE, AS I SAID, IS YOURS. BUT YOUR AID COULD NOT HURT HIM, AND IT MIGHT CON-CEIVABLY HELP.
HURRAY, HURRAY! THAT WAS SO WONDROUS!
HOW DID YOU DO THAT? CAN YOU SHOW ME HOW TO DO THAT? I CAN ONLY EVER SAY ONE THING AT ONCE.
HELLO?
HELLO?
BUT DESTINY HAS GONE. AND, EVENTUALLY, FINDING NO FURTHER ANSWERS TO HER QUESTIONS, HIS SISTER PICKS A PATH FOR HERSELF, AND WALKS IT, AND LEAVES THAT PLACE.
11

THERE WE GO, HIPPOLYTA. IN HERE...

YOU'D BETTER *STAY* ON THE BED.

I'LL JUST HAVE TO MAKE UP A BED FOR MYSELF IN THE BATHTUB. TCH.

WELL, I'VE *FOUND* YOU. THEY CAME THROUGH ON *THAT* MUCH.

I WONDER WHERE YOU ARE...

I CAN *FEEL* YOU, FAR AWAY.

CAN *YOU* FEEL *ME?*

WELL, IT DOESN'T MATTER IF YOU CAN OR NOT, REALLY, *DOES* IT?

NOW. YOU NEED PROTECTION.

12

DILL FRONDS AND LAUREL LEAVES AND ROSE PETALS, CRUSHED IN A HONEY BASE. IT'S A BIT STICKY, AND IT'S VERY SIMPLE, BUT IT *WILL* TAKE CARE OF YOU, TO START OFF WITH.

LET'S SMEAR IT ON. THEEERE WE GO.

WELL, *THAT* WILL HOLD YOU AGAINST *MOST* OF THE THINGS YOU'RE LIKELY TO RUN INTO.

NOW WE JUST HAVE TO LOOK AFTER YOU *HERE*, IN CASE ANY-ONE COMES CALLING...

COME ON... *OUT* WE GO...

DO YOU *KNOW* HOW HARD IT IS TO FIND A BLACK LAMB IN WEST HOLLYWOOD? I HAD TO ORDER *THIS* ONE FROM AN EXOTIC PET SHOP.

SHE'S GOING TO BE YOUR GUARDIAN.

WAK!

OW.

BLOOD FOR BLOOD, EH, LITTLE LAMB?

IT'S BEEN *TOO* LONG SINCE I'VE NEEDED TO SACRIFICE ANYTHING LARGER THAN A RABBIT. TCH... THERE, LET THAT BE A LESSON FOR ME, LYTA, AND FOR YOU TOO, IF YOU CAN HEAR ME: NOTHING IS HARMLESS.

NOTHING IS TOO CUTE AND SWEET TO BE DANGEROUS.

NOTHING IS SAFE.

CHK

IF THERE ARE HUNGRY SHADES ABOUT ME, LET THEM WAIT AND STARE UNFED.

IF LONELY AGING GODS THERE BE HERE, LET THEM LOOK ELSEWHERE FOR FOOD.

AEMINAEROTHERRETHORABEANIMEA, PTOUMOU LALAPSA, PHORBEA NEREATO BRIMO...

I CONSECRATE THIS CIRCLE TO HER WHO WAITS BENEATH THE EARTH, AND TO HER WHO MAKES LIFE ON THE EARTH, AND TO HER WHO SHINES COLDLY ABOVE THE EARTH.

I DEMAND THEIR PROTECTION FOR THE WOMAN WITHIN.

THERE.

THERE. I'VE DONE ALL I CAN, FOR NOW. TRIVIA OF THE CROSSWAYS ATTEND THEE ON THY TRAVELS, GIRL.

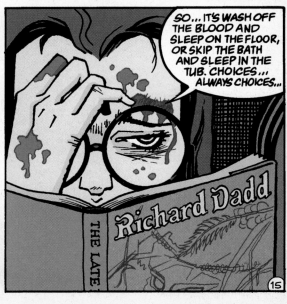

SO... IT'S WASH OFF THE BLOOD AND SLEEP ON THE FLOOR, OR SKIP THE BATH AND SLEEP IN THE TUB. CHOICES... ALWAYS CHOICES...

15

HER TOES SEARCH FOR CREVICES AND HOLLOWS. HER FINGERS BRAZENLY FORCE THEIR WAY INTO THE TINIEST FINGERHOLDS.

DESCENDING IS ALWAYS HARDER THAN ASCENDING, AND THIS DESCENT IS THE HARDEST LYTA HAS MADE.

TERROR EXISTS; THE KNOWLEDGE OF HOW EASY IT WOULD BE TO TUMBLE OFF AND AWAY INTO THE DARKNESS.

ALL JOURNEYS LEAVE MARKS ON US.

HER CLOTHES TEAR. HER SKIN IS GRAZED. MUSCLES ACHE AND BURN.

THE FALL, SHE KNOWS WITH A DARK CERTAINTY, WILL KILL HER.

SO SHE INCHES DOWNWARD, A MOMENT AT A TIME, BRUISED AND SKINNED AND SCARED.

I'M **SO** TIRED.

THEN STOP.

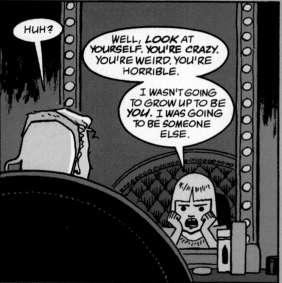

HUH?

WELL, **LOOK** AT YOURSELF. YOU'RE CRAZY. YOU'RE WEIRD. YOU'RE HORRIBLE.

I WASN'T GOING TO GROW UP TO BE **YOU**. I WAS GOING TO BE SOMEONE ELSE.

MAYBE WHEN **I** GROW UP I'LL BE A PRINCESS, OR A DANCER, OR A MOVIE STAR.

NOT A CRAZY WOMAN.

I'M NOT CRAZY.

OF **COURSE** I'M NOT CRAZY. I'M ONE OF THE **GOOD** GUYS.

I AM THE FURY. MY FEET ARE FIRMLY PLANTED ON THE GROUND. THIS IS PROBABLY JUST SOME SUPER-VILLAIN'S MIND-CONTROL-RAY EXPERIMENT...

RESIST, LYTA! **RESIST!**

"YOU DON'T **HAVE** TO GO THROUGH WITH THIS. YOU CAN OPEN YOUR EYES, CLIMB OFF THIS BED, WALK OUT THE DOOR, PUT YOUR LIFE BACK TOGETHER AGAIN.

"THERE'S ALWAYS THE CHOICE."

NOT ALWAYS.

17

SOMETIMES THERE JUST AREN'T ANY CHOICES AT ALL....

HELLO?

AT LAST, MY SISTER.

THERE, MY POSSET. WE'VE BEEN EXPECTING YOU.

HMMPH. IT TOOK HER LONG ENOUGH TO GET HERE.

WE *SAID* WE'D SEE YOU AGAIN....

18

AH. IT'S YOU. I THOUGHT I'D SEE YOU HERE, EVENTUALLY.

Mm. HOW PERCEPTIVE OF YOU.

NOW, THAT'S UNWORTHY OF YOU.

Perhaps it is.

YOU KNOW... YOU ARE THE SECOND PERSON TODAY TO EXPRESS THEIR DISAPPOINTMENT WITH ME.

DO YOU MEAN THAT, GILBERT?

AM I REALLY THAT DISAPPOINTING?

THERE, WELL AND YOU'RE HERE NOW. YOU'VE COME A LONG WAY.

COME IN. SIT DOWN. MAKE YOURSELF NICE AND COMFORTABLE.

WE'LL MAKE YOU A HOT CUP OF TEA. ARE YOU HUNGRY?

I ...YES. A LITTLE.

A FORTUNE COOKIE.

READ IT FIRST. THEN EAT THE COOKIE.

"LET ALL THAT DO ILL TAKE THIS PRECEDENT: 'MAN MAY HIS FATE FORE-SEE, BUT NOT PREVENT.' AND OF ALL AXIOMS THIS SHALL WIN THE PRIZE, 'TIS BETTER TO BE FORTUNATE THAN WISE'."

NOW, ISN'T THAT HELPFUL?

19

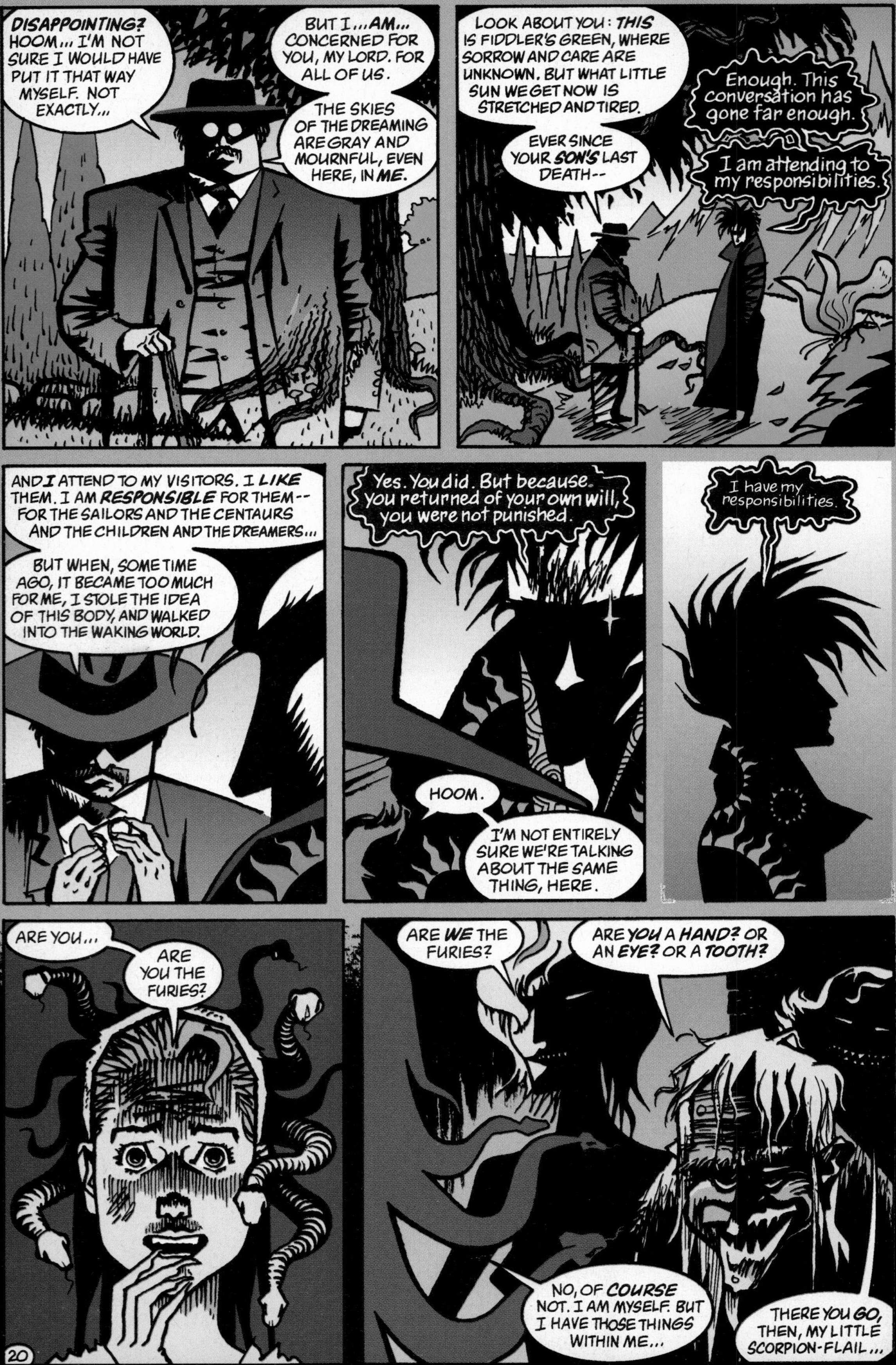
DISAPPOINTING? HOOM... I'M NOT SURE I WOULD HAVE PUT IT THAT WAY MYSELF. NOT EXACTLY...
BUT I...AM... CONCERNED FOR YOU, MY LORD. FOR ALL OF US.
THE SKIES OF THE DREAMING ARE GRAY AND MOURNFUL, EVEN HERE, IN ME.
LOOK ABOUT YOU: THIS IS FIDDLER'S GREEN, WHERE SORROW AND CARE ARE UNKNOWN. BUT WHAT LITTLE SUN WE GET NOW IS STRETCHED AND TIRED.
EVER SINCE YOUR SON'S LAST DEATH--
Enough. This conversation has gone far enough.
I am attending to my responsibilities.
AND I ATTEND TO MY VISITORS. I LIKE THEM. I AM RESPONSIBLE FOR THEM-- FOR THE SAILORS AND THE CENTAURS AND THE CHILDREN AND THE DREAMERS...
BUT WHEN, SOME TIME AGO, IT BECAME TOO MUCH FOR ME, I STOLE THE IDEA OF THIS BODY, AND WALKED INTO THE WAKING WORLD.
Yes. You did. But because you returned of your own will, you were not punished.
HOOM.
I'M NOT ENTIRELY SURE WE'RE TALKING ABOUT THE SAME THING, HERE.
I have my responsibilities.
ARE YOU...
ARE YOU THE FURIES?
ARE WE THE FURIES?
ARE YOU A HAND? OR AN EYE? OR A TOOTH?
NO, OF COURSE NOT. I AM MYSELF. BUT I HAVE THOSE THINGS WITHIN ME...
THERE YOU GO, THEN, MY LITTLE SCORPION-FLAIL...
20

There is a heath upon which cold winds blow.

There is a house upon that heath, built of dead rock and dry bone, in which one woman lives, or three, or none.

She is sustained, or they are, by the stream of blood that runs beside the house. Once it was a river, but that was many years ago.

The smell of cordite drifts on the air here; fragments of shrapnel and bone glint in the red earth.

There will always be sacrifices to the Morrigan, the lady of war...

A raven walks slowly about her house, its frock-coated gait that of an elderly gentleman, leaning forward as it struts.

A black hound waits by the door.

In the garden by the stream a little girl plays with something yellowed and round that might, conceivably, be a ball.

Ravens are solitary birds: they do not flock; they travel apart.

The bird looks up.

It pushes itself up into the harsh gray sky with beats of its huge wings; and it rides the cold wind, far away from the house on the heath.

I HAVE COME A VERY LONG WAY. FURTHER THAN I'VE EVER GONE BEFORE.

I AM SEEKING THE FURIES.

NOT THE FURIES, MY LOBELIA. THAT'S SUCH A NASTY NAME. IT'S ONE OF THE THINGS THEY CALL WOMEN, TO PUT US IN OUR PLACE...

TERMAGANT.

SHREW.

VIXEN.

VIRAGO.

WITCH.

BITCH.

DO WE LOOK FURIOUS TO YOU?

NO. YOU LOOK VERY KIND. VERY WISE. VERY GENTLE.

21

WELL, SO *THIS* IS WHERE THEY LIVE, EH?

YES. AARRKK...

WHAT DO WE DO IF ANYONE *FINDS* US HERE? MAYBE WE NEED SOME KIND OF *COVER STORY.*

YEAH? TELL 'EM WE'RE COPS.

SO WHAT AM I? *UNDERCOVER?* GIVE ME A *BREAK...*

YOU CAN JUST *CAW* AND FLY AWAY. OR NOT, AS YOU WILL. ANYWAY, WHO *CARES?* IF THEY'RE A *PROBLEM,* I CAN ALWAYS *KILL* THEM.

WILL YOU LAY OFF THAT KINDA TALK?

OKAY. OKAY. NO PROBLEM. IF YOU FEEL *THAT* STRONGLY, *YOU* CAN KILL THEM.

HMM... ODD... LOCKS'RE BUSTED...

DOESN'T SMELL LIKE THERE'S BEEN ANYONE AROUND FOR DAYS.

I CAN'T SMELL THE KID AT ALL...

HE'S DEFINITELY NOT HERE. WHAT DO WE DO *NOW?*

YOU'RE ASKING *ME?* FOR *ADVICE? COOOL.* YOU'RE *LEARNING,* BIRDIE.

LISTEN, *CREEP...*

UH.

BRRRRRR.

S'MATTER?

THIS WEIRD FEELING: LIKE SOMEONE JUST DANCED ON MY *GRAVE.*

I... I HAVE TO GO *HOME.*

UH *UH.* YOU'RE STAYING WITH ME UNTIL WE FIND THE BOY. THE *BOSS* SAID.

BUT--

YOU'RE MY *PARTNER,* LIKE IT OR NOT. WALK OUT ON ME *NOW,* BIRD, AND I *WRING* YOUR SCRAWNY NECK.

THERE, AND *THAT'S* A GOOD GIRL, WITH A PLEASANT TONGUE IN HER HEAD.

WE DO WHAT WE *HAVE* TO DO. THAT'S THE MOST ANYONE *CAN* DO.

WE DON'T *BOTHER* ANYONE. WE *HATE* TO BE A BOTHER, NOT UNLESS THERE'S A GOOD *REASON* TO BOTHER SOMEBODY.

THERE'S A... *MAN.*

I WANT TO DO *MORE* THAN BOTHER HIM. I WANT TO *DESTROY* HIM.

22

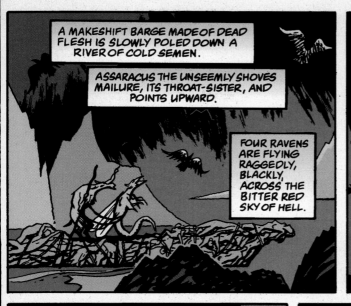

A MAKESHIFT BARGE MADE OF DEAD FLESH IS SLOWLY POLED DOWN A RIVER OF COLD SEMEN.

ASSARACUS THE UNSEEMLY SHOVES MAILURE, ITS THROAT-SISTER, AND POINTS UPWARD.

FOUR RAVENS ARE FLYING RAGGEDLY, BLACKLY, ACROSS THE BITTER RED SKY OF HELL.

MAILURE OPENS HER WINGS AND SPEEDS UPWARD, TRAILING FLESH, HER WET MOUTHS OPEN AS WIDE AS THEY CAN GO.

THE RAVENS BEAT THEIR BLACK WINGS HARD AGAINST THE SKY, AND FLY FASTER.

IN ENGLAND A WOMAN WHO LOOKS YOUNGER THAN HER TRUE AGE WRITES A LETTER, AND HALF LISTENS TO THE NEWS ON HER HOTEL ROOM TV.

THE THIRD ITEM OF NEWS IS THAT THE RAVENS HAVE LEFT THE TOWER OF LONDON. THE RAVENS' WINGS HAVING BEEN CLIPPED TO PREVENT THEIR FLYING AWAY, IT IS ASSUMED THEY HAVE BEEN STOLEN.

THE GOVERNMENT SPOKESMAN ANNOUNCES THAT THEY WILL NOT SUBMIT TO TERRORISTS, AND SAYS THEY HAVE ORDERED A DOZEN RAVEN CHICKS FROM ZOOS AROUND THE COUNTRY. THEY FEAR DAMAGE TO THE TOURIST TRADE.

THE REPORTER ASKS ABOUT THE KINGDOM FALLING, AND IS ASSURED THAT, IN THIS DAY AND AGE, ONE MUST TAKE SUCH SUPER-STITIONS WITH A GRAIN OR TWO OF SALT.

EVERYBODY LAUGHS.

WHY?

HE KILLED MY SON. HE *STOLE* AND *KILLED* MY SON. HE KILLED MY HUSBAND, TOO. ISN'T *THAT* REASON ENOUGH?

NO, DEARIE. IT'S NOT.

YOU SEE, MY GOSLING, THE LADIES YOU WERE TALKING ABOUT CAN REALLY ONLY AVENGE *BLOOD-DEBTS.*

THAT'S ONE OF THE *RULES.*

IT'S THE *OLDEST* RULE.

23

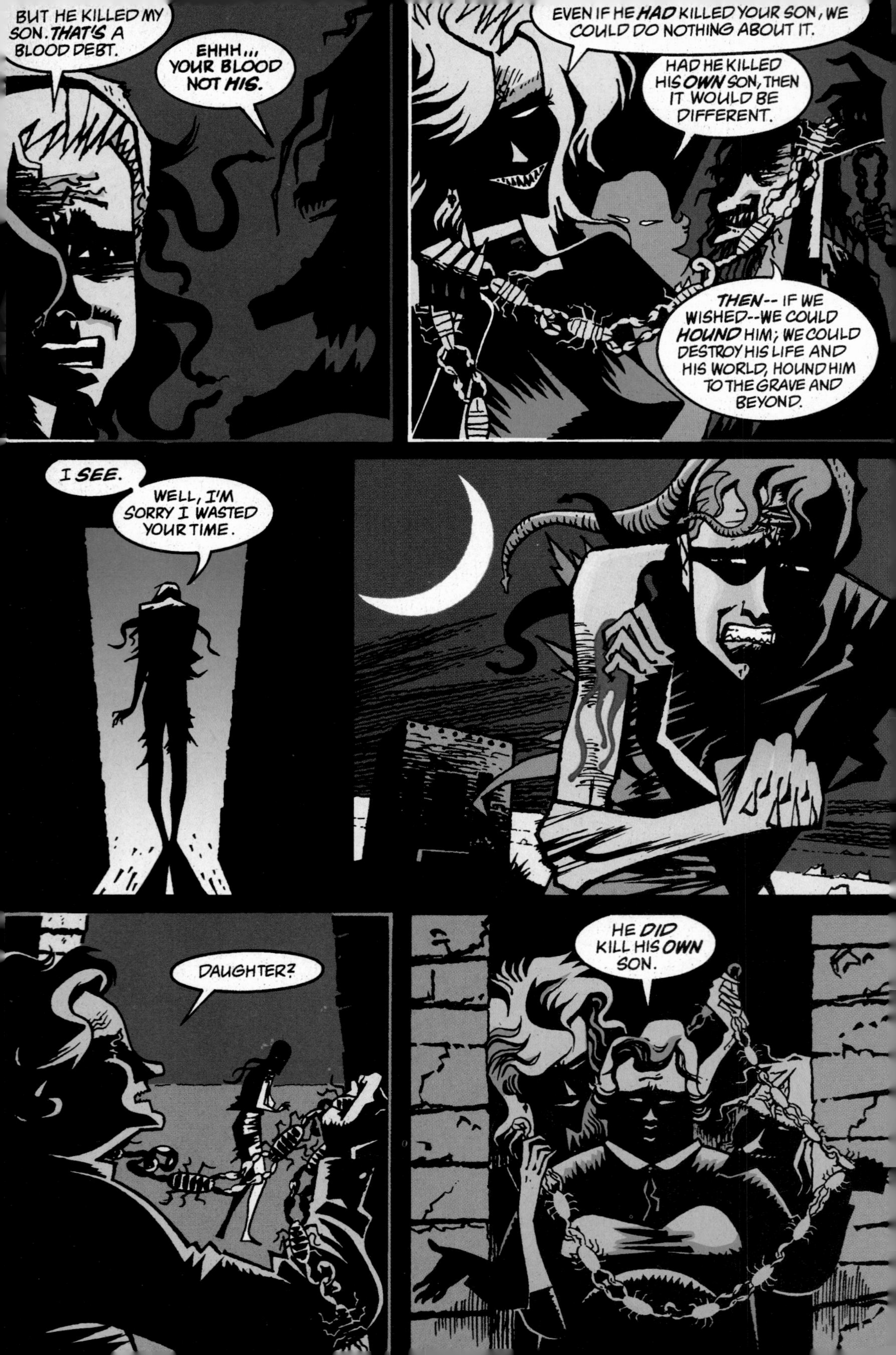
BUT HE KILLED MY SON. THAT'S A BLOOD DEBT.
EHHH... YOUR BLOOD NOT HIS.
EVEN IF HE HAD KILLED YOUR SON, WE COULD DO NOTHING ABOUT IT.
HAD HE KILLED HIS OWN SON, THEN IT WOULD BE DIFFERENT.
THEN-- IF WE WISHED--WE COULD HOUND HIM; WE COULD DESTROY HIS LIFE AND HIS WORLD, HOUND HIM TO THE GRAVE AND BEYOND.
I SEE.
WELL, I'M SORRY I WASTED YOUR TIME.
DAUGHTER?
HE DID KILL HIS OWN SON.

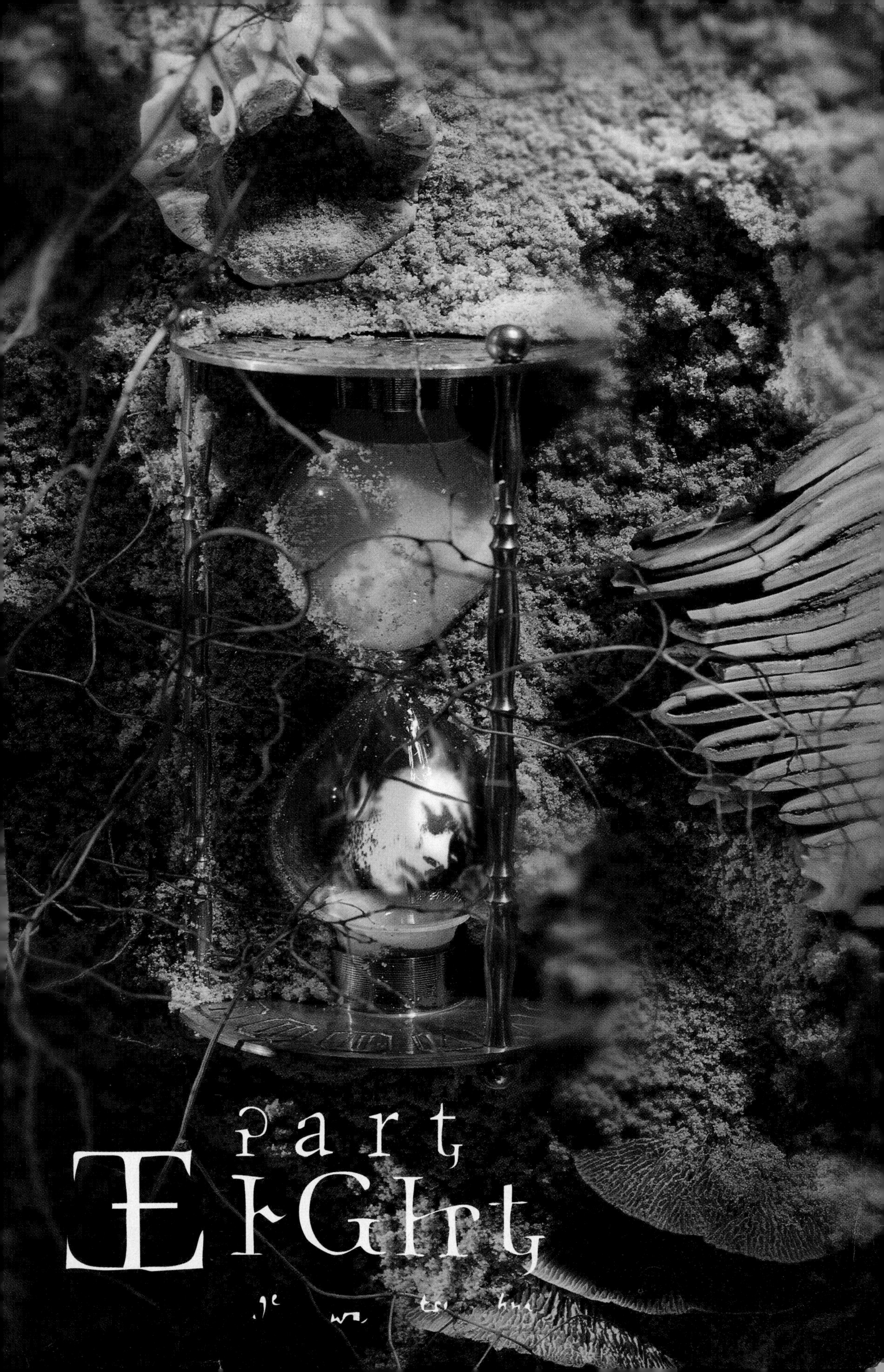
part
Eight

ON MOONDAY, THE KING OF DREAMS GAVE AN AUDIENCE TO FIVE SMALL CHILDREN, WHO HAD TRAVELLED A LONG WAY, SEEKING THEIR LOST MOTHER.

HE MET THEM IN A HALL FILLED WITH SCARECROWS, WHO WHISPERED AMONG THEMSELVES IN THE VOICES OF THE STARS OF THE SILENT SCREEN.

DANCING SALAMANDERS BROUGHT THE CHILDREN SILVER PLATES PILED WITH EXOTIC ICE-CREAMS OF VARIOUS FLAVORS, AND WITH FRUITS THEY HAD NEVER SEEN BEFORE AND WOULD NEVER SEE AGAIN...

ALTHOUGH THEY WOULD DREAM OF THEM, ON RARE OCCASIONS, UNTIL THEY DIED.

GRAVELY, THE LORD OF DREAMS LISTENED TO EACH CHILD PLEAD AND BEG; AND THEN, AT THE END, HE DREW A DOOR IN THE AIR WITH HIS FINGER, AND THE CHILDREN WALKED THROUGH IT, INTO THE REST OF THEIR STORY.

1

AND ON MOONDAY, HE ARBITRATED IN A DISPUTE BETWEEN THE KNIGHT OF CLOUDS AND THE BODY POLITIC.

HE AWARDED THE MAGIC LANTERN SHOW TO THE KNIGHT OF CLOUDS, ALTHOUGH HE PERMITTED THE BODY POLITIC TO RETAIN CUSTODY OF THE SIX SCREAMING STONES AND THE SNOWS OF YESTERDAY.

HE WALKED FROM HIS CASTLE TO THE DREAMS OF A SMALL BOY IN HONG KONG. HE REMAINED THERE FOR SOME MINUTES, OBSERVING QUIETLY. THEN HE LEFT.

HE ATE IN THE DREAM OF THE HEAD CHEF IN THE BEST HOTEL IN SRI LANKA, A DREAM OF A CERTAIN MEAL DESCRIBED TO THE CHEF BY HIS GRANDFATHER. THE MEAL CONSISTED OF ALMOST FIFTY SEPARATE COURSES, AND OVER TWO HUNDRED DISHES.

THE KING OF DREAMS TASTED SPARINGLY OF A VEGETABLE DISH, AND A LITTLE PLAIN RICE, AND WAS CONTENTED BY THE PERFECTION OF EACH.

HE HAD BEEN ASKED TO PERMIT THE SENDING OF A DREAM OF WARNING TO A TEENAGED GIRL IN SOUTH AFRICA. WITH THIS DREAM TO DRIVE HER, THE GIRL WOULD GROW UP TO TAKE CHARGE OF THE COUNTRY, TO UNITE ALL DIVIDED FACTIONS; WITHOUT IT, SHE WOULD BECOME A NURSE.

HE CAME TO HIS OWN DECISION, AND RELAYED IT TO THE TRIBAL GODS FROM WHOM THE REQUEST HAD COME. HIS DECISION BROOKED NO ARGUMENT, HAD NO APPEAL.

AND THEN, TO CONCLUDE THE DAY'S WORK, HE GAVE AN ELDERLY TORTOISE, ALONE ON HER ISLAND THESE PAST TWO CENTURIES, A DREAM OF HER LOVE, ROASTED BY PASSING SAILORS LONG SINCE FOR HIS RICH GREEN FLESH.

2

ON TRUESDAY, THE PRINCE OF STORIES LISTENED TO THE TALE OF A NIGHTMARE IT HAD CREATED A HANDFUL OF YEARS BEFORE, AND SENT OUT INTO THE WORLD.

THE NIGHTMARE BROUGHT GIFTS: A PHOTOGRAPH OF A SMILE, A HANDFUL OF DRIED THYME, AND A CLAMMY, FAT SILVER-AND-RED CLOWN TOY, MADE OF SOMETHING NOT UNLIKE RUBBER.

HE GAVE IT WORDS OF APPROVAL IN RETURN, AND IT BLUSHED BLACK WITH PLEASURE.

THEN THE PRINCE OF STORIES WALKED THE BOUNDS OF THE DREAMING, BEGINNING WITH THE SHORES OF NIGHT, AND FROM THERE TO THE BORDERS OF THE SHIFTING PLACES.

HE TOOK SHIP IN THE ARCHIPELAGO, AND INSPECTED THE SKERRIES, TALLYING EACH ONE, NO MATTER HOW INSIGNIFICANT.

HE RODE A BLACK HORSE ACROSS THE LAKE OF DAWN; AND RODE A WHITE HORSE THROUGH THE MANDRAKE WOOD; AND RODE A SCREECH OWL OVER THE VIA LACRIMAE.

HE WALKED THROUGH THE LOVE FIELDS, AND FROM THERE HE WALKED ON INTO NIGHTMARE.

3

THE KINDLY ONES:8

ON WODENSDAY, HE WALKED THE CASTLE. THE HEART OF THE DREAMING IS AS LARGE AS THE DREAMING ITSELF.

HE BEGAN IN THE CELLARS BENEATH THE CASTLE, WHERE ONCE MANY WINES AND JARS AND DISTILLATES WERE STORED. HE TOOK COUNSEL WITH THE GREAT SPIDERS, AND EXCHANGED QUIET WORDS WITH MANY-LEGGED SCUTTLING THINGS, WHO VIEWED HIM AS ONE OF THEMSELVES.

THIS WAS INTERRUPTED BY THE ARRIVAL OF THE LORD OF THIS DAY. HE SPOKE TO THE DREAM KING AND LEFT.

4

IN THE AFTERNOON, THE LORD SHAPER WALKED THROUGH THE ROOMS OF THE CASTLE ABOVE THE GROUND, TALKING TO EACH OF THE STAFF IN TURN, HEARING THEIR GRIEVANCES, ACKNOWLEDGING THEIR SERVICE AND THEIR WORK.

HE SPOKE TO THE SCAR-DANCERS, TO THE STRAW-DUST-WOMEN, TO THE OLD MAN WITH A SWAN'S ARM WHO TENDS THE BACK STAIRS, TO THE THREE CHILDREN OF THE AUTOPSY, TO THE PAINTERS AND THE SCRIVENERS AND THE WALLS.

HE SPOKE TO PEOPLE MADE OF THIN TWIGS, AND TO THE DREAM GHOSTS WHO LEFT GLOWING FOOTPRINTS AS THE ONLY EVIDENCE OF THEIR PASSAGE.

HE SPOKE TO THE EMBRYONIC SILICON DREAMS WHO CLUSTERED IN A FAR BALLROOM, AND WHISPERED TO THEM, BRIEFLY, ABOUT THE OTHER MACHINES THAT HAD DREAMED IN THE DISTANT PAST.

WHEN THIS DAY WAS ALMOST OVER HE WENT INTO THE THRONE ROOM, AND TOOK STOCK OF CERTAIN ITEMS THERE, INCLUDING THOSE THINGS HE KEEPS IN THAT ROOM, BEHIND COLORED GLASS: THE RAW STUFF, UNTAMED, THAT IS CENTRAL TO THE DREAMING.

ON THIRSTDAY, THE KING OF DREAMS WALKED IN THE WAKING WORLD. HE STOOD, BRIEFLY, AT THE SIDE OF THE HALL, WATCHING A YOUNG WOMAN WITH A GUITAR TELL AN AUDIENCE OF A DREAM SHE HAD HAD, IN SONG.

HE STOOD IN FRONT OF A PAINTING SPRAY-PAINTED ON A WALL SOON TO BE DEMOLISHED, AND, AFTER STARING FOR SOME TIME, HE NODDED, AS IF IN APPROVAL.

IN A SMALL PARK IN CENTRAL EUROPE, HE STOPPED TO FEED THE PIGEONS, BECAUSE IT GAVE HIM PLEASURE SO TO DO, ALTHOUGH HE STOPPED WHEN IT WAS POINTED OUT TO HIM THAT A SIGN SAID "DO NOT FEED THE PIGEONS."

A GALAMBOKAT ETTENI TILOS!

HE WALKED ACROSS THE PARK, AND WATCHED AN OPEN-AIR PERFORMANCE OF A MIDSUMMER NIGHT'S DREAM. HE WAS MILDLY DISAPPOINTED BY THE TRANSLATION.

HE WAS, HOWEVER, EXTRAORDINARILY AMUSED BY THE PERFORMANCE OF THE ACTOR PLAYING THE PART OF BOTTOM.

LATER THAT DAY, HE VISITED EACH OF HIS PROPERTIES IN THE WAKING WORLD, CHECKING THE UPKEEP AND CONDITION OF EACH; AND THEN HE RETURNED TO THE DREAMING.

6

ON FIRE'S DAY, DREAM WAS REVIEWING CERTAIN OF THE VARIOUS TREATIES AND AGREEMENTS BETWEEN THE DREAMING AND OTHER STATES AND BOUNDARIES AND ENTITIES, WHEN HE WAS DISTURBED.

RIGHT. I'M DOING THIS PROPERLY. I'M IN MY PLACE WHERE THE THINGIES ARE AND I'M TALKING TO THE ONE WITH YOUR SIGGY THING ON IT AND I'M TALKING TO IT PROPERLY. CAN I COME AND SEE YOU NOW?

If you must.

I REALLY MUST.

UM. HI.

I'M LOOKING FOR MY DOGGY. DO YOU REMEMBER MY DOGGY? I GOT HIM ON THE DAY THAT I ATE ALL THE CHERRIES ALL UP.

FROM OUR BROTHER.

I have not forgotten.

WELL, I SPOKE TO OUR BROTHER AND HE SAID... THERE'S A STATUE OF YOU THAT LOOKS ALL SADLY IN THE GARDEN.

You saw him? Destruction said that?

SAID WHAT?

That there was a...statue of me that looked "all sadly."

HE NEVER SAID THAT. I SAID THAT.

Indeed. But you saw Destruction?

DESTINY, NOT DESTRUCTION. I SAW DESTINY. HE SAID YOU'D KNOW ABOUT BARNABAS. HE SAID IT COULDN'T HURT TO COME AND SEE YOU.

HE TOLD ME NOT TO COME AND SEE YOU, TOO.

HE SAID IT BOTH.

WILL YOU HELP ME FIND MY DOGGY? YOU AND ME, WE HAD SUCH A NICE TIME THE LAST TIME WE WENT LOOKING FOR SOMEONE.

DID WE?

DIDN'T WE?

7

SO, CAN YOU COME WITH ME? AND LOOK?

Sister, I have responsibilities. I cannot leave the Dreaming at this time.

YOU USE THAT WORD SO MUCH. RESPONSIBILITIES. DON'T YOU EVER THINK ABOUT WHAT IT MEANS? I MEAN, WHAT DOES IT MEAN TO YOU? IN YOUR HEAD?

Well, I use it to refer to that area of existence over which I exert a certain amount of control and influence.

In my case, the realm and action of dreaming.

HUMP. IT'S MORE THAN THAT. THE THINGS WE DO MAKE ECHOES. S'POSE, F'RINSTANCE, YOU STOP ON A STREET CORNER AND ADMIRE A BRILLIANT FORK OF LIGHTNING--ZAP!

WELL FOR AGES AFTER PEOPLE AND THINGS WILL STOP ON THAT VERY SAME CORNER, STARE UP AT THE SKY, THEY WOULDN'T EVEN KNOW WHAT THEY WERE LOOKING FOR.

SOME OF THEM MIGHT SEE A GHOST BOLT OF LIGHTNING IN THE STREET. SOME OF THEM MIGHT EVEN BE KILLED BY IT.

OUR EXISTENCE DEFORMS THE UNIVERSE.

THAT'S RESPONSIBILITY.

Delirium...?

8

I KNOW *LOTS* OF THINGS. PEOPLE THINK I *DON'T* BUT I REALLY DO. I KNOW MORE *ABOUT US* THAN ANY OF US. THAT'S JUST *ONE* OF THE THINGS I KNOW.

I JUST *DON'T* KNOW WHERE *MY DOGGY* IS...

HE CONSCRIPTED A SMALL, BUT HIGHLY CONSCIENTIOUS NIGHTMARE TO HELP HIS SISTER FIND HER COMPANION, AND SENT THEM ON THEIR WAY.

AND IF HE WAS SHAKEN INSIDE, OR DISTURBED IN ANY WAY BY THIS MEETING, HE GAVE NO EVIDENCE OF THIS.

Friday. Dear Journal. Well. Big news. I'm writing this by hand, so as not to wake up Jack.

Which is my big news.

It started with a late lunch, in a village pub, today.

... WELL, THE VILLAGE *ITSELF* IS IN THE DOMESDAY BOOK. I DON'T KNOW ABOUT THE *GRIFFIN.* PROBABLY GOES BACK ABOUT FIVE HUNDRED YEARS. I'LL ASK THE LANDLORD FOR YOU.

MM. TELL ME ABOUT MR. MCGUIRE.

PAUL? HE LIVES IN THE GATEHOUSE OF A MANOR DOWN THE ROAD. BIG DECAYING PILE--THE SORT YOU USED TO BE ABLE TO FLOG TO ROCK BANDS AND MULTINATIONALS, BUT THESE DAYS YOU SPLIT UP INTO A COUPLE OF DOZEN HIGH-CLASS FLATS.

HE INVITED ME TO GO AND SEE IT.

MM. YOU *OUGHT* TO.

9

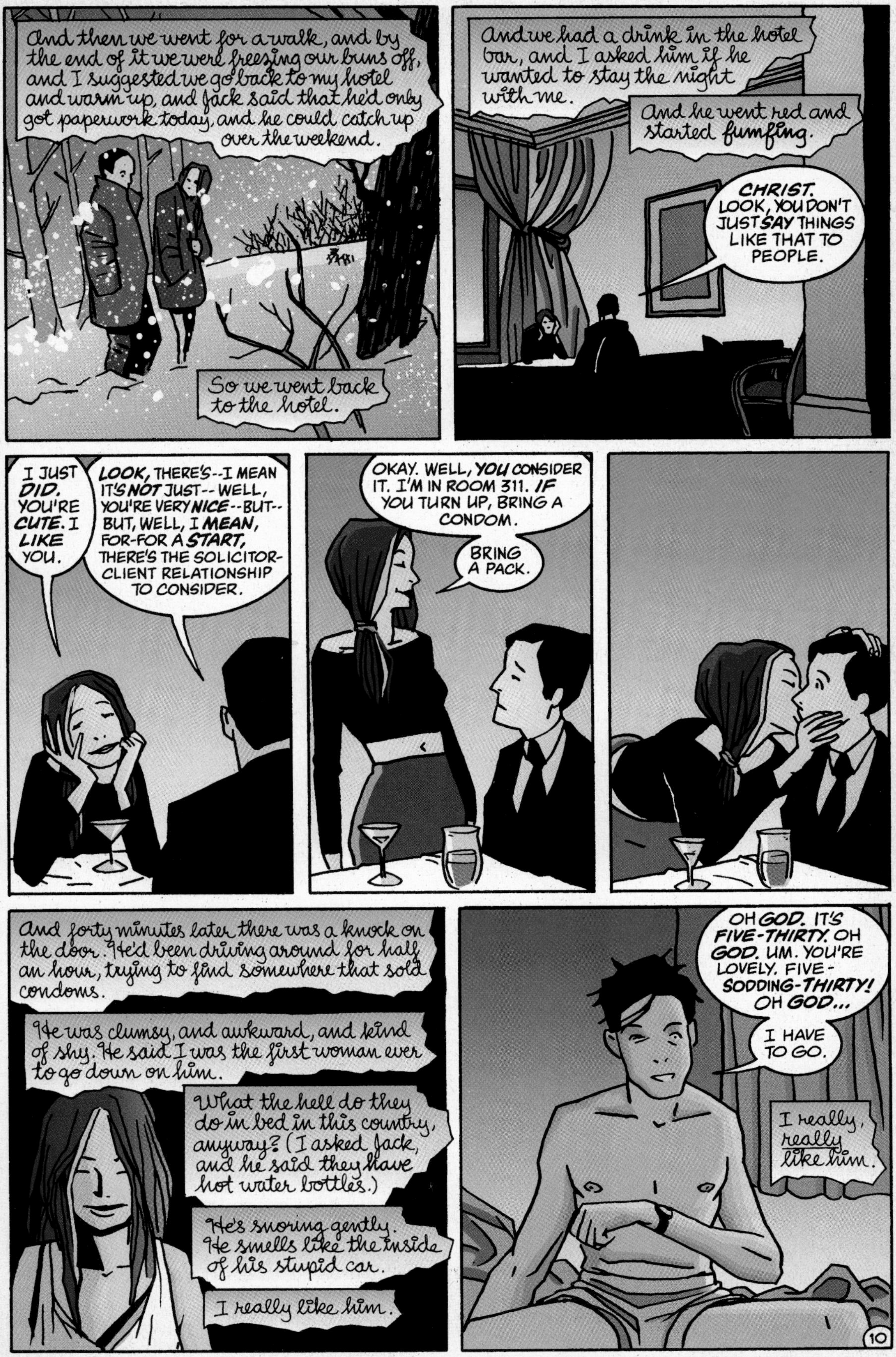

And then we went for a walk, and by the end of it we were freezing our buns off, and I suggested we go back to my hotel and warm up, and Jack said that he'd only got paperwork today, and he could catch up over the weekend.
So we went back to the hotel.
And we had a drink in the hotel bar, and I asked him if he wanted to stay the night with me.
And he went red and started fumfing.
CHRIST. LOOK, YOU DON'T JUST SAY THINGS LIKE THAT TO PEOPLE.
I JUST DID. YOU'RE CUTE. I LIKE YOU.
LOOK, THERE'S--I MEAN IT'S NOT JUST--WELL, YOU'RE VERY NICE--BUT--BUT, WELL, I MEAN, FOR-FOR A START, THERE'S THE SOLICITOR-CLIENT RELATIONSHIP TO CONSIDER.
OKAY. WELL, YOU CONSIDER IT. I'M IN ROOM 311. IF YOU TURN UP, BRING A CONDOM.
BRING A PACK.
And forty minutes later there was a knock on the door. He'd been driving around for half an hour, trying to find somewhere that sold condoms.
He was clumsy, and awkward, and kind of shy. He said I was the first woman ever to go down on him.
What the hell do they do in bed in this country, anyway? (I asked Jack, and he said they have hot water bottles.)
He's snoring gently. He smells like the inside of his stupid car.
I really like him.
OH GOD. IT'S FIVE-THIRTY. OH GOD. UM. YOU'RE LOVELY. FIVE-SODDING-THIRTY! OH GOD...
I HAVE TO GO.
I really, really like him.

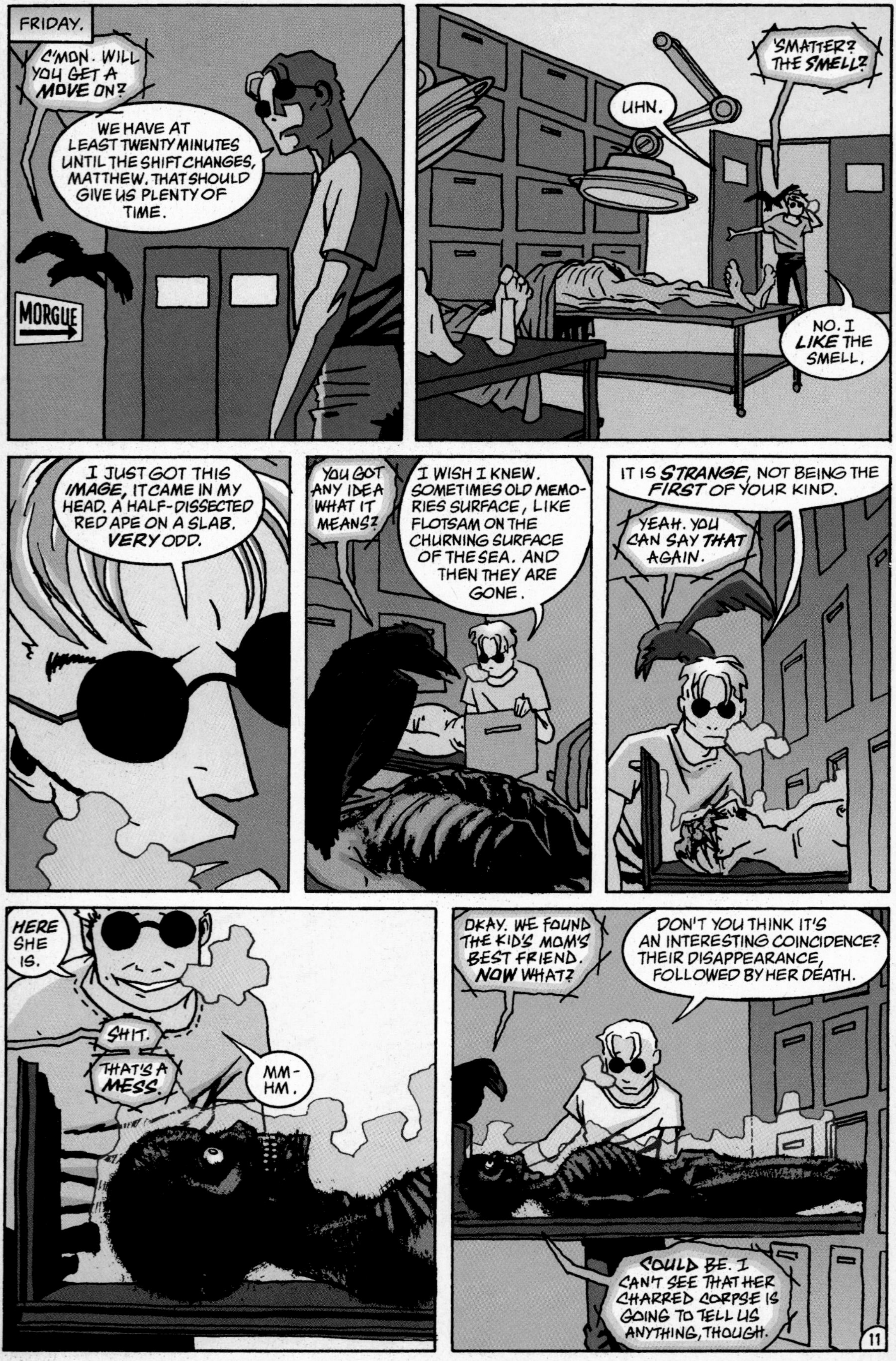
FRIDAY.
C'MON. WILL YOU GET A MOVE ON?
WE HAVE AT LEAST TWENTY MINUTES UNTIL THE SHIFT CHANGES, MATTHEW. THAT SHOULD GIVE US PLENTY OF TIME.
MORGUE
UHN.
'SMATTER? THE SMELL?
NO. I LIKE THE SMELL.
I JUST GOT THIS IMAGE, IT CAME IN MY HEAD. A HALF-DISSECTED RED APE ON A SLAB. VERY ODD.
YOU GOT ANY IDEA WHAT IT MEANS?
I WISH I KNEW. SOMETIMES OLD MEMORIES SURFACE, LIKE FLOTSAM ON THE CHURNING SURFACE OF THE SEA. AND THEN THEY ARE GONE.
IT IS STRANGE, NOT BEING THE FIRST OF YOUR KIND.
YEAH. YOU CAN SAY THAT AGAIN.
HERE SHE IS.
SHIT.
THAT'S A MESS.
MM-HM.
OKAY. WE FOUND THE KID'S MOM'S BEST FRIEND. NOW WHAT?
DON'T YOU THINK IT'S AN INTERESTING COINCIDENCE? THEIR DISAPPEARANCE, FOLLOWED BY HER DEATH.
COULD BE. I CAN'T SEE THAT HER CHARRED CORPSE IS GOING TO TELL US ANYTHING, THOUGH.

YOU KNOW, IN DAYS GONE BY THEY HAD *MANY* BELIEFS ABOUT VIOLENT DEATH. THEY BELIEVED THAT A *CORPSE* WOULD BEGIN TO BLEED AGAIN, WHEN ITS MURDERER WALKED BY.

THEY BELIEVED THAT THE *LAST* THING ONE SAW BEFORE ONE DIED WAS RECORDED -- FROZEN -- ON THE INSIDE OF THE VICTIM'S EYES ...

THAT'S *BULLSHIT.*

NO, THAT'S THE TRUTH. IT'S JUST NO ONE KNOWS HOW TO *DEVELOP* THE IMAGES ...

YOU'RE SICK.

NO. I AM A VISIONARY.

WHAT DID YOU SEE?

I SAW HER DIE. I SAW WHAT SHE SAW AS SHE BURNED. AND I SAW OTHER THINGS.

I SAW A HOTEL ROOM BURNING. I SAW FIRE ENGULF A CITY BUILT OF GLASS.

SKUMPF

CLUMP

YOU THINK THOSE ARE CLUES?

I THINK THEY'RE ECHOES, OR RIPPLES OR...

I....I DO KNOW WHO KILLED HER.

I KNOW WHO TOOK DANIEL HALL.

AND ON FIRE'S DAY THE PRINCE OF STORIES NOTED, WITHOUT CONCERN, BUT WITH A SMALL AMOUNT OF SURPRISE, THE ARRIVAL OF A NUMBER OF RAVENS IN HIS REALM.

SOME WERE LARGER THAN EAGLES. SOME WERE OLDER THAN GODS.

THEY STAYED IN THE SHADOWS, KAWWING AND TOKKING.

WAITING.

ON SATYRDAY, THE CASTLE RECEIVED A VISITOR.

WE ARE HERE TO TALK TO YOUR MASTER.

OUR MASTER IS SEEING NO ONE THIS DAY.

YOU *WILL* LET US IN TO THE CASTLE. OR YOU WILL SUFFER FOR IT.

LADY. LEAVE THIS PLACE. WE ARE THE GUARDIANS OF THE GATE, AND WE SHALL FULFILL OUR FUNCTION.

WILL YOU NOT LEAVE?

THEN RUN AWAY, LADY. RUN VERY *FAST.*

14

GRYPHON, YOU ARE OLD.

YOUR FLESH IS MEAT, AND THE MEAT IS DECAYING. YOUR BONES ARE DRY AND BRITTLE. WITHIN YOU NOW, LION AND EAGLE ABANDON THEIR BATTLE FOR DOMINANCE, AND SURRENDER TO TIME AND TO THE GRAVE.

LORD... I CANNOT FEEL YOU, LORD...

YOU KILLED HIM.

THERE. YES. WE *DID*.

NOW. WE NEED TO TALK TO YOUR MASTER. WE WILL *NOT* HARM HIM DIRECTLY AT THIS TIME. HE HAS MANY CHOICES, WE NEED MERELY TO *TALK* TO HIM. THIS WE SWEAR.

IF YOU *WISH*, YOU MAY ATTACK ME, DEFENDING THE GATE. YOU WILL *DIE*, LIKE YOUR FRIEND. *OR* YOU MAY LET ME PASS. WHICH COURSE WILL YOU TAKE?

LORD? SHALL I *KILL* HER?

NO, WYVERN.

Let her through. I will not have either of you endangered. She has sworn her oath.

Your friend has not died in vain.

I HAVE SPOKEN TO THE LORD OF THIS REALM. HE HAS GIVEN YOU PERMISSION TO ENTER THE CASTLE, AND WILL GRANT YOU AUDIENCE.

I AM HONOR-BOUND TO WARN YOU TO STAY ON THE PATH THROUGH THE CASTLE. STRAYING FROM THE PATH COULD MEAN YOUR DESTRUCTION.

YOU KILLED MY FRIEND, WOMAN.

STRAY FROM YOUR PATH.

16

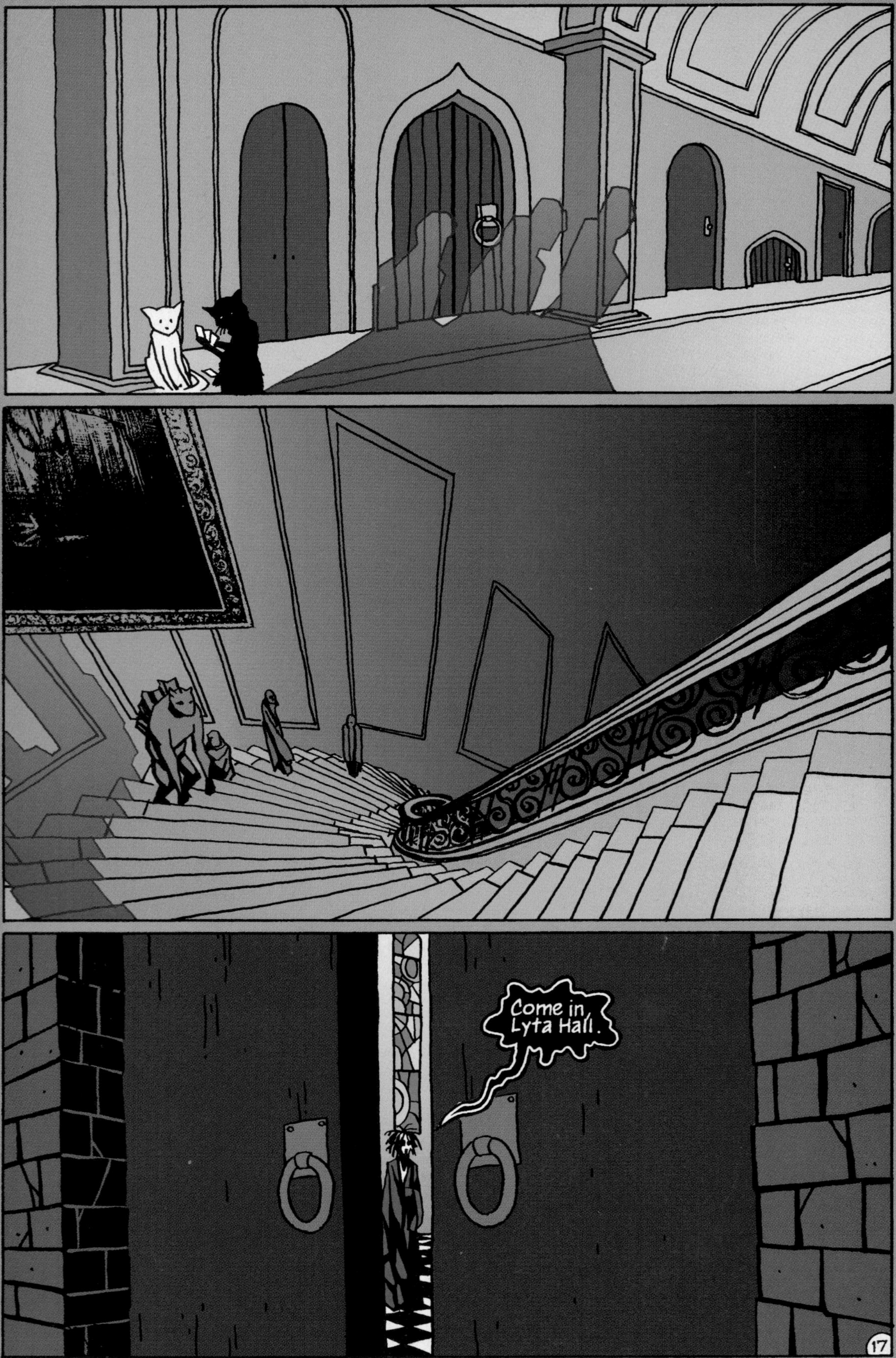
Come in Lyta Hall.

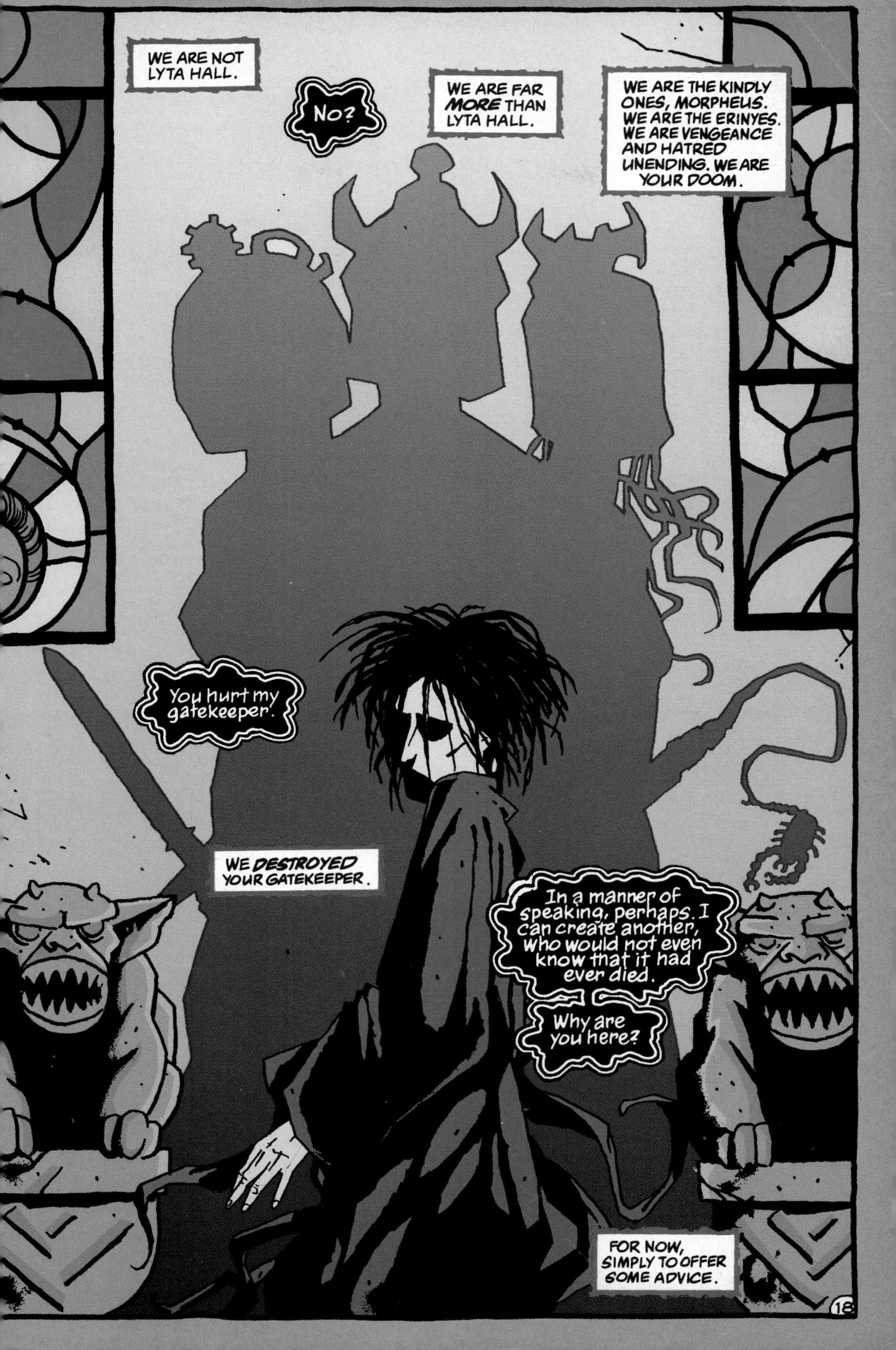

WE ARE NOT LYTA HALL.
No?
WE ARE FAR MORE THAN LYTA HALL.
WE ARE THE KINDLY ONES, MORPHEUS. WE ARE THE ERINYES. WE ARE VENGEANCE AND HATRED UNENDING. WE ARE YOUR DOOM.
You hurt my gatekeeper.
WE DESTROYED YOUR GATEKEEPER.
In a manner of speaking, perhaps. I can create another, who would not even know that it had ever died.
Why are you here?
FOR NOW, SIMPLY TO OFFER SOME ADVICE.
18

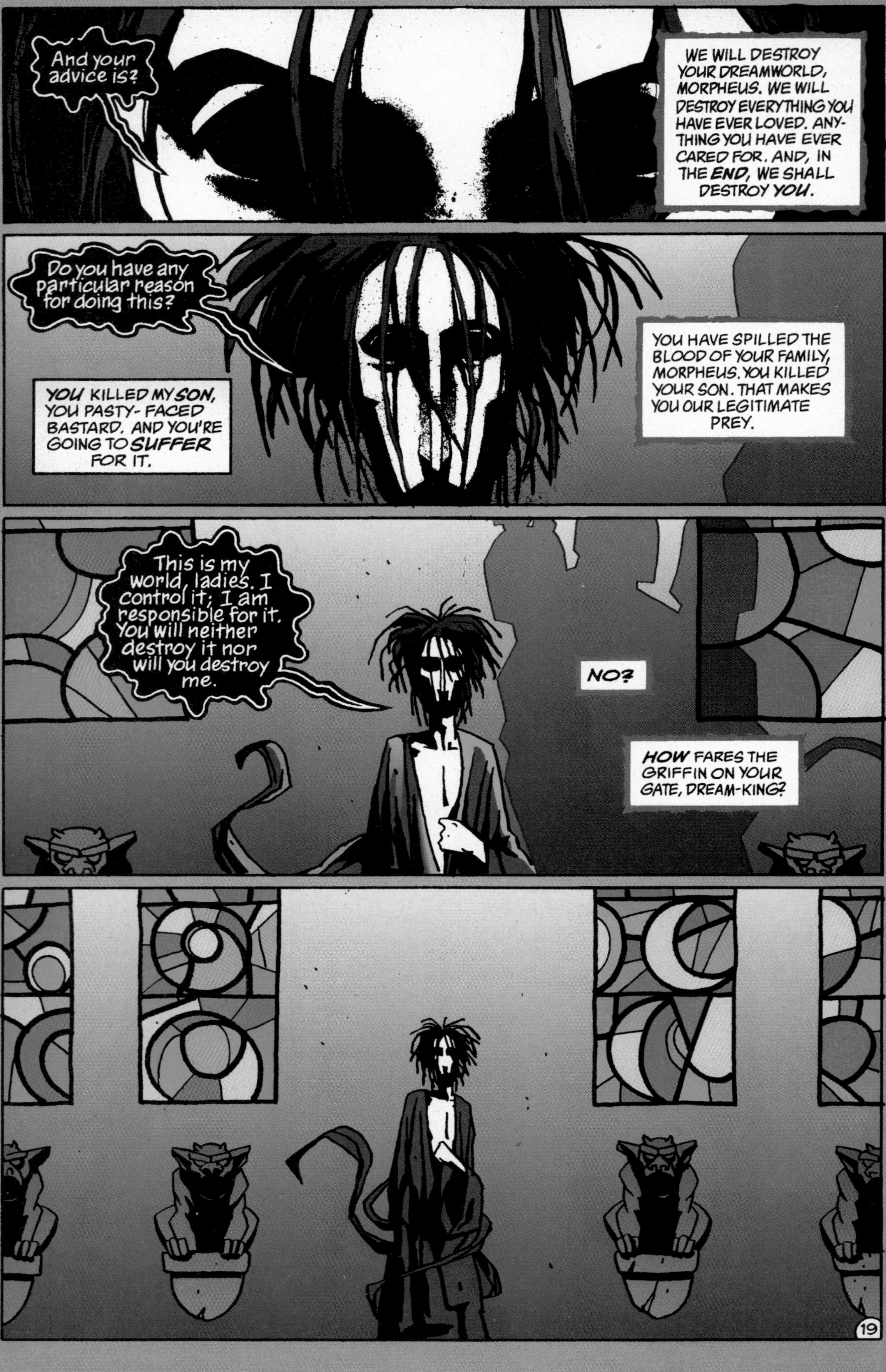
And your advice is?
WE WILL DESTROY YOUR DREAMWORLD, MORPHEUS. WE WILL DESTROY EVERYTHING YOU HAVE EVER LOVED. ANYTHING YOU HAVE EVER CARED FOR. AND, IN THE END, WE SHALL DESTROY YOU.
Do you have any particular reason for doing this?
YOU KILLED MY SON, YOU PASTY-FACED BASTARD. AND YOU'RE GOING TO SUFFER FOR IT.
YOU HAVE SPILLED THE BLOOD OF YOUR FAMILY, MORPHEUS. YOU KILLED YOUR SON. THAT MAKES YOU OUR LEGITIMATE PREY.
This is my world, ladies. I control it; I am responsible for it. You will neither destroy it nor will you destroy me.
NO?
HOW FARES THE GRIFFIN ON YOUR GATE, DREAM-KING?

Matthew?

HI, BOSS. THAT *IS* YOU, ISN'T IT?

Indeed. It has been five days now. The boy is not here. I am extremely unimpressed.

UH. WE'RE MAKING *PROGRESS*, BOSS.

HE'S *RIGHT*, SIRE.

Where are you two? You are not in the waking world. I sent you to the waking world.

THE CHILD IS NO *LONGER* IN THE WAKING WORLD, LORD. WE *WILL* FIND HIM, AND BRING HIM TO YOU, AS YOU COMMANDED.

SOON.

...I see.

I have a certain amount of faith and confidence in both of you. It would disappoint me exceedingly to find that it had been misplaced.

20

JESUS...

I ...I'VE NEVER *HEARD* THE BOSS SOUND LIKE THAT. HE SOUNDED SO ...*COLD*...

I JUST HOPE YOU KNOW WHAT YOU'RE DOING, CORINTHIAN.

SO DO I, LITTLE RAVEN. THAT *SHOULD* BE IT UP AHEAD.

"YONDER LIES DA PALACE OF MY *FADDER*," EH? LET'S HOPE WE'RE NOT EXPECTED.

WOLF!

KRAK

DO YOU THINK IT WAS A *REAL* WOLF? OR DO YOU THINK WE'RE *EXPECTED?*

WE'RE A *LONG* WAY FROM THE *REAL* WORLD NOW, MATTHEW. I THINK WE CAN ASSUME THAT WE *ARE* EXPECTED.

BUT REAL OR NOT, THAT WAS *STILL* MY FIRST KILL OF THIS LIFE, MATTHEW.

AND THE EYES ARE *MINE.*

21

AND, AS SATURDAY CONCLUDED,

...LUCIFER PLAYED A MEDLEY OF LITTLE-KNOWN COLE PORTER SONGS, BEGINNING WITH MILDLY RISQUÉ SONGS, SUCH AS "PETS," "MY MOST INTIMATE FRIEND" AND "AFTER ALL, I'M ONLY A SCHOOLGIRL," AND CONCLUDING WITH THREE SONGS PORTER HAD EVER ONLY PLAYED TO INTIMATES AT EXTREMELY PRIVATE PARTIES.

HE WAS STARTING TO FIND HIMSELF BORED BY MUSIC; AND HE FOUND HIMSELF, DURING THE FINAL CHORUS OF "SHE NEVER WENT DOWN ON THE TITANIC," OBSERVING WITHIN HIMSELF THE URGE TO MOVE ON.

...THE WITCH-WOMAN WHO NOW CALLED HERSELF LARISSA LAY ON THE CAMP-BED IN HER ROOM, READING AN IMPROVING BOOK, AND PICKING AT A BOWL OF LAMB STEW.

SHE IGNORED THE MOANS OF HER NEW HOUSEMATE.

THE CAMP-BED WAS NEW. IT HAD COST HER $70, AND THAT, TOGETHER WITH THE OTHER EXPENSES SHE HAD RECENTLY INCURRED, HAD PRETTY MUCH CLEANED OUT HER SAVINGS.

SHE HAD NOTICED CERTAIN PECULIARITIES OF THE STARLINGS' FLIGHT AT DUSK THAT EVENING; LARISSA WAS A MORE-THAN-COMPETENT AUGUR, AND SHE WAS CONCERNED ABOUT HER VISITOR OF THE FOLLOWING DAY.

JOHN BAUER

...NUALA SAT IN THE GARDEN OF HER CITADEL ON THE EDGE OF THE FOREST BY TIR-NA-NOG, TRYING TO RECALL WHAT SHE HAD DONE WITH HER TIME, IN THE DAYS BEFORE THE DREAMING.

SHE HAD DANCED, AND SUNG, AND FLIRTED. SOMETIMES SHE WOULD CURSE, OTHER TIMES SHE WOULD BESTOW SMALL FAVORS. TIME PASSED.

SHE HAD HAD NO PURPOSE THEN; AND STILL, SHE HAD BEEN CONTENT.

SHE FINGERED THE STONE AROUND HER NECK, UNCONSCIOUSLY, AND RECALLED HAPPINESS.

22

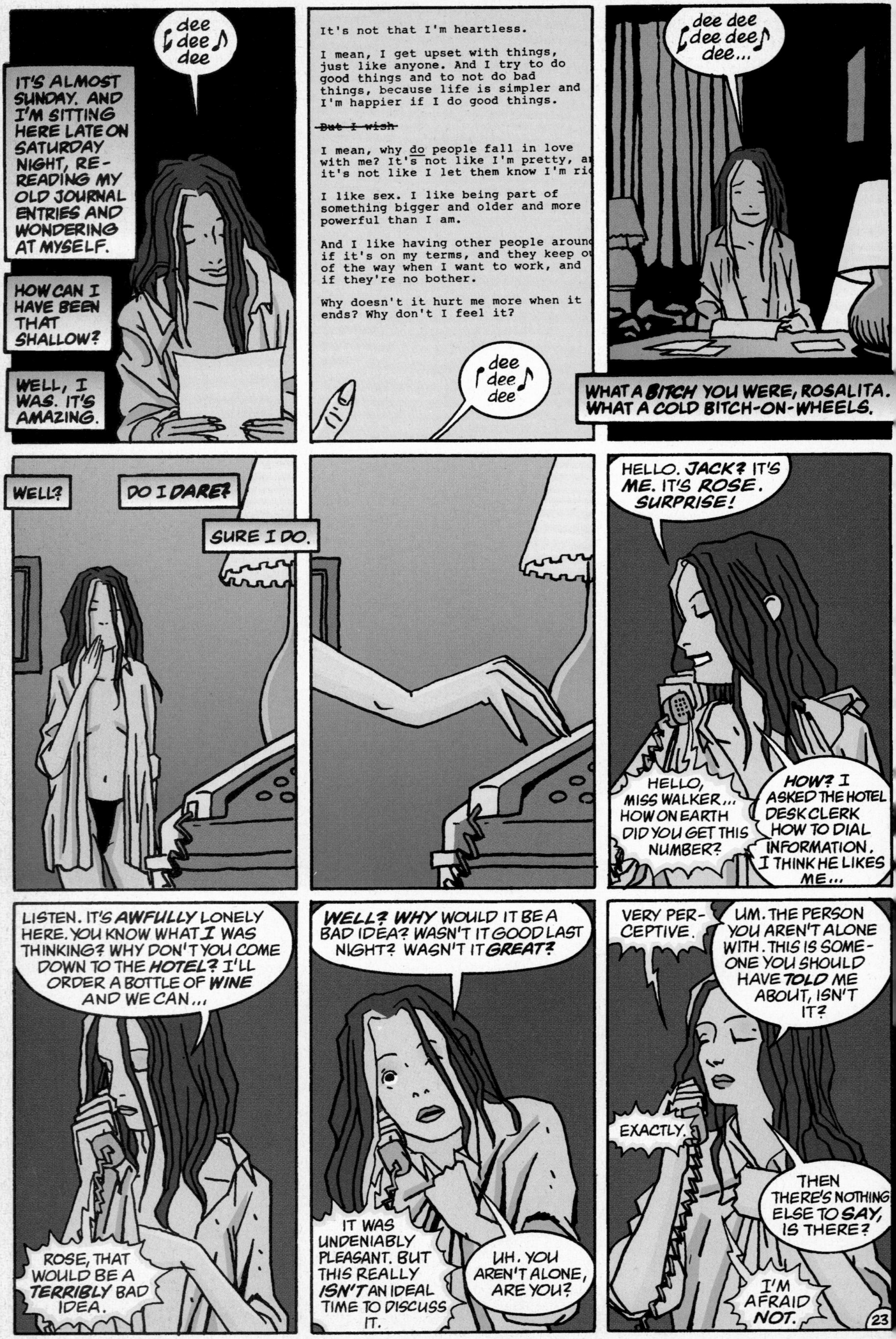

dee dee dee
IT'S ALMOST SUNDAY. AND I'M SITTING HERE LATE ON SATURDAY NIGHT, RE-READING MY OLD JOURNAL ENTRIES AND WONDERING AT MYSELF.
HOW CAN I HAVE BEEN THAT SHALLOW?
WELL, I WAS. IT'S AMAZING.
It's not that I'm heartless.
I mean, I get upset with things, just like anyone. And I try to do good things and to not do bad things, because life is simpler and I'm happier if I do good things.
~~But I wish~~
I mean, why do people fall in love with me? It's not like I'm pretty, a it's not like I let them know I'm ri
I like sex. I like being part of something bigger and older and more powerful than I am.
And I like having other people aroun if it's on my terms, and they keep o of the way when I want to work, and if they're no bother.
Why doesn't it hurt me more when it ends? Why don't I feel it?
dee dee dee
dee dee dee dee dee...
WHAT A BITCH YOU WERE, ROSALITA. WHAT A COLD BITCH-ON-WHEELS.
WELL?
DO I DARE?
SURE I DO.
HELLO. JACK? IT'S ME. IT'S ROSE. SURPRISE!
HELLO, MISS WALKER... HOW ON EARTH DID YOU GET THIS NUMBER?
HOW? I ASKED THE HOTEL DESK CLERK HOW TO DIAL INFORMATION. I THINK HE LIKES ME...
LISTEN. IT'S AWFULLY LONELY HERE. YOU KNOW WHAT I WAS THINKING? WHY DON'T YOU COME DOWN TO THE HOTEL? I'LL ORDER A BOTTLE OF WINE AND WE CAN...
ROSE, THAT WOULD BE A TERRIBLY BAD IDEA.
WELL? WHY WOULD IT BE A BAD IDEA? WASN'T IT GOOD LAST NIGHT? WASN'T IT GREAT?
IT WAS UNDENIABLY PLEASANT. BUT THIS REALLY ISN'T AN IDEAL TIME TO DISCUSS IT.
UH. YOU AREN'T ALONE, ARE YOU?
VERY PERCEPTIVE.
UM. THE PERSON YOU AREN'T ALONE WITH. THIS IS SOMEONE YOU SHOULD HAVE TOLD ME ABOUT, ISN'T IT?
EXACTLY.
THEN THERE'S NOTHING ELSE TO SAY, IS THERE?
I'M AFRAID NOT.

AND ON SON'S DAY, THEY HELD THE FIRST FUNERAL.

part

NINE

ALMOST TIME.

NEARLY. *VERY* NEARLY.

SUNDAY MORNING... ♫

HELLO, MISTER McGUIRE.

ROSE? ROSE *WALKER?* WHAT A PLEASURE. I'M JUST CLEANING THE SIGN. ALMOST FINISHED. COME INSIDE. PLEASE COME IN.

YOU SAID I COULD COME AND SEE YOU.

OF COURSE I DID. OF *COURSE.* DELIGHTED YOU TOOK ME UP ON IT. CAN I OFFER YOU SOME TEA?

NO THANK YOU.

WINE?

SURE.

HOW GO YOUR RESEARCHES?

THEY *SUCK.* THE WHOLE *THING* SUCKS.

OH, I *AM* SORRY TO HEAR THAT.

S'OKAY. S'NOT YOUR PROBLEM.

SO, UM. THIS IS THE GATEHOUSE. IT'S MORE OR LESS MY BACHELOR FLAT. NOT VERY EXCITING, THOUGH.

WOULD YOU LIKE TO TAKE A LOOK AROUND THE MANOR HOUSE ITSELF? BIT OF A GUIDED TOUR?

YEAH. SURE. *GREAT.* THANKS.

FAWNEY RIG. IT SOUNDS LIKE A VERY *OLD* NAME. WHAT *IS* THIS PLACE? IT MUST BE *HUNDREDS* OF YEARS OLD, RIGHT?

THE *BODY* OF THE MANOR IS REGENCY, BUT THERE WERE CONTINUOUS ADDITIONS OVER THE NEXT COUPLE OF HUNDRED YEARS. ALEX'S FATHER ADDED CERTAIN MODIFICATIONS OF HIS OWN, IN HIS UNIQUELY DEPLORABLE ARCHITECTURAL TASTE.

THE HOUSE WAS KNOWN AS WYCH MANOR-- A WYCH IS, IF MEMORY SERVES, AN ELM TREE, NOTHING TO DO WITH POINTY HATS AND BROOMSTICKS. WHEN BURGESS BOUGHT IT, IN THE LATE 1890'S, HE RENAMED IT "FAWNEY RIG."

KEYS...*KEYS*...

2

COME ON IN.

THIS IS THE ENTRANCE HALL.

IT'S A BIT GRUNGY, I'M AFRAID. I HAVE A CLEANING LADY WHO COMES IN ONCE A WEEK AND SWEEPS A LITTLE.

UNDER THE SHEETS ARE SOME RATHER NICE PIECES OF FURNITURE.

THROUGH HERE.

THIS IS THE *LIBRARY*. I'VE NEVER BEEN MUCH OF A READER, I'M AFRAID. THESE ARE ALEX'S BOOKS, AND HIS FATHER'S. NOT THE RARE OCCULTY ONES --THEY'RE KEPT ELSEWHERE, AFTER SOME PROBLEMS WE HAD A FEW YEARS BACK.

HEY, IS THIS A COMPLETE STORISENDE EDITION OF JAMES BRANCH CABELL?

I'M SURE IT IS.

AND THIS YEATS BOOK. *"THE PATHS OF GOLD."* I'VE NEVER *HEARD* OF IT...

HEY, IT'S SIGNED *"TO RODERICK BURGESS WITH ADMIRATION."* IS THIS SIGNATURE REALLY YEATS'S?

I WOULD IMAGINE SO.

THIS PLACE IS LIKE THE LIBRARY OF MY DREAMS.

WELL, IF YOU HAVE ANY SPARE TIME BEFORE RETURNING, FEEL FREE TO COME DOWN AND BROWSE.

YOU CAN'T TAKE ANYTHING AWAY, THOUGH, I'M AFRAID. THE BOOKS BELONG TO ALEX.

WHEN MONEY GOT A BIT TIGHT, IN THE LATE SEVENTIES, I SUGGESTED WE SELL SOME OF THE BOOKS -- HE WOULDN'T HEAR OF IT...

WOUND UP SELLING OFF TWENTY ACRES OF PRIME WOODLAND TO DEVELOPERS INSTEAD.

3

I THINK I MAY BE GOING BACK TO LA TOMORROW.

RESEARCHES ALL DONE?

YOU COULD SAY THAT.

DINING ROOM.

MM. HOW DID YOU MEET ALEX?

I WAS A YOUNG AND BEAUTIFUL UNDER-GARDENER. HE WAS A REPRESSED OLD MAID OF FORTYISH.

I PERSUADED HIM TO TAKE ADVANTAGE OF ME BEHIND THE POTTING SHED.

REALLY?

OR THE SUMMER HOUSE. I FORGET.

THIS WAS ALEX'S STUDY.

THIS ROOM THROUGH HERE IS CALLED THE ROSE ROOM. IT'S A SORT OF CONSERVATORY.

ROSES? IN WINTER?

I'VE BEEN GROWING THEM HERE FOR FOUR DECADES. WOULD YOU LIKE ONE?

THAT'S VERY SWEET OF YOU.

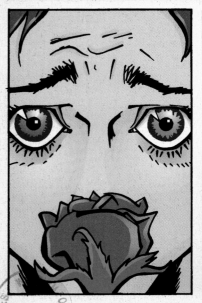

KITCHEN. BIG, ISN'T IT? REALLY, A KITCHEN LIKE THIS ONLY WORKS WITH A HUGE HOUSEHOLD STAFF. I...

I'M SORRY. I'M GOING TO HAVE TO SIT DOWN. BIT-- BIT OUT OF BREATH. YOU POKE ABOUT ALL YOU WANT TO. I'LL BE HERE WHEN YOU'VE SEEN ENOUGH.

ARE YOU...?

I'M FINE, THANK YOU.

SOMEHOW, I CAN'T BRING MYSELF TO DO A "HE LOVES ME, HE LOVES ME NOT" WITH HOTHOUSE ROSE PETALS.

SO WE'LL JUST ASSUME THAT HE *DOESN'T* LOVE ME.

HELLO, UGLY.

KLIK

OH C'MON...

MR. McGUIRE! I JUST OPENED SOME KIND OF SECRET STAIRWAY UP HERE.

OH, *THAT.* YES. IT JUST LEADS DOWN TO THE CELLAR. IT OUGHT TO BE *QUITE* SAFE. THERE'S A LIGHT-SWITCH AS YOU GO IN.

THANKS!

HELLO, GRAND-DAUGHTER.

5

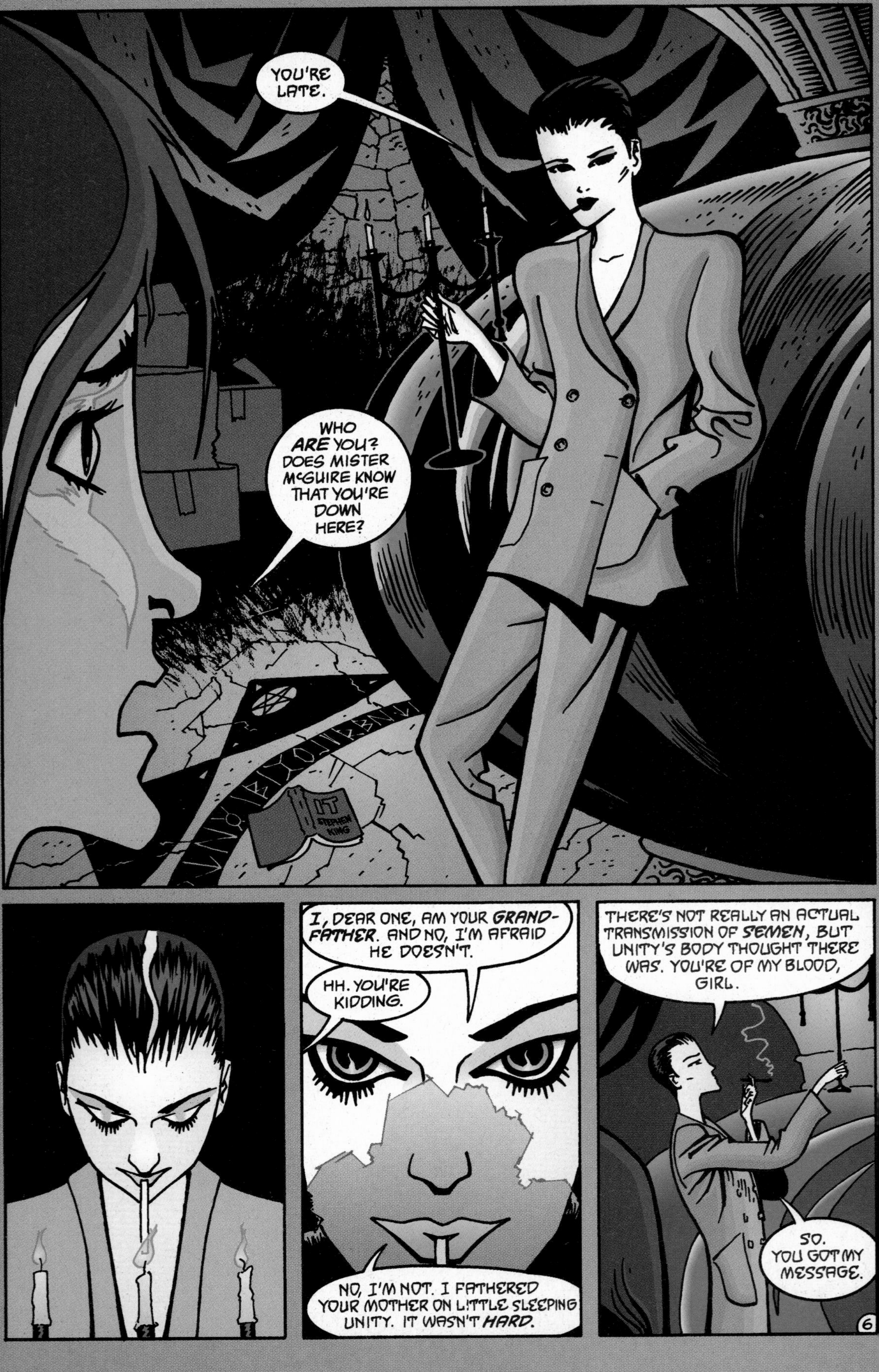
YOU'RE LATE.
WHO ARE YOU? DOES MISTER McGUIRE KNOW THAT YOU'RE DOWN HERE?
IT STEPHEN KING
I, DEAR ONE, AM YOUR GRANDFATHER. AND NO, I'M AFRAID HE DOESN'T.
HH. YOU'RE KIDDING.
NO, I'M NOT. I FATHERED YOUR MOTHER ON LITTLE SLEEPING UNITY. IT WASN'T HARD.
THERE'S NOT REALLY AN ACTUAL TRANSMISSION OF SEMEN, BUT UNITY'S BODY THOUGHT THERE WAS. YOU'RE OF MY BLOOD, GIRL.
SO. YOU GOT MY MESSAGE.
6

WEIRD *SHIT*. THIS IS JUST ONE OF THOSE WEIRD SHIT MOMENTS, ISN'T IT?

YOU MIGHT SAY THAT.

ARE YOU GOING TO *HURT* ME? *KILL* ME? *MESS* ME UP?

NO MORE THAN USUALLY; NO; AND PERHAPS, A LITTLE. BUT ONLY WITH *LOVE*.

LOVE...

HAVE YOU EVER BEEN IN LOVE?

YOU MIGHT SAY THAT.

HORRIBLE, ISN'T IT?

IN WHAT WAY?

IT MAKES YOU SO VULNERABLE. IT OPENS YOUR CHEST AND IT OPENS YOUR HEART AND IT MEANS SOMEONE CAN GET INSIDE YOU AND MESS YOU UP.

YOU BUILD UP ALL THESE DEFENSES. YOU BUILD UP THIS WHOLE ARMOR, FOR YEARS, SO NOTHING CAN HURT YOU, THEN ONE STUPID PERSON, NO DIFFERENT FROM ANY OTHER STUPID PERSON, WANDERS INTO YOUR STUPID LIFE...

YOU GIVE THEM A PIECE OF YOU. THEY DON'T ASK FOR IT. THEY DO SOMETHING DUMB ONE DAY LIKE KISS YOU, OR SMILE AT YOU, AND THEN YOUR LIFE ISN'T YOUR OWN ANYMORE.

7

LOVE TAKES HOSTAGES. IT GETS INSIDE YOU. IT EATS YOU OUT AND LEAVES YOU CRYING IN THE DARKNESS, SO A SIMPLE PHRASE LIKE "MAYBE WE SHOULD JUST BE FRIENDS" OR "HOW VERY PERCEPTIVE" TURNS INTO A GLASS SPLINTER WORKING ITS WAY INTO YOUR HEART.

HOW PICTURESQUE.

IT HURTS. NOT JUST IN THE IMAGINATION. NOT JUST IN THE MIND. IT'S A SOUL-HURT, A BODY-HURT, A REAL GETS-INSIDE-YOU-AND-RIPS-YOU-APART PAIN.

NOTHING SHOULD BE ABLE TO DO THAT.

ESPECIALLY NOT LOVE.

I HATE LOVE.

I THINK I PREFERRED YOU, GRANDDAUGHTER, WHEN YOU WERE STOICALLY COMPLAINING ABOUT NOT FEELING ANYTHING.

WHY...WHY AM I TELLING YOU ALL THIS? WHO ARE YOU...?

I THOUGHT I'D COME DOWN AND SEE HOW YOU WERE DOING.

WHAT DO YOU THINK OF THE SANCTUM SANCTORUM THEN?

I'M SORRY, MR. McGUIRE... I THINK I MUST HAVE FALLEN ASLEEP OR SOMETHING.

FUNNY PLACE TO FALL ASLEEP, DEAR.

8

I'M SORRY. I DIDN'T EVEN REALIZE I'D FALLEN ASLEEP.

WELL, YOU *MUST* HAVE BEEN *DOWN* HERE FOR ALMOST HALF AN HOUR...

REALLY? I HAD THIS DREAM...

IT WAS REALLY *WEIRD.*

THERE WAS THIS *PERSON* IN IT, AND I COULDN'T TELL IF IT WAS A *MAN* OR A *WOMAN.* AND HE--SHE-- KEPT LIGHTING CIGARETTES ALL THE TIME...

AND SHE WAS *GOING* TO TELL ME ALL THESE SECRET THINGS. I MEAN, REALLY *IMPORTANT* THINGS. AND ALL I HAD TO DO WAS SHUT UP AND LISTEN.

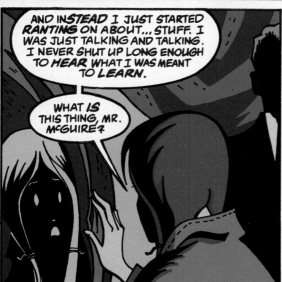

AND IN*STEAD* I JUST STARTED *RANTING* ON ABOUT... STUFF. I WAS JUST TALKING AND TALKING. I NEVER SHUT UP LONG ENOUGH TO *HEAR* WHAT I WAS MEANT TO *LEARN.*

WHAT *IS* THIS THING, MR. M°GUIRE?

A *BOX,* DEAR. ALEX'S FATHER KEPT SOME- THING VALUABLE TO HIM IN IT FOR A LONG TIME.

OH.

OOPS-A-DAISY. YOU *DROPPED* SOMETHING.

I *DID?*

IT'S A LIGHTER, ISN'T IT? ART DECO, EH? VERY NICE.

HERE YOU GO. DON'T WANT TO GO *LOSING* IT AGAIN, DO YOU?

9

SWARTALFHEIM.

YOU GOT ANY *BETTER* IDEAS?

WELL, *I* DON'T KNOW. *MAYBE.*

HOW ABOUT *THIS:* I'LL FLY IN AND SCOUT THE PLACE OUT. FLY BACK HERE, WE'LL *SNEAK* YOU IN, MAYBE DISGUISE YOU AS SOMETHING...

IT,... IT'S *HAPPENING* AGAIN...

SOMETHING'S PULLING ME BACK TO THE DREAMING...

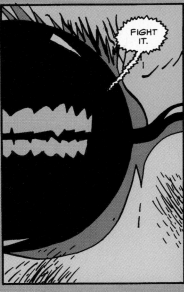

FIGHT IT.

NO, LET US JUST *DO* IT. IF WE ARE EXPECTED, *THEN* WE ARE EXPECTED. AND I HAVE NO *TALENT* FOR DISGUISE.

ANY IDEA WHAT THIS *THING* IS? I'VE SEEN A FEW A THEM IN THE DREAMING FROM TIME TO TIME. ACROSS THE SKY.

THE CORD? I THINK,...THEY CAN HELP YOU FIND YOUR WAY BACK TO YOUR BODY. SOMETHING LIKE THAT...

HUSH NOW.

THERE'S SOMEONE HERE.

10

WE HAVE COME FOR THE CHILD DANIEL.

WHERE *IS* HE?

Matthew. You and your friend have done well. I am proud of you both. You have won through all the trials and travails that I created to test your loyalty.

You may both now return to the Dreaming to receive your reward.

BOSS...?

THAT ISN'T HIM.

SOUNDS KIND OF LIKE HIM, THOUGH.

YOU ARE NOT OUR LORD. YOU ARE NOT MY CREATOR. WE CANNOT BE FOOLED THAT EASILY.

NO?

If you believe me to be other than what I am, then you are indeed a fool. But such foolishness can easily be remedied...

Rest easy. I am indeed your creator, little nightmare.

SOUNDS EXACTLY LIKE HIM.

THEN *UNCREATE* ME NOW, IF YOU HAVE THE POWER. FOR I SHALL STAND AGAINST YOU. I AM YOUNG, TRUE. BUT I HAVE AGE WITHIN ME.

AND YOU ARE *NOT* MY LORD.

11

Please...you must not...

ARE YOU?

NO. I AM *NOT* YOUR LORD. I AM SOMETHING *MUCH* WORSE. I AM YOUR *RUIN*. YOUR *DEATH*. YOUR *END*.

LET *GO* OF ME, AND I SHALL LET YOU *LIVE*.

HOW...CAN YOU *DO* THIS...TO YOUR-SELF?

OH, PLEASE. CREDIT ME AT *LEAST* WITH THE WIT TO KNOW WHICH ONE OF US I AM.

OWW.

THAT'S *MUCH* MORE IMAGINATIVE, BUT STILL NOT CONVINCING.

I SHALL *NOT* LET YOU GO, OLD GOD.

LET ME...*PLEASE* LET ME GO...CHOKING...

I WILL GIVE YOU...A *RING*...FORGED BY THE DWARFS...IT WILL LET YOU FIND HIDDEN TREASURE, AND KNOW WHAT OTHERS...ARE THINKING...

...GIVE YOU... A SWORD...A HAMMER... AN EAGLE... A TINDER-BOX...

12

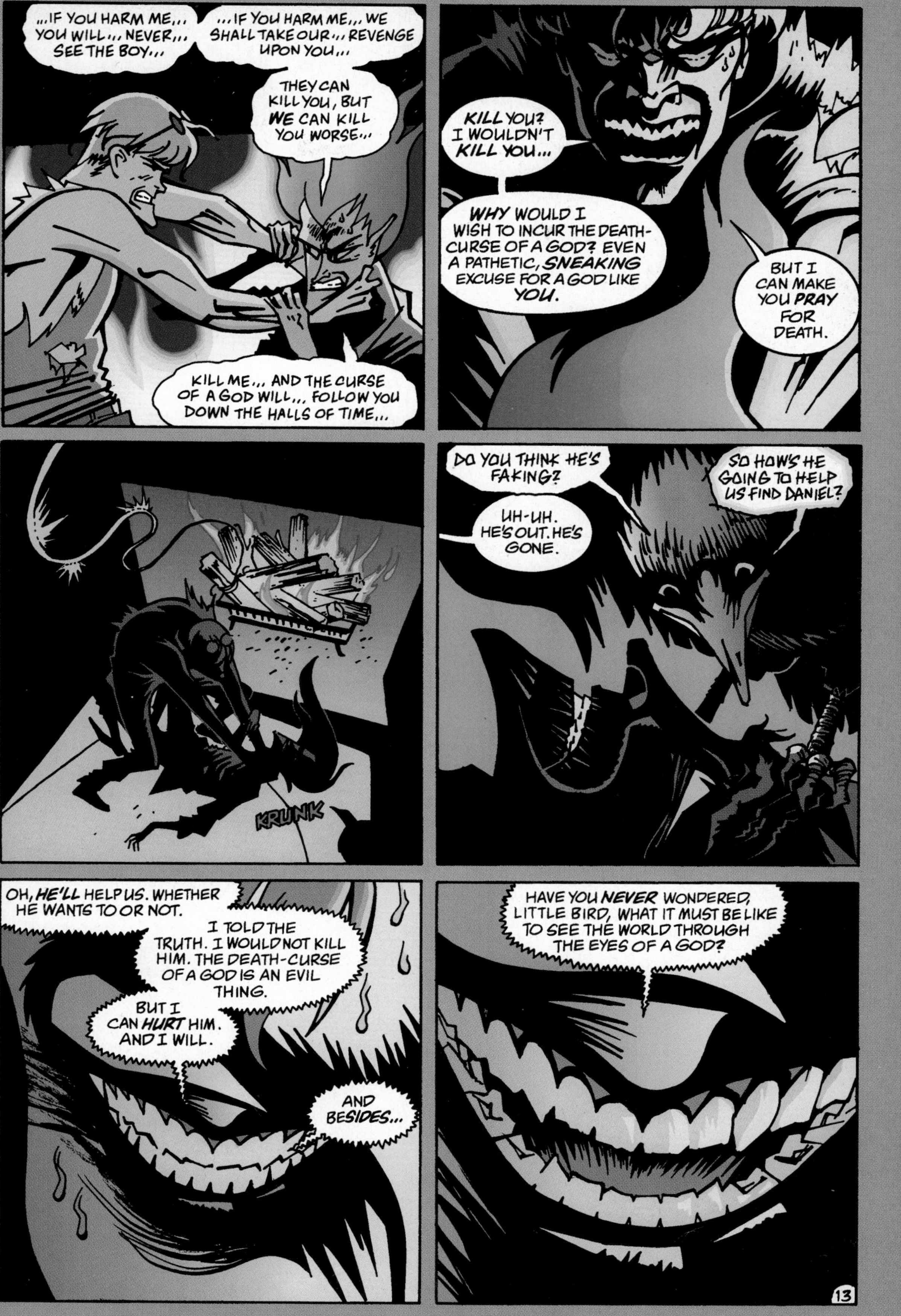
...IF YOU HARM ME,.. YOU WILL... NEVER,.. SEE THE BOY...
...IF YOU HARM ME,.. WE SHALL TAKE OUR... REVENGE UPON YOU...
THEY CAN KILL YOU, BUT WE CAN KILL YOU WORSE...
KILL ME... AND THE CURSE OF A GOD WILL... FOLLOW YOU DOWN THE HALLS OF TIME...
KILL YOU? I WOULDN'T KILL YOU...
WHY WOULD I WISH TO INCUR THE DEATH-CURSE OF A GOD? EVEN A PATHETIC, SNEAKING EXCUSE FOR A GOD LIKE YOU.
BUT I CAN MAKE YOU PRAY FOR DEATH.
KRUNK
DO YOU THINK HE'S FAKING?
UH-UH. HE'S OUT. HE'S GONE.
SO HOW'S HE GOING TO HELP US FIND DANIEL?
OH, HE'LL HELP US. WHETHER HE WANTS TO OR NOT.
I TOLD THE TRUTH. I WOULD NOT KILL HIM. THE DEATH-CURSE OF A GOD IS AN EVIL THING.
BUT I CAN HURT HIM. AND I WILL.
AND BESIDES...
HAVE YOU NEVER WONDERED, LITTLE BIRD, WHAT IT MUST BE LIKE TO SEE THE WORLD THROUGH THE EYES OF A GOD?
13

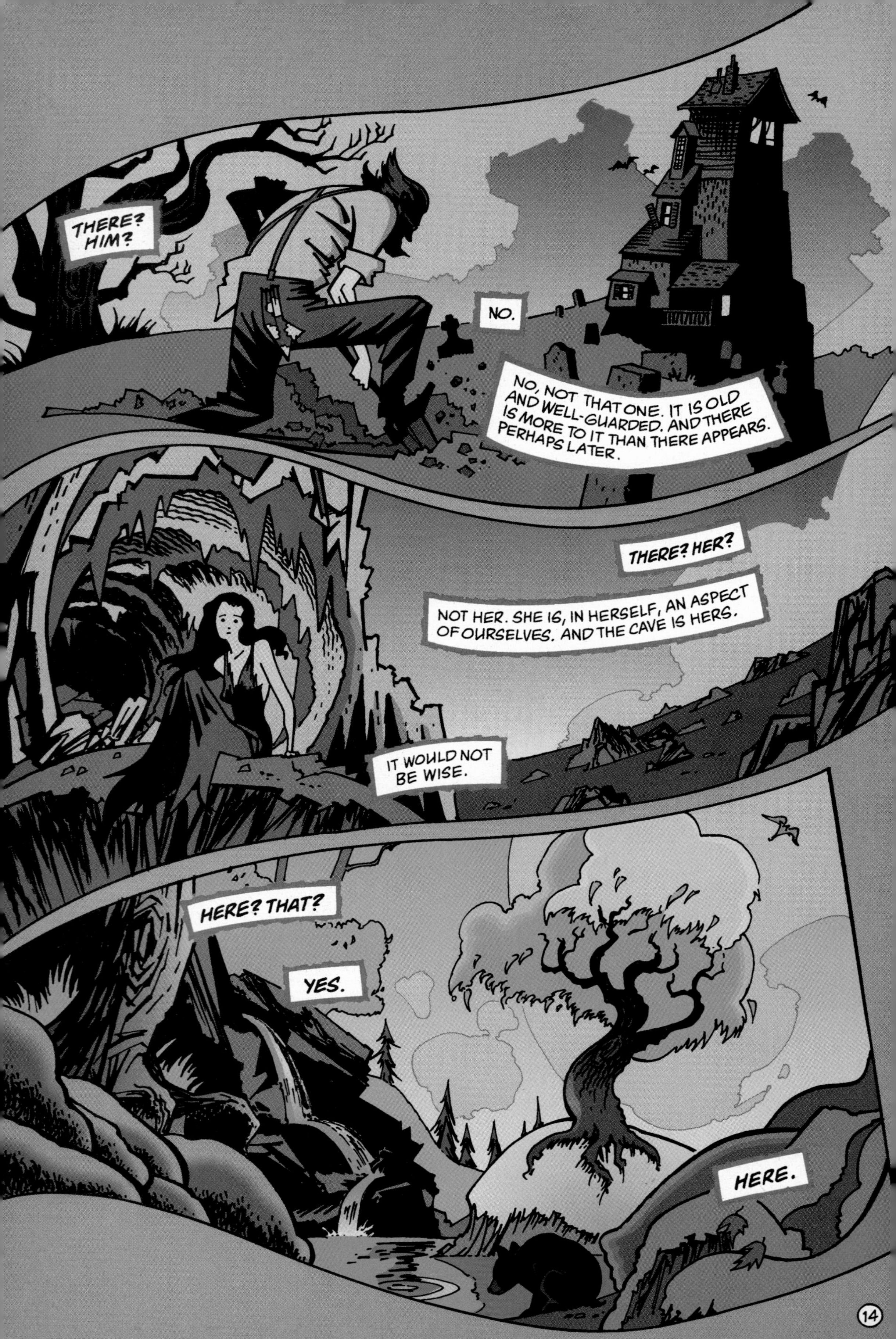
THERE? HIM?
NO.
NO, NOT THAT ONE. IT IS OLD AND WELL-GUARDED. AND THERE IS MORE TO IT THAN THERE APPEARS. PERHAPS LATER.
THERE? HER?
NOT HER. SHE IS, IN HERSELF, AN ASPECT OF OURSELVES. AND THE CAVE IS HERS.
IT WOULD NOT BE WISE.
HERE? THAT?
YES.
HERE.

NOW TO THE ACT OF BLOOD...

THERE IS NO FITTER OFFERING.

AAAAAARK!

MADAME: WHILE I WELCOME GUESTS AND VISITORS OF EVERY KIND, MANNER AND DESCRIPTION, I DO NOT APPRECIATE DAMAGE AND DESTRUCTION TO MY REGULAR INHABITANTS...

DO YOU KNOW WHO WE ARE?

DO YOU?

DO YOU KNOW WHAT WE CAN DO?

NO, MADAME. I DO NOT BELIEVE I HAVE HAD THE PLEASURE...

15

MADAME... I DO **NOT** KNOW YOUR GRIEVANCE, BUT I **DO** WISH THAT WE COULD HAVE **TALKED** ABOUT IT BEFORE YOU RESORTED TO VIOLENCE...

BUT THEN, IF I **HAVE** TO DIE, I HAVE LIVED AN INTERESTING LIFE ...**AND A VARIED** ONE...

AND I... TAKE WITH ME THE **MEMORIES** OF ALL THE THINGS THAT HAVE MOVED ME... TOLD ME I WAS **ALIVE**.

THE GREEN PLAY OF SUNLIGHT THROUGH BIRCH LEAVES...

A **KISS**... ONCE... ON THE **CHEEK**... FROM A **FRIEND**...

I SUPPOSE... I **HAD** ALWAYS HOPED THAT I WOULD DIE QUIETLY, ON MY OWN ... OR THAT I WOULD DIE FOR A **REASON**.

IT OCCURS TO ME **NOW**... THAT ONLY THINGS THAT ARE TRULY **UNREASONABLE** HAVE **REASONS** ... PERHAPS ONLY THE INCONSE... QUENTIAL NEED... **CONS**EQUENCES ...

STILL, I **DO** SO RATHER WISH IT HAD HAPPENED ANOTHER WAY...

HOOM...

16

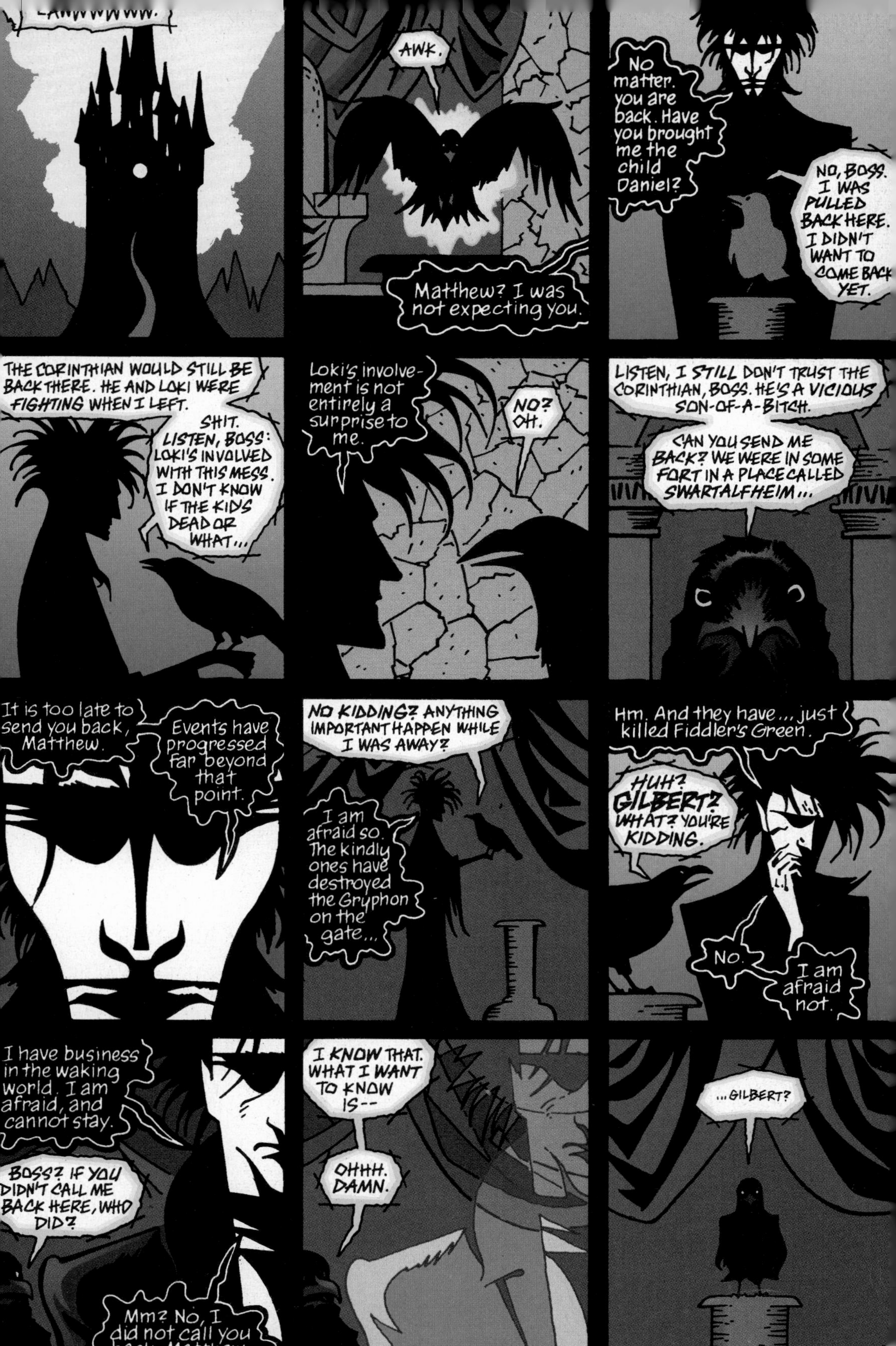
AWK.
Matthew? I was not expecting you.
No matter. you are back. Have you brought me the child Daniel?
NO, BOSS. I WAS PULLED BACK HERE. I DIDN'T WANT TO COME BACK YET.
THE CORINTHIAN WOULD STILL BE BACK THERE. HE AND LOKI WERE FIGHTING WHEN I LEFT.
SHIT. LISTEN, BOSS: LOKI'S INVOLVED WITH THIS MESS. I DON'T KNOW IF THE KID'S DEAD OR WHAT...
Loki's involvement is not entirely a surprise to me.
NO? OH.
LISTEN, I STILL DON'T TRUST THE CORINTHIAN, BOSS. HE'S A VICIOUS SON-OF-A-BITCH.
CAN YOU SEND ME BACK? WE WERE IN SOME FORT IN A PLACE CALLED SWARTALFHEIM...
It is too late to send you back, Matthew.
Events have progressed far beyond that point.
NO KIDDING? ANYTHING IMPORTANT HAPPEN WHILE I WAS AWAY?
I am afraid so. The kindly ones have destroyed the Gryphon on the gate...
Hm. And they have... just killed Fiddler's Green.
HUH? GILBERT? WHAT? YOU'RE KIDDING.
No.
I am afraid not.
I have business in the waking world. I am afraid, and cannot stay.
BOSS? IF YOU DIDN'T CALL ME BACK HERE, WHO DID?
Mm? No, I did not call you back, Matthew.
I KNOW THAT. WHAT I WANT TO KNOW IS--
OHHH. DAMN.
...GILBERT?

LOS ANGELES.

RIPPED DREAM FACES, FLESH ANATOMICAL, HANGING FROM SILVER CHAINS (THE MOON METAL)--A SLICK GLIMPSE OF THE BAR BEHIND--A FLICKER OF SORROW, A FLASH OF REGRET--OLD MEMORIES THAT BEGIN TO STIR AND ARE SUPPRESSED BEFORE THEY CAN TOUCH HER--

--SHE KNOWS, SOMEHOW, THAT SHE DREAMS--

--THEN THE DARKNESS TAKES SHAPE AND FORM; AND, BEFORE SHE IS REQUIRED TO PUT A NAME TO IT, SHE FORCES HER- SELF TO WAKE--

OH. IT'S YOU.

18

SO. HOW HAVE YOU BEEN?

Perfectly satisfactory.

YOU *LOOK* TERRIBLE.

Thank you. You, for your part, look much as I remember. This is where you are living, nowadays?

I WAS AT SCHOOL IN CHICAGO FOR A WHILE. BUT THE *UCLA* LIBRARY FACILITIES ARE BETTER, SO I TRANSFERRED OUT HERE.

YOU WANT TEA? I HAVE *RED ZINGER, MINT MADNESS,* OR A *CRAMP-BARK* AND *CHAMOMILE* BLEND OF MY OWN.

No, thank you.

I am here to end the matter of Lyta Hall. She is causing... damage... to the Dreaming.

TO END THE MATTER? TO *KILL* HER, YOU MEAN?

MM. I *NEVER* UNDERSTOOD YOUR DISLIKE OF KILLING, WHEN IT WAS NECESSARY.

No. You never did, did you?

She has already caused a great deal of trouble. I have little choice in the matter.

YOU HAVE *LESS* CHOICE THAN YOU MIGHT IMAGINE.

I see.

Your handiwork, I presume.

WELL? AREN'T YOU GOING TO STEP *OVER* IT? *KILL* HER? SHE'S JUST ONE RATHER UNDERFED MORTAL WOMAN. SHE WOULDN'T LAST THREE MINUTES AGAINST YOU.

I cannot cross the borders of the circle.

NO, YOU CAN'T.

19

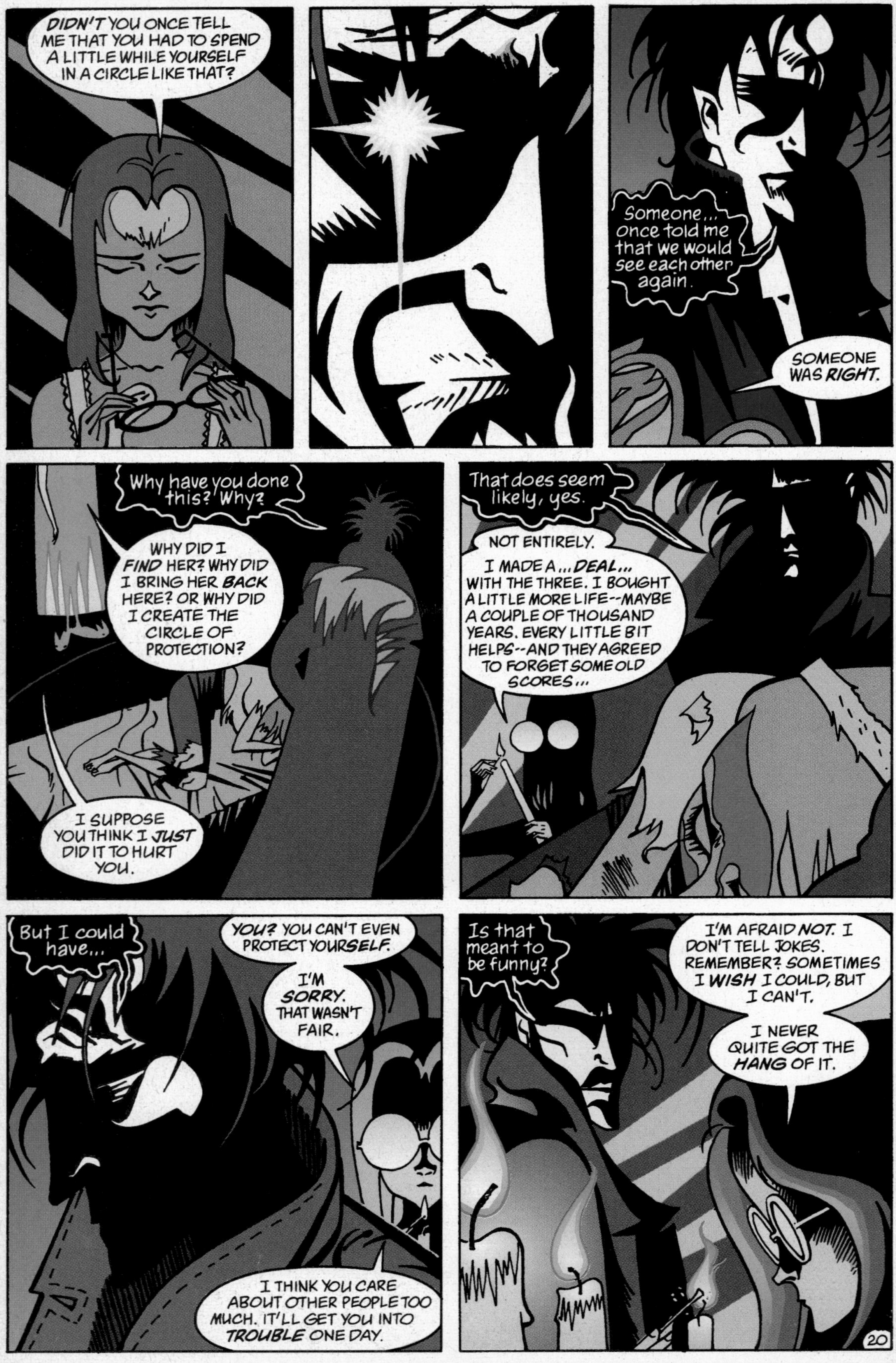
DIDN'T YOU ONCE TELL ME THAT YOU HAD TO SPEND A LITTLE WHILE YOURSELF IN A CIRCLE LIKE THAT?
Someone... once told me that we would see each other again.
SOMEONE WAS RIGHT.
Why have you done this? Why?
WHY DID I FIND HER? WHY DID I BRING HER BACK HERE? OR WHY DID I CREATE THE CIRCLE OF PROTECTION?
I SUPPOSE YOU THINK I JUST DID IT TO HURT YOU.
That does seem likely, yes.
NOT ENTIRELY.
I MADE A...DEAL... WITH THE THREE. I BOUGHT A LITTLE MORE LIFE--MAYBE A COUPLE OF THOUSAND YEARS. EVERY LITTLE BIT HELPS--AND THEY AGREED TO FORGET SOME OLD SCORES...
But I could have...
YOU? YOU CAN'T EVEN PROTECT YOURSELF.
I'M SORRY. THAT WASN'T FAIR.
I THINK YOU CARE ABOUT OTHER PEOPLE TOO MUCH. IT'LL GET YOU INTO TROUBLE ONE DAY.
Is that meant to be funny?
I'M AFRAID NOT. I DON'T TELL JOKES. REMEMBER? SOMETIMES I WISH I COULD, BUT I CAN'T.
I NEVER QUITE GOT THE HANG OF IT.
20

...OH, BUT THE STARS STILL SHINE...

I could kill her. There are many ways to end a human life. I could do it without breaking the circle.

WITHOUT BREAKING THE CIRCLE, PERHAPS. BUT WITHOUT BREAKING THE *RULES?*

...no. I must do it myself, directly.

YOUR KIND ARE SO BOUNDED BY YOUR IDIOT RULES...

EXCEPT FOR YOUR BIG SISTER. SHE DOES WHATEVER SHE PLEASES. SHE'S A *COLD* BITCH, THAT ONE.

OF COURSE, I COULD BREAK THE CIRCLE FOR YOU. I COULD EVEN *KILL* HER FOR YOU. I AM BOUND BY NO RULES. AND I OWE *HER* NOTHING.

BUT WE *HAVE* ESTABLISHED THAT THERE IS NOTHING YOU COULD GIVE ME I WOULD WANT.

I... I did not intend to hurt you.

AND WHAT IF YOU DID *NOT?* INTENT AND OUTCOME ARE SO *RARELY* COINCIDENT.

I simply wanted you to know.

HOW *SWEET.* WELL, IT WAS NICE OF YOU TO DROP BY. IF YOU NEED ME, YOU KNOW WHERE TO FIND ME.

I'LL BE TAKING CARE OF LYTA HERE. TAKING EXTREMELY *GOOD* CARE OF HER.

May your gods be with you.

OH, THEY WILL BE. THERE'S NEVER BEEN ANY DOUBT ABOUT THAT.

21

HOW CHILDISH. MEN!

SO. HELLO, YOUNG RAVEN. I DON'T BELIEVE I'VE HAD THE PLEASURE...?

I'M MATTHEW. MATT. MATTHEW. YOU ARE?

JUST CALL ME RAVEN. NOAH DID.

YOU WERE NOAH'S RAVEN? ONE OF A COUPLE, EH?

VERY FUNNY. ONE OF SEVEN, ACTUALLY.

NOAH. THE OLD LUSH. YES. HIS NAME WAS UTNAPISHTIM BACK THEN, MIND YOU.

HE HAD MORE LUCK WITH THE DOVES. THEY COME BACK. RAVENS GO WHERE THEY WANT TO. BUT I WAS HIS FIRST. AND I WAS HIS, FIRST.

SO. WHERE WERE YOU CALLED HERE FROM?

SWARTALFHEIM. BUT I LIVE HERE.

WELL, SOMEBODY'S GOT TO, I SUPPOSE.

YOU'VE NOT BEEN A RAVEN LONG, HAVE YOU?

ABOUT FIVE YEARS, I THINK. IS THAT LONG?

HEHHH. YOU'RE PRACTICALLY A CHICK.

22

THE THING YOU OUGHT TO REMEMBER ABOUT RAVENS, IS THAT WE BELONG EQUALLY TO BOTH GENDERS. YOU DON'T SEE THAT EVERY DAY. BUT WE'RE AS LIKELY TO BE THE MORRIGAN'S AS ODIN'S, AS LIKELY TO BE EVE'S AS DREAMS.

OTHER THAN THAT WE HAVE NOTHING IN COMMON, SAVE A LOVE OF FINE CONVERSATION, AND A TENDENCY TO VIEW A BATTLE AS A PRELUDE TO FINE DINING...

KAAAAR.

SO, YOUNG MATTHEW. YOU WANT TO GO FIRST?

I CAN'T. HE WAS MY FRIEND. I JUST CAME DOWN TO SAY GOODBYE.

SO? LISTEN, AN EYE'S JUST AN EYE. A FEW MORE DAYS, AND HE'LL BE SOMETHING NOT EVEN A RAVEN WOULD EAT. OVER TO THE ANTS...

I SAID NO.

I DON'T KNOW IF THINGS DO ROT IN DREAMS OR NOT. YOU'D THINK I'D KNOW THAT, BUT I DON'T.

KAAAWR. SMELLS REAL TASTY.

POOR GUY. ANYWAY... I'M AFRAID THERE'S GOING TO BE LOTS MORE WHERE THAT CAME FROM.

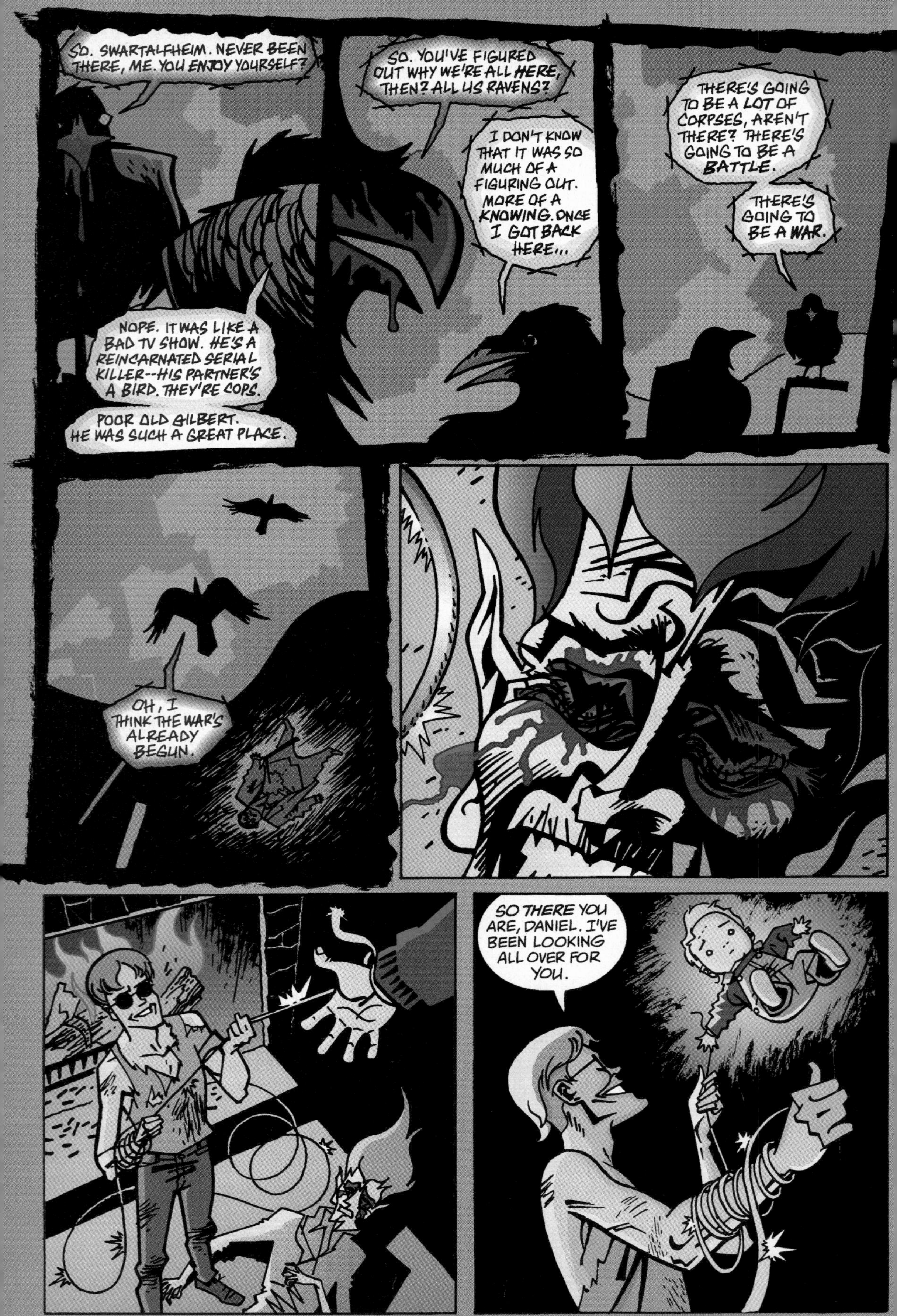
SO. SWARTALFHEIM. NEVER BEEN THERE, ME. YOU ENJOY YOURSELF?
NOPE. IT WAS LIKE A BAD TV SHOW. HE'S A REINCARNATED SERIAL KILLER--HIS PARTNER'S A BIRD. THEY'RE COPS.
POOR OLD GILBERT. HE WAS SUCH A GREAT PLACE.
SO. YOU'VE FIGURED OUT WHY WE'RE ALL HERE, THEN? ALL US RAVENS?
I DON'T KNOW THAT IT WAS SO MUCH OF A FIGURING OUT. MORE OF A KNOWING. ONCE I GOT BACK HERE...
THERE'S GOING TO BE A LOT OF CORPSES, AREN'T THERE? THERE'S GOING TO BE A BATTLE.
THERE'S GOING TO BE A WAR.
OH, I THINK THE WAR'S ALREADY BEGUN.
SO THERE YOU ARE, DANIEL. I'VE BEEN LOOKING ALL OVER FOR YOU.

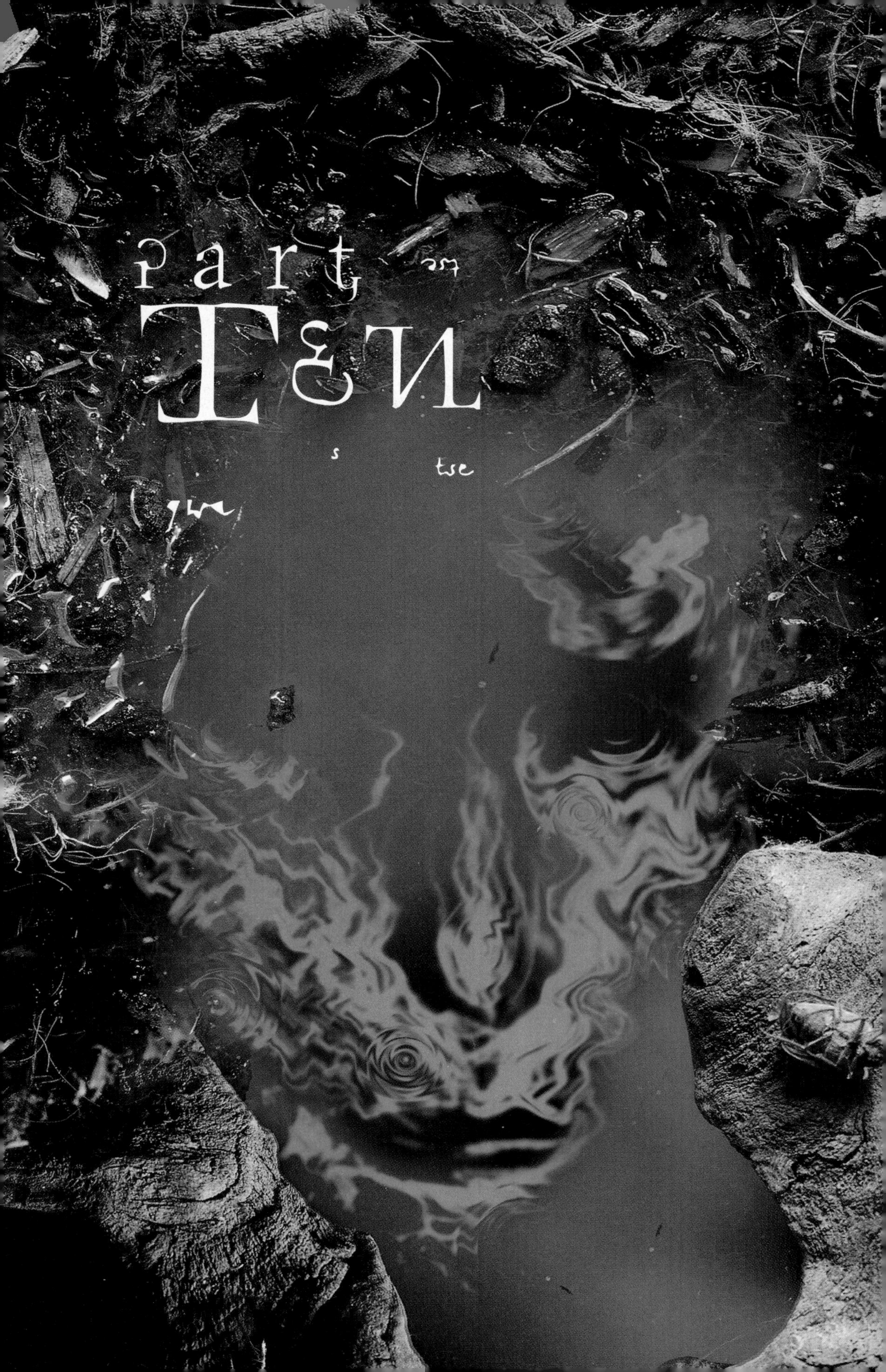
part
TEN

THERE WE GO, YOUNG DANIEL. SO, WHAT HAVE YOU BEEN DOING, EH? OFF HAVING LITTLE ADVENTURES?

WELL, I'VE BEEN SENT TO BRING YOU TO THE DREAMING, AND THAT'S *JUST* WHERE WE'RE GOING.

THERE.

deeming?

THAT'S RIGHT. THERE WAS A BIRD HERE SOMEWHERE, ALTHOUGH HE SEEMS TO HAVE GOOFED OFF ON US. BUT DON'T WORRY.

WE'LL GIVE HIM A GOOD *TELLING-OFF,* EH?

YOU MIGHT AS WELL SHOW YOURSELF. I'VE GOT THE BOY, NOW.

HOW DID YOU KNOW THAT I WAS *HERE?*

YOU BREATHE TOO LOUDLY, LITTLE CREATURE.

WHAT MANNER OF THING ARE YOU, ANYWAY?

I AM THE *PUCK,* CALLED *ROBIN GOODFELLOW.* I AM A TRICKSTER, AN ANTIC PRANKSTER, A WILL O' THE WISP.

"THINGS FALL APART, THE CENTRE CANNOT HOLD, MERE ANARCHY IS LOOSE UPON THE WORLD."

THAT'S ME.

EX-JESTER TO THE KING OF FAERIE.

I AM KNOWN AS THE CORINTHIAN. WHY DID YOU STEAL THIS BOY?

NONE O' YOUR BEESWAX. I'VE STOL'N MANY A CHILD IN MY TIME, LEFT MANY A CHANGELING IN ITS CRIB TO STARE WITH OLD EYES FROM A BABY'S FACE.

WHO WERE YOU WORKING FOR? WHO TOLD YOU TO STEAL THE BOY?

I COULD ANSWER YOU ENDLESSLY, AND PERHAPS YOU EXPECT ME TO; BUT I LACK THE TIME AND THE INCLINATION, AND THUS I CHOOSE TO KEEP MY REASONS --AND MY PRINCIPALS -- TO MYSELF.

YOU'VE GOT THE LADDIE NOW, AND A PRETTY CHILD HE IS TOO.

SO THE WOLF AND THE RAVEN ARE VERY PRETTY FOOLS WHEN THEY ARE YOUNG... EH?

MOUSE, MOUSE, GO BACK TO YOUR HOUSE, YOUR DAUGHTER'S A STRUMPET, AND SO IS YOUR SPOUSE.

WE BURNED AWAY MOST OF HIS MORTALITY, YOU KNOW.

NOT ALL OF IT.

BUT ANOTHER FEW DAYS, ANOTHER FEW FIRES, AND WE WOULD HAVE HAD IT ALL.

SO. DO WE FIGHT NOW, ROBIN GOODFELLOW?

A PUCK IS HARDER BY FAR TO HURT THAN SOME LITTLE LORD OF MALICE FROM THE LAND OF ICE AND SNOW. WE PUCKS ARE OLD AND HARD AND WILD...

BUT NO; I'LL LEAVE, I THINK, TAKE MY ADIEUS OF THIS DULL SPHERE.

I'LL RETURN TO FAERIE, PERHAPS. FOR A SHORT WHILE. VEX MY LORD AUBERON; PLAGUE MAB, MAEVE, TITANIA, OR ONE OF THE OTHER FACETS OF THE QUEEN...

CREATION IS MY PLAYGROUND, AFTER ALL.

pway?

2

IT WAS A *DELIGHT* TO MAKE YOUR ACQUAINTANCE, MESSIRE THE CORINTHIAN. AND I SHALL RESTRAIN MYSELF FROM ENQUIRING WHETHER YOU TAKE YOUR NAME FROM THE LETTERS, THE PILLARS, THE LEATHER, THE PLACE, OR THE MODE OF BEHAVIOR...

YOU GAINED CONSCIOUSNESS TWO MINUTES BACK. YOUR BREATHING BETRAYS YOU TOO, LOKI.

KILL ME.

GIVE ME BACK MY EYES. OR KILL ME.

NO. I SHALL KEEP THE EYES, AND I SHALL LET YOU LIVE.

GOODNIGHT.

PLEASE... PLEASE, KILL ME...

3

HEH, LOKI SKY-WALKER. I LEFT ONE EYE WITH MIMIR THE BODILESS, TRADED IT FOR WISDOM. YOU'VE NOW LOST BOTH EYES, BUT I FEAR YOU HAVE HAD THE WORST OF THE BARGAIN.

GRIMNIR? BLOOD BROTHER? ...MY FRIEND?

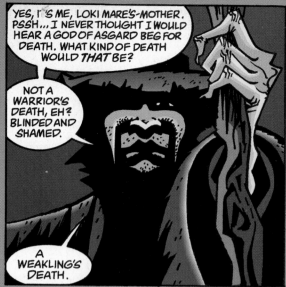

YES, IT'S ME, LOKI MARE'S-MOTHER. PSSH... I NEVER THOUGHT I WOULD HEAR A GOD OF ASGARD BEG FOR DEATH. WHAT KIND OF DEATH WOULD THAT BE?

NOT A WARRIOR'S DEATH, EH? BLINDED AND SHAMED.

A WEAKLING'S DEATH.

ODIN... THIS IS NOT WHAT IT APPEARS TO BE.

OH, SO?

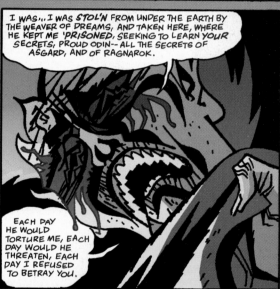

I WAS... I WAS STOL'N FROM UNDER THE EARTH BY THE WEAVER OF DREAMS, AND TAKEN HERE, WHERE HE KEPT ME 'PRISONED, SEEKING TO LEARN YOUR SECRETS, PROUD ODIN-- ALL THE SECRETS OF ASGARD, AND OF RAGNAROK.

EACH DAY HE WOULD TORTURE ME, EACH DAY WOULD HE THREATEN, EACH DAY I REFUSED TO BETRAY YOU.

FINALLY HE SENDED HIS CUTTHROAT, TO TEAR MINE EYES FROM MY HEAD, WOULD I NEVER REVEAL TO HIM THE SECRETS OF ODIN.

KILL ME, I SAID TO HIM. I WOULD PROUDLY DIE, RATHER THAN BETRAY A SINGLE CONFIDENCE.

HMPH. AND THAT'S THE TRUTH YOU TELL ME, LOKI? ANSWER ME HONESTLY. FOR IF THIS IS TRUE, THEN IT'S WAR BETWEEN ASGARD AND THE DREAMING.

TRUE AS I BREATHE.

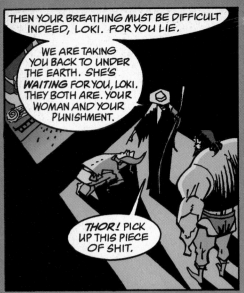

THEN YOUR BREATHING MUST BE DIFFICULT INDEED, LOKI. FOR YOU LIE.

WE ARE TAKING YOU BACK TO UNDER THE EARTH. SHE'S *WAITING* FOR YOU, LOKI. THEY BOTH ARE. YOUR WOMAN AND YOUR PUNISHMENT.

THOR! PICK UP THIS PIECE OF SHIT.

CARRY IT. CAREFULLY, MIND.

PSST!...YOUR WIFE, THOR. THE LADY *SIF,* SHE HAS A BIRTHMARK, HIGH ON THE INSIDE OF HER THIGH, IN THE SHAPE OF AN ANVIL.

HOW DO *YOU* KNOW THAT?

QUIET, BACK THERE! DO NOT *TALK* TO HIM, THOR.

SHE LET ME *LICK* IT. SHE LET ME DO FAR MORE THAN THAT. SHE WENT DOWN ON HER KNEES, AND SWORE TO BE MY SLAVE. SHE LET ME WHIP HER WITH A WHIP OF OILED LEATHER.

SHE LET ME EXPLORE EVERY CREVICE OF HER BODY. SHE LET ME *DO* THINGS SHE SWORE BLIND SHE HAD NEVER LET YOU DO TO HER. AND WHEN I WAS *SATED,* SHE *BEGGED* ME-- SHE PLEADED WITH ME TO COME BACK TO HER AND DO IT *AGAIN*...

I ... I WILL *KILL* YOU, SMASH YOUR *SKULL* LIKE A *STONE*...

5

THOR! STOP IT!

BUT HE SAID--

HE *WANTS* YOU TO *KILL* HIM, THOR. HE WANTS TO *DIE*. HE WAS LYING TO YOU. HE *TELLS LIES*. YOU *KNOW* THAT.

HIS PUNISHMENT IS *WORSE* THAN DEATH. DEATH WOULD BE *SO* EASY.

PUT HIM DOWN, HERE.

I *BIND* YOU, LOKI SKY WALKER, MALICE-MONGER. I BIND YOU WITH THE GUTS OF NARVI, YOUR SON. I BIND YOU WITH FROST AND WITH FIRE, AND WITH THE WEIGHT OF THE WORLD.

WOMAN. SIGYN LOKI'S-WIFE. HE TREATED YOU ILL. HE LEFT YOU HERE BENEATH THE EARTH WHILE HE WANDERED FREE.

HE LOST HIS EYES, AND HIS NECK HAS BEEN BROKEN. HE HAS DISGRACED HIMSELF.

YOU DO NOT *HAVE* TO STAY HERE. *LET* THE SNAKE DRIP ITS POISON INTO THE SOCKETS OF HIS EYES. LET HIM *TAKE* HIS PAIN. HE *DESERVES* IT.

VERY WELL. *SNAKE!* LET FLOW YOUR VENOM.

6

DRIP

ODIN? HE NEVER TOUCHED HER, DID HE? MY SWEET SIF? HE NEVER DID THAT STUFF?

YOU *BELIEVED* HIS LIES, THOR? EVEN FOR A MOMENT?

HH. 'COURSE NOT.

AS THE FIRST DROPS OF POISON STRIKE LOKI'S FACE, BURNING THEIR WAY INTO THE EMPTY SOCKETS IN A FRENZIED EXPLOSION OF COLOR AND PAIN, HE BEGINS TO CURSE HER.

DRIP

HE DISSECTS HER WITH HIS WORDS, WHIPS HER WITH OBSCENITIES AND BRUISES HER WITH CURSES. SHE BEGINS TO CRY, SOFTLY, DEEP IN HER THROAT; THEN TEARS WELL UP AND BURN HER PALE EYES, WHICH SHE HAD IMAGINED FAR BEYOND TEARS. THE SALT-WARM DROPS FALL ON HER HUSBAND'S FACE, AND HE WINCES AT EACH DROP...

DRIP

EACH WORD IS LIKE A SLAP, A BLOW, A KICK, A BURN.

DRIP

AND SHE TAKES IT.

SLOWLY THE SILVER BOWL BEGINS TO FILL WITH POISON ONCE MORE. HE IS TIED, HE REALIZES, BY HIS CHILD; HE CANNOT LEAVE. HE WILL NOT LEAVE UNTIL THE WORLD ENDS...

I'M PLEASED YOU CAME BACK, MY LOVE, WHISPERS HIS WIFE.

...AND HE BEGINS TO LAUGH INANELY, HIGH AND WORDLESS.

HE TAKES A DEEP BREATH AND THEN, BROKEN-NECKED—HEAD LOLLING, EYESOCKETS BLOODIED AND HOLLOWED, HE BEGINS TO CURSE HER ONCE MORE.

DRIP

YUHYUHYUHYUH YOU CUHCAN'T KILL ME.

LITTLE FAT MAN, YOU SMELL LIKE POPCORN AND SWEAT. OF COURSE WE CAN KILL YOU.

YOU'RE THE FUHFURIES.

I NUHKNOW THE RULES. YOU DON'T KERKILL ANYONE. YOU DON'T HURT ANYONE. YOU FUHFIND SOMEONE WHO SPILLED FAMILY BLOOD, AND YOU DRIVE THEM TO SUICIDE OR TO RERERE-PENTANCE.

I NUHNEVER SPILLED FAMILY BLOOD. THAT WAS...

I MUHMEAN. YOU CAN'T KILL ME.

arwk?

WE CAN. IF WE WANT TO.

"YOU SCARCELY EXIST. YOU'RE A DREAM OF A GHOST OF A MEMORY OF SOMEONE WHO, ONE SUSPECTS, NEVER EXISTED IN THE FIRST PLACE. YOUR DEATH WILL HARDLY BE A REAL DEATH."

"NONE OF YOU ARE TRULY DEAD UNTIL MORPHEUS HIMSELF IS DEAD. ARE YOU?"

AND THIS WILL HARDLY BE YOUR FIRST DEATH, WILL IT?

YOU MUSTN'T KILL ME. YOU DON'T LOVE ME.

YOU D-DON'T EVEN KNOW ME.

"*FAERIE* (WHICH IS A *PLACE*, BUT PERHAPS ALSO, I LIKE TO THINK, AN *ATTITUDE*) IS, LIKE *ALL* PLACES, INHABITED BY PEOPLE (A WORD I USE HERE IN ITS WIDEST POSSIBLE SENSE), GOVERNED *ONLY* BY RULES OF ETIQUETTE, BY FORMALITIES AND MODES OF BEHAVIOR: IN SHORT, BY *CUSTOM*."

CUSTOMS HAVE *POWER*, AND ONLY THE TRULY BRAVE, OR THE TRULY *DANGEROUS*, WILL *DEFY* THEM. ONE MUST *NOT* OFFEND AGAINST THE NOTIONS OF ONE'S NEIGHBORS.

BUT *CLURACAN*: WE ARE CREATURES OF *ANARCHY* AND *MADNESS*. *WE* ARE *THE WILD*. HOW CAN YOU *POSSIBLY* DESCRIBE US AS CREATURES OF *CUSTOM*?

LOOK YOU-- HERE AT OUR REVELS, SOME OF US GAVOTTE, OTHERS MINUET, OTHERS LURCH AND SPIN AND JIG.

THERE IS *NO* ORDER HERE, NO PATTERN, NO...*CUSTOM.*

SOME OF US ARE IN *RAGS*, SOME IN *TAGS*, SOME IN *VELVET GOWNS.* WHERE IS THE CONVENTIONAL HERE? I SEE NOTHING BUT *DIVERSITY.*

REALLY? I SEE NOTHING BUT DULL ROUTINE.

9

FRANKLY, MENTON, I WOULD FIND IT DIFFICULT TO IMAGINE ANY ACTION HERE THAT WOULD SO MUCH AS DRAW COMMENT. WERE THE QUEEN *HERSELF* TO PICK SOME WITLESS HUMAN FROM THE CROWD AND ANNOUNCE THAT SHE WAS TAKING HIM AS A LOVER--

THEN NO ONE WOULD BE THE *SLIGHTEST* BIT SHOCKED. OR EVEN SURPRISED.

WELL, *THERE'S* SOMETHING TO SURPRISE!

"THAT *CAN'T* BE HIM."

"OH, THAT'S *HIM*, ALL RIGHT. HE HASN'T CHANGED."

"HMPH. HE WAS NEVER HER PET BEFORE."

"NOR IS HE NOW."

SEE, CLURACAN. *THAT* WAS A WONDER.

SEE? WHAT AM I MEANT TO SEE? A PRODIGAL PUCK RETURNS AFTER THREE HUNDRED YEARS, AND *STILL* IT CAUSES NO MORE THAN RAISED EYEBROWS.

BY THE SILVER APPLES OF THE MOON--

WHAT HAS SHE *DONE?*

10

"WHO in AVALON is THAT?"

"THAT LITTLE ELF-THING. Is SHE invited to the QUEEN'S REVELS? SURELY NOT."

"WHO IS SHE? CLURACAN, do you KNOW THAT CREATURE?"

"THAT IS MY SISTER, NUALA."

"BUT SHE HAS NO GLAMOUR on her! HOW DARE she appear here, like that. WHAT CAN SHE be THINKING?"

NUALA. IS THIS A DELIBERATE INSULT?

UH, NO. NO, YOUR MAJESTY.

I GAVE THE MATTER A CERTAIN AMOUNT OF THOUGHT, AND DECIDED I FELT MOST COMFORTABLE WITHOUT. UM. GLAMOUR.

OF COURSE, SHE'S A DREAM OF A GIRL. GOOD-HEARTED. AND SHE'S FAMILY.

JUST MAKES IT MORE PAINFUL TO WATCH HER DIG HERSELF IN SO DEEP.

AH. SHE'LL TAKE BANISHMENT HARD, I'LL WAGER.

YOU...FELT... COMFORTABLE?

CLOTHE YOURSELF, NUALA. IMMEDIATELY.

BUT MAJESTY, I--

I DON'T-- I, YOUR MAJESTY, I WILL NOT BE.... I....

OH.

MM. I SUPPOSE THAT'S BETTER.

BUT--YOUR *MAJESTY*--

NUALA!

WHAT MY SISTER WAS *ABOUT* TO SAY, MAJESTY, IS THAT *SHE* HAS WON OUR *BET*.

I, UH, I WAGERED NUALA THAT THERE WAS *NOTHING* SHE COULD DO NOR WEAR SO OUTRÉ AS TO CAUSE COMMENT AT OUR REVELS, AND SHE SWORE TO PROVE ME WRONG.

NUALA, YOU *WITTY* LITTLE MINX, UPSTAGING EVEN THE *PUCK* BY YOUR ENTRANCE...

SO THIS WAS *YOUR* FAULT, CLURACAN?

YOU'VE FOUND ME OUT? AYE ME. I SHALL TAKE MY BANISHMENT MANFULLY.

IF THE *PUCK* CAN VANISH FOR THREE CENTURIES, I AM SURE I CAN FIND SOMETHING TO KEEP ME OCCUPIED.

AND WHILE I THINK OF HIM, WHERE *IS* OUR *MERRY* WONDERER OF THE NIGHT?

AH! *THERE* YOU ARE, SIRRAH, SKULKING AND LURKING.

NOW, GOOD FELLOW-- SURELY THE TWO TOASTS OF OUR REVELS SHOULD TREAD A MEASURE TOGETHER? I MUST DISCUSS THE DETAILS OF MY IMPENDING PUNISHMENT WITH OUR MOST GRACIOUS QUEEN.

NOW, MAJESTY. BANISHMENT, DECAPITATION, OR SOMETHING LINGERING WITH BOILING OIL IN IT SOMEWHERE?

CLURACAN, YOU ARE A *RASCAL*...

MILADY? MAY I HAVE THE PLEASURE?

AS IF I HAVE A *CHOICE?* CERTAINLY I WILL DANCE WITH YOU, PUCK.

12

SO...YOU HAVE RETURNED TO FAERIE?

AYE, BUT NOT FOR LONG. IT *BORES* ME. VEXING NIXIES AND PESTERING BOGGARTS LACKS ANY SPICE.

WHY DO YOU TAKE SUCH *JOY* IN CONFUSION, ROBIN GOODFELLOW?

BECAUSE I AM TRUE TO MY NATURE, LADY NUALA.

HOW WAS YOUR SERVITUDE WITH THE LORD SHAPER?

IT WAS... EDUCATIONAL. THE LORD SHAPER IS... MOST *SINGULAR*.

A PALE AND PRISSY, POMPOUS, PREENING PRIG. A PRICK-ME-DAINTY POPINJAY. A PIG.

THE LORD SHAPER IS *NONE* OF THOSE THINGS.

WAS NONE OF THOSE THINGS.

WAS?

MORE OR LESS, LADY. WE SET THE FURIES AROUND HIS EARS, MY ASSOCIATE AND I. IF HE IS NOT YET GONE, HE WILL BE SOON.

THERE. IS THAT NOT *FINE* REVENGE FOR TAKING A FAIRY LADY AS HIS SCULLERY MAID?

YOU *HURT* HIM... FOR *ME?*

NO. I CARE *NOTHING* FOR YOU. NOT ONE *FIG* NOR *JOT* NOR *TITTLE*. I DID IT BECAUSE... IT *AMUSED* ME.

HM. YOUR OAFISH BROTHER HAS MOLLIFIED YOUR QUEEN, I SEE.

MY BROTHER -- WHO IS NO OAF-- COULD MOLLIFY A MINOTAUR.

YOU WERE WEARING YOUR TRUE SHAPE. IS THAT BECAUSE THE LATE DREAM KING *LIKED* IT?

...YOU ARE SIMPLY TRYING TO UPSET ME...

NOTHING COULD HURT MY LORD SHAPER. YOU HAVE LOST YOUR TALENT TO VEX IN THREE CENTURIES, PUCK.

AND *YOU* ARE A *VERY* STUPID CREATURE.

I *SWEAR* ON MY *NAME*. SOON HE WILL BE REMEMBERED ONLY BY ANTIQUARIES. BUT THEN, WE ARE *ALL* IMPROVED BY THE GLOW OF MEMORY.

"WHERE IS THE LADY NUALA GOING?"

13

"A MURDER OF RAVENS HAUNTS THE DREAMING: SLOW WINGS FLAPPING BLEAKLY LIKE SHADOWS OR OLD MEN STUMBLING, BATTLE-BIRDS, DARK DWELLERS IN THE AFTERMATH."

"WE CROAK OUR RAVEN SECRETS, EACH TO EACH, SHARE OUR GRIM JOY AND SHARE OUR HISTORIES, AS HIDDEN KINGS, LOST GODS, DARK THOUGHTS, BEADED EYES, RIDING COLD WINDS AND STORMS."

UNSATISFIED, WE PICK AT RANDOM CORPSES. CREATURES OF DEATH, CERTAIN OF FEASTS TO COME, OF CARRION: THE SPOILS OF THE NIGHT.

A MURDER OF RAVENS: DARK--

--HERALDS OF MISFORTUNE...

THPLAT!

KAAR!

YAGETTOUTTAHERE! GWAN! SHOO!

JESUS. AND I THOUGHT THE BOSS'S BIRDS WAS BAD. AT LEAST NONE OF THEM THOUGHT THEY WAS POETS.

YEAH, YEAH. POINT TAKEN. EXCEPT WHATSISNAME.

OKAY. ARISTEAS OF MARMORA. LIKE I GIVE A TOSS. SO NOW THAT THE BEAK'S OUTTA THE WAY, IF I C'N HAVE YOUR ATTENTION...?

14

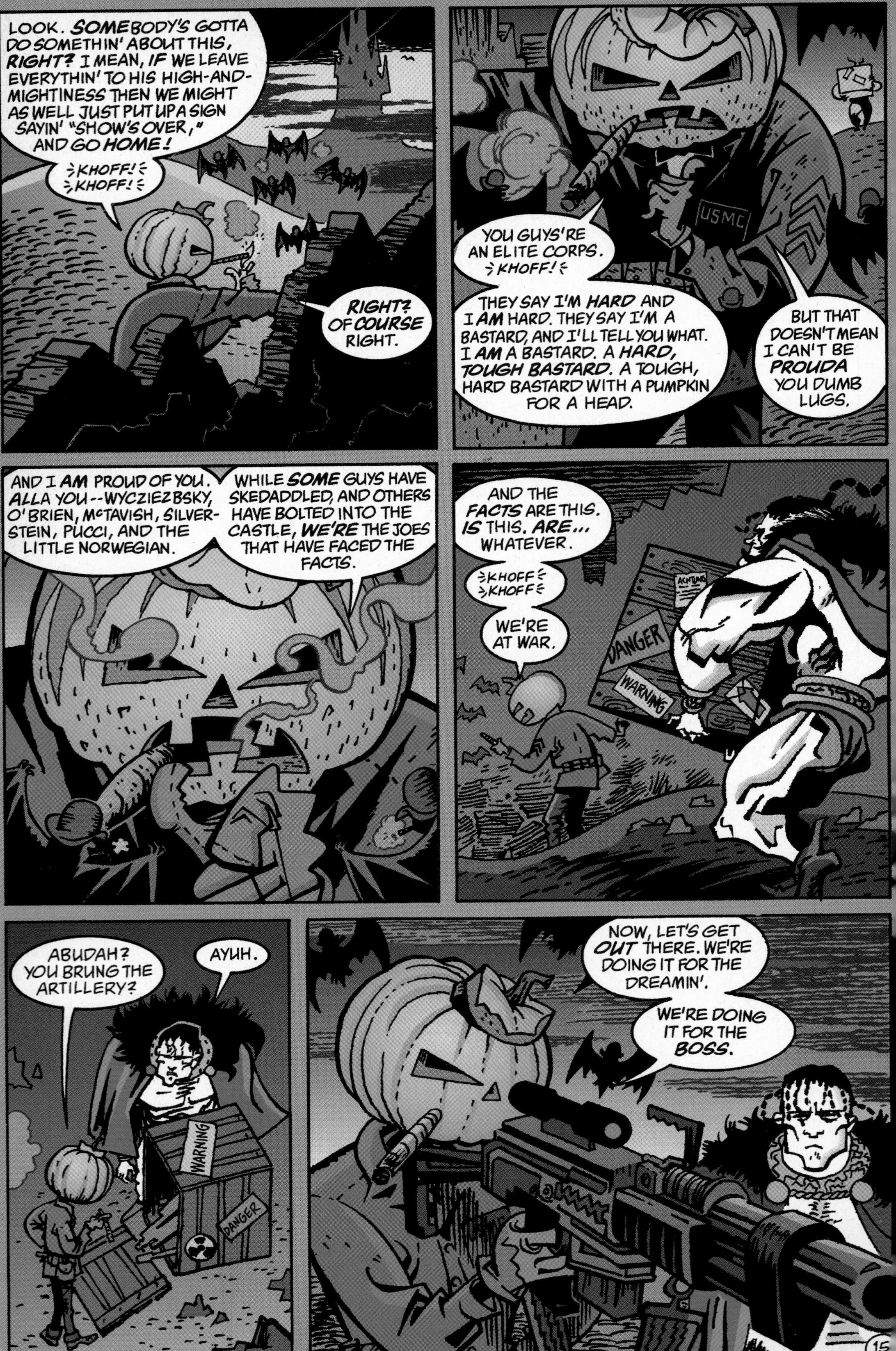
LOOK. SOMEBODY'S GOTTA DO SOMETHIN' ABOUT THIS, RIGHT? I MEAN, IF WE LEAVE EVERYTHIN' TO HIS HIGH-AND-MIGHTINESS THEN WE MIGHT AS WELL JUST PUT UP A SIGN SAYIN' "SHOW'S OVER," AND GO HOME!
KHOFF! KHOFF!
RIGHT? OF COURSE RIGHT.
YOU GUYS'RE AN ELITE CORPS. KHOFF!
THEY SAY I'M HARD AND I AM HARD. THEY SAY I'M A BASTARD, AND I'LL TELL YOU WHAT. I AM A BASTARD. A HARD, TOUGH BASTARD. A TOUGH, HARD BASTARD WITH A PUMPKIN FOR A HEAD.
BUT THAT DOESN'T MEAN I CAN'T BE PROUDA YOU DUMB LUGS.
USMC
AND I AM PROUD OF YOU. ALLA YOU--WYCZIEZBSKY, O'BRIEN, McTAVISH, SILVERSTEIN, PUCCI, AND THE LITTLE NORWEGIAN.
WHILE SOME GUYS HAVE SKEDADDLED, AND OTHERS HAVE BOLTED INTO THE CASTLE, WE'RE THE JOES THAT HAVE FACED THE FACTS.
AND THE FACTS ARE THIS. IS THIS. ARE... WHATEVER.
KHOFF KHOFF
WE'RE AT WAR.
ACHTUNG
DANGER
WARNING
ABUDAH? YOU BRUNG THE ARTILLERY?
AYUH.
WARNING
DANGER
NOW, LET'S GET OUT THERE. WE'RE DOING IT FOR THE DREAMIN'.
WE'RE DOING IT FOR THE BOSS.

LET'S GO!

≴KHOFF KHOFF KHOFF...≵

HEY! I CAN SEE YOU.

GAARRR.

THROW DOWN YOUR WEAPONS. JUST SURRENDER PEACEFULLY AND NO ONE'LL GET HURT.

YOU? WHAT ARE YOU?

ME? LADY, I'M YOUR *WORST NIGHTMARE*-- A PUMPKIN WITH A GUN.

WE *HAVE* NO NIGHTMARES.

WE ARE THE HOUNDS OF HADES.

GODS FEAR US, DEMONS FEAR US. WE HAVE HOUNDED KINGS AND ANGELS. WE HAVE TAKEN VENGEANCE ON WORLDS AND ON UNIVERSES.

WE ARE THE KINDLY ONES. WE ARE THE EUMENIDES.

YEAH? WELL, EUMENIDES THIS!

BUDDABUDDABUDDABUDDA!

16

MERVYN'S DEAD.

Yes.

HOW... HOW **DARE** YOU LET THAT HAPPEN, LORD? **HOW DARE YOU?**

You will not speak to me like that, Lucien.

I DOUBT I'LL BE ALIVE TOMORROW, LORD. ON THAT BASIS I FIND IT PARTICULARLY EASY TO SAY **EXACTLY** WHAT I THINK...,

I CANNOT BE**LIEVE** THAT YOU COULD LET **HIM** --OF ALL PEOPLE... MERVYN WAS A FINE SOUL...

"He is far from the only one."

"HE **DIDN'T** DESERVE IT."

"...none of you deserve it."

YOU CAN'T JUST **SIT** HERE WHILE THEY HURT US, TO HURT YOU.

WHY AREN'T YOU RESTORING THE THINGS THEY DESTROY?

SO ARE YOU GOING TO **LET** THEM KILL US ALL? ARE YOU GOING TO LET THEM PULL THE DREAMING DOWN AROUND YOUR EARS?

They will not leave until I am destroyed, by my own hand or another's.

I... I knew what I was going to do, Lucien. I was going to remove the mortal woman Lyta Hall. She is what powers this aspect of the Furies.

That proved... impractical.

AND **NOW**, LORD?

Now, I am... considering.

17

WHERE IS THE LADY NUALA GOING? THE LADY NUALA IS GOING TO WALK IN THE *WOOD BETWEEN* THE *WORLDS.*

AND *WHY* IS *THAT?* BECAUSE THE LADY NUALA IS *SICK* OF FAERIE, AND THE LADY NUALA *LACKS* THE AUTHORITY TO *LEAVE* THE DAMNED PLACE.

SO THE LADY NUALA IS MAKING THE BEST OF UN-WELCOME CIRCUM-STANCES, WHICH *IS,* IN AN EGGSHELL, THE STORY OF LADY NUALA'S LIFE SO FAR.

And to *whom* would the lady Nuala be *talking*?

LEAVE ME BE, BOGGART.

hrr'hem-- let's see...

You crippled you with pain and lies You're hurting all the time; and elf, You built your prison cell yourself then schemed and dreamed of open skies--

GO...AWAY...YOU ARE A *NASTY,* LYING LITTLE BOGGART. IF YOU DO NOT GO, THEN I WILL *HURT* YOU. VERY, *VERY* BADLY.

But lady...

NOW!

⸘snf.⸘

⸘snf.⸘

YOU CUT IT.

OF COURSE I CUT IT.

BUT HE'S STILL *THERE,* ISN'T HE, MY PIGSNEY?

HMMM. SOMETIMES IT TAKES THEM A LITTLE WHILE TO *NOTICE*...

ATROPOS? IS THERE SOMETHING YOU AREN'T *TELLING* US?

18

I DON'T **KNOW.**

WHAT DO YOU **MEAN,** YOU DON'T **KNOW?**

HELLO.

HELLO.

WE'RE LOOKING FOR MY DOGGIE.

THAT'S NICE.

SO FAR WE'VE FOUND **LOTS** OF CLUES. **HERE'S** A LITTLE SWAN MADE OF ICE...

AND A TOFFEE...AND A TONGUE-STUD.

AND A **WORD** THAT MEANS RED OR GREEN AT THE SAME TIME.

OH. **THIS** IS THE BORGHAL RANTIPOLE. BORGHAL RANTIPOLE, **THIS** IS A LADY I DON'T KNOW EITHER.

MY NAME IS **NUALA,** AN' IT PLEASES YOU.

CHARMED.

MY LADY DELIRIUM-- WHAT DO YOU **KNOW** ABOUT YOUR BROTHER, THE LORD SHAPER?

UHN. STUFF? THINGS? ODDMENTS?

I ... WAS **TOLD** TODAY THAT HE WAS IN GREAT TROUBLE. IS THAT **TRUE?**

...HE IS IN TROUBLE.

ISN'T THERE ANYTHING *YOU* CAN DO ABOUT IT?

I DON'T *KNOW*... I *TRIED* TO MAKE HIM COME *WITH* ME, AND LOOK FOR MY *DOGGIE*. BUT HE *GAVE* ME THE *BORGHAL RANTIPOLE* INSTEAD, TO HELP.

I COULDN'T *GET* HIM TO LEAVE THE DREAMING. I *DID* TRY.

YOU...HAVEN'T SEEN A DOGGIE HERE, ANYWHERE?

HE--HE'S *BLACK* AND *BROWN* AT THE *SAME* TIME. HE'S A *NICE* SORT OF DOGGIE EXCEPT WHEN HE'S *GRUMPY.*

NO...

BUT...

UM,

WELL...

WHERE DID YOU *LEAVE* IT?

THAT IS SO *EXTREMELY* CLEVER. I NEVER *THOUGHT* OF *THAT.* THANK YOU, PRETTY FAIRY. I THINK YOU *MUST* BE MY *GOOD* FAIRY.

...I *WISH* I COULD GIVE YOU A PRESENT.

DO YOU NEED A *WORD* THAT MEANS RED *AND* GREEN AT THE *SAME* TIME?

NO THANK YOU.

YOU... DON'T WANT A PRESENT?

I ALREADY *HAVE* ONE.

20

I HAD AN *AUNT* WHO WENT TO AMERICA, BEFORE THE *WAR*. SHE USED TO SEND US PICTURE POSTCARDS, WHEN WE WERE LITTLE. MY DAD SAID SHE WAS NO BETTER THAN SHE SHOULD HAVE BEEN.

THAT'S MY DAD FOR YOU. WELL, HE'S DEAD NOW, OF COURSE.

WHAT'RE *YOU* READING? I'M READING *PRINCESS DAISY*. IT'S LOVELY.

IT'S CALLED *HERE COMES A CANDLE*. IT'S A NOVEL BY SOME DEAD WHITE MALE.

A FRIEND I MET GAVE IT TO ME TO READ ON THE PLANE. I HAVE TO SEND IT BACK WHEN I'VE FINISHED IT. IT'S BEEN OUT OF PRINT FOR YEARS.

"YOU GOING HOME, THEN?"

"YUP."

"WERE YOU IN ENGLAND ON HOLIDAY?"

"NOT REALLY. *KIND* OF."

"I'M GOING TO *AMERICA* ON HOLIDAY. I'VE GOT A PEN PAL."

WHAT'S IT ABOUT?

IT'S ABOUT AN ARTIST WHO DREAMS OF A WOMAN.

AND ONE DAY HE *MEETS* THE WOMAN HE'S BEEN DREAMING OF, SO HE LOCKS HER UP IN HIS CELLAR, WHICH HE MAKES INTO A KIND OF COZY CELL. AND EVERY NIGHT HE GOES DOWN AT MIDNIGHT AND HE *STARES* AT HER THROUGH THE BARS AND SHE TELLS HIM WHAT TO PAINT...

IT SOUNDS A WEE BIT... RACY.

NOT REALLY. I MEAN, I *THINK* THEY'RE SCREWING, BUT IT WAS WRITTEN BACK IN THE DAWN OF TIME, SO THEY DO IT IN ROWS OF ASTERISKS, OR BETWEEN CHAPTERS.

OH.

ACTUALLY, IT'S A PRETTY GOOD BOOK. I'VE NEVER HEARD OF THE AUTHOR. HE'S KIND OF A CROSS BETWEEN ROBERT AICKMAN AND I DUNNO... SHIRLEY JACKSON, MAYBE, IN HER *WE HAVE ALWAYS LIVED IN THE CASTLE* MODE.

YOU KNOW SHIRLEY JACKSON?

UM. NOT REALLY.

21

I'M MAKING A LIST OF WORDS TO LOOK UP WHEN I GET HOME TO MY DICTIONARY.

SINOPLE. LUSK. BLOATER.

WELL, A BLOATER'S LIKE A KIPPER, REALLY. YOU KNOW, A SMOKED HERRING. LIKE YOU HAVE FOR BREAKFAST.

NOT ME. I'M MORE OF A CORNFLAKES GIRL, MYSELF.

HEY... I DON'T KNOW YOUR NAME.

CELIA. CELIA CRIPPS.

I'M ROSE. HI.

CELIA,.. WHEN *YOU* WERE A LITTLE KID. DID YOU EVER FOLLOW YOUR PARENTS AROUND, LIKE DOWN TO THE MALL OR SOMETHING, AND YOU'RE FOLLOWING YOUR MOM, AND THEN SHE TURNS AROUND, AND YOU REALIZE IT'S *NOT* YOUR MOM.

IT'S LIKE SOME *OTHER* WOMAN WITH THE SAME GREEN DRESS.

DID *THAT* EVER HAPPEN TO *YOU*?

ONCE. FOLLOWING MY DAD AROUND MARKS AND SPARKS IN CRAWLEY. *WHY*?

I DON'T KNOW. BECAUSE THAT'S HOW MY VISIT TO ENGLAND FELT, I SUPPOSE.

LIKE I WAS WAITING FOR THE LADY IN THE GREEN DRESS TO TURN AROUND.

THAT'S WHY I LIKE JUDITH KRANTZ, REALLY. YOU DON'T HAVE TO LOOK UP ANY WORDS WITH JUDITH KRANTZ.

22

LORD MORPHEUS... LORD SHAPER? HELLO?

THIS IS ME, NUALA THE ELF. I DON'T KNOW IF YOU REMEMBER ME. I MEAN, I'M SURE YOU DO REMEMBER ME, BUT NOW I LOOK LIKE I DID WHEN YOU FIRST MET ME, NOT LIKE I LOOKED WHEN YOU KNEW ME, AND I'D TAKE IT OFF, EXCEPT MY BROTHER PUT IT ON, AND SO HE'LL HAVE TO TAKE IT OFF...

I WORKED FOR YOU, FOR A WHILE.

WHEN I LEFT YOUR SERVICE, YOU DID ME THE FAVOR OF CONFERRING A GIFT UPON ME.

YOU SAID THAT I COULD CALL YOU. AND YOU'D COME. AND I COULD HAVE A BOON.

SO HERE AND NOW, DO I CALL YOU, LORD SHAPER.

Nuala?

YES, LORD.

I am no longer your lord.

NO, LORD. OF COURSE YOU AREN'T. I'M SORRY.

This is exceedingly inconvenient, Nuala.

Can we not postpone it to another time?

NO, MY LORD. WE CANNOT.

My Lady Nuala, I must most earnestly beseech you...

"IF IN NEED, HOLD THE STONE WITH BOTH HANDS, AND CALL ME. I WILL COME TO YOU; YOU MAY HAVE ONE BOON."

23

MY *LORD?*

You do me a disservice, Nuala.

PLEASE, MY LORD?

I am here, Nuala.

WELCOME TO THE DWELLING, LORD SHAPER. CAN I OFFER YOU *WINE?* OR *PASTRIES?* IF YOU ATE FLOWERS, I WOULD OFFER YOU FLOWERS.

NO WINE. NO PASTRIES. AND I DO NOT EAT FLOWERS. STATE YOUR BOON AND I WILL GRANT IT.

MY LORD,,, THE *PUCK* TELLS ME THAT THE *DIRAE* ARE SET AGAINST YOU.

HE SAYS YOU ARE IN *TROUBLE.* THE LADY DELIRIUM, YOUR SISTER, WORRIES ABOUT YOU.

The Puck says many things.

The Lady Delirium, while she has many fine features, also says many things.

ARE YOU IN TROUBLE?

Yes. I suppose that I am.

However, as long as I remain in the Dreaming, no real harm can occur.

MY *LORD...*

YOU ARE NO LONGER IN THE DREAMING.

No.

I am not.

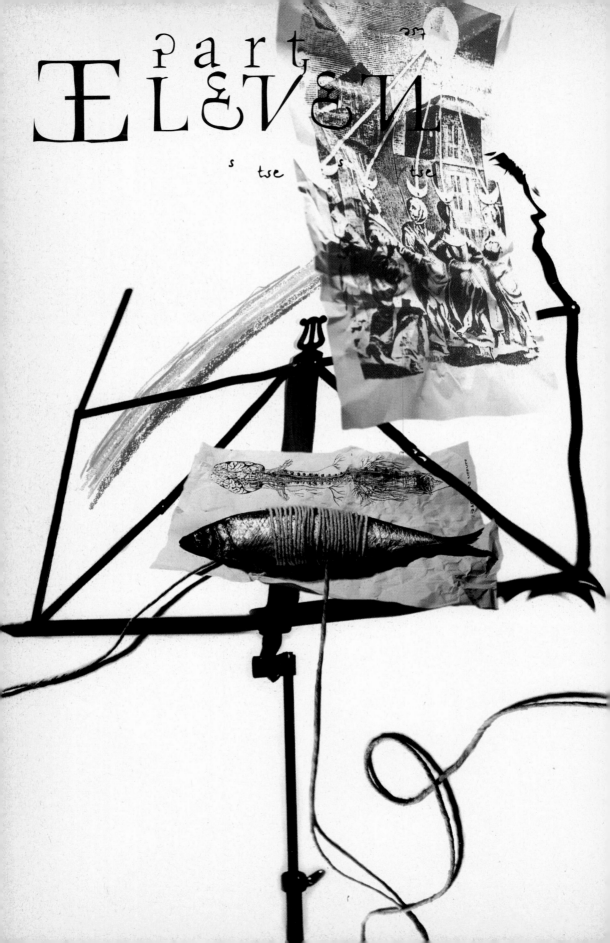

part
Œ LEVEN

s tse s tse

WHO'S THERE?

AND WHO WOULD *THAT* BE, ASKING FOR MY NAME? AND WOULD YOU BE *FRIEND* OR FOE?

I AM THE CORINTHIAN. I TRAVEL TOWARD THE CASTLE OF HIS DARKNESS, THE LORD MORPHEUS OF THE ENDLESS.

AH. THE CORINTHIAN. I KNEW YOUR *FATHER*. WELL, NOT FATHER... FORMER SELF? PRIOR INCARNATION? PREVIOUS INCUMBENT? *HMPH*...

I AM *CAIN*. PURVEYOR OF FINE NIGHTMARES, PENNY DREADFULS, SHILLING SHOCKERS, BLOOD AND THUNDERS...

I, UH... I, UH...

THINGS HAVE *CHANGED*. SINCE YOU'VE BEEN AWAY.

SO I SEE.

BAD THINGS HAVE HAPPENED... MY BROTHER...

THEY WOULDN'T *HURT* ME.

NOBODY'S ALLOWED TO HURT *ME*.

THAT WAS MY PUNISHMENT. NOT BEING HURT...

WHO'S THE SPRAT?

HIS NAME'S DANIEL.

AH *YES*. WE'VE MET BEFORE. IN MY BROTHER'S HOUSE. IN HAPPIER TIMES.

THERE'S A BOY. THERE'S A LADDIE.

I AM TAKING HIM TO THE CASTLE.

OH DEAR.

"OH DEAR"?

EXACTLY. OH DEAR. TWO WORDS INTENDED TO INDICATE THAT THE JOURNEY TO THE CENTER OF THE DREAMING IS CURRENTLY PROBLEMATIC, TO SAY THE LEAST.

THINGS HAVE BEEN A LITTLE *TURBULENT* HERE OF LATE.

LATE BEING THE OPERATIVE WORD.

WELL, IF YOU'RE GOING TO GO TO THE CASTLE, I SUPPOSE I OUGHT TO GO WITH YOU. SAFETY IN NUMBERS, ALL THAT.

I CAN LOOK AFTER MYSELF, CAIN.

BUT *CAN* YOU LOOK AFTER THE BRATLING?

HOW *LONG* HAVE YOU BEEN GONE?

I AM UNSURE. SEVERAL DAYS? A WEEK, PERHAPS? THE RAVEN, MATTHEW, WAS WITH ME. HE DESERTED ME.

HAS HE RETURNED TO THE DREAMING? I HAVE A *BONE* TO PICK WITH HIM.

ᛉTCH.ᛉ YOU DIDN'T *FINISH* THAT PROPERLY. YOU SHOULD HAVE SAID SOMETHING LIKE, "A BONE TO PICK WITH HIM--HIS WISHBONE." OR SOMETHING ABOUT PICKING HIS FLESH-- FROM HIS BONES... HEHEHEH...

DO YOU THINK I SOUND LIKE VINCENT PRICE?

WHO?

NOT IMPORTANT.

I'LL TELL YOU A *SECRET*. A RAVEN CREATED THE WORLD. WHEN NOAH SENT HIM OUT TO FIND LAND, HE COULDN'T FIND ANY. IT HAD ALL BEEN WASHED AWAY. SO HE CREATED IT. HE *SHAT* THE DRY LAND AND HE *PISSED* THE FRESH WATER. THEN HE FLEW OFF, LAUGHING FIT TO BURST.

SO THE WORLD WAS THERE FOR THE *DOVE* TO FIND.

2

CORRECT ME IF I MISREMEMBER, FRIEND CAIN, BUT IT SEEMS TO ME THAT YOUR STORIES ARE *MYSTERIES*, NOT *SECRETS*.

THAT WASN'T ONE OF *MY* STORIES. THAT WAS ONE OF MY B... ONE OF MY *BROTHER'S* STORIES.

REALLY?

THEY DON'T *ADMIT* TO IT, OF COURSE. WHO WANTS TO BE *BLAMED* FOR CREATING THE WORLD?

AND WHERE *IS* YOUR BROTHER?

I DON'T *KNOW* WHERE HIS NIBS IS.

I *DO* HAVE CERTAIN OPINIONS OF MY OWN ABOUT THE ADVISABILITY OR OTHERWISE OF JUST *BOPPING* OFF ON LITTLE JAUNTS WHILE INSANE PRIMEVAL FORCES DESTROY YOUR KINGDOM AND ITS LUCKLESS INHABITANTS, BUT THEN, *THAT'S* THE KIND OF FELLOW I AM.

WE'LL TAKE THE BOY TO THE CASTLE. HE'LL COME BACK.

THAT WAS EASIER THAN I HAD HOPED. BUT HIS LORDSHIP ISN'T *THERE*, YOU KNOW.

WHERE?

AT THE CASTLE. HE'S NOT *THERE*. HE *LEFT*.

THEN WHERE *IS* HE? HE TOLD ME TO BRING THE CHILD TO HIM.

I ASK AGAIN: WHERE IS HE?

OPINIONATED.

CORINTHIAN, YOU ARE WELCOME HERE. WE HAVE BEEN EXPECTING YOU.

CAIN? DO YOU *ALSO* SEEK REFUGE?

SHELTER, PERHAPS. *NOT* REFUGE. *I* STILL HAVE A HOUSE TO CALL MY OWN, AFTER ALL.

I HAVE THE CHILD I WAS SENT TO FETCH. WHERE IN THE CASTLE SHOULD I WAIT FOR OUR LORD'S RETURN?

WAIT WHERE YOU WILL, CORINTHIAN. IT IS ALL ONE TO US.

THERE *WERE* TO BE APARTMENTS BUILT FOR YOU, IN THE CASTLE, CORINTHIAN. BUT THEY WERE NEVER CON- STRUCTED. AND NOW THERE IS NO ONE LEFT TO CONSTRUCT THEM.

WE ARE *SORRY.* WHEN OUR LORD COMES BACK, ALL WILL BE MADE *WELL* AGAIN.

ENTER, THE FOUR OF YOU, AND BE SAFE.

SO, WE'RE HERE. NOTHING TO DO NOW BUT WAIT FOR HIM, AND KEEP OUR FINGERS CROSSED. AND BY THE WAY...

FOUR OF US, CAIN?

WELL, I COULDN'T JUST *LEAVE* IT THERE.

eeple.

doggie!

4

I came, Nuala. Because I promised that I would come, if you summoned me; and you did summon me.

But I would that you had done otherwise.

I DID NOT REALIZE THAT I COULD HARM YOU BY TAKING YOU FROM THE DREAMING.

I THOUGHT I WAS HELPING YOU.

THE PUCK SAID THAT THE DIRAE WERE *HOUNDING* YOU.

The Kindly Ones? Yes, they are now in the Dreaming.

BUT SURELY SUCH AS *THEY* HAVE NO POWER OVER SUCH AS *YOU*, MY LORD?

There are old rules, Nuala. Rules that were old when time was young. The ladies have power to avenge blood-crimes...

And I killed my son.

I killed him twice. Once, long ago, when I would not help him; and once... more recently... when I did...

The ladies are empowered to hound those who spill family blood. I have Orpheus's blood on my hands, Nuala.

I killed my son. It was what he wanted...what he craved. In my pride I abandoned him for several thousand years; and then, at the last, I killed him.

YOU...YOU *WANT* THEM TO PUNISH YOU, *DON'T* YOU? YOU *WANT* TO BE PUNISHED FOR ORPHEUS'S DEATH.

Have you ever been imprisoned, Nuala? I was... I spent over eighty years in a glass bottle, like a genie... or a city... I could have waited until the earth crumbled to dust. But still, I waited.

I told Ishtar that she was wrong. That I was not changed. That I did not change. But in truth, I think I lied to her.

6

I DID NOT MEAN TO HARM YOU.

I know that, Nuala. But, as has recently been pointed out to me, intent and outcome are rarely coincident.

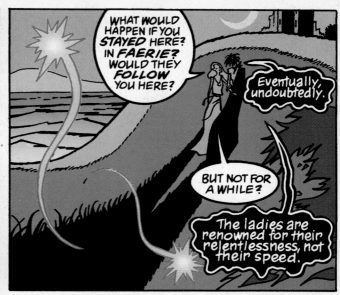

WHAT WOULD HAPPEN IF YOU STAYED HERE? IN FAERIE? WOULD THEY FOLLOW YOU HERE?

Eventually, undoubtedly.

BUT NOT FOR A WHILE?

The ladies are renowned for their relentlessness, not their speed.

YOU COULD KEEP MOVING. YOU COULD GO FROM FAERIE TO SOMEWHERE ELSE, TO, TO SOMEWHERE ELSE AGAIN. THEY'D NEVER CATCH YOU.

I COULD COME WITH. I COULD HELP...

I AM... SORRY I CALLED YOU HERE, LORD. WHAT WILL YOU DO NOW?

I shall return to my Realm. And I shall do what I have to do.

I AM TRULY, TRULY SORRY--

Please. Nuala. No more apologies.

YES. OF COURSE. SORRY.

UM. SORRY I SAID "SORRY." I MEAN.

SORRY.

Before I take my farewell of you, Nuala, there is one thing left for me to do, is there not?

IS THERE?

I still owe you a boon, Lady.

WELL...

7

Did you have a particular boon in mind? When you summoned me here?

I WANTED YOU TO STAY. I...

I WANTED YOU TO *LOVE* ME.

And do you think that love is a gift? Like a bauble, or a trinket? Something I can reach into a pouch and present to you?

I GAVE ALL *MY* LOVE TO YOU. YEARS AGO.

Did you? I did not realize...

On reflection, while I cannot give you the thing itself, I could give you a dream of my love.

I ALREADY HAVE THAT, MY LORD.

PLEASE GO.

8

ZELDA? NO. **NO ONE** TOLD ME. WHEN DID IT **HAPPEN?** I WAS ONLY--

I'M SORRY. IT'S JUST A **SHOCK**...

WE **DID** TRY TO PHONE YOUR HOME. THE MESSAGE ON YOUR MACHINE SAID YOU WERE IN ENGLAND, MS. WALKER. IT'S HOSPICE POLICY NOT TO LEAVE MESSAGES ON MACHINES.

YOUR FRIEND ZELDA PASSED AWAY IN THE WEE HOURS OF SUNDAY MORNING.

RECEPTION

IF YOU WISH TO TAKE CHARGE OF HER EFFECTS, THEY CAN BE RELEASED TO YOU AS SOON AS YOU'VE SETTLED HER FINAL BILL.

WILL YOU BE SEEING TO THE FUNERAL ARRANGEMENTS?

I--I DON'T KNOW. I SUP**POSE**. I MEAN I **HAVE** TO, **DON'T** I? SHE DOESN'T **HAVE** ANYONE ELSE.

WELL, FIRST YOU'LL NEED TO SETTLE THINGS WITH MRS. BURROWS IN CREDIT AND ACCOUNTS, DOWN THE HALL THERE. PAST THE DOUBLE DOORS.

MS. **WALKER?** OH, MS. WALKER?

DON'T FORGET, WE TAKE MASTERCARD **AND** VISA.

9

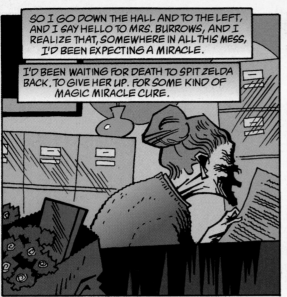

SO I GO DOWN THE HALL AND TO THE LEFT, AND I SAY HELLO TO MRS. BURROWS, AND I REALIZE THAT, SOMEWHERE IN ALL THIS MESS, I'D BEEN EXPECTING A MIRACLE.

I'D BEEN WAITING FOR DEATH TO SPIT ZELDA BACK, TO GIVE HER UP. FOR SOME KIND OF MAGIC MIRACLE CURE.

BUT THERE AREN'T ANY MIRACLES. AND ONCE YOU'RE DEAD, YOU'RE DEAD.

DEATH MEANS I HAVE TO SIGN FOR AN ITEMIZED LIST OF PERSONAL POSSESSIONS INCLUDING THREE DISPLAY CASES OF STUFFED SPIDERS, A HUMAN SKULL AND SEVERAL PHOTOGRAPHS, AND I HAVE THE CHOICE OF TAKING HER BOOKS HOME WITH ME OR DONATING THEM TO THE HOSPICE LIBRARY, WHICH IS WHAT I DO.

DEATH MEANS I SIGN AN INDEMNIFYING WAIVER, TWICE, BY THE LITTLE CROSSES.

NO MIRACLES.

AND THEN I PUT ZELDA'S DEATH ON MY VISA CARD AND THAT MAKES IT FINAL.

THE FUNERAL WILL BE THE DAY AFTER TOMORROW. I'LL NEED TO MEET THE PEOPLE FROM THE FUNERAL HOME THIS AFTERNOON AND SIGN ANOTHER VISA SLIP.

AND ALL THE WEIRD SHIT TUMBLES INTO PERSPECTIVE. IT DOESN'T MATTER AND IT ISN'T REAL.

NO MIRACLES.

NO MAGIC.

NO DREAMS.

JUST PAIN AND DEATH, AND VISA SLIPS.

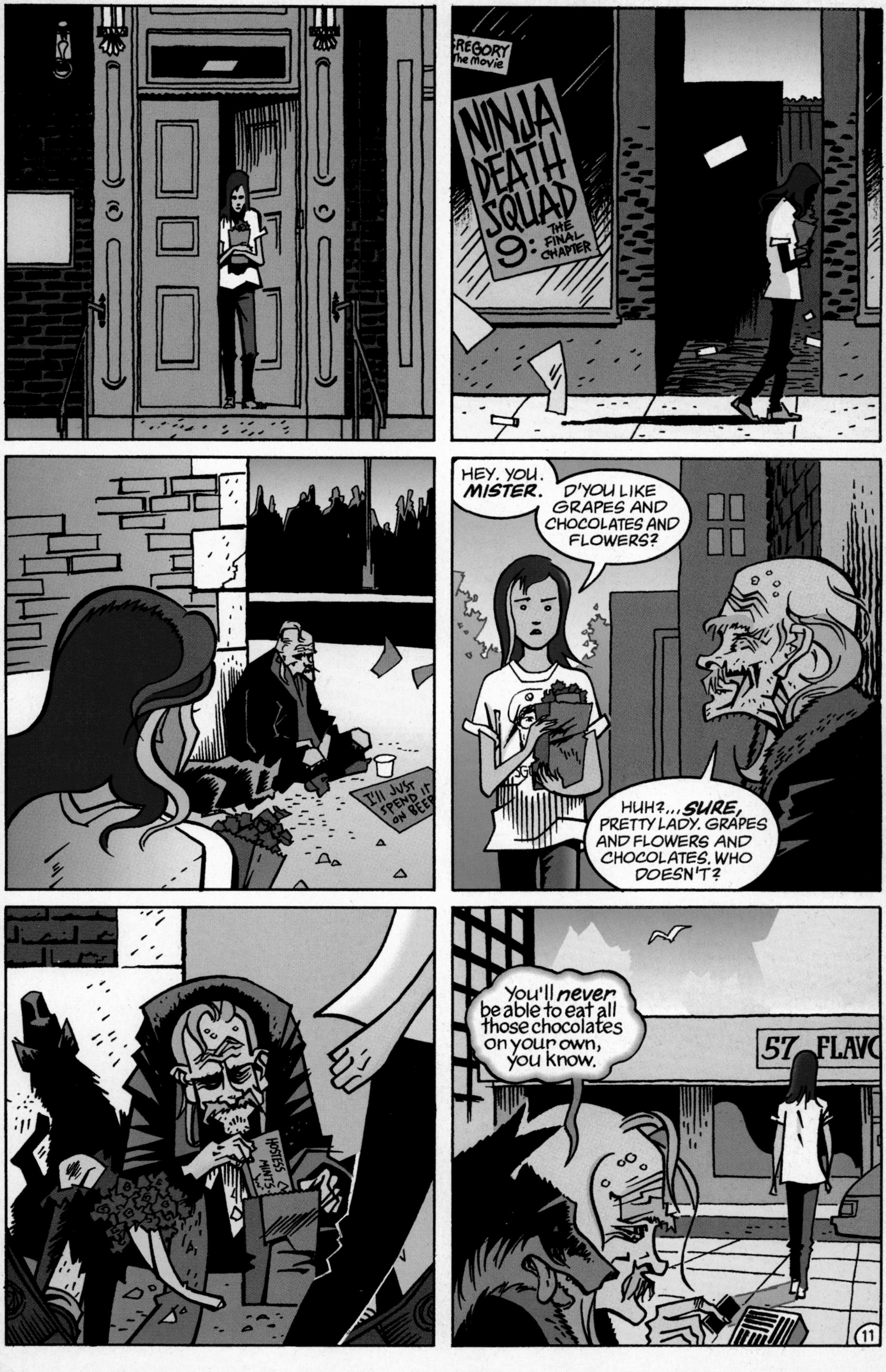
GREGORY The Movie
NINJA DEATH SQUAD 9: THE FINAL CHAPTER
I'LL JUST SPEND IT ON BEER
HEY. YOU. MISTER.
D'YOU LIKE GRAPES AND CHOCOLATES AND FLOWERS?
HUH?... SURE, PRETTY LADY. GRAPES AND FLOWERS AND CHOCOLATES. WHO DOESN'T?
HOSTESS MINTS
You'll never be able to eat all those chocolates on your own, you know.
57 FLAVO
11

OF COURSE HE'LL BE BACK.

EVENTUALLY, PERHAPS.

CAIN, YOU'RE BEING RIDICULOUS.

REALLY? WHAT ABOUT LAST TIME?

LAST TIME?

WE ALL WAITED FOR HIM TO COME BACK LAST TIME. HE WAS GONE MORE THAN SIXTY YEARS. REMEMBER?

I...I REMEMBER.

I...I REMEMBER WAITING FOR HIS RETURN. I REMEMBER THE STRANGE STRAINED GRAY DAYS THAT STRETCHED INTO YEARS AND INTO DECADES. THE SLOW CRUMBLING OF WALLS ...THE ROOMS THAT WERE NO LONGER THERE...

I REMEMBER THE DAY THAT I REALIZED I COULD SIMPLY WALK INTO THE WAKING WORLD, SHOULD I WISH TO SO DO,... THAT I COULD DO WHAT- EVER I WISHED, WITHOUT FEAR OF RETRIBUTION,...

AND THEN... I REMEMBER NO MORE.

THEY AREN'T YOUR MEMORIES.

THEY ARE ALL I HAVE.

owie!

THERE, NOW. YOU'RE ALL RIGHT. NO BONES BROKEN.

I REMEMBER THOSE DAYS.

WE WAITED FOR HIM, WHILE THE CASTLE FELL APART ABOUT OUR EARS, WHILE THE WORDS FLED FROM MY BOOKS AND SCURRIED OFF DOWN THE CORRIDORS IN TWOS AND THREES, OR FADED INTO OBLIVION AND OBSCURITY.

12

THOSE OF THE STAFF WHO TOOK THEIR POWER DIRECTLY FROM OUR LORD, THE GATEKEEPERS AND SUCHLIKE, BECAME INSUBSTANTIAL, OR CEASED TO EXIST ENTIRELY.

SOME OF US KEPT BUSY.

SOME OF US DID, YES. BUT MOST DID NOT.

STILL, HE'LL COME BACK.

OF COURSE HE WILL. EVENTUALLY.

IS THERE ANYTHING HERE FOR THE BOY TO PLAY WITH?

THIS IS THE THRONE ROOM OF THE KING OF DREAMS, NOT THE GARDEN OF WONDERFUL TOYS.

BUT HERE.

CAIN, YOU REALLY OUGHTN'T LET HIM PLAY WITH THAT. WE COULD ALL GET INTO THE MOST FRIGHTFUL TROUBLE...

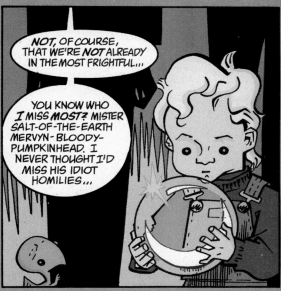

NOT, OF COURSE, THAT WE'RE NOT ALREADY IN THE MOST FRIGHTFUL...

YOU KNOW WHO I MISS MOST? MISTER SALT-OF-THE-EARTH MERVYN-BLOODY-PUMPKINHEAD. I NEVER THOUGHT I'D MISS HIS IDIOT HOMILIES...

MAYBE WE SHOULD FIND HIM SOMETHING ELSE TO PLAY WITH.

13

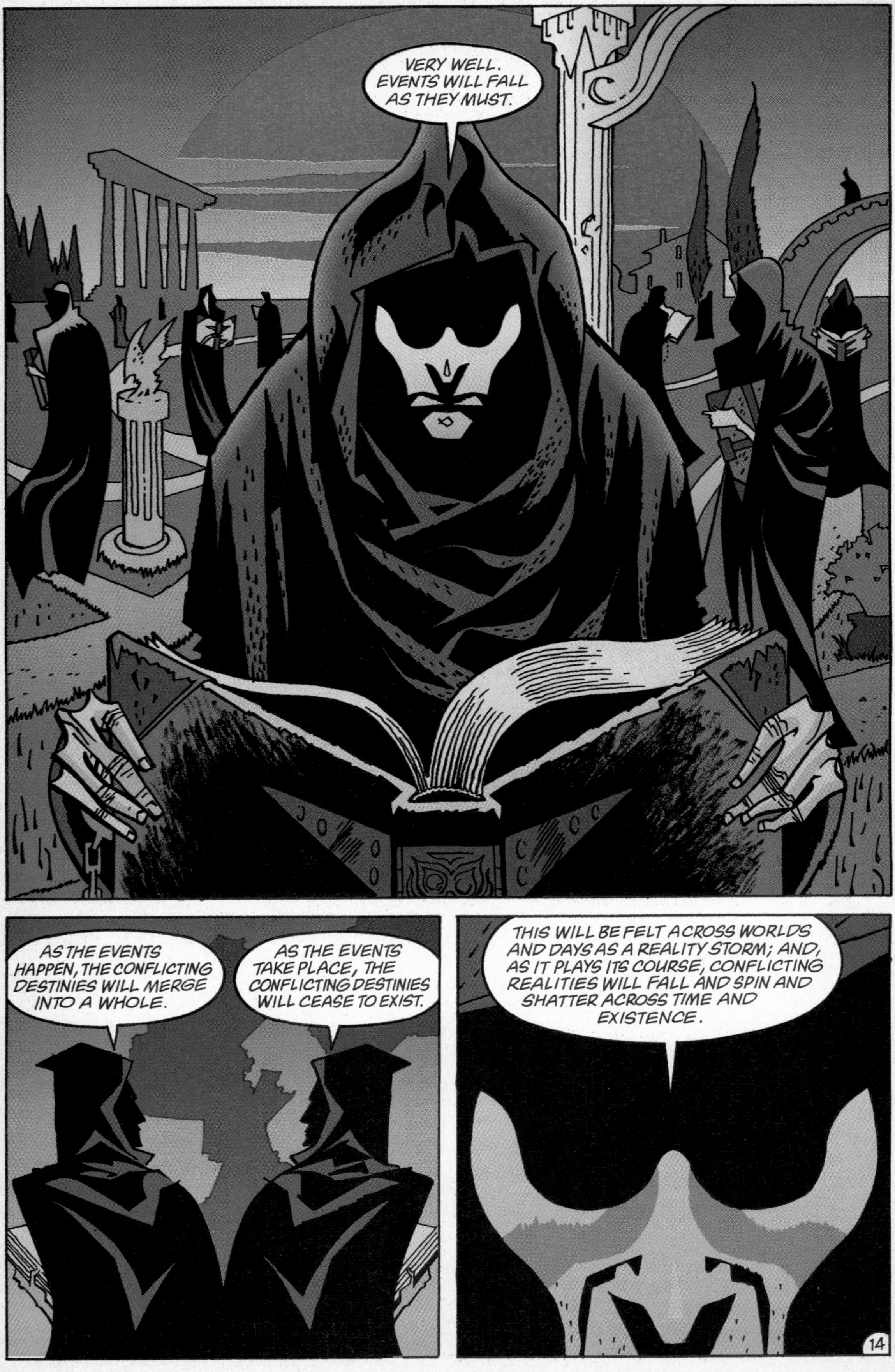
VERY WELL. EVENTS WILL FALL AS THEY MUST.
AS THE EVENTS HAPPEN, THE CONFLICTING DESTINIES WILL MERGE INTO A WHOLE.
AS THE EVENTS TAKE PLACE, THE CONFLICTING DESTINIES WILL CEASE TO EXIST.
THIS WILL BE FELT ACROSS WORLDS AND DAYS AS A REALITY STORM; AND, AS IT PLAYS ITS COURSE, CONFLICTING REALITIES WILL FALL AND SPIN AND SHATTER ACROSS TIME AND EXISTENCE.

ALL THIS IS DESTINED TO HAPPEN.

EVENTS THAT NEVER DID HAPPEN AND NOW NEVER SHALL, WILL CAST THEIR CONCLUSIONS AND OCCURRENCES OUT INTO THE WORLDS.

CAUSE AND EFFECT WILL JOSTLE, UNABLE TO TELL QUITE WHICH CAME FIRST. THE EVENT HORIZON WILL COME CLOSER AND CLOSER. WRECKS AND MIRAGES OF TIME AND OCCASION...

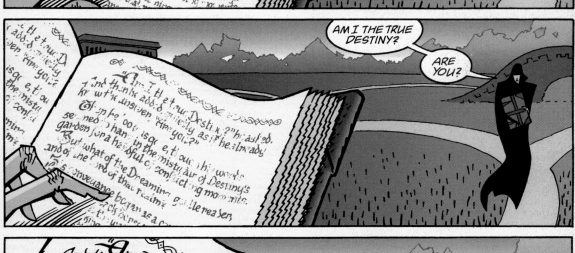

AM I THE TRUE DESTINY?

ARE YOU?

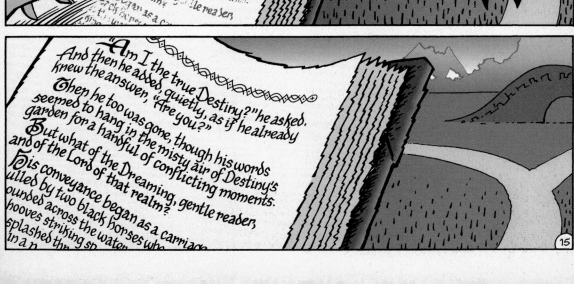

"Am I the true Destiny?" he asked. And then he added, quietly, as if he already knew the answer, "Are you?"

Then he too was gone, though his words seemed to hang in the misty air of Destiny's garden for a handful of conflicting moments.

But what of the Dreaming, gentle reader, and of the Lord of that realm?

His conveyance began as a carriage, pulled by two black horses who... ...ounded across the water, ...hooves striking sp... ...splashed th... ...in an...

15

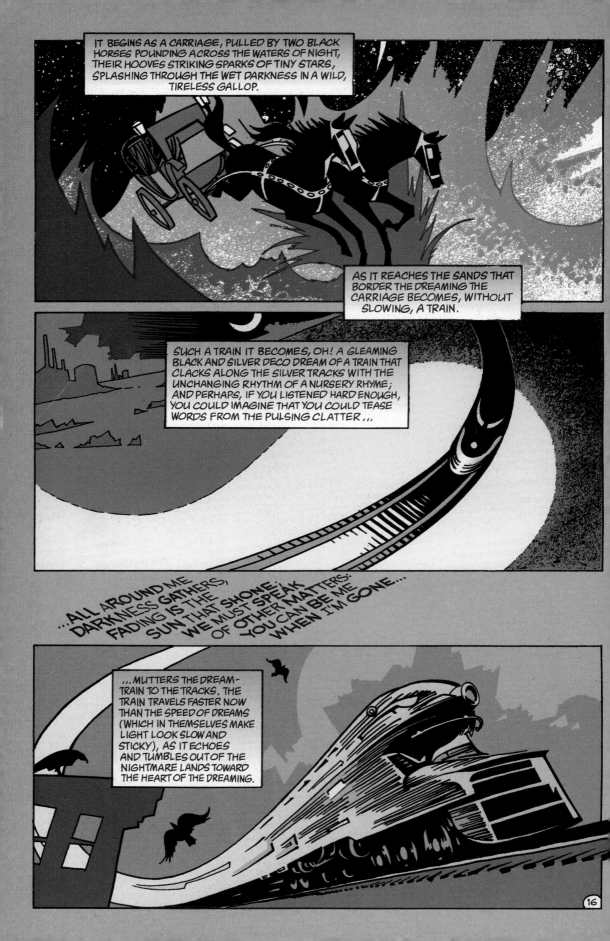

IT BEGINS AS A CARRIAGE, PULLED BY TWO BLACK HORSES POUNDING ACROSS THE WATERS OF NIGHT, THEIR HOOVES STRIKING SPARKS OF TINY STARS, SPLASHING THROUGH THE WET DARKNESS IN A WILD, TIRELESS GALLOP.

AS IT REACHES THE SANDS THAT BORDER THE DREAMING THE CARRIAGE BECOMES, WITHOUT SLOWING, A TRAIN.

SUCH A TRAIN IT BECOMES, OH! A GLEAMING BLACK AND SILVER DECO DREAM OF A TRAIN THAT CLACKS ALONG THE SILVER TRACKS WITH THE UNCHANGING RHYTHM OF A NURSERY RHYME; AND PERHAPS, IF YOU LISTENED HARD ENOUGH, YOU COULD IMAGINE THAT YOU COULD TEASE WORDS FROM THE PULSING CLATTER...

...ALL AROUND ME DARKNESS GATHERS, FADING IS THE SUN THAT SHONE, WE MUST SPEAK OF OTHER MATTERS: YOU CAN BE ME WHEN I'M GONE...

...MUTTERS THE DREAM-TRAIN TO THE TRACKS. THE TRAIN TRAVELS FASTER NOW THAN THE SPEED OF DREAMS (WHICH IN THEMSELVES MAKE LIGHT LOOK SLOW AND STICKY), AS IT ECHOES AND TUMBLES OUT OF THE NIGHTMARE LANDS TOWARD THE HEART OF THE DREAMING.

16

THE CASTLE OF DREAMS SHIVERS AND RE-FORMS AS THE TRAIN APPROACHES.

WHAT WAS A FORTRESS IS NOW A TERMINUS.

ABOVE THE ENTRANCE IS A FRIEZE: A WYVERN AND A WINGED HORSE ARE FROZEN IN BAS RELIEF, AND THERE IS AN EMPTY SPACE, WHERE A THIRD CARVING MIGHT ONCE HAVE BEEN.

Gentlemen?

I have returned. I am afraid I must apologize for the delay.

17

MY LORD...

I know, Lucien. I know. I should have left neither the Dreaming nor the castle at this time.

I see the castle is no longer being a place of refuge. My apologies.

Corinthian. I am pleased to see you.

Cain.

THERE IS A MATTER I BELIEVE WE NEED TO *DISCUSS*, SIRE.

IT CONCERNS MY BROTHER, MY LORD. AND HIS MURDER.

Soon, Cain. Soon. Not now.

MY *LORD*! *I* AM THE MURDERER HERE! I HAVE A *CONTRACT*! MY POOR *BROTHER* HAD A *CONTRACT*!

I WAS THE *FIRST* MURDERER! I HAVE *CERTAIN* RIGHTS AND PRIVILEGES!

WE MUST *TALK*!

Cain. I have no interest in discussing this matter at this time.

LATER, THEN, SIRE. OF COURSE.

Young man. A pleasure finally to meet you, after all this time.

Madame. Ladies.

Good afternoon.

THEY'RE *HERE*?

DREAM KING.

WE ARE HERE.

18

Madame? I must ask you to leave this place.

YOU WERE GONE FROM HERE, DREAM KING. THIS CASTLE IS OURS, NOW, TO DO WITH AS WE WILL.

SHALL WE FREE YOUR PRISONERS TO TORMENT YOU?

SHALL WE SHATTER THE PRETTY WINDOWS THAT HIDE YOUR POWER AND YOUR MADNESS?

You shall do none of these things.

You will leave. Now.

19

You dare?

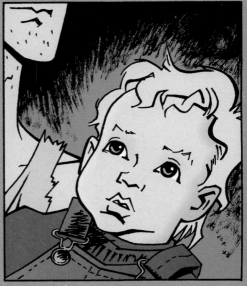

BUT... THAT'S DANIEL. ISN'T IT? THAT'S DANIEL. MY BABY.

PARTLY, YES.

HE ISN'T DEAD.

WHERE ARE THEY GOING?

HE IS NO LONGER ALIVE.

20

HE ISN'T *DEAD*. DON'T YOU *SEE*? WE DON'T HAVE TO *DO* THIS. WE DON'T HAVE TO *KILL* HIM--

WE DON'T KILL. WE *CAN'T*. HAVEN'T YOU BEEN *LISTENING*?

WE HAVE TO RESCUE DANIEL. BRING HIM BACK. WE DON'T HAVE TO HURT *ANYONE* ANYMORE.

WE DO NOT RESCUE, MY LITTLE SMELFUNGUS. WHAT DO YOU THINK WE *ARE*?

AFTER ALL, HE *KILLED* HIS *SON*.

¿PTEU!¿

AND WE HATED HIS SON.

WHAT?

HE MADE US *WEEP*. HE MADE THE LADIES WEEP WITH HIS SONGS AND HIS THINGS THAT NEVER WERE AND NEVER *SHALL* BE. STORIES.

MADE-UP RUBBISHY STORIES.

MAKES YOU SICK.

WE HAVE TO RESCUE HIM.

I TOLD YOU *ONCE*. I WON'T *TELL* YOU *AGAIN*. WE *DON'T* RESCUE. WE REVENGE.

...I don't know. I don't know any more. I don't know anything any more.

Heaven. The Silver City. Do we *tell* them? I *have* been telling them. Is anyone *listening*? They send no response. But what obligation *has* our Creator to respond to us?

We *must* have faith, my angel. We must *keep* our faith.

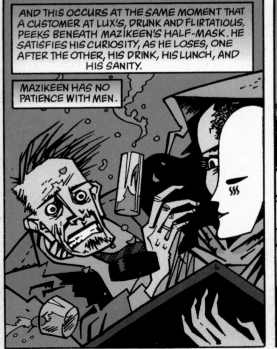

AND THIS OCCURS AT THE SAME MOMENT THAT A CUSTOMER AT LUX'S, DRUNK AND FLIRTATIOUS, PEEKS BENEATH MAZIKEEN'S HALF-MASK. HE SATISFIES HIS CURIOSITY, AS HE LOSES, ONE AFTER THE OTHER, HIS DRINK, HIS LUNCH, AND HIS SANITY.

MAZIKEEN HAS NO PATIENCE WITH MEN.

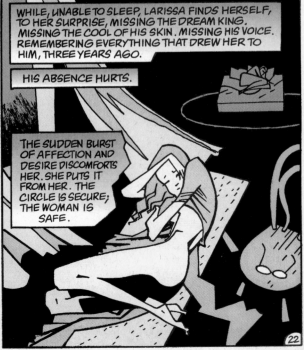

WHILE, UNABLE TO SLEEP, LARISSA FINDS HERSELF, TO HER SURPRISE, MISSING THE DREAM KING. MISSING THE COOL OF HIS SKIN. MISSING HIS VOICE. REMEMBERING EVERYTHING THAT DREW HER TO HIM, THREE YEARS AGO.

HIS ABSENCE HURTS.

THE SUDDEN BURST OF AFFECTION AND DESIRE DISCOMFORTS HER. SHE PUTS IT FROM HER. THE CIRCLE IS SECURE; THE WOMAN IS SAFE.

22

KNOCK KNOCK!

Enter.

ARE THEY STILL HERE, LORD?

NO, Lucien. They have withdrawn, for now.

VERY GOOD, LORD. WILL YOU BE KEEPING THE SCAR?

I do not know. I suppose so. For now. Aliahora foretold that I would receive my scars, in my turn, like the one I left on her cheek, like the one I left on her heart.

She knew it then.

WHAT ARE YOU GOING TO DO NOW, LORD?

Do? I am going to do whatever I can do.

I will do what I must.

23

First, I will need to see the boy Daniel. Before I confront the ladies. There are matters I need to discuss with him.

Will you bring him here to me, Lucien?

CERTAINLY, LORD.

In the reflectory there is a small wooden box, which contains an Eagle Stone...

THE EMERALD, LORD?

Exactly. Please bring that to me also.

AT ONCE, LORD.

"You could keep moving. You could go from Faerie to somewhere else, to, to somewhere else again. They'd never catch you."

Rules and responsibilities: these are the ties that bind us.

We do what we do, because of who we are. If we did otherwise, we would not be ourselves.

I will do what I have to do.

And I will do what I must.

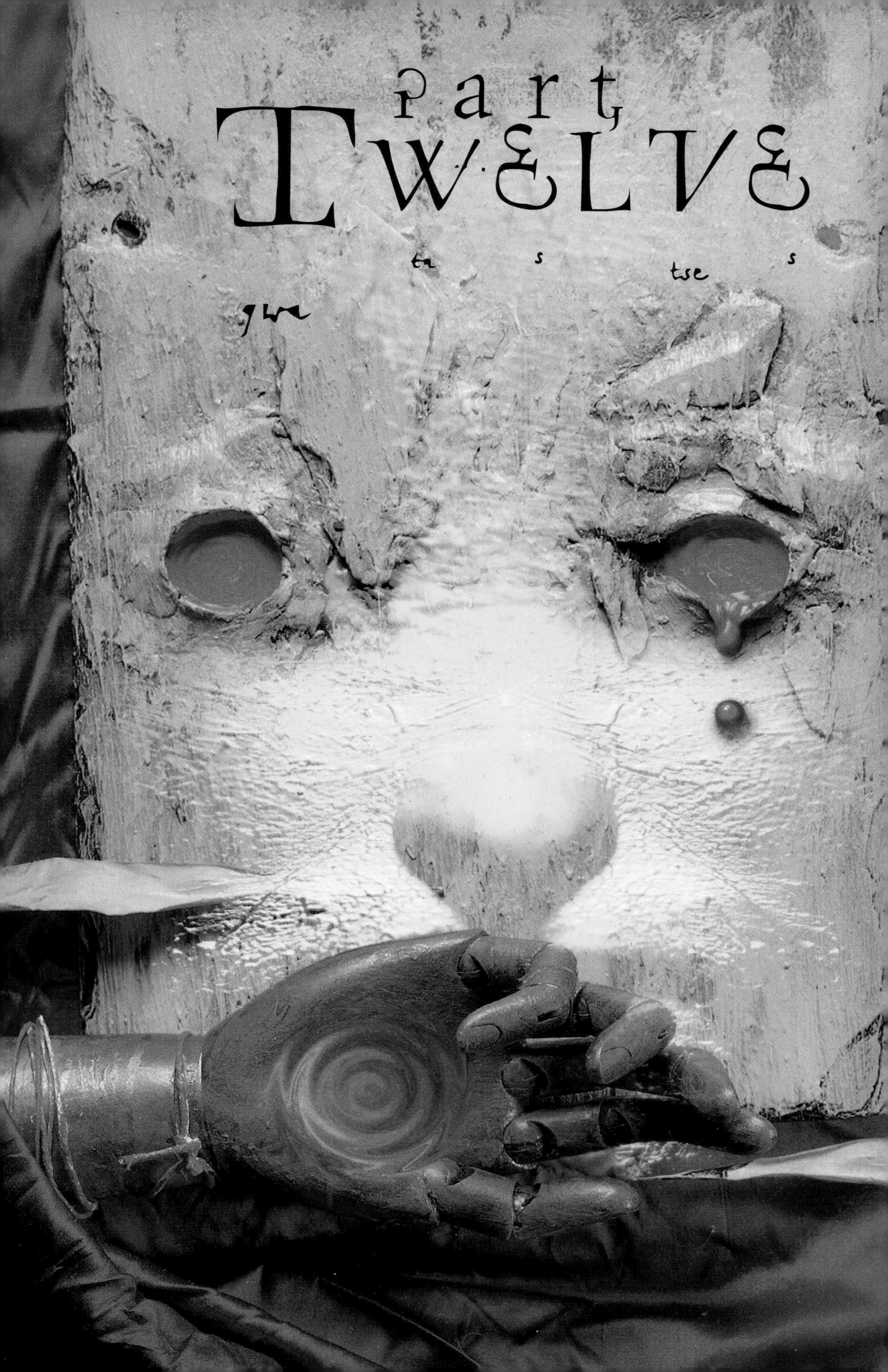
part
TWELVE

STILL HERE, THEN?

SO IT WOULD APPEAR, YES.

SO, WHAT'S *NEW?* ANYTHING MUCH HAPPEN WHILE I WAS GONE?

I have decided to confront the Ladies of the Fury, though it could mean my doom; and I will be leaving shortly so to do; I already have spoken to young Daniel of certain matters...

I am currently contemplating this emerald. And, by the by, the Corinthian has sworn to destroy you for deserting him.

I'M HONESTLY KINDA SORRY I ASKED.

CAN HE *HURT ME?* THE *CORINTHIAN?* CAN ONE DREAM HURT *ANOTHER?*

COULD HE *KILL ME?*

Kill you? Certainly. Not permanently. But for a while.

It wasn't my *fault*, though. I didn't *ask* to be pulled back here. Why don't you *tell* him *that*? Just tell him that it wasn't my *idea*.

I can tell him, yes.

Penny for your thoughts.

You have no pennies, Matthew.

I was contemplating this emerald. It was one of the twelve Dreamstones I created, long, long ago.

The greatest of them, the one into which I put most of myself, was the Ruby. There were others—a Rose-Quartz I gave to poor Alianore, a Fire-Opal, a Black Pearl, a Topaz...

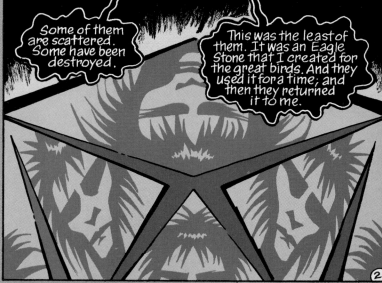

Some of them are scattered. Some have been destroyed.

This was the least of them. It was an Eagle Stone that I created for the great birds. And they used it for a time; and then they returned it to me.

②

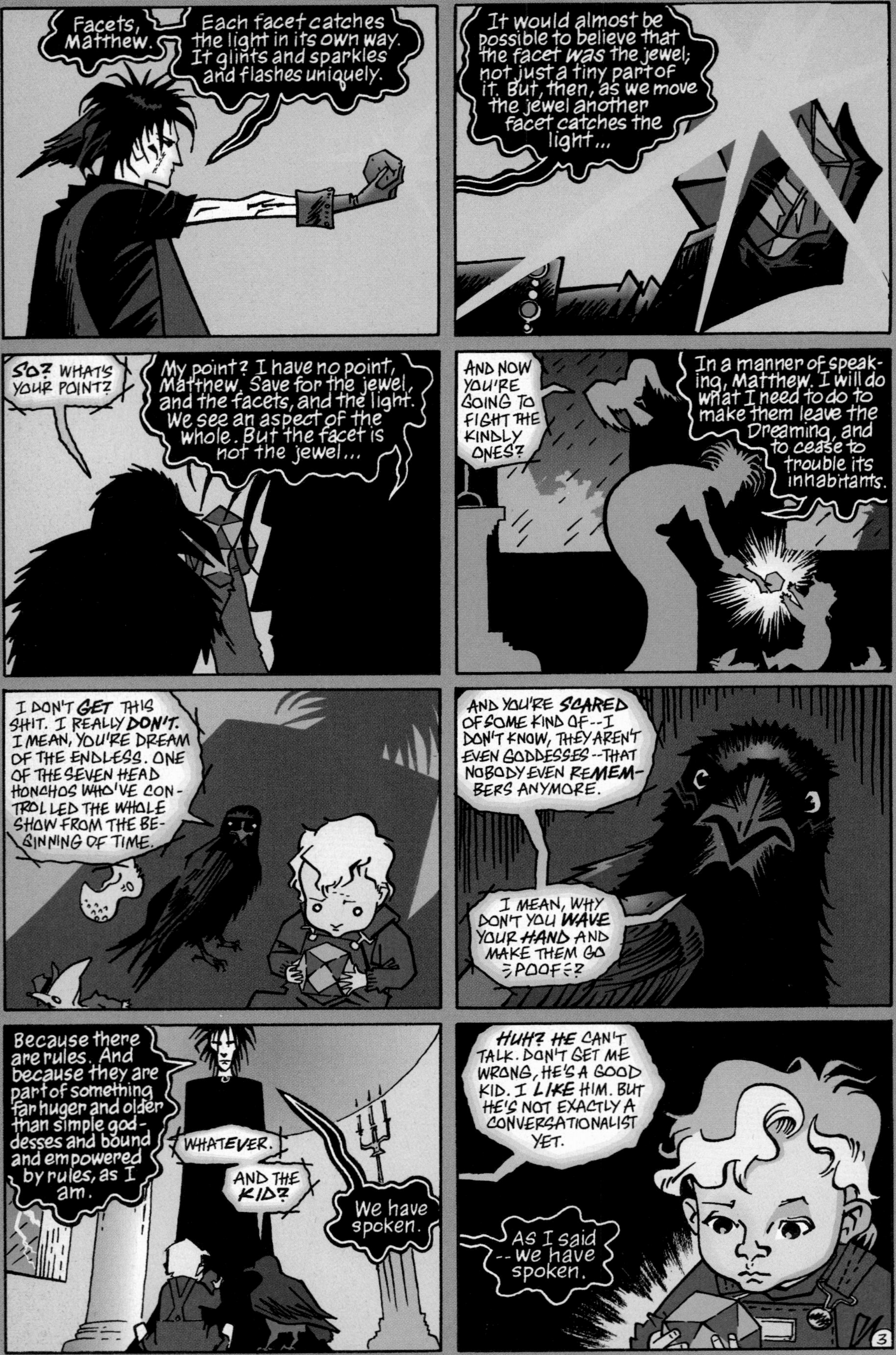
Facets, Matthew.
Each facet catches the light in its own way. It glints and sparkles and flashes uniquely.
It would almost be possible to believe that the facet WAS the jewel; not just a tiny part of it. But, then, as we move the jewel another facet catches the light...
SO? WHAT'S YOUR POINT?
My point? I have no point, Matthew. Save for the jewel, and the facets, and the light. We see an aspect of the whole. But the facet is not the jewel...
AND NOW YOU'RE GOING TO FIGHT THE KINDLY ONES?
In a manner of speaking, Matthew. I will do what I need to do to make them leave the Dreaming, and to cease to trouble its inhabitants.
I DON'T GET THIS SHIT. I REALLY DON'T. I MEAN, YOU'RE DREAM OF THE ENDLESS. ONE OF THE SEVEN HEAD HONCHOS WHO'VE CONTROLLED THE WHOLE SHOW FROM THE BEGINNING OF TIME.
AND YOU'RE SCARED OF SOME KIND OF--I DON'T KNOW, THEY AREN'T EVEN GODDESSES--THAT NOBODY EVEN REMEMBERS ANYMORE.
I MEAN, WHY DON'T YOU WAVE YOUR HAND AND MAKE THEM GO =POOF=?
Because there are rules. And because they are part of something far huger and older than simple goddesses and bound and empowered by rules, as I am.
WHATEVER.
AND THE KID?
We have spoken.
HUH? HE CAN'T TALK. DON'T GET ME WRONG, HE'S A GOOD KID. I LIKE HIM. BUT HE'S NOT EXACTLY A CONVERSATIONALIST YET.
As I said --we have spoken.
3

SO WHAT **NOW?**

NOW, I BID FAREWELL TO YOU, AND THE BOY, AND THE EMERALD, AND THE CASTLE. I SHALL SEND YOU AWAY. AND I SHALL GO AND DO WHAT NEEDS TO BE DONE WITH THE LADIES...

FARE YOU WELL, MATTHEW. I SHALL NOT FORGET YOU.

MATTHEW? I SENT YOU AWAY.

NOT IF I DON'T **WANT** TO GO. IT DIDN'T WORK THE **LAST** TIME, REMEMBER? SOMETIMES I THINK IT'S ALL I GOT LEFT. NOT GOING.

4

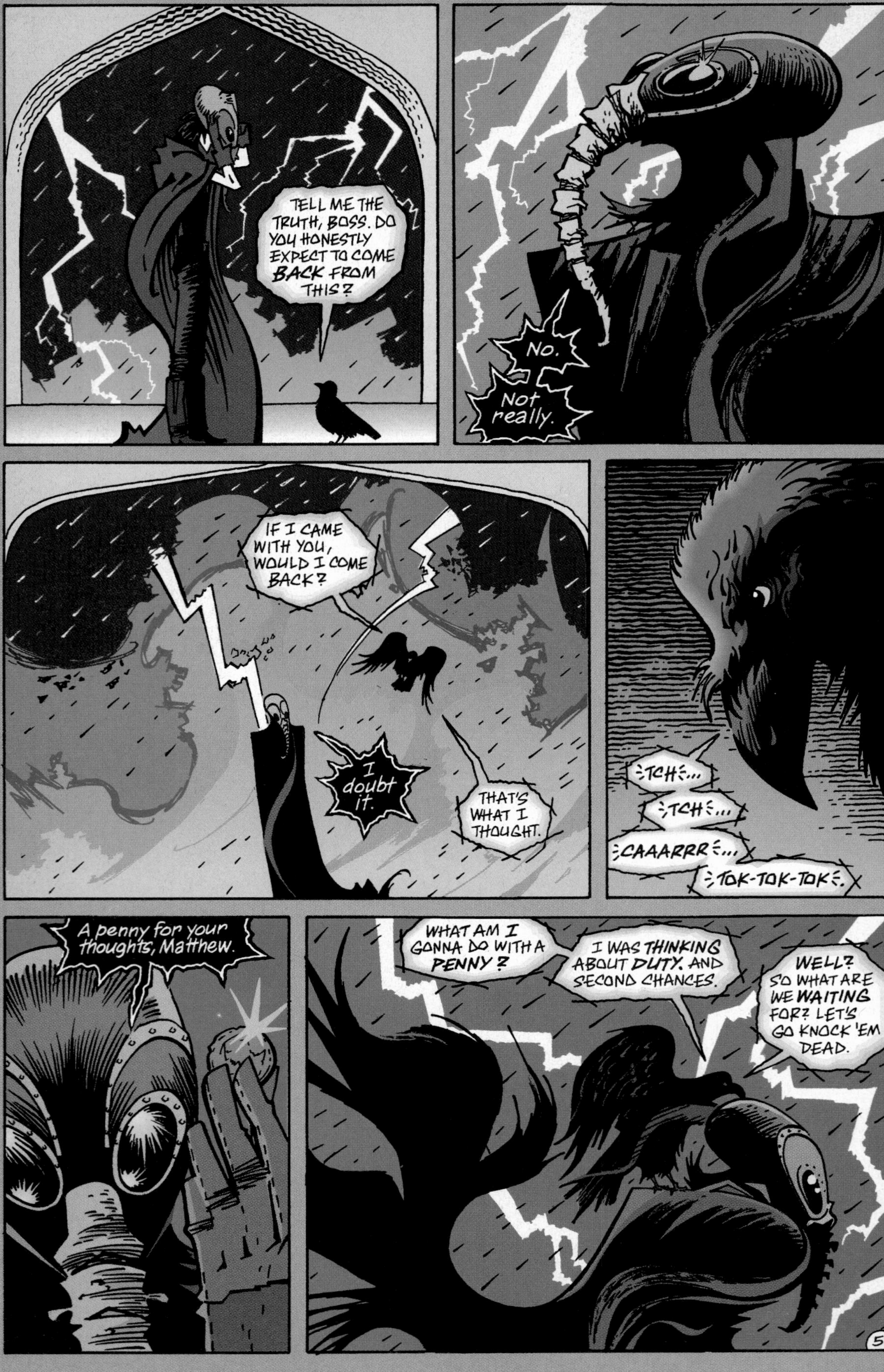

TELL ME THE TRUTH, BOSS. DO YOU HONESTLY EXPECT TO COME BACK FROM THIS?
No.
Not really.
IF I CAME WITH YOU, WOULD I COME BACK?
I doubt it.
THAT'S WHAT I THOUGHT.
TCH...
TCH...
CAAARRR...
TOK-TOK-TOK.
A penny for your thoughts, Matthew.
WHAT AM I GONNA DO WITH A PENNY?
I WAS THINKING ABOUT DUTY. AND SECOND CHANCES.
WELL? SO WHAT ARE WE WAITING FOR? LET'S GO KNOCK 'EM DEAD.
5

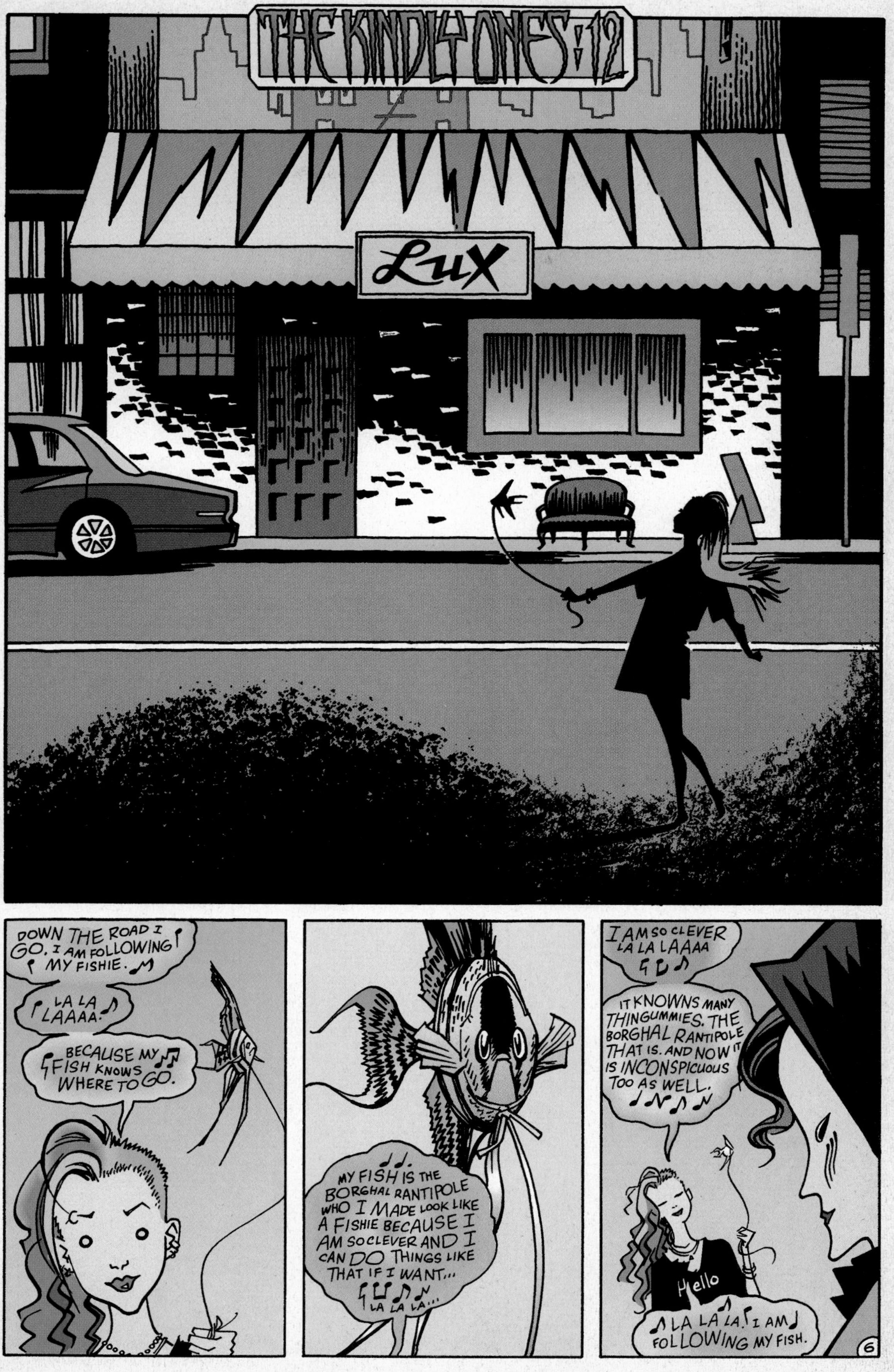
THE KINDLY ONES : 12
LUX
DOWN THE ROAD I GO. I AM FOLLOWING MY FISHIE.
LA LA LAAAA.
BECAUSE MY FISH KNOWS WHERE TO GO.
MY FISH IS THE BORGHAL RANTIPOLE WHO I MADE LOOK LIKE A FISHIE BECAUSE I AM SO CLEVER AND I CAN DO THINGS LIKE THAT IF I WANT...
LA LA LA...
I AM SO CLEVER LA LA LAAAA
IT KNOWNS MANY THINGUMMIES. THE BORGHAL RANTIPOLE THAT IS. AND NOW IT IS INCONSPICUOUS TOO AS WELL.
Hello
LA LA LA. I AM FOLLOWING MY FISH.
6

EXIT

NGO ARAY.

HELLO PRETTY LADY. I AM FOLLOWING MY FISH. LOOKING FOR MY DOGGIE. *BOTH.* AT THE SAME TIME.

Hello

IGH ROU GOWNK NGHO ARAY HAI RIRR KHORR ZHE PFOREEZSCH.

WHAT WILL YOU CALL THE POLICE?

GHO ARAY.

HMPH. IF YOU DON'T LET ME IN, I WILL TURN *YOU* INTO A DEMON HALF-FACE WAITRESS NIGHT-CLUB LADY WITH A CRUSH ON HER BOSS, AND I'LL MAKE IT SO YOU'VE *BEEN* THAT FROM THE BEGINNING OF TIME TO *NOW* AND YOU'LL NEVER *EVER* KNOW IF *YOU* WERE ANYTHING *ELSE* AND IT WILL ITCH INSIDE YOUR HEAD WORSE THAN LITTLE BUGSES.

EXIT

mazikeen? LET HER COME THROUGH.

Hello

NGO ING ZHENG. HE DEZSHERGZS HEOU.

IF HE DESERVES ME HE MUST HAVE BEEN VERY *VERY* GOOD INDEED.

I AM FOLLOWING MY FISH.

7

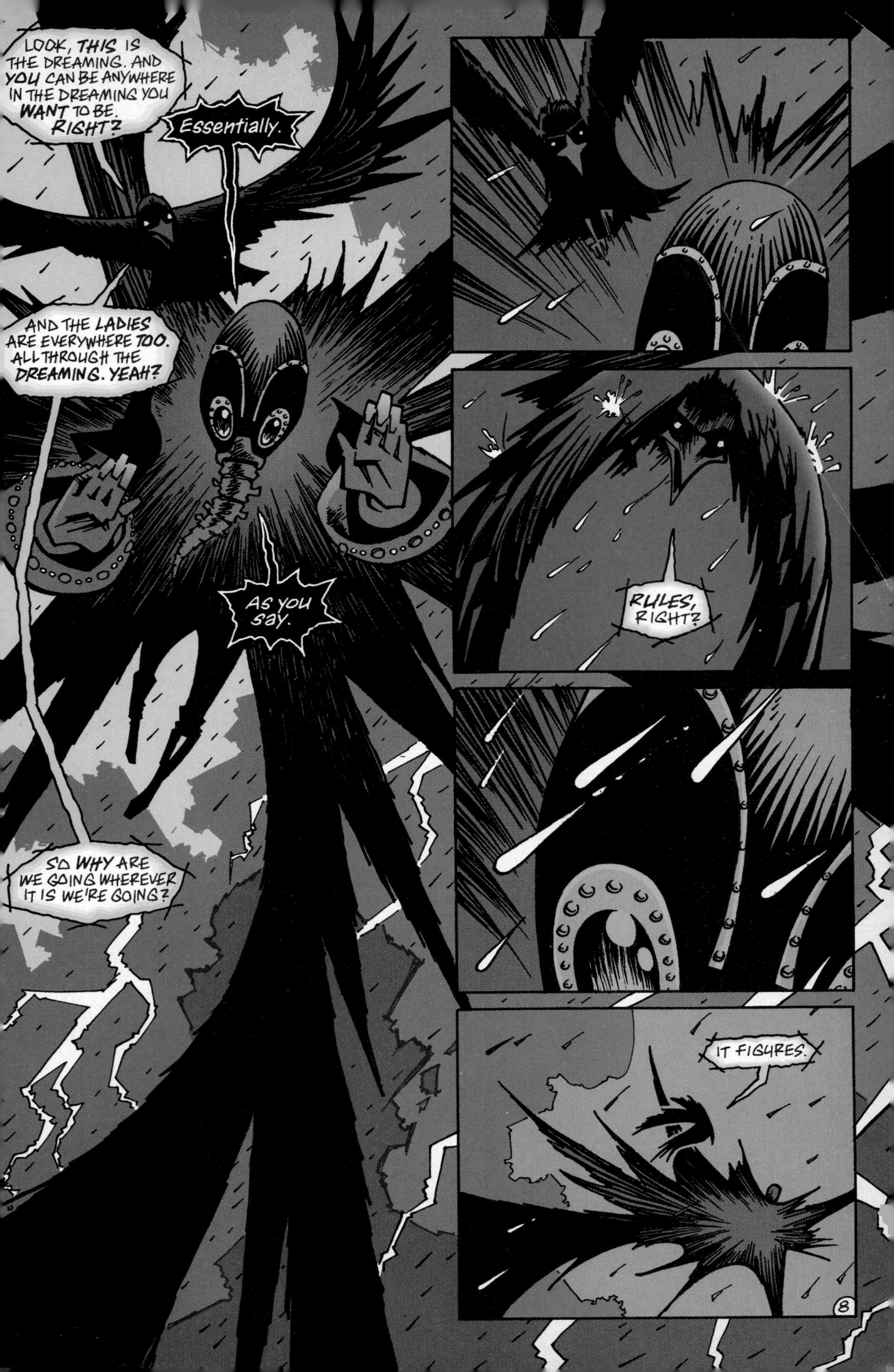
LOOK, THIS IS THE DREAMING. AND YOU CAN BE ANYWHERE IN THE DREAMING YOU WANT TO BE. RIGHT?
Essentially.
AND THE LADIES ARE EVERYWHERE TOO. ALL THROUGH THE DREAMING. YEAH?
As you say.
SO WHY ARE WE GOING WHEREVER IT IS WE'RE GOING?
RULES, RIGHT?
IT FIGURES.
8

NOW, VIXEN, IT SAYS HERE THAT YOUR NEW SHOW HAS BEEN PICKETED BY SOME LESBIAN GROUPS? IS THAT *RIGHT?*

OHHH, *MARY,* DON'T GET ME *STARTED*--THE PROBLEM I SEE WITH LESBIANS IS SELF-IMAGE. AT LEAST GAY MEN HAD ROCK HUDSON AND OSCAR WILDE--

--THE BEST *LESBIANS* COULD MUSTER WAS MISS HATHAWAY FROM *THE BEVERLY HILLBILLIES.*

TELL ME, VIXEN, DID YOU SET OUT TO BECOME CONTRO-VERSIAL?

CONTROVERSIAL? *MOI?* I *PREFER* TO THINK OF MYSELF AS A BIOLOGICAL WEAPON IN THE WAR BETWEEN THE SEXES.

OR THE FIFTH COLUMN, PERHAPS? *VIXEN,* LADIES N' GENTLEMEN. AND CONGRATU-LATIONS AGAIN ON THE SUCCESS OF THE *CD.*

VIXEN WILL BE APPEARING LIVE AT THE COMEDY CAVERN FOR THE NEXT THREE WEEKS IN HER ONE-WOMAN REVUE 'DON'T GET ME STARTED!'

BE*LIEVE* IT OR *NOT,* A GLENDALE DENTAL HYGIENIST CLAIMS AN *ANGEL* TOLD HER THE DATE OF THE *NEXT* L.A. EARTHQUAKE --AND THAT *THIS* ONE'LL BE THE *BIG* ONE. SHE'LL TELL US *ALL* ABOUT THAT, AFTER THE BREAK. *I'M* MARY GENTIAN, AND *THIS* IS 'MARY IN THE MORNING'--DON'T GO 'WAY NOW.

THAT *WAS GREAT,* VIXEN. SO, UH, MISS HATHAWAY WAS A *LES*BIAN?

MM-HMM.

IS THAT, LIKE, THE ONE ON THE *TV,* OR THE ONE IN THE *MOVIE?*

YOU KNOW WHAT THEY *SAY,* SUGAR: "IF YOU HAVE TO ASK ..."

EXIT

GUEST DRESSING ROOM A

HOW THE *HELL* DID *YOU* GET IN HERE?

9

HUNDRED-DOLLAR BILLS, HAL. YOU *GIVE* THEM TO PEOPLE, THEY LET YOU WANDER AROUND BACKSTAGE. I TOLD THEM I WAS AN OLD FRIEND AND WANTED TO SURPRISE YOU.

AND, OF COURSE, I *AM* AN OLD FRIEND. AND I *DID* WANT TO SURPRISE YOU.

WELL, SUR*PRISE*, SURPRISE.

SO WHY ARE *YOU* HERE? I THOUGHT AFTER OUR LAST CONVER-SATION THAT LITTLE MISS ROSE POLITICALLY CORRECT WALKER FOUND ME JUST *TOO* SOCIALLY *MONSTROUS* TO BE *TOLERATED*.

THAT'S NOT TRUE, HAL. AND YOU KNOW IT. LOOK, I DON'T WANT TO ARGUE. THAT'S NOT WHY I CAME.

UH, ZELDA'S DEAD.

SO: EXEUNT THE SPIDER WOMEN, STAGE *LEFT.* LOOK ON THEIR *WORKS*, YE MIGHTY, AND CLEAN YOURS WITH BLEACH.

YOU *MAY* BE AMUSED TO KNOW THAT, WHILE *THEY* ARE PUSHING UP THE DAISIES, *I,* ACCORDING TO THE LATEST SET OF TESTS, AM STILL GLORIOUSLY--*MAGNIF*ICENTLY--*HIV* NEGATIVE.

THAT'S NOT *FUNNY*, HAL.

OH, IT'S FUNNY ENOUGH, COSMICALLY SPEAKING. IF YOU TAKE THE *BROAD VIEW*. BE A GOOD GIRL AND UNZIP ME.

10

WELL, ZELDA *ISN'T* PUSHING UP THE DAISIES--*YET*. THE FUNERAL'S TOMORROW.

YOU WERE HER ONLY OTHER FRIEND.

I THOUGHT THAT *THIS* MIGHT BE AN OPPORTUNITY TO LET, Y'KNOW, BYGONES BE BYGONES, BETWEEN US, AND WITH WHATEVER HAPPENED BETWEEN YOU AND CHANTAL AND ZELDA.

SHE'S *GOT* NO FAMILY. IF *YOU* DON'T COME, I'M GOING TO BE THE *ONLY* ONE AT THE SERVICE.

SO, WHAT DO YOU SAY?

TWO LETTERS. STARTS WITH AN *N*, RHYMES WITH BLOWJOB, IF YOU LOSE THE JOB AT THE END.

HAL!

SORRY, SWEETHEART. I DON'T *DO* FUNERALS. LIFE IS, AS THEY SAY, TOO SHORT.

AND I CAN'T WEAR *BLACK*. I'M AN *AUTUMN*.

ASSHOLE, HAL. THE WORD YOU'RE LOOKING FOR IS ASSHOLE.

11

This is the place.

LOOK. *BOSS.* I'M NOT SURE I'M GOING TO *GET* ANOTHER CHANCE TO SAY THIS. OR... HELL. YOU KNOW WHAT I MEAN.

SO. WHATEVER HAPPENS.

IT WAS *GOOD BEING YOUR RAVEN.*

REALLY. I MEAN...

IT WAS GOOD BEING YOUR FRIEND.

Friend?

YEAH. FRIEND. SHIT. I DON'T KNOW. WHAT-EVER.

Ladies? I am here. It is time to settle this matter for good.

12

WELCOME, LADY DELIRIUM. COME IN, COME IN. CAN I *GET* YOU ANYTHING?

I KNOW YOU.

I KNOW WHO YOU ARE.

AND I KNOW WHO *YOU* ARE TOO, LADY.

YOU'RE THE DEE EE VEE EE um EYE EL.

NOT ANY *MORE.* I STOPPED. "QUOTH THE RAVEN..."

WHATEVER.

NOW I'M JUST TAKING THINGS EASY. PLAYING A LITTLE PIANO, AND RUNNING THE BEST DAMNED NIGHTCLUB AND RESTAURANT IN THIS WHOLE CITY OF THE ANGELS.

ANY REQUESTS?

YES. I WANT MY *DOGGIE* BACK.

AND I WANT MY *BROTHER* ALL RIGHT. I DON'T WANT HIM HURT OR ANYTHING.

THAT'S MY REQUEST. PLEASE.

13

I **TOLD** him, you know.

I told him **YEARS AGO.**

IT WAS AT THE END OF MY REIGN. I CLOSED THE FINAL DOOR TO HELL, AND I TOLD HIM...

I TOLD HIM THAT I OWED HIM MUCH FOR HAVING GIVEN ME THE IMPETUS TO GO.

I TOLD HIM THAT THERE WAS **ALWAYS** FREEDOM, EVEN THE ULTIMATE FREEDOM. THE FREEDOM TO LEAVE.

YOU DON'T HAVE TO STAY **ANYWHERE** FOREVER.

I **LEAVE** PLACES.

I AM SURE YOU DO.

BUT **DREAM** DOESN'T. I DON'T THINK HE CAN.

YOU KNOW, I SWORE TO DESTROY HIM. YOUR BROTHER.

NO. I MEAN, I **DIDN'T** KNOW.

WHY?

OH, HE EMBARRASSED ME... HE SAID SOMETHING HE THOUGHT WAS CLEVER... IT'S **NOT** THAT IMPORTANT.

AND NOW... NOW I FEEL ALMOST **SORRY** FOR HIM.

WHAT SHOULD I **DO?**

GO AND FIND YOUR **DOG,** CHILD. GO AND FIND YOUR DOG; IT IS TOO LATE TO HELP YOUR BROTHER.

14

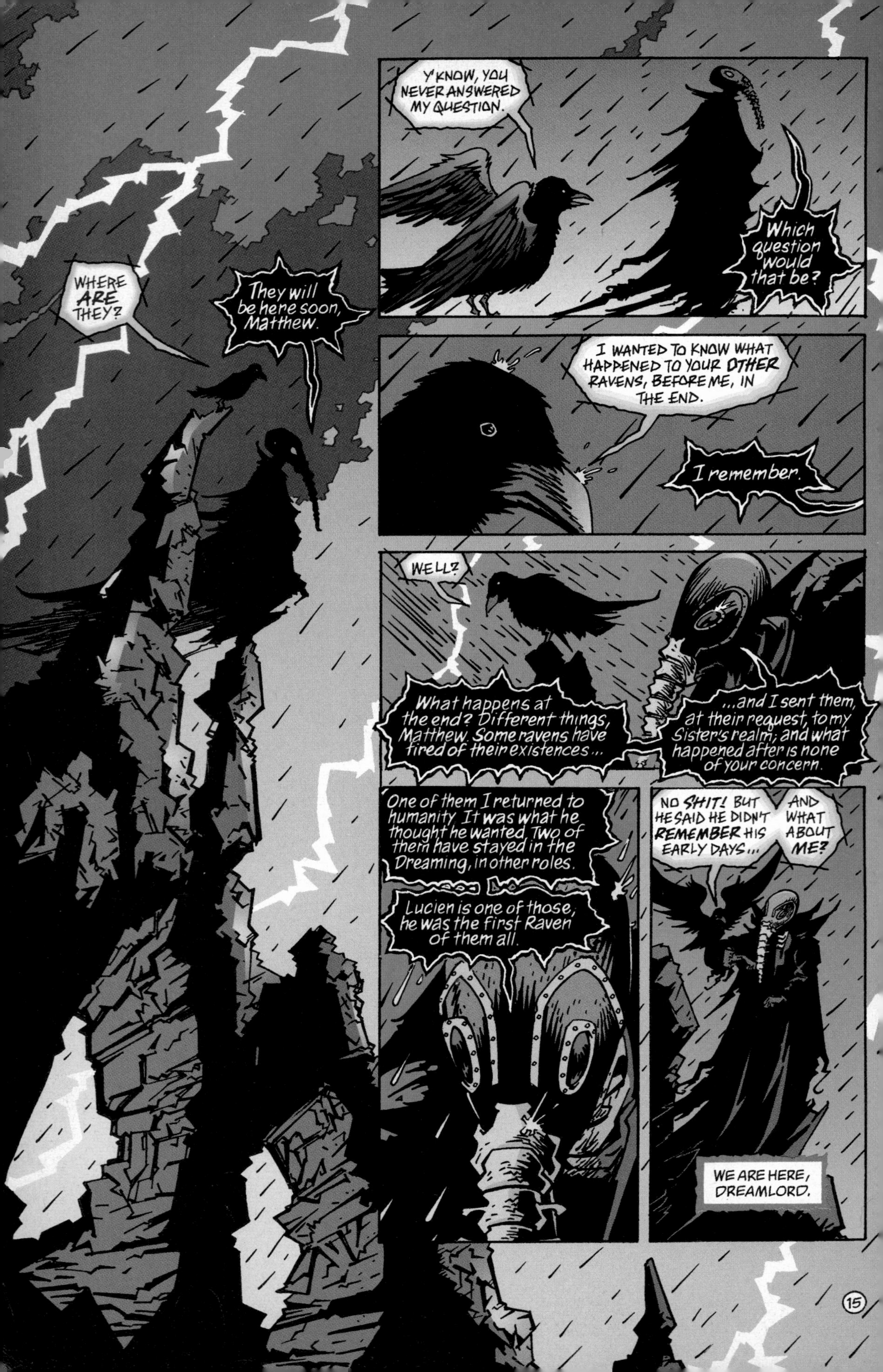
WHERE ARE THEY?
They will be here soon, Matthew.
Y'KNOW, YOU NEVER ANSWERED MY QUESTION.
Which question would that be?
I WANTED TO KNOW WHAT HAPPENED TO YOUR OTHER RAVENS, BEFORE ME, IN THE END.
I remember.
WELL?
What happens at the end? Different things, Matthew. Some ravens have tired of their existences...
...and I sent them, at their request, to my Sister's realm; and what happened after is none of your concern.
One of them I returned to humanity. It was what he thought he wanted. Two of them have stayed in the Dreaming, in other roles.
Lucien is one of those, he was the first Raven of them all.
NO SHIT! BUT HE SAID HE DIDN'T REMEMBER HIS EARLY DAYS...
AND WHAT ABOUT ME?
WE ARE HERE, DREAMLORD.

Faerie

@hem, lady...
To conclude my
poem, the Envoi.

Princess! The river holds the trout;
so does the world take care of me.
And if you do not choose to see
that what we are, we choose to be,
It's hard, but is all one to me.

The rule is cruel, but there's
no doubt--
I'll dream tonight of
storms at sea...
Be sure your sins
will find
you out.

There. That's my
poem done, lady.

Well?

Well?
What did
you
think?

16

I--I DO NUHNOT *CARE* FOR YOUR POETRY, CLURACAN.

NUHNOR FOR YOUR --->snf! --MODE OF DELIVERY.

HOW DID YOU KNOW IT WAS *ME*?

THE POETRY'S-*SOUND*ED LIKE YOURS. AND YOU'RE VAIN ENOUGH TO WANT TO SEE THE REACTION OF YOUR INTENDED AUDIENCE.

YOU'RE MY *BROTHER*, FOR OUR LADY'S SAKE. IT'S THE KUH*KIND* OF STUPID THING YOU'D *DO*.

NOW, *GO* AWAY.

YOU'RE *CRYING*.

LORD SHAPER IS IN DIRE *NEED*. AND HE DOESN'T LOVE ME.

WOULD IT BE BETTER IF HE WAS IN DIRE NEED AND *DID* LOVE YOU?

AND *LOOK* AT ME. THIS IS WHAT YOU MADE ME.

I *SAVED* YOU FROM *BANISHMENT*. OR *WORSE*. YOU COULD HAVE BEEN SENT AWAY....

YES. >snnnf.< THANK YOU FOR THE POEM.

CLURACAN? WILL YOU GIVE ME MY *TRUE* SHAPE BACK, FOR MY *JOURNEY*?

....JOURNEY?

AS YOU *SAID* IN YOUR SILLY POEM. WHAT WE *ARE*, WE *CHOOSE* TO BE.

I CHOOSE TO *LEAVE*.

BROTHER? WILL YOU GIVE ME BACK MY *FACE?*

17

SO. YOU HAVE COME TO RECKON WITH US...

Yes.

I want you to leave my realm.

I want you to stop harming the entities who live here under my protection.

WE *WILL* DO WHAT WE *SHALL* DO. EH, DREAMER?

WE WILL DO WHAT WE *MUST*.

AND WE *CANNOT* LEAVE UNTIL OUR TASK IS DONE.

THIS WOULD BE ONE OF THOSE RULES DEALS AGAIN, WOULDN'T IT?

Hush, Matthew.

And if I fought you? And if I took a stand, here? What then?

THEN NOTHING WOULD CHANGE, DREAM-KING. HOW WILL YOU *FIGHT* US? YOU CANNOT EVEN *TOUCH* US.

TAKE YOUR STAND. WE CARE NOT. WE WILL CONTINUE TO RIP APART YOUR WORLD, *BIT BY BIT*, *SHRED* BY SHRED.

YOUR SON'S *BLOOD* IS ON YOUR HANDS.

As you say. So...you will not be satisfied with anything less, then?

WHAT DO *YOU* THINK?

LESS THAN *WHAT?* WHAT ARE THEY *ASKING?*

Hush, Matthew, hush. That is none of your concern.

18

SO *YOU'RE* DANIEL.

HELLO.

KEEP AWAY FROM HIM.

YOU'RE THE *CORINTHIAN,* AREN'T YOU? THE *NEW* ONE. *HI.*

WHO ARE YOU?

I'M YOUR MASTER'S SISTER.

I *KNOW* YOU. IF YOU TRY TO TOUCH THE CHILD, I WILL TRY TO *STOP* YOU, THOUGH IT MEANS *MY* DEATH ALSO.

I'M NOT HERE FOR *EITHER* OF YOU.

WHERE'S MY BROTHER?

19

OUR LORD IS WITH THE *LADIES,* MADAM.

THANK YOU, LUCIEN.

UM.

I *LIKED* THE LAST BOOK YOU GAVE ME.

MISS MIRRLEES HER*SELF* WAS MOST FOND OF THE BOOK AS WELL, YOU KNOW: SHE WOULD THINK ON IT FOR *HOURS* BEFORE SHE WENT TO SLEEP AT NIGHT; BUT SHE NEVER *WROTE* MORE OF IT THAN A COUPLE OF PARAGRAPHS.

I *ALSO* HAVE HER SEQUELS TO A FLY IN AMBER, SOMEWHERE, A BIT DRY, OF COURSE, NOT FICTION, BUT IF YOU'RE INTERESTED I COULD GO AND--

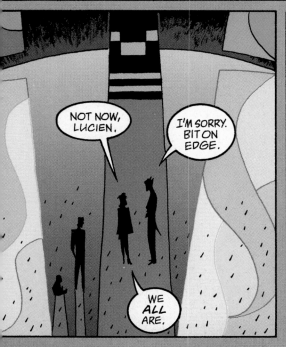

NOT NOW, LUCIEN.

I'M SORRY. BIT ON EDGE.

WE *ALL* ARE.

WELL, *I* CAN WAIT.

20

I have no alternative, do I?

NO.

I see.

You are doing something that is extremely inadvisable, and will certainly have repercussions.

YOU DO NOT SCARE US.

I do not intend to scare you. There are, however, matters of balance to consider.

We make choices.

No one else can live our lives for us. And we must confront and accept the consequences of our actions.

BOSS? WHAT'RE YOU-- ARE YOU CRAZY, BOSS?

No, Matthew, but I appreciate your concern.

And I have a task for you.

UH-UH. I'M NOT GOING ANYWHERE. I'M STAYING HERE WITH YOU.

This is the last thing I will ask of you, Matthew. Will you deny it to me?

UH. WHAT DO YOU NEED?

Take them.

PLEASE.

I'm sorry...?

Here. Take these back to the castle. Guard them well.

My sister will be there. Ask her to meet me here.

THEY'RE... KIND OF BIG FOR ME TO CARRY.

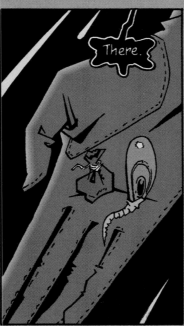

There.

22

"TAKE THEM, *PLEASE.*"

I apologize. Will you take them? Please?

OKAY. SURE. NO PROBLEM.

And wait with them.

I DON'T GET TO COME BACK?

I'm afraid not.

I... I'LL SEEYA, THEN. WHEN YOU COME BACK TO THE CASTLE. I'LL WAIT FOR YOU THERE.

Goodbye, Matthew.

HE SAID YOU'D BE HERE.

HE WANTS YOU TO GO TO HIM.

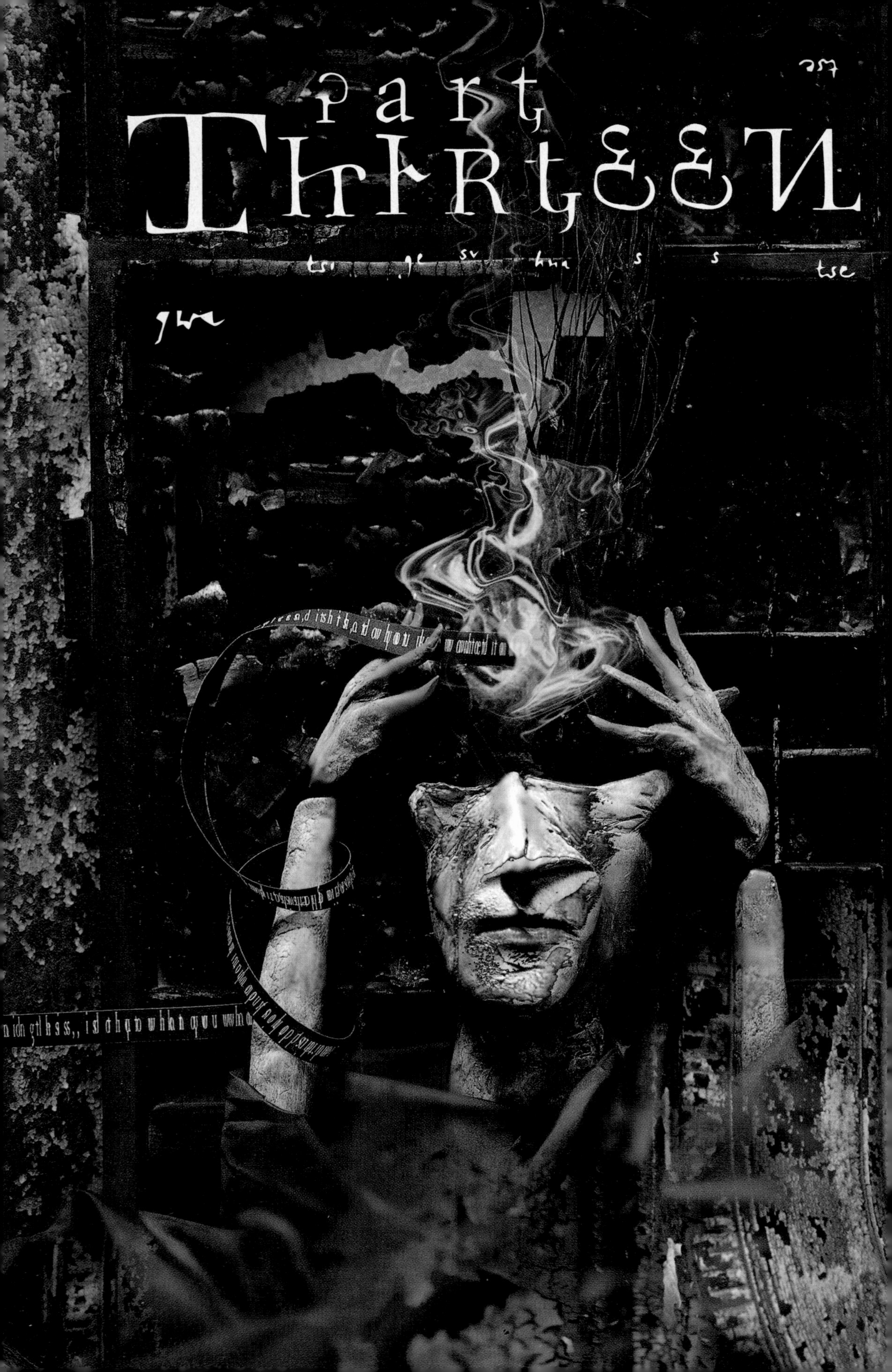
part
Thirteen

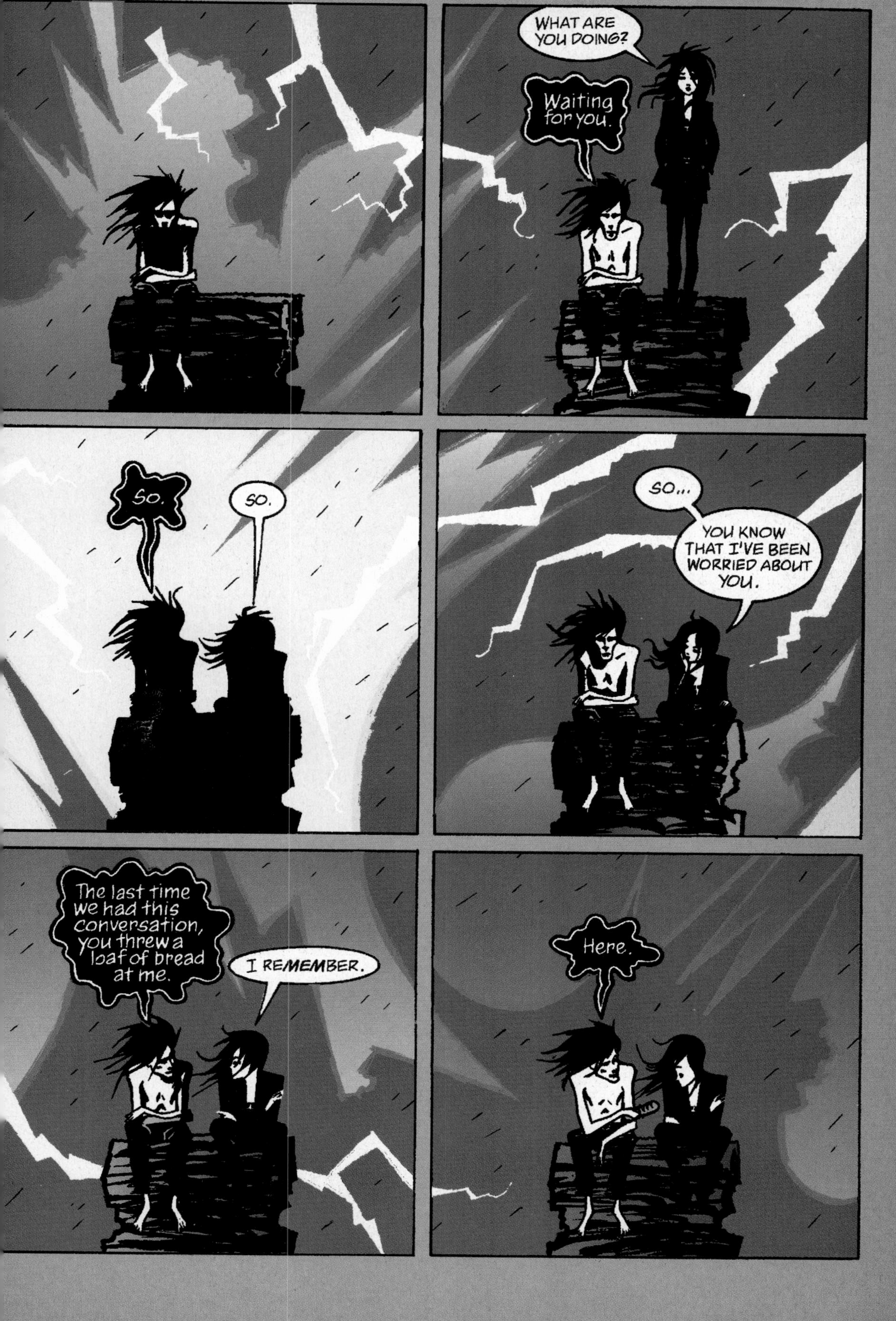
WHAT ARE YOU DOING?
Waiting for you.
So.
SO.
SO...
YOU KNOW THAT I'VE BEEN WORRIED ABOUT YOU.
The last time we had this conversation, you threw a loaf of bread at me.
I REMEMBER.
Here.

HM. YOU WANT TO MAKE SOME PIGEONS?

If that is what you wish.

I was expecting you to throw it at me--to tell me off; to shout at me.

IT'S TOO LATE FOR THAT, MY BROTHER. IT'S MUCH TOO LATE FOR THAT.

I am tired, my sister. I am very tired.

HEY! MATTHEW?

UH?

SHIT!

=KAAR=

STAY OUT OF REACH OF ITS MOUTH, I THINK WE CAN ASSUME THAT IT'S POISON- OUS.

WHAT THE HELL WAS THAT?

I HAVE NO IDEA.

IT WAS CALLED NYBBAS. OR POSSIBLY IT IS MERELY A NYBBAS, I FORGET.

IT WAS ONE OF LORD MORPHEUS'S PRISONERS. ALL OF THEM WERE FREED ABOUT AN HOUR AGO --I PRESUME BY THE LADIES.

A COUPLE OF THEM TOOK REFUGE IN THE LIBRARY. I.... DEALT WITH THEM....

3

SHIT. THEY'RE *ALL* FREE?

THE ONES THAT WERE IN DARKNESS. THE THINGS HE PUT IN THE CHEST ARE STILL SAFE.

HOW MANY OF THEM ARE LEFT IN THE CASTLE?

A *FEW.* I'VE DEALT WITH THOSE THAT TRIED TO HARM ME OR THE BOY. MOST OF THEM FLED.

YOU AND YOUR SWISS ARMY KNIFE TAKE ON THE WORLD, HUH?

SO: YOU GOING TO TRY AND *KILL* ME NOW?

I *OUGHT* TO. BUT... HELL, BIRD. LIFE'S TOO *SHORT.*

WELL, *THANKS.* I THINK.

SO WHERE'S THE BOY? WHERE'S *DANIEL?* HE *OKAY?*

HE'S *FINE.* SAY HI TO MATTHEW, DANIEL.

HEY, KID. ATTABOY. YOU REMEMBER ME?

birdee.

KIND OF A LATE DEVELOPER, HUH?

MATTHEW? WHAT HAS BEFALLEN OUR LORD, EH? HOW CROAKS THE RAVEN?

HE'S OFF ON THE BORDERS OF NIGHTMARE. HE SENT ME BACK HERE WITH SOME OF HIS *STUFF.* TO WAIT WITH IT, UNTIL HE COMES *BACK.*

HOW DOES IT GO...?

"THERE'S BUT THREE FURIES FOUND IN SPACIOUS HELL; BUT IN A GREAT MAN'S BREAST THREE THOUSAND DWELL."

WHAT*EVER.*

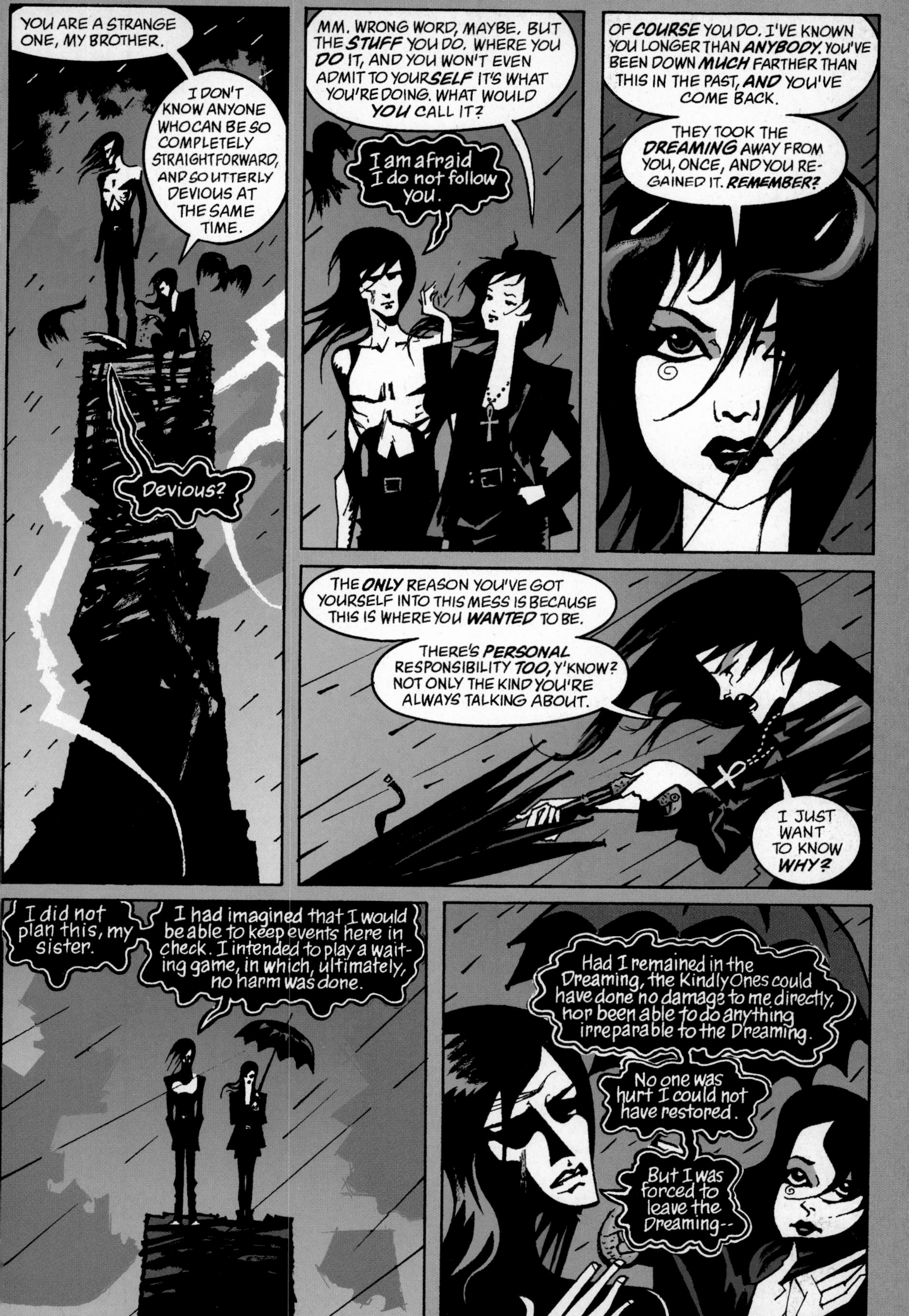

YOU ARE A STRANGE ONE, MY BROTHER.
I DON'T KNOW ANYONE WHO CAN BE SO COMPLETELY STRAIGHTFORWARD, AND SO UTTERLY DEVIOUS AT THE SAME TIME.
Devious?
MM. WRONG WORD, MAYBE, BUT THE STUFF YOU DO. WHERE YOU DO IT, AND YOU WON'T EVEN ADMIT TO YOURSELF IT'S WHAT YOU'RE DOING. WHAT WOULD YOU CALL IT?
I am afraid I do not follow you.
OF COURSE YOU DO. I'VE KNOWN YOU LONGER THAN ANYBODY. YOU'VE BEEN DOWN MUCH FARTHER THAN THIS IN THE PAST, AND YOU'VE COME BACK.
THEY TOOK THE DREAMING AWAY FROM YOU, ONCE, AND YOU RE-GAINED IT. REMEMBER?
THE ONLY REASON YOU'VE GOT YOURSELF INTO THIS MESS IS BECAUSE THIS IS WHERE YOU WANTED TO BE.
THERE'S PERSONAL RESPONSIBILITY TOO, Y'KNOW? NOT ONLY THE KIND YOU'RE ALWAYS TALKING ABOUT.
I JUST WANT TO KNOW WHY?
I did not plan this, my sister.
I had imagined that I would be able to keep events here in check. I intended to play a waiting game, in which, ultimately, no harm was done.
Had I remained in the Dreaming, the Kindly Ones could have done no damage to me directly, nor been able to do anything irreparable to the Dreaming.
No one was hurt I could not have restored.
But I was forced to leave the Dreaming--
5

DON'T YOU START BLAMING NUALA FOR THIS. YOU DIDN'T *HAVE* TO LEAVE. YOU DIDN'T *HAVE* TO DO ANYTHING.

No... you are right, of course...

It has nothing to do with Nuala.

It has everything to do with me.

Since I killed my son... the Dreaming has not been the same... or perhaps *I* was no longer the same. I still had my obligations...

But even the freedom of the Dreaming can be a cage, of a kind, my sister.

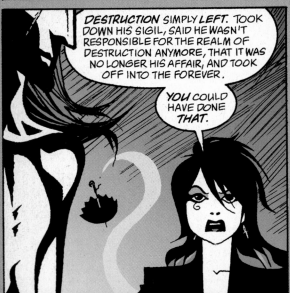

DESTRUCTION SIMPLY *LEFT.* TOOK DOWN HIS SIGIL, SAID HE WASN'T RESPONSIBLE FOR THE REALM OF DESTRUCTION ANYMORE, THAT IT WAS NO LONGER HIS AFFAIR, AND TOOK OFF INTO THE FOREVER.

YOU COULD HAVE DONE *THAT.*

No. I could not.

NO, YOU COULDN'T, COULD YOU?

6

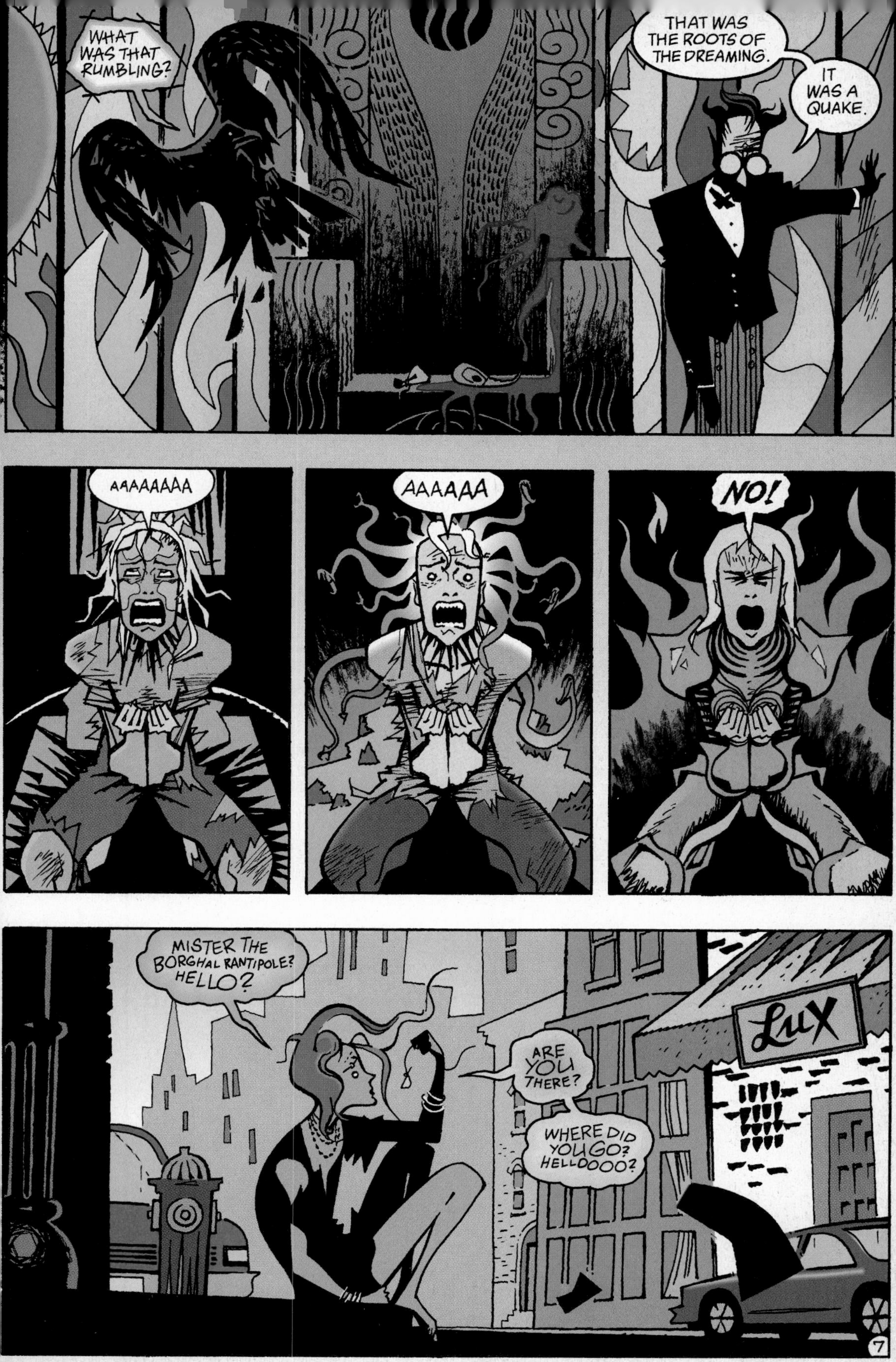
WHAT WAS THAT RUMBLING?
THAT WAS THE ROOTS OF THE DREAMING.
IT WAS A QUAKE.
AAAAAAAA
AAAAAA
NO!
MISTER THE BORGHAL RANTIPOLE? HELLO?
ARE YOU THERE?
WHERE DID YOU GO? HELLOOOO?
LUX

AND NUALA SPIES THE HILL-PORTAL, AND URGES HER PONY TOWARD IT; AND THE WIND IS ICE IN HER FACE.

AND THIS IS PASSING STRANGE IN FAERIE, WHERE IT IS ALWAYS MOST CLEMENT AND GENTLE.

AND THE POISON SPILLS INTO LOKI'S MOUTH AND EYES; HE WRITHES, AND A CITY FALLS: AND IN THE MOMENT OF PAIN HE GAINS A CERTAIN CLARITY.

THE MASTER MANIPULATOR REALIZES HOW, ULTIMATELY-- HOW STRANGELY, HOW ELEGANTLY-- HE TOO HAD BEEN MANIPULATED.

PERHAPS THE SOUND HE MAKES IS LAUGHTER.

AND A HUNDRED HUGE RAVENS FLAP THEIR WINGS IN YOUR DREAMS AND RAISE THEIR BLACK EYES TO THE STORM, EXPECTANTLY.

8

DID YOU FEEL THAT, DREAM KING?

WE ARE RIPPING YOUR WORLD APART.

I felt it.

WE HAVE FREED THE POWERS THAT YOU HAD CAGED.

I know.

DREAM-KING, WE ARE DESTROYING THE DREAMING. CAN YOU NOT FEEL IT?

Yes. I can.

WHAT WILL YOU DO, TO STOP US?

WHAT *CAN* YOU DO?

ENOUGH! I HAVE HAD *QUITE* ENOUGH OF THIS.

WE ARE MERELY PERFORMING OUR FUNCTION, LADY.

LEAVE US ALONE. THIS IS BETWEEN ME AND MY BROTHER.

THERE.

9

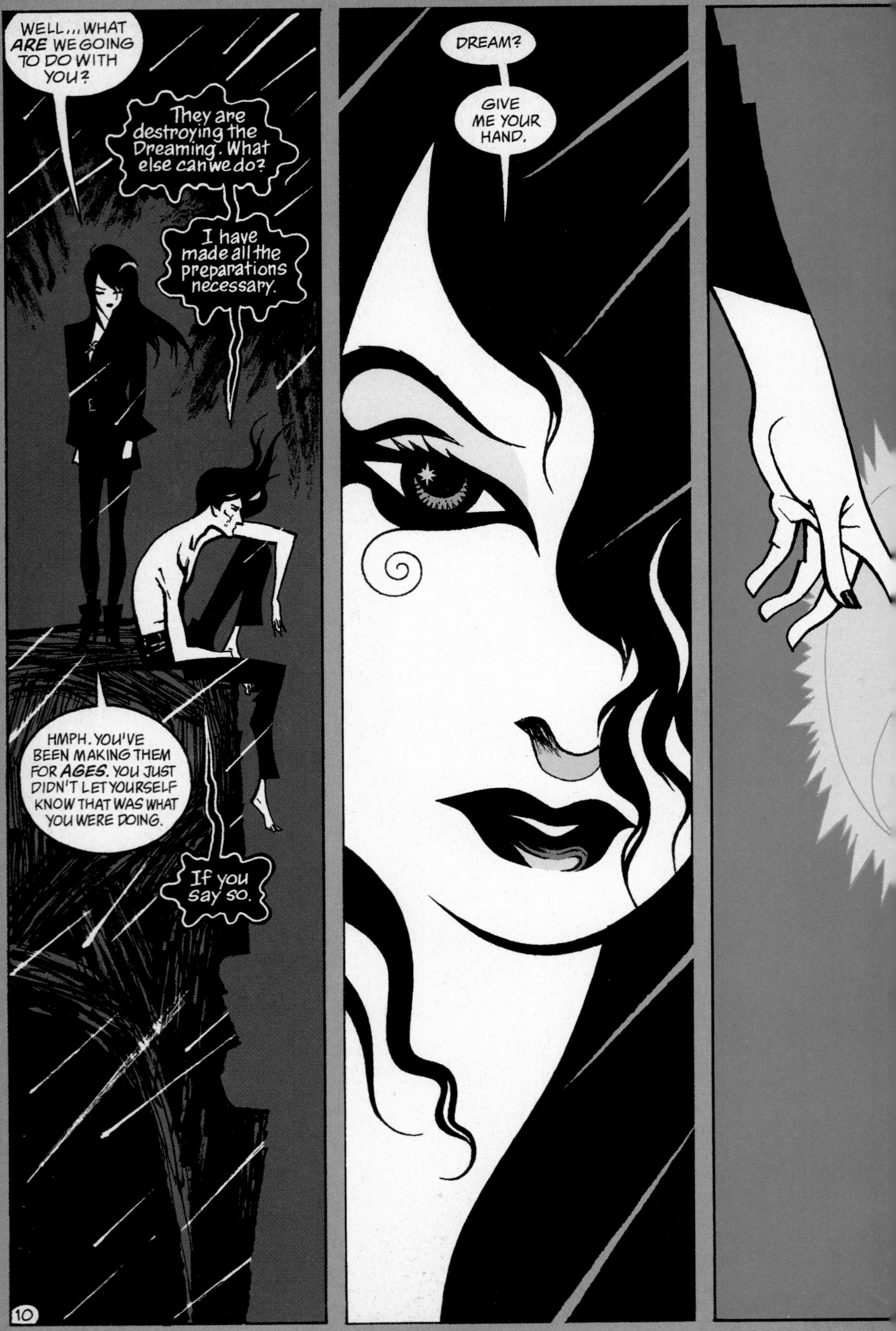

WELL... WHAT ARE WE GOING TO DO WITH YOU?
They are destroying the Dreaming. What else can we do?
I have made all the preparations necessary.
HMPH. YOU'VE BEEN MAKING THEM FOR AGES. YOU JUST DIDN'T LET YOURSELF KNOW THAT WAS WHAT YOU WERE DOING.
If you say so.
DREAM?
GIVE ME YOUR HAND.

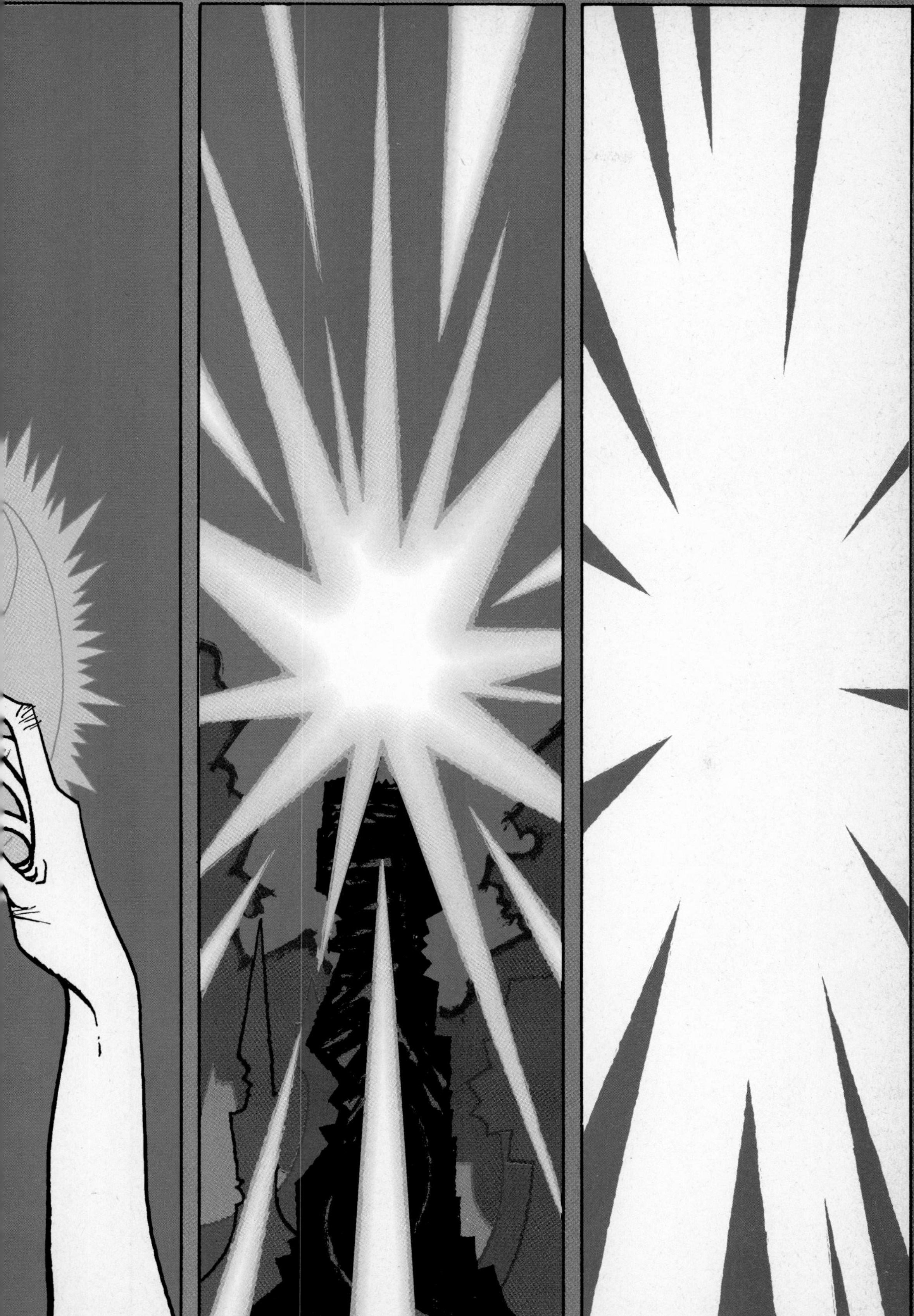

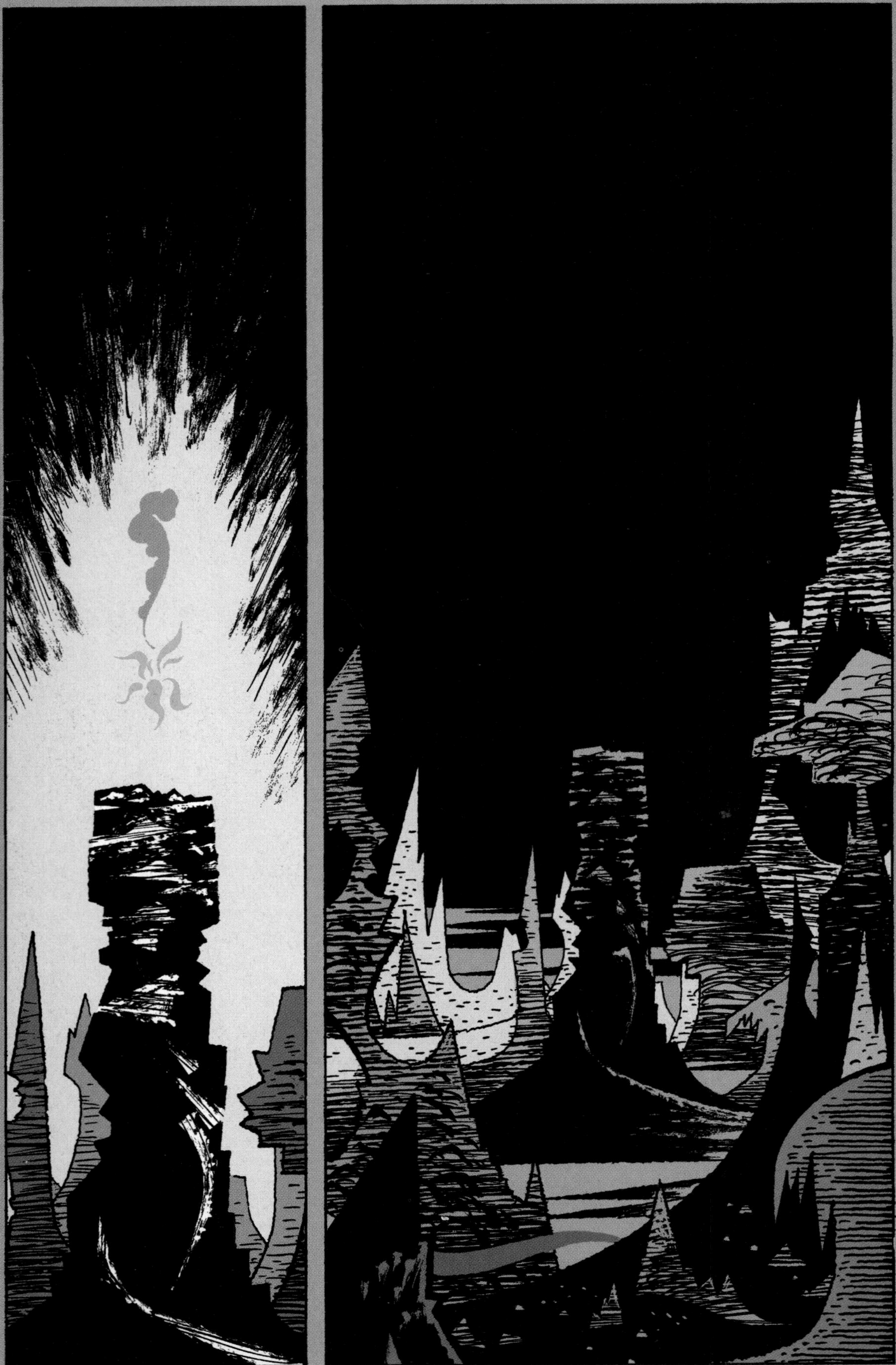

THE LADY NUALA. **WHERE** ARE YOU GOING?

I HAVE NO PATIENCE FOR THOSE WHO WOULD REJECT MY GUARDIANSHIP, AND DO NOT RECALL HAVING GIVEN YOU PERMISSION TO LEAVE THE BOUNDS OF FAERIE...

MY LADY.

I **AM** LEAVING. LET ME GO, OR IMPRISON ME, OR DESTROY ME; FOR I SHALL NOT WILLINGLY **STAY** HERE A MOMENT MORE.

YOU UNGRATEFUL **WRETCH.** I'LL MAKE YOU WISH YOU HAD NEVER BEEN--

IT WAS **TRUE**, THEN, CLURACAN. YOUR FORETELLING.

LADY, I HAD HOPED IT WOULD NOT BE SO...

GO AWAY. GO WHERESOEVER YOU WISH. I CARE NOT.

13

Hullo. You're late.

BARNABAS? I THOUGHT YOU WERE LOSTED.

I will never *ever*-- as long as I *live*--let you out of my sight again for a single, solitary *second*.

It's not even like they *have* proper ice creams at Disneyland anyway-- running off like that after a chocolate-covered banana... I *ask* you...

It's been *two weeks. Two weeks.*

BUT I *DID* LOOK FOR YOU. ALL OVER.

14

Hmph. *Where were* you looking? Patagonia? Mars? The Emerald City?

UM. PLACES *LIKE* THAT.

I spent over a week on the run. I nearly *starved* to *death*. This kind gentleman took pity on my plight.

HE'S A *GOOD* DOG, MISSIE. THE LITTLE DOG LAUGHED TO SEE SUCH FUN, BUT HE'S NOT *SO* LITTLE. AND HE TALKS PRETTY GOOD, FOR A DOG.

I MUST GIVE YOU A *PRESENT*, FOR FINDING MY. DOGGIE.

HMMMMM MMMMMM.

DO YOU WANT *PALACES* AND GOLDEN *TOUCHES* AND, OH! NEVER DYING AND THINGS?

NOPE, UH-UH. NO WAY. NOT ME, MA'AM.

WHAT *DO* YOU WANT?

I *KNOW* YOU, MISSY, I THINK I DO. I'M KIND OF YOURS ANYWAY, AIN'T I?

KIND OF.

T'AIN'T *SAFE* TO ASK FAVORS OF YOUR KIND, EVEN IF I *EARNED* 'EM. OTHERWISE I COULD FIND MYSELF SPITTING OUT FLOWER PETALS AND SILVER DOLLARS EVERY TIME I SPEAK.

THAT'S AS I UNDERSTAND IT, ANYHOW.

I'M HAPPY WITH JUST A THANK-YOU-KINDLY, AND MAYBE SOMETIMES THE BARNEY-DOG CAN COME FIND ME AND GAB A BIT.

I THINK I'M GOING TO *MISS* HIM.

WELL, OKAY.

OH, BARNABAS. I *AM* SO PLEASED TO SEE YOU. I THINK *BAD* THINGS HAVE HAPPENED. I FEEL THEM IN MY SOCKS.

YOU REMEMBER MY BROTHER? DREAM-WHO-YOU-MET?

Tall, officious, rather stuffy? Looks like he doesn't get *out* enough?

UM. YES. HIM.

Hello

HE'S *GONE*. HE'S NOT IN MY *MIND* ANY MORE.

I'm sure he can take care of himself.

I..., I DON'T *THINK* SO...

I OPENED THIS NIGHT SPOT FOR MY OWN ENTERTAINMENT. AND, FOR A WHILE, IN THE NIGHT, IT ENTERTAINED ME.

BUT THE DIVERSION BEGINS TO PALL. ONCE AGAIN, I PERCEIVE THE VOID BENEATH THE SURFACE OF ALL THINGS.

ALL THAT KEEPS ME GOING NOW IS THE DESIRE TO SEE HOW IT ALL COMES OUT.

HEOW *WOSH* CUNNZSH OUGK?

OH, YOU KNOW...THE WHOLE THING. THE UNIVERSE.

I HAD THE HUBRIS ORIGINALLY TO REGARD MYSELF AS A COLLABORATOR, AS A CO-AUTHOR...

VERY RAPIDLY I FOUND MYSELF REDUCED TO THE STATUS OF CHARACTER, FOLLOWING SOMETHING OF A DISAGREEMENT IN THE FUNDAMENTAL DIRECTION OF THE CREATION.

NOW I SOMETIMES FEEL I'M SIMPLY WAITING AROUND TO SEE WHICH OF US WAS RIGHT, WHICH WAS WRONG.

BUT EVEN IF IT TURNS OUT THAT I *WAS* RIGHT, WHAT GOOD DOES IT DO ME?

SO--WHAT--I GET THE THRILL OF STANDING AT THE END OF THE UNIVERSE, AND SAYING "SEE, I WAS RIGHT ALL THE TIME?" NO, I'M BETTER OFF OUT OF IT.

ONE MORE NIGHT. AND THEN THAT'S *IT* FOR LUX, I THINK.

AND WHAT *THEN?* AYE. THERE'S THE RUB.

RHERH ARE HEOU GKOINGH ZISS TCHINE?

EXIT

WHERE? ANYWHERE. EVERYWHERE. I DON'T KNOW.

I RRIW VFORROW HEOU VFORR EFFER...I NGUSSKKHH.

IF YOU MUST.

EXIT

AM I **LATE?**

HAL, YOU'D BE LATE TO YOUR OWN FUNERAL. NOW, TAKE THOSE FUCKING SHADES OFF.

PUSH BUTTON FOR ADMITTANCE

LANGUAGE, SWEETIE.

SO: WE'LL JUST ASSUME EVERYTHING **YOU** SAID YESTERDAY WAS RIGHT, AND THAT EVERYTHING **I** SAID WAS WRONG, **SHALL** WE? EASIER THAT WAY.

WHY, **HAL.** THAT'S THE SWEETEST APOLOGY ANYONE'S EVER MADE TO ME.

MM.

SAY, LISTEN, YOU KNOW WHAT YOU SAID ABOUT CLEANING YOUR WORKS? **THAT** WASN'T HOW THE SPIDER WOMEN DIED. THEY DIDN'T HAVE ANY DRUG... EXCEPT EACH OTHER...

CHAPEL

TCH. LOCKED.

WELL, YOU DON'T GET IT FROM TOILET SEATS, YOU KNOW.

CHANTAL HAD A KIDNEY REPLACEMENT IN APRIL 1989.

THE DONOR WAS **HIV** POSITIVE, ALTHOUGH SHE PROBABLY DIDN'T **KNOW** IT. SOME WOMAN WHO DIED IN A SHOOTING. BITS OF HER WERE RUSHED TO HOSPITALS ALL OVER. ONE OF HER KIDNEYS WENT INTO CHANTAL.

IT COULDN'T HAPPEN NOW. IT WAS A **FLUKE** IT WASN'T CAUGHT **THEN.**

NOT ALL THE TRANSPLANTEES GOT **AIDS.** EIGHT OUT OF FIFTY-SEVEN PEOPLE, SOMETHING LIKE THAT.

HOW DO YOU KNOW?

ZELDA'S MEDICAL RECORDS.

17

SO YOU SEE, IT *WAS* INNO-CENT. IT REALLY WAS. JUST BAD LUCK.

ROSALITA,,,THERE *ISN'T* ANY INNOCENT. THERE ISN'T ANY *GUILTY*. THERE'S JUST *DEAD*.

EXCUSE ME, BUT WOULD YOU BE THE MIDDAY SERVICE?

THAT'D BE US.

HOW GOES THE QUEST FOR THE TRIPLE GODDESS IN TV SITCOMS?

I HAVEN'T DONE ANYTHING ON THE BOOK FOR *AGES*.

UMMMM...

HAL, I THINK I'M PREGNANT.

SO WE DON'T BELIEVE IN BIRTH CONTROL ANY-MORE, THEN?

WE *DO*. BUT WE DIDN'T USE ANY SPERMICIDE, AND ONE OF THE CONDOMS BROKE.

THERE WE *GO*, THEN. IN THE MIDST OF DEATH, WE ARE IN LIFE.

LET'S GO AND SAY BYE-BYE TO ZELDA.

AFTER *YOU*.

18

IN A NURSING HOME A LITTLE OUTSIDE THE TOWN OF WYCH CROSS, IN THE COUNTY OF SUSSEX, IN THE SOUTH OF ENGLAND, MRS. SHORE, WHO IS ON NIGHT DUTY, IS ROUSED FROM A RESTLESS DOZING DREAM IN WHICH HER FATHER (DEAD THESE MANY YEARS) FELL FROM A CLIFF, SLIPPING THROUGH HER HANDS TO HIS DEATH; AND SHE WAKES WITH HOT TEARS BURNING HER CHEEKS.

Evening H
LOCAL SOLICITOR KILLS HIMSELF WHEN GAY LO WALKS OU

SHE RISES, AND WALKS THE HALLS OF THE HOME. STRANGE NOTIONS CAN TAKE HOLD OF YOU, IN THE SMALL HOURS OF THE MORNING, AND SHE FANCIES HERSELF, FOR A MOMENT, IN HELL.

PERHAPS IT IS SIMPLY THE FULL OF THE MOON, SHE THINKS; BUT THE HOWLS AND THE MOANS THAT ASSAIL HER FROM EVERY ROOM ARE MORE THAN MERE LUNACY.

THEY HOWL IN THEIR SLEEP LIKE FURIES, SHE THINKS, LIKE BANSHEES, LIKE HARPIES.

SHE CONFIRMS FOR HERSELF THAT THEY STILL SLEEP, THOUGH THEY WRITHE AND MOAN LIKE WOMEN POSSESSED.

THEN SHE HEARS A VOICE, RUSTY AND HOARSE WITH DISUSE, PLEADING THROUGH THE SHADOWS.

HELLO? NURSE? PAUL? *HELLO?* IS ANYBODY *THERE?*

MISTER BURGESS? BLESS ME, IT *IS* YOU.

I ...I WAS ASLEEP, WASN'T I? I HAD SUCH DREAMS. THERE WAS A *CAT*, WHO BECAME A MAN, THE MAN MY FATHER CAUGHT... IT'S A STRANGE... OH, BUT IT'S GONE...

WHERE'S *PAUL?*

YOU MUST BE A *NEW* NURSE. I DON'T *KNOW* YOU I DON'T...

PAUL? IS THIS ANOTHER NIGHTMARE? *IS* IT? IS IT ANOTHER BAD DREAM?

HUSH NOW, DEARIE.

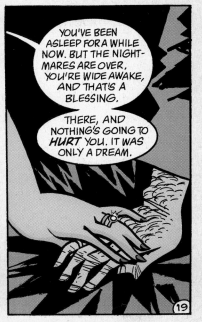

YOU'VE BEEN ASLEEP FOR A WHILE NOW. BUT THE NIGHTMARES ARE OVER, YOU'RE WIDE AWAKE, AND THAT'S A BLESSING.

THERE, AND NOTHING'S GOING TO *HURT* YOU. IT WAS ONLY A DREAM.

19

WELCOME BACK, HIPPOLYTA.

WHO... WHERE...

I SMELL LIKE SHIT. I...

WHERE *AM* I?

WHAT'S *HAPPENED* TO ME?

WHAT HAPPENED? THE LAST THING I REMEMBER IS...

DANIEL... THEY TOOK *DANIEL!*

I MUST HAVE HAD SOME KIND OF BREAK-DOWN.

WHO ARE *YOU?* HOW DO YOU KNOW *ME?*

I'M CALLED LARISSA.

AND YOU... ARE A PAWN... WHO BRIEFLY BECAME A KNIGHT ...OR A QUEEN. AND YOU'VE JUST BEEN TAKEN OFF THE BOARD.

YOU'RE TALKING *NONSENSE.*

AS I UNDERSTAND IT, YOUR ACTIONS HAVE ENSURED THAT YOU WILL NEVER SEE DANIEL AGAIN.

WAS I *DRUGGED,* OR SOMETHING? I WAS LOOKING FOR DANIEL...

HERE. IT'S RED ZINGER.

I'D TAKE A SHOWER, AND THEN START RUNNING, IF I WERE YOU.

LOTS OF PEOPLE ARE GOING TO WANT TO HURT YOU OR KILL YOU FOR WHAT YOU'VE DONE.

INCLUDING ME.

20

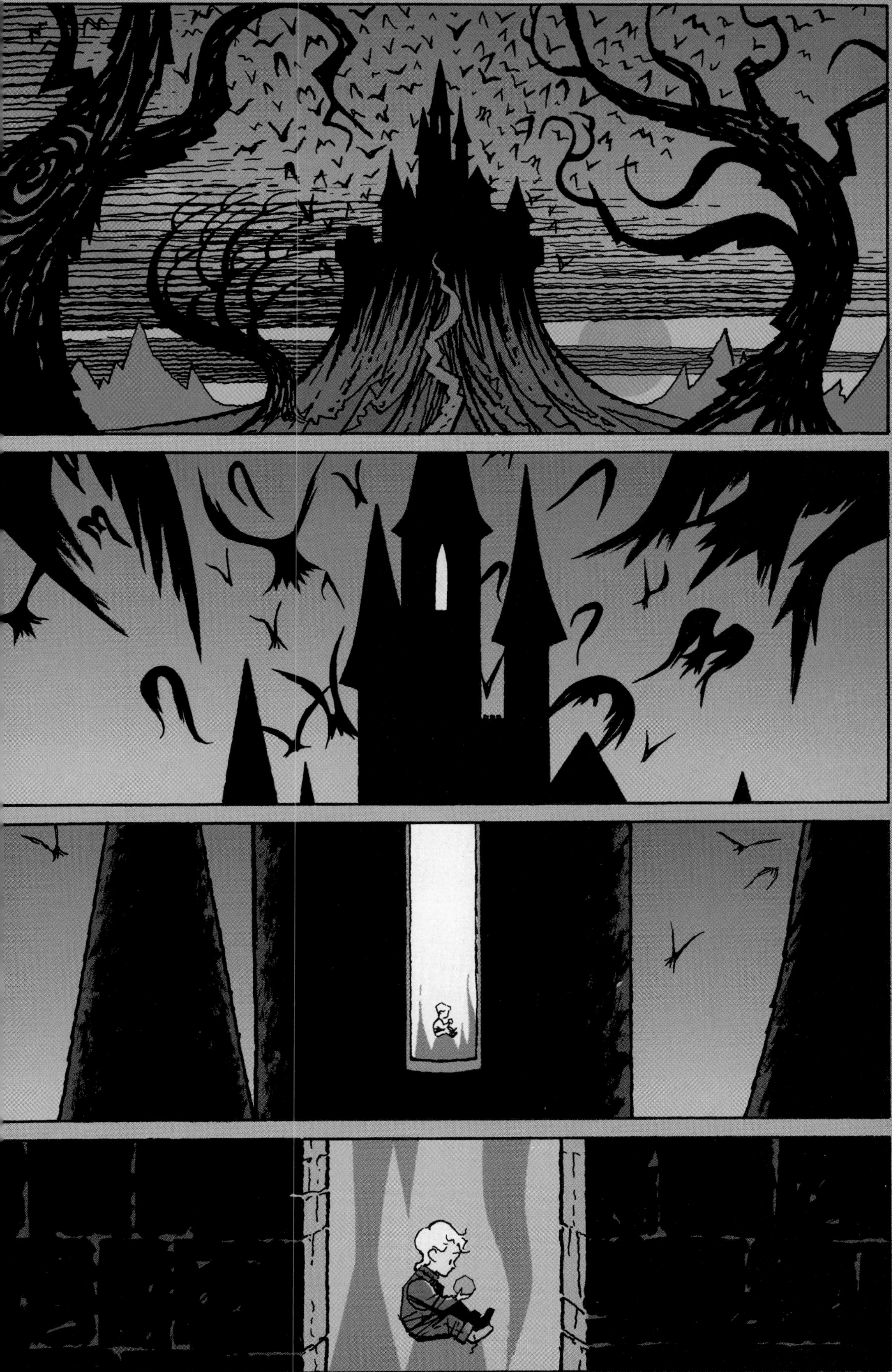

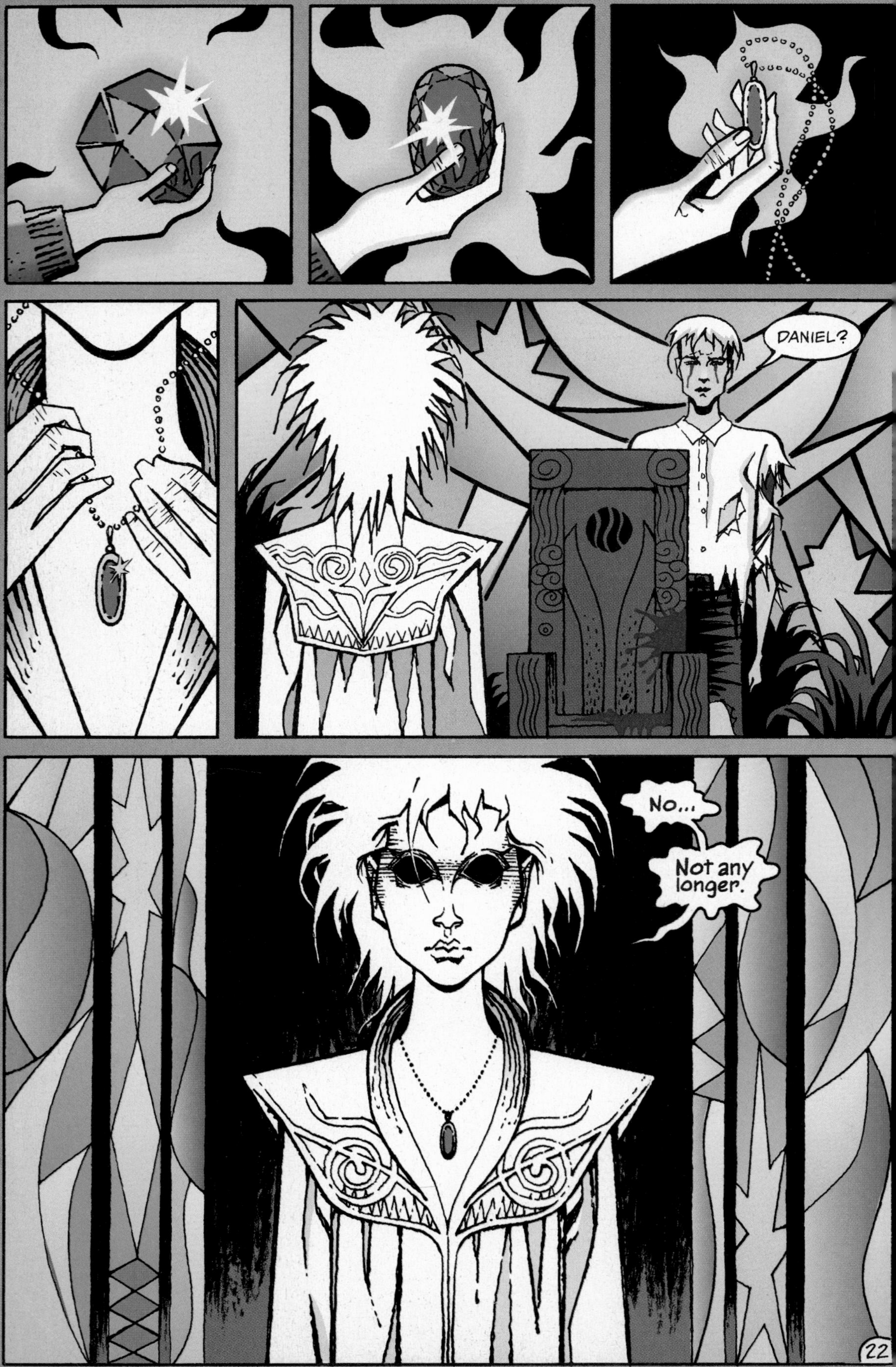
DANIEL?
No...
Not any longer.

SO, IT'S FINISHED.

YES.

WHAT DID WE MAKE? WHAT *WAS* IT, IN THE END?

WHAT IT *ALWAYS* IS. A HANDFUL OF YARN; A LITTLE WEAVING AND STITCHING; SOME EMBROIDERING PERHAPS. A FEW LOOSE ENDS, BUT THAT'S ONLY TO BE EXPECTED...

IT'S THE SAME OLD STORY... WHATEVER IT TURNS INTO ON THE WAY, WHATEVER IT IS YOU ORIGINALLY UNDERTAKE TO SPIN OR KNIT OR WEAVE, KEEP IT GOING LONG ENOUGH AND, IN THE END, MY LILIES, IT'S ALWAYS A WINDING SHEET...

ARE YOU *SATISFIED*?

NIMINY PIMINY, MY PIGEON, REFLECT: AND HOW COULD I *EVER* BE SATISFIED?

IT'S LIKE WE TOLD THAT YOUNG LADY, I TOLD HER, I SAID, YOU'VE MADE YOUR BED AND NOW YOU MUST EAT IT.

EH WELL, NO REST FOR THE WICKED.

HERE WE GO, TEA FOR THREE. I FOUND A FLORENTINE, A FORTUNE COOKIE, AND A SHIP'S BISCUIT. WHO'S FOR WHAT?

I'LL HAVE THE FLORENTINE.

I'LL HAVE THE SHIP'S BISCUIT. THERE'S MAGGOTY PROTEIN IN THERE, GOOD FOR EYES AND TEETH.

AND THERE WAS DAYS WHEN WE'D BUT A SINGLE EYE AND A TOOTH BETWEEN US... OR *WAS* THAT US? I DON'T REMEMBER...

I'LL TAKE THE FORTUNE COOKIE, MY CORACLE, AND HAVE DONE WITH IT.

23

WELL? WHAT DOES IT SAY?

HMPH. IT'S NOT WHAT I'D CALL A *PROPER* FORTUNE.

I *LIKED* THE LAST ONE, IS IT THE *LAST* ONE AGAIN? THE ONE ABOUT THE CLASH AND THE FRAY?

IT'S SILLY RUBBISH.

FLOWERS GATHERED IN THE MORNING, AFTERNOON THEY BLOSSOM ON, STILL ARE WITHERED BY THE EVENING: YOU CAN BE ME WHEN I'M GONE.

IT'S NOT EVEN VERY GOOD POETRY.

I WONDER HOW *THAT* GOT IN THERE?

MORE OF A *MOTTO* THAN A *FORTUNE.*

⧗snf⧗ AT*LEAST* IT'S NOT A MORAL. WORSE THAN BEGINNINGS, MORALS. I'VE GOT *NO* TIME FOR THEM. NO TIME AT ALL.

NEVER MIND.

THERE. FOR GOOD OR BAD.

IT'S DONE,

THE KINDLY ONES

"Was it a bear,
or a Russian,
or what?"

I had planned originally to use this page to list the unanswered questions raised by the kindly ones; all the answerable ones, like who were Loki and Puck actually working for? and what was Remiel's problem anyway? and the unanswerable, like how could anyone play, let alone win, Mrs. Crupp and Mrs. Treadgold's game of draughts (a.k.a. checkers)? or even so was that really Piglet in the bed?

But you can make your own list.

Some of your questions may be answered in the last Sandman book, the wake, which follows this, and others may be answered in the earlier seven Sandman collections. and for those that aren't answered anywhere, all i can do is quote Cain, quoting Robert Aickman, quoting Saccheverel Sitwell. it is the mystery that lingers, they have all told us, at one time or another, and not the explanation.

This was the longest of all the Sandman stories, and it was in many ways the hardest to write. through everything, Shelly Roeberg got pages out of me and out of the artists, and saw them through the production process. she was always there, and i cannot thank her enough.

Thanks to the artists: Marc Hempel, Richard Case and D'Israeli, Glyn Dillon, Dean Ormston, Teddy Kristiansen and Charles Vess. thanks to Kevin Nowlan.

Thanks to Danny Vozzo for the colors, and to Todd Klein for making everyone talk, and over and above it all, thanks to Dave McKean for the covers, the design, and being a sane friend in a delightfully crazy world.

Karen Berger reigns on high like Juno, and Bob Kahan scuttles around in the depths like Vulcan, hammering the thirteen episodes of the story into the correctly colored, relatively goof-free volume you hold in your hands; together they are our editors.

Thanks to Paul Levitz and Jenette Kahn for letting the story end. thanks to John Webster for seeing the skull beneath the skin, and to Matthew the raven, for being the kind of fictional character one can rely on.

I still do not know how successful the kindly ones was, how close i got or how far i came from what i set out to say. still, it's the heaviest of all of these volumes, and thus, in hardback at least, could undoubtedly be used to stun a burglar; which has always been my definition of real art.

Neil Gaiman
Out in the cold woods
November 1995

Who's who?

"No Future" (not in that tie)

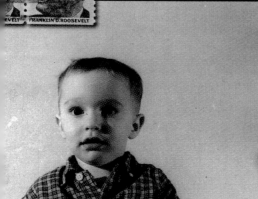

'Put the knife down, Daddy'

Our little professor

he Nice Vess boy.

small Dane with bobble hat

David's
~ile
g the shaving cream incident.

"Ow! Glyn hurt his arm!"

Master Case could teach
Marc and Matt to smile!

serious hair and
drums, Dean.

Is that Kevin on the right?

mighty iron lungs!

Young Matt does 'The shining'.

Who
knew?

Young Todd - lovely penmanship.

"One scoop or seven, Bob?"

Keeps coloring things in.

Little Miss Roeberg
tap-dances her way
into yr hearts.

Backlist
the sandman library

also available from vertigo:

for the nearest comics shop carrying collected editions and monthly titles from dc comics, call 1-888-comic book.

970430